```
JX
1398      Miner          66-9644
M5        Fight for the Panama
1966      route
```

JUL 2000
Date Due JUN 2004

FEB 25 '69			JUN 09	
MAR 11 '69				
WITHDRAWN			JUL X X 2015	

THE FIGHT FOR
THE PANAMA ROUTE

THE FIGHT FOR
THE PANAMA ROUTE

THE STORY OF THE SPOONER ACT
AND THE HAY-HERRÁN TREATY

By Dwight Carroll Miner

1966
OCTAGON BOOKS, INC.
New York

Copyright 1940 Columbia University Press

Reprinted 1966
by special arrangement with Columbia University Press

OCTAGON BOOKS, INC.
175 FIFTH AVENUE
NEW YORK, N. Y. 10010

LIBRARY OF CONGRESS CATALOG CARD NUMBER: 66-18054

Printed in U.S.A. by
NOBLE OFFSET PRINTERS, INC.
NEW YORK 3, N. Y.

To Molly

FOREWORD

The story of the North American acquisition of the Panama Canal Zone is one which, far more complex than has usually been supposed, deserves the fullest exploration and the most careful exposition. Not only is it rich in dramatic incident, but it carries several important lessons to our democracy. Few events in our history illustrate more emphatically the dangers inherent in the assumption that an important and beneficent end justifies the use of dubious means; few do more to demonstrate the moral penalties of haste and arrogance in diplomatic affairs; few are better adapted to chasten the feeling of superior rectitude with which we sometimes regard other nations. Theodore Roosevelt, a few years after the taking of Panama, complacently said that while the controversy about his course went on, so did the building of the canal. His statement requires a reversal of emphasis. For decades to come, while the use of the canal goes on it will be accompanied by a feeling of moral uneasiness, a sense that the great achievement was clouded by a deplorable and wholly unnecessary blemish. It will take long for the political leaders of Hispanic America to forget the episode; it will take still longer for historians in all parts of the world to forget it.

This story is here told by Dr. Miner with a completeness, an exactitude, and a comprehension of every element, every point of view, that give his treatment a close approach to finality. At several points he adds new matter of primary importance. In particular, he analyzes the situation in Colombia, full as it was of intricate political, economic, and social factors, with a thoroughness that is highly profitable. It has long been agreed that Colombia had her side of the controversy, and a far more tenable side than that of the Roosevelt administration. It has long been agreed that the Colombian Senate had every right to refuse to ratify the Hay-Herrán Treaty, just as the United States Senate had recently declined to ratify the first Hay-Pauncefote Treaty.

It has long been agreed that the Hay-Herrán Treaty gave Colombia a low payment for the Canal Zone, and that, as so unsparing a critic of Colombia as Philippe Bunau-Varilla admitted, it seriously restricted the nation's sovereignty in Panama. But Dr. Miner sets forth with a new precision and clarity the political situation in the half-isolated republic; explains the personality and attitude of the octogenarian dictator, President Marroquín, and all the other important leaders; elucidates the motives of the Colombian Senate; shows for the first time the tremendous difficulties under which Colombia's representatives in Washington labored; and gives us a convincing analysis of public opinion in Colombia.

It becomes clear from Dr. Miner's volume that the Panama affair was on both sides largely a tragedy of errors. The government at remote Bogotá, afflicted with administrative disorganization, poorly advised, and incapable of understanding the Anglo-Saxon mind, comprehended neither the position of the Roosevelt administration nor the international situation. Roosevelt (to whom Secretary Hay ultimately surrendered the management of the matter) did not understand the politics of Bogotá, the pride of the ruling class in Colombia, or the mentality of Hispanic Americans generally. He did not even try to. Both sides were guilty of miscalculation and error. But Dr. Miner makes it clear that while Bogotá was not without some greediness, while the Congress there was not so pure or representative as it might have been, and while the aged Marroquín was sadly inept, the difficulties in obtaining a satisfactory agreement with Colombia were far from insuperable. Showing patience and good will, Roosevelt could have obtained a clear title without much friction, and with no aftermath of ill will. The few additional millions which it might have cost would have brought golden returns in South American confidence. But ignorance, impatience, and arrogance in Washington, complicated by political motives arising from the imminence of the election of 1904, defeated the hope of an amicable agreement.

One of the most interesting parts of Dr. Miner's book is his account of the way in which the New Panama Canal Company succeeded, against huge odds, in defeating the Nicaraguan route, committing Congress, the State Department, and the President to Panama, and reaping the utmost financial advantage from the bankrupt property it held. It is a remarkable adventure story in politics and high finance. In less than five years the New Company's astute attorney, William Nelson Cromwell, and the adroit engineer, Bunau-Varilla, accomplished what many would have thought impossible. Mr. Cromwell contributed his $60,000 (or rather, the company's $60,000) to the Republican campaign fund in 1900 with just the right gesture. The company dropped its price to $40,000,000 in just the nick of time. Bunau-Varilla made just the right contacts with Hay, Hanna, and Roosevelt, and just the right use of the Pelée eruption and the Nicaraguan stamps picturing an active volcano. And finally, the New Company's attorney executed a masterly stroke in arranging that, while the United States should make a financial deal with the Company, Colombia should have no right to do so. It is an astonishing story, this of the skillful salvaging of the wreck left by de Lesseps; and Dr. Miner, adding new facts, brings out all its values.

A series of writers, in 1903–1904 and afterward, attempted to defend and excuse Roosevelt's headlong and arbitrary course. But the opinion of impartial and judicious historians has long since been decisively pronounced. Dr. Miner offers evidence which, while explaining the policy of the Roosevelt administration more fully than before, confirms the judgment already entered; and no one can read his interesting book without a new conviction of the unprofitability as well as the indefensibility of Rough Rider methods in diplomacy. To outrage a sister republic, to offend twenty other nations of the Americas, to deliver a blow to the great cause of the fair and moderate settlement of international disputes, to leave a blot on the national escutcheon—this was a heavy price to pay for the gain of a few months or years in building an isthmian waterway.

ALLAN NEVINS

Columbia University
February, 1940

AUTHOR'S PREFACE

No INCIDENT in Theodore Roosevelt's terms of office gave rise to more protracted controversy, national and international, than the secession of Panama from Colombia in 1903. The literature of protest and justification quickly reached voluminous proportions, but it was not until after the Bogotá and Washington governments had finally adjusted their differences in 1921 that commentators began to discard the partisan's axe for the historian's probe. Since 1927, when Howard C. Hill's *Roosevelt and the Caribbean* appeared, a number of studies have been completed in this country and on the Isthmus which throw valuable light upon the events that brought the Panama Canal site under United States control.

Understandably enough, emphasis has, in most cases, been placed upon the circumstances immediately connected with the outbreak in Panama, thereby obscuring to a certain extent the significance of earlier occurrences in Colombia and the United States which prepared the way for the dramatic climax on the Isthmus. It is the primary purpose of this volume to present a critical analysis of the more important of these earlier developments. Specifically, they include the achievement of the New Panama Canal Company in procuring the adoption by the United States Congress of the Panama route, popularly associated with French failure and corruption, in preference to the so-called "national" route across Nicaragua; the diplomatic maneuvers and Colombian domestic pressures which led to the signing of the Hay-Herrán treaty; the rise of protest against the pact in Colombia; and the combination of factors which resulted in the rejection of the treaty by the Bogotá legislature. These are the elements that form the main theme of the book, although the course of the narrative moves on into the Panama Revolution by such natural channels that the pertinent aspects of that coup and its aftermath have, of necessity, been treated in scarcely less detail. This distribution of emphasis reflects the author's conviction that the explanation of the secession of Panama is to be found not merely in the plottings of the *junta* or the prejudicial action of the United States naval forces on the Isthmus but also, very importantly, in the tragic ineptitude of the Washington and Bogotá authorities in handling the previous canal negotiations.

The author has utilized primary sources to the full extent that these have been available to him, both in the United States and Colombia. Some of this material is here offered for the first time, some of it has been published but has been difficult of access, and some of it has been employed previously in cursory fashion or without adequate checking. The critical reader will have no difficulty in discovering the various respects in which the present volume falls short of being definitive. Something more than crumbs remains for tomorrow's student. Sources now sealed will undoubtedly be opened to future investigators. New depositories of information will probably be brought to light. Should William Nelson Cromwell's papers be published or the Paris archives of the New Panama Canal Company be released from legal restrictions; should the actual nature and extent of the transcontinental railroads' lobbying activities in connection with the canal bills be disclosed; or should access be granted to the private papers of the Colombian leaders of the period, parts of this work may well require remedial surgery. The author can only hope that when that time arrives the emendator's knife will be wielded with kindly skill and scholarly intent.

Aside from the omission of the accent from Panama, only one intentional departure has been made from Hispanic-American usage regarding personal and place names. During his sojourn in Washington as minister plenipotentiary, Dr. Carlos Martínez Silva apparently came to be known to Cromwell and others as Dr. Silva. Correctly, of course, this constituted only that part of his surname which referred to his mother's family. This shortened form has, however, found its way into so many of the source materials bearing upon that period and occurs so frequently in passages quoted directly from them in the present volume that it has seemed less confusing to adhere to it consistently.

In reviewing the sources from which friendly assistance has come in the preparation of this work, the librarians and archivists seem clearly entitled to first place. The author takes this opportunity to express his gratitude for able guidance and ungrudging help to Mrs. Natalia Summers of the National Archives, Washington, D. C., to the officials of the Columbia University Library, the New York Public Library, the Huntington Library at San Marino, California, and the Biblioteca Nacional, the Biblioteca de la Academia Nacional de Historia, and the library of the Ministry of Foreign Affairs, all at Bogotá, Colombia. A special word of thanks is due Miss Nora E. Cordingley, in charge of the Roosevelt House Library in New York City, for her unfailing patience and coöperation. Above all, the author is indebted to Dr. St. George L. Sioussat, Chief of the Manuscripts Division of the Library of Congress, and to Dr. Thomas Martin, Assistant Chief, for kindly interest and efficient help.

For access to the Spooner and Root Papers in the Library of Congress the author expresses his thanks to Mr. Charles P. Spooner and Mr. Elihu Root, respectively. Permission to reproduce certain letters of John Hay has been graciously granted by Mrs. James W. Wadsworth and Mrs. Payne Whitney. The right to quote materials from the Theodore Roosevelt Papers in the Library of Congress has been obtained from the family estate through the kind efforts of Colonel Theodore Roosevelt. Among the many agreeable personal experiences which the present work has involved, none has been more pleasant and valuable than the privilege of consulting with Professor John Bassett Moore. The author is deeply grateful for the permission granted to make full use of the Memorandum of August, 1903, and of certain letters to Theodore Roosevelt.

For suggestions and assistance of various kinds the author acknowledges indebtedness to Dr. Leo S. Rowe, Director-General of the Pan-American Union, Dr. Tyler Dennett, Dr. Raymond Leslie Buell; Professors David S. Muzzey, Frank Tannenbaum, and John A. Krout, of Columbia University; Dr. Raimundo Rivas, Dr. Victor M. Londoño, Dr. Luis A. Cuervo, and Señor Jorge Cuervo, of Bogotá; Mr. Phanor J. Eder, Mr. Frank Rebuelta; and Mr. Samuel Dickson and Mr. Benjamin Muse of the Department of State. Mr. Hugh Harvey has, throughout the course of preparing and revising this work, devoted his time and resourcefulness unsparingly to its technical improvement. Professor Harry J. Carman of Columbia University has been an unfailing source of encouragement and help, for which a simple statement of gratitude must stand in all its inadequacy here. Finally, the author wishes to express his deep indebtedness to Professor Allan Nevins of Columbia University and a warm appreciation of the generosity and graciousness with which Professor Nevins has placed his advice and vast research knowledge at the disposal of others.

Acknowledgment is hereby made to the following publishers for kind permission to quote from works published by them: Dodd, Mead and Company, *John Hay* by Tyler Dennett; E. P. Dutton and Company, *Adventures in American Diplomacy* by Alfred L. P. Dennis; Harcourt, Brace and Company, *Theodore Roosevelt* by Henry F. Pringle; Harper and Brothers, *The Principles of American Diplomacy* by John Bassett Moore; Houghton Mifflin Company, *The Life of Lord Pauncefote* by R. B. Mowat and *The Life and Letters of John Hay* by William Roscoe Thayer; Robert M. McBride and Company, *Panama: The Creation, Destruction, and Resurrection* by Philippe Bunau-Varilla; The Macmillan Company, *A History of Spain* by Charles E. Chapman and *Marcus Alonzo Hanna* by Herbert Croly; Charles Scribner's Sons, *Theodore Roosevelt and His Time* by Joseph Bucklin Bishop, *An Autobiography* by Theodore Roosevelt, and *Selections from the Correspondence of Theodore Roosevelt and Henry Cabot Lodge.*

AUTHOR'S PREFACE

Permission to quote material has also been generously granted by the publishers of the New York *Times*, the New York *Sun* (for excerpts from the New York *Herald*), *The Nation*, and *Popular Science Monthly*.

DWIGHT C. MINER

Columbia University
March, 1940

CONTENTS

	FOREWORD BY ALLAN NEVINS	vii
	AUTHOR'S PREFACE	xi
I	FROM COLUMBUS TO MCKINLEY	3
II	THE COLOMBIAN BACKGROUND	33
III	THE BATTLE OF THE ROUTES	75
IV	THE PASSAGE OF THE SPOONER ACT	117
V	THE NEGOTIATION OF THE HAY-HERRÁN TREATY	157
VI	THE COLOMBIAN DOCTOR'S DILEMMA	200
VII	THE RISE OF PROTEST IN COLOMBIA	241
VIII	PRESSURE DIPLOMACY	273
IX	THE DEFEAT OF THE TREATY	298
X	REVOLUTION IN PANAMA	335
XI	THE TRIUMPH OF PANAMA	371
	APPENDIX A: THE HAY-CONCHA MEMORANDUM OF APRIL 18, 1902	397
	APPENDIX B: THE SPOONER ACT	408
	APPENDIX C: THE HAY-HERRÁN TREATY	413
	APPENDIX D: THE JOHN BASSETT MOORE MEMORANDUM OF AUGUST, 1903	427
	BIBLIOGRAPHY	435
	INDEX	451

MAPS

I   CENTRAL AMERICA: ROUTES MOST FREQUENTLY PROPOSED FOR THE INTEROCEANIC CANAL   5

II   THE CONTINENTAL DEPARTMENTS OF COLOMBIA IN 1902   35

III   THE ISTHMUS OF PANAMA IN 1903   167

THE FIGHT FOR
THE PANAMA ROUTE

I

FROM COLUMBUS TO McKINLEY

If, in tracing the historical roots of the story of the Panama Canal, we venture back into the period of the Spanish dominion, we meet with few projects for linking the Atlantic and Pacific until the very century of the conquest. While Coronado sought the Cities of Cíbola in the north and Pizarro plundered the Inca's treasure-houses in Peru, certain men of vision urged the feasibility of a canal across the Isthmus.[1] The eastern Indies were still undespoiled, and an artificial waterway in Central America would greatly facilitate an advance in that direction.

These proposals reflected a declining faith in the theory that somewhere in the tropics a natural passage pierced the continental barrier. Nevertheless, until this hope finally died the "secret of the strait" remained a primary objective of Spanish exploration. Columbus devoted his fourth voyage to it. His tiny, storm-battered ships turned back to Cuba at a point not far from the Caribbean entrance to the present canal.[2] Other leaders continued the search, scouring the coast line from La Plata to Yucatan. In 1513 Balboa located the South Sea, but it was left for Magellan seven years later to demonstrate its vast extent and the true geographical isolation of the Americas.

Magellan's passage was inconvenient and dangerous, but year by year the reports of expeditions made it clearer that no passage existed closer to Cuba. Nevertheless, rumors of a corridor were current until after 1525. The council of pilots and cartographers, assembled at Badajoz in 1524 to correlate the available facts about the New World, believed an all-water route would eventually

[1] The most prominent among these were: Cortés, Saavedra Ceron, Galván, López de Gómara, Gil González Dávila, Salcedo, Esquivel, and Mercado. See Chapman, *History of Spain*, p. 350.
[2] Harrisse, *Discovery of North America*, p. 693.

be found somewhere between Newfoundland and Darien.[3] Contemporary maps portray an unbroken coast line with greater frequency about this time, although a Central American strait is still included in some charts of the next decade.[4]

Alvaro de Saavedra Ceron, a companion of Balboa at Darien and subsequently a lieutenant of Cortés, is generally credited with being the first to suggest the construction of a canal through the Isthmus. Between 1517 and 1529 Ceron is supposed to have engaged in extensive surveys which led him to urge the practicality of routes closely approximating those most frequently recommended by later engineers, namely, from Nombre de Dios to Panama, from Urabá to the Gulf of San Miguel, through Lake Nicaragua, and, finally, across Tehuantepec. He died in 1529 before submitting his official report.[5] About this time Pedrarias, as governor of Nicaragua, considered cutting canals to link Lake Nicaragua with the oceans, but more immediate matters interposed.

For a while Charles V interested himself in the Panama route which linked Peru with the rest of the Empire. The Chagres River was made navigable from the Atlantic to Cruces in 1534, and surveys were ordered for a canal from that point to the Pacific, but reports were not encouraging and the project lapsed.[6] In general, the Spaniards were more eager to expend their energies in exploration and exploitation than in pushing a ditch through a fever-ridden jungle. "As engineers," Chapman remarks, "Spaniards lagged behind other European peoples; engineering works were not greatly involved in the colonization of the Americas." [7] So it happened that for nearly three hundred years jingling pack trains carried the burden of Spain's com-

[3] Bennett, *History of the Panama Canal*, p. 96.
[4] Winsor, *Narrative and Critical History*, II, 121, 219, 221; Harrisse, *Discovery of North America*, pp. 279–280.
[5] Bennett, *History of the Panama Canal*, p. 97; Johnson, *Four Centuries of the Panama Canal*, p. 31.
[6] Bishop, *Panama Gateway*, pp. 27–29. According to Bishop the order of Charles V regarding the Chagres River is the first official step on record toward the building of an isthmian canal.
[7] *History of Spain*, p. 350.

I. CENTRAL AMERICA: ROUTES MOST FREQUENTLY PROPOSED FOR THE INTEROCEANIC CANAL

merce with Peru along the stone-paved roads which connected Nombre de Dios, Cruces, and, later, Portobello, with Panama.[8]

Charles's successor, Philip II, at first showed interest in the possibilities of the Nicaragua route, but after receiving an unfavorable report on it in 1567, ceased to push the matter. Advancing age focused his attention more and more on considerations of the next world and his decisions in matters of state not infrequently reflected this preoccupation. He is reported to have concluded that it would be impious to join the waters of the mighty oceans which Providence had seen fit to place asunder and, according to some accounts, he ended further discussion of the subject by decreeing the death penalty for anyone attempting to open a new route across the Isthmus.[9]

It is very unlikely, however, that the almost uninterrupted support which Philip's successors gave this negative policy for the next two centuries was due solely to a scattering of unfavorable surveys or to the whim of a royal fanatic.[10] Other reasons intimately connected with its position as a world power gradually

---

[8] A post road was constructed about 1521 between the old city of Panama and Nombre de Dios. Thirteen or fourteen years later a station, known as Cruces, or Santa Cruz, was established at the head of navigation on the Chagres River. For the next half-century the easiest and cheapest way to cross the Isthmus from the Atlantic side, except during the dry season, was to ascend the river for eighteen leagues to Cruces and then follow the *Camino Real* for five leagues to Panama. About the end of the sixteenth century, however, after the destruction of Nombre de Dios, the Atlantic terminus of the treasure route was shifted to Portobello. See Merriman, *Rise of the Spanish Empire*, III, 633–634; Lindsay, *Panama and the Canal Today*, pp. 9–10.

[9] Bishop, *Panama Gateway*, p. 30; Johnson, *Four Centuries of the Panama Canal*, pp. 33–34. Johnson attributes the story of Philip's religious fear of joining the oceans to the Jesuit historian, José de Acosta. The account of the death-penalty decree may be legendary. Lucien N. B. Wyse was unable to find any trace of it in his investigations in the Spanish archives half a century ago. On this point see Rudolph J. Taussig's article on "The American Inter-Oceanic Canal, an Historical Sketch of the Canal Idea" in *The Pacific Ocean in History*, p. 121.

[10] In 1616 Philip III ordered a survey of the Damaquiel and Atrato River routes, but there is no record of a report; the Tehuantepec route was surveyed in 1715 and 1774, and the Nicaragua in 1779; Manuel Milla's project by way of Caledonian Bay in 1788 was as fruitless as the others.

Alexander von Humboldt attracted widespread attention to the possibilities of an interoceanic canal as a result of his observations in his American travels in 1799–1804. He outlined nine routes, scattered from the Missouri River to Patagonia, and particularly emphasized the practicality of those in Central America.

impelled Spain to alter its whole attitude toward the canal project. With the passage of time the royal advisers in Madrid had come to regard the New World less as an unfortunate obstacle to the coveted Indies than as a veritable Eldorado in its own right. As such, the task of subjugation and control had completely absorbed what energy the nation could give to overseas expansion. Not alone Magellan, but Cortés and Pizarro as well, had made the East seem far away indeed.

From still another standpoint the canal scheme lost its chief attraction for Spain as time wore on. By the early seventeenth century the Indies were no longer to be had for the taking. The English, French, and Dutch had ensconced themselves in the choice places and offered only prospects of trouble to an advance in that quarter. Nor could Castile still account herself the unchallenged mistress of the seaways. The fleets of Holland and England had grown formidable; the latter had already badly singed His Catholic Majesty's beard. Under the circumstances a canal at Panama would only increase the vulnerability of the Spanish colonial empire. It would likewise endow the Isthmus with a commercial value that would almost inevitably lead to a conflict with England for possession.

With the exception of a period of temporary regeneration during the reign of Charles III, the effectiveness and prestige of the colonial administration underwent a slow decline throughout the seventeenth and eighteenth centuries. Popular unrest due to local social and economic conditions was quickened by the successful revolutionary movements in France and North America in the last quarter of the eighteenth century and by the politico-social doctrines which accompanied them. Before the next century was a decade old rebellion had broken out in many parts of Spain's American empire. In 1814 the Madrid government, in a final effort to retain the loyalty of its American subjects, ordered the construction of a canal. It was a gesture of despair, and it came too late. Before work could begin the revolt had spread beyond control and Spain's grip relaxed on the New World to which it had shown the way.

II

For a time it seemed that the elimination of Spain from Central America would facilitate the building of a canal. But it soon became apparent that the struggling republics which occupied the region were utterly lacking in the stability and resources to carry through so unprecedented a design, or even to protect a private concessionary.

Numerous surveys were made during the nineteenth century, but only two projects reached the pick-and-shovel stage. The chronic political chaos in Central America, among other reasons, made it difficult to attract the necessary capital. Few of these ventures were regarded seriously by the commercial nations. Each failure, nevertheless, emphasized the fact that, for success, the work would have to be undertaken by treaty arrangement with some more powerful nation, or else by a private company under international protection. Either alternative would introduce delicate questions of local sovereignty, with the prospect of endless misunderstandings. Either method would burden a difficult engineering feat with complex considerations of "world diplomacy."

This separation of sovereignty and enterprise constituted the cardinal fact in the canal problem during the nineteenth century. It was responsible for making that problem an international one. It gave rise, in consequence, to the doctrine of a "free and neutral canal." Until after 1865, at least, the question of who should build the canal was subordinated by the great powers to the question of who should control it.[11]

Great Britain was, of course, among those most concerned in the future of the Isthmus. Her interest there went back more than a century and a half before the expulsion of Spanish authority to the days when her freebooting subjects took to cutting logwood along the Gulf of Honduras when spoil was scarce on the Spanish Main. Indeed, from time to time the British government had interfered to protect their settlements at Belize and

---

[11] Latané, *History of American Foreign Policy*, pp. 306–307.

on the Bay Islands from the attempts of the Spaniards to dislodge them.

Further south, between Cape Gracias a Dios and the San Juan River, English traders had befriended the Mosquito "nation," a Carib people with African and European infusions, whom the conquerors of Guatemala had never fully subdued. The Mosquitoes helped the English to establish a flourishing trade with the interior of Central America in contravention of the strict mercantile code of Spain, and they received protection in return. In 1740 they surrendered their sovereignty to the governor of Jamaica for safekeeping. There it remained until the British government agreed by treaty with Spain in 1786 to withdraw from the Mosquito Coast and the Bay Islands, and even acknowledged Spain's sovereignty over the logwood concession at Belize. This treaty was still operative when the Spanish colonies revolted.[12]

Downing Street was fully alive to the commercial opportunities presented by the new republics. Foreign Secretary Canning not only refused to assist Spain in their recovery but proposed to the United States a joint opposition to any attempt of the Holy Alliance to reconquer them. Under his direction English activities in Central America gradually quickened. The promulgation of the Monroe Doctrine without consultation with Great Britain annoyed him and aroused his suspicions of North American designs on the Isthmus.[13] He and his successors, therefore, shaped their policy to prevent the Latin-American countries from looking to the United States for aid or alliances.[14]

With the breakup of the Central American Federation in 1839 British agents became more aggressive and worked actively from Belize to foster faction and advance British influence. Perhaps to avoid arousing public opinion to the north, the Foreign Office three times between 1834 and 1846 refused the request of the English residents that Belize be converted into British Hon-

[12] Williams, *Anglo-American Isthmian Diplomacy*, pp. 2–25.
[13] Perkins, *Monroe Doctrine, 1823–1826*, pp. 181–184, 248–251.
[14] Rippy, *Latin America in World Politics*, pp. 54–57; Williams, *Anglo-American Isthmian Diplomacy*, pp. 27–28.

duras. The time was not ripe. In 1841, however, the less important Bay Islands were virtually made a protectorate. Along the Mosquito Coast the advance went steadily forward. After 1830 the custom of giving presents to the Indians was revived. Then Nicaragua was forced to recognize the "independence" of the region, and finally, in 1840, British officials took temporary possession of the mouth of the San Juan River over the protest of the Central American states.[15]

Meanwhile the government at Washington gave no official sign of uneasiness over these encroachments. From time to time it dispatched private agents to Guatemala or Nicaragua, but their reports make no mention of British activities.[16] As a matter of fact, during the quarter-century that followed the War of 1812 the United States was but moderately interested in Central American politics south of Mexico. The prowling of a few British agents through the wilderness of Nicaragua was of small concern beside the great movement into the West and the portentous struggles over constitutional authority involving internal improvements, the Bank, slavery, and the tariff.

United States trade contacts with Latin America at this period were valued but not vital. Generally speaking, North American interest in that region consisted chiefly in a desire to see other exponents of the republican ideal prosper, with an admixture of pro-slavery imperialism that hardly extended to the San Juan River.[17] Nor was the Department of State searching to the southward for another controversy with Great Britain to add to the outstanding difficulties over matters of trade and boundaries.

[15] Williams, *Anglo-American Isthmian Diplomacy*, pp. 30-41.
[16] *Ibid.*, pp. 28-30.
[17] Perkins, *Monroe Doctrine, 1823-1826*, pp. 40-41, 43-46. Commerce between the United States and Great Colombia in the early twenties seemed to offer bright prospects of future development, in spite of the early headway made by the British. For the two decades following 1825, however, trade decreased drastically, falling from $3,858,446 in 1825 to $203,510 in 1845. Political disorders in Colombia, discriminatory duties, and a poor consular service appear to have been important contributing factors. Attempts of the North American chargés at Bogotá to negotiate a treaty placing United States commerce on a footing equal to that of Great Britain proved fruitless until 1846. See Parks, *Colombia and the United States*, pp. 115, 169-177.

The question of communication with the Pacific did not become important at Washington until westward migration and the temper of the forties pointed toward the speedy consummation of California's "manifest destiny."

Despite its preoccupation with its own affairs the United States on several occasions in this period indicated interest in the construction of an isthmian canal. In no case, however, did the government show any desire to monopolize the enterprise. When, in 1825, the envoy of the Central American Republic suggested to Secretary of State Clay a treaty which would ensure to his country and the United States the control of a Nicaraguan canal, Clay expressed "deep interest," not in the treaty but in the project of a canal.[18] The next spring, in instructing the administration representatives to the Panama Congress that a canal across Central America would be a proper subject for discussion, the secretary wrote that the enterprise "should not be left to the separate and unassisted efforts of any one power" nor the benefits "exclusively appropriated to any one nation, but [they] should be extended to all parts of the globe upon the payment of a just compensation or reasonable tolls." [19]

In 1835 the Senate adopted a resolution favoring negotiations with other nations, "particularly with the governments of Central America and New Granada, for the purpose of effectually protecting, by . . . treaty . . . such individuals or companies as may undertake to open . . . a ship canal across the isthmus . . . and of securing forever . . . the free and equal right of navigating such a canal to all nations." [20] President Jackson accordingly dispatched one Charles Biddle to investigate the Nicaragua, Guatemala, and Panama routes. Instead of complying with instructions, Biddle journeyed direct to Panama and thence to Bogotá where, in June, 1836, he obtained for himself and a number of associates a concession to establish a land-and-water

---

[18] Johnson, *Four Centuries of the Panama Canal*, p. 44. Clay also instructed the United States chargé d'affaires in Central America to collect all data relative to the cost and practicability of the Nicaragua route.
[19] Moore, *Digest of International Law*, III, 2.
[20] *Senate Journal*, 23rd Cong., 2nd Sess., p. 238.

communication across the Isthmus. Jackson was infuriated by this use of an official mission for the furtherance of personal interests and, in all probability, only Biddle's death the following December saved him from a severe reprimand. The chief executive informed Congress early the next year that he was convinced that negotiations for the protection of a canal were not "expedient" at that time.[21] Three years later the upper house expressed "deep interest" in the subject of a canal built through international coöperation. Van Buren's confidential agent, John L. Stephens, reported in 1839 in favor of the Nicaragua route, which he estimated would cost $35,000,000, but he advised delay until the country was less troubled.

The elections of 1844 carried James K. Polk into office pledged to the "reannexation of Texas" and the "reoccupation of Oregon." The country was recovering from the effects of the 1837 panic and expansionist feeling was running high. War with somebody was in the air. The administration wisely chose to compromise with Great Britain and fight Mexico, with the result that within three years of Polk's inauguration Texas, New Mexico, California, and southern Oregon had been acquired, and the national domain stretched unbroken across the continent.

The president had meanwhile given rather hesitant endorsement to an arrangement with New Granada for improving access to the Pacific coast. On February 10, 1847, he transmitted to the Senate for ratification a treaty signed at Bogotá the previous December by Benjamin Bidlack and Foreign Minister Manuel María Mallarino.[22] It concerned chiefly a transit privilege for citizens and merchandise across the Isthmus of Panama. Polk's explanatory message read in part:

It will be perceived by the thirty-fifth article of this treaty that New Granada proposes to guarantee to the Government and citizens

---

[21] Richardson, *Messages and Papers*, III, 272–273; Parks, *Colombia and the United States*, pp. 185–189.

[22] Malloy, *Treaties*, I, 302. Bidlack had been sent to Bogotá in June, 1845, with instructions to oppose any canal privileges to other powers which might prove injurious to the United States. The New Granadan government, having failed

of the United States the right of passage across the Isthmus of Panama over the natural roads and over any canal or railroad which may be constructed to unite the two seas, on condition that the United States shall make a similar guaranty to New Granada of the neutrality of this portion of her territory and her sovereignty over the same. . . . The importance of this concession to the commercial and political interests of the United States cannot easily be overrated. The route by the Isthmus of Panama is the shortest between the two oceans, and . . . it would seem to be the most practicable for a railroad or canal. . . . We are more deeply and directly interested in the subject of this guaranty than New Granada herself or any other country.

This guaranty, as the message proceeded to point out, was confined to the "single Province of the Isthmus of Panama," and the treaty itself was not "an alliance for a political object, but for a purely commercial interest." The president felt that such a guaranty as Article 35 provided was "almost indispensable to the construction of a railroad or canal across the territory," and anticipated that France and Great Britain, at least, would subscribe to the pledge of neutrality.[23] A further important object of the treaty to which Polk called attention was the termination of the discriminating commercial duties which had hampered

---

shortly before to obtain treaty guaranties of the neutrality of the Isthmus from France and Great Britain, opened negotiations with the North American chargé d'affaires in the fall of 1846. See Bemis, *American Secretaries of State*, V, 305.

[23] Richardson, *Messages and Papers*, IV, 513. It was this guaranty of isthmian neutrality which had caused Polk to hesitate about sending the convention to the Senate. Bidlack had negotiated and signed the treaty without instructions from Washington, actuated by fear that the opportunity for securing such important advantages might be lost by delay (Parks, *Colombia and the United States*, pp. 202 *et seq.*). The Taylor administration, which came into office in March, 1849, was not at all anxious to bear the responsibility for protecting the transit singlehanded. Secretary Clayton expressed his readiness to share the guaranty and its benefits with Great Britain and even instructed Minister Lawrence to assist the Granadan envoy in securing a British pledge of protection similar to that in the 1846 pact (*ibid.*, p. 214). In the fall of 1848 he wrote to his representative in Mexico City: "The guarantee in the treaty with New Granada is a conspicuous exception to our usual cautious and wise policy. That treaty was concluded without instructions from this department. There is reason to believe that it was reluctantly submitted to the Senate. . . . It cannot be deemed a safe precedent" (Clayton to Letcher, Sept. 18, 1849, quoted from *ibid.*, pp. 214–215).

United States trade with New Granada for a score of years. After several postponements the convention was rushed through a single day's debate and ratified without amendments in June, 1848.[24]

The British clearly foresaw the result of the war with Mexico and hastened to secure their interests in Central America against future Yankee imperialism in that direction. Acting through the "council" of the Mosquito king, Palmerston ordered Nicaragua to withdraw from the mouth of the San Juan River by January 1, 1848, or be expelled by force. That country, incapable of armed protest, appealed to Washington for aid after Great Britain had refused to negotiate.[25]

Although the Department of State made no immediate reply to the Nicaraguans, the administration was aroused. The English needed only possession of Tigre Island, commanding the Bay of Fonseca on the Pacific side, to control the termini of one of the most promising canal routes. Polk made pointed reference to British activity in his annual message of December, 1847,[26] and early the next year sent Elijah Hise to Guatemala to encourage the Central American states to united opposition. Hise found them in political confusion. Honduras, Nicaragua, and Salvador

[24] Richardson, *Messages and Papers*, IV, 513. Bidlack informed the State Department that the unfavorable duties could not have been abolished without the guaranty of isthmian sovereignty. See Hill, *Roosevelt and the Caribbean*, pp. 40–41.

The treaty made possible the extensive use of the Panama route at the time of the gold rush. Polk's diary mentions the bad state of the roads across the Isthmus in 1849 and his decided opposition on constitutional grounds to a scheme proposed by W. H. Aspinwall and others to construct a railroad there for the transport of the mails and public property for a twenty-year subsidy of $250,000 per annum (*Polk: Diary*, p. 372).

The Aspinwall group formed a company in New York in April, 1849, and obtained a concession from New Granada in 1850 for an isthmian railroad to be completed in six years with reversion to that government forty-nine years after opening to traffic. It ran its first train from ocean to ocean in January, 1855. Dr. F. N. Otis, in his *Illustrated History of the Panama Railroad*, graphically recounts the struggles of these pioneers with tropical wilderness and disease. Their sufferings and achievements have been unduly overshadowed by the magnitude and notoriety of the de Lesseps fiasco. The mortality among the workers was over 6,000. Financially the venture was profitable from the very beginning.

[25] Williams, *Anglo-American Isthmian Diplomacy*, pp. 46–49.
[26] Richardson, *Messages and Papers*, IV, 539–540.

looked to the United States for aid while Costa Rica and Guatemala were under British influence.[27]

Convinced that Palmerston sought exclusive control over a future Nicaragua canal, Hise proceeded without instructions to conclude a convention with Nicaragua in June, 1849, granting to the United States, "or to a company of the citizens thereof," the exclusive right to construct a canal or railroad across Nicaragua and to fortify and protect it. In return, the United States was to protect Nicaragua in all the territory rightfully hers.[28] It was a complete challenge to British pretensions.

The news of this convention did not reach Washington until after the new Taylor administration had dispatched E. G. Squier to replace Hise with more guarded instructions and words of friendly promise to Nicaragua.[29] The California gold rush was in full swing, and the dangers of British monopoly of any trans-isthmian route were now graphically exposed. The issue could be delayed no longer. Squier found Chatfield, the energetic British consul in Guatemala, on the alert to frustrate his plans.[30] Despite this opposition, he obtained another transit treaty from Nicaragua by which the United States recognized Nicaragua's sovereignty over the canal route only, and guaranteed the neutrality of any canal constructed by United States citizens as long as it was in their hands.[31] He also obtained a concession and act of incorporation in favor of the American Atlantic and Pacific Ship Canal Company, a Vanderbilt project.[32]

On receiving news shortly afterwards of a Chatfield plot to occupy Tigre Island, Squier hastily concluded a treaty with Honduras ceding the island to the United States for eighteen

[27] Williams, *Anglo-American Isthmian Diplomacy*, pp. 54–56.
[28] *House Exec. Docs.*, 31st Cong., 1st Sess., No. 75, pp. 110–117.
[29] *Ibid.*, p. 132. The Hise convention was disregarded at Washington.
[30] Williams, *Anglo-American Isthmian Diplomacy*, pp. 59–62.
[31] *House Exec. Docs.*, 31st Cong., 1st Sess., No. 75, pp. 152–154, 168–171.
[32] This company absorbed the Compañía de Tránsito de Nicaragua, organized by New York capitalists in March, 1849. In 1851, under the name of the Accessory Transit Company, it established a steamboat and coach service across Nicaragua which was much frequented until outclassed by the improvement of the facilities of Panama. No serious effort was made to construct a canal and the concession finally lapsed.

months. Chatfield countered by seizing the disputed territory without authorization in October, 1849, and remained there until ordered out by Admiral Hornby, commander of the British West Indian squadron. Both envoys were subsequently rebuked by their governments for their part in the affair.[33]

When intelligence of this incident reached Washington diplomatic conversations were already well under way between the two nations. Neither was disposed to go to war over the canal route. Indeed, both had repeatedly expressed a desire to aid the enterprise, but each feared exclusion by the other. The United States still held that no one power should control the San Juan in the event of its becoming a world highway.[34] Palmerston, on the other hand, had convinced W. C. Rives, the American representative in London, that his motive in seizing the San Juan was to prevent control of the Pacific from passing to the United States through a monopoly of the proposed passage.[35]

Although Sir Henry Bulwer came in December to Washington to forward the negotiations, progress was tediously slow. The British stubbornly insisted that the convention remain vague concerning their Mosquito protectorate. Other delays followed. Finally, in exasperation, Taylor prepared to push the Squier Nicaragua treaty through the Senate. This move spurred Sir Henry to action and on April 19, 1850, the Clayton-Bulwer treaty was signed. The Senate concurred the following July.[36] By its terms neither signatory was exclusively to control a Nicaraguan canal or fortify the route; neither was to take possession of, fortify, colonize, or exercise dominion over any part of Central America; both were to guard the safety and neutrality of the proposed canal and invite other nations to do the same; both would support any satisfactory company which should undertake the work; and these specific points were to be considered as a "gen-

[33] Williams, *Anglo-American Isthmian Diplomacy*, pp. 63–66.
[34] Bemis, *American Secretaries of State*, VI, 50; Johnson, *Four Centuries of the Panama Canal*, p. 57.
[35] Williams, *Anglo-American Isthmian Diplomacy*, pp. 80, 82.
[36] Bemis, *American Secretaries of State*, VI, 52–63.

eral principle" applicable to all isthmian canals or railroads in Panama or Tehuantepec as well as in Nicaragua.[37]

III

Throughout the half-century of its existence, the Clayton–Bulwer treaty proved a source of irritation to the United States. The timeliness of its service in bridging a major crisis with Great Britain was quickly lost to view in the flood of criticism that followed. "Probably no other diplomatic document to which the United States was a party," writes John Bassett Moore, "has given rise to discussions at once so complicated and so prolonged." [38]

Most of the dissatisfaction expressed in the years preceding the Civil War related to the failure of the treaty to force the British definitely from the Mosquito Coast.[39] The triumph of Union arms in 1865, however, abruptly heightened the self-assurance of the government and the press in dealing with foreign affairs. The whole principle of international control over the proposed isthmian waterway now came in for direct attack. In its place the doctrine of "an American canal under American control" met with constantly growing public favor in the United States.[40] The result of the mounting opposition to the coöperative spirit of the Clayton-Bulwer treaty had the effect of converting that agreement into a most formidable instrument of obstruction. It retained this latter character until its abrogation in 1901.

Grant was the first president to embody the "exclusive control" principle in his foreign policy.[41] He soon had Secretary Hamilton Fish at work on a Colombian canal treaty to replace that of Janu-

---

[37] Malloy, *Treaties*, I, 662.
[38] *Principles of American Diplomacy*, pp. 122–123.
[39] Williams, *Anglo-American Isthmian Diplomacy*, pp. 106–107.
[40] Moore, *Principles of American Diplomacy*, p. 125. Interestingly enough, this was the basis of Stephen A. Douglas's opposition to the Clayton-Bulwer treaty during the secret debates on ratification in the Senate. (Reported by Douglas to a kinsman in 1859. See *Sen Docs.*, 56th Cong., 2nd Sess., No. 41.)
[41] It is significant, however, that several weeks before Grant's inauguration, Secretary Seward wrote the Colombian minister at Washington that it was his "very deliberate conviction" (1) that "henceforth neither any foreign government nor the capitalists of any foreign nation, except the Government and capitalists of the United States, will ever undertake in good faith to build a canal across the

ary, 1869, which the Senate had failed to ratify.⁴² Fish summarized the president's attitude in a dispatch to the United States minister at Bogotá the following September: "He regards [the canal] as an American enterprise, which he desires to be undertaken under American auspices, to the benefit of which the whole commercial world should be fully admitted." ⁴³

The new convention, signed at Bogotá, January 26, 1870, assigned the sole right to construct a Panama canal to the United States, which in turn recognized Colombia's sovereignty over the region and guaranteed the work against hostile acts. Such other nations as wished might join in this guaranty. War vessels of nations engaged in hostilities with either signatory were to be excluded.⁴⁴ The Colombian senate ratified the treaty with certain amendments unacceptable to the United States Senate,⁴⁵ and in consequence the 1846 treaty continued to define the isthmian relations between the two countries until 1903.

The public interest that greeted the opening of the Suez Canal in 1869 was heightened by Disraeli's acquisition of the controlling shares in the canal company in 1875. In February of the following year Grant's interoceanic canal commission terminated its four-year study of seven outstanding isthmian routes with a report giving unanimous preference to the Greytown-Brito line across Nicaragua.⁴⁶ Its length, one hundred and seventy miles, as

---

Isthmus of Darien"; (2) that "the neutrality most desirable for Colombia is to be found in a combination of the power, authority and influence of the United States of America and the power, authority and influence of the United States of Colombia to protect the canal . . ."; and (3) that "not only would the United States be unwilling to enter into an entangling alliance with other foreign nations for the construction and maintenance of a passage through the Isthmus, but also that the idea that other commercial powers could and would consent to enter into a combination with the United States of America for that purpose is impracticable and visionary." (Cited from Moore, *Digest of International Law*, III, 21.)

⁴² *Sen. Docs.*, 56th Cong., 1st Sess., No. 237, pp. 45–51. This treaty granted the United States the exclusive right to build the canal and to defend it, if necessary, by military force, with full recognition of Colombia's sovereignty.

⁴³ *Sen. Exec. Docs.*, 46th Cong., 2nd Sess., No. 112, p. 46.

⁴⁴ *Sen. Docs.*, 56th Cong., 1st Sess., No. 237, pp. 51–61.

⁴⁵ Bemis, *American Secretaries of State*, VII, 207.

⁴⁶ *Sen. Exec. Docs.*, 46th Cong., 1st Sess., No. 15. The report was not transmitted to Congress until April, 1879, when it was called for by a resolution of the Senate.

compared with fifty at Panama, was compensated for, in the opinion of the commission, by an elevation considerably lower than that at Culebra. Its chief drawbacks lay in the absence of natural terminal harbors and the excessive rainfall at Greytown (San Juan).

As a result of this report and of the failure of the earlier negotiations with Colombia, the Department of State turned its attention once more to Nicaragua. Late in 1876 Secretary Fish attempted to secure a revision of the Dickinson-Ayon treaty of 1867. By this pact the United States had acquired the right of transit across the territory of the smaller republic, including the transport of troops and munitions under certain conditions, in return for protecting the line of communication.[47] Several months of futile discussion produced a deadlock over points touching Nicaragua's sovereignty and no alterations were made.

These diplomatic disappointments were soon followed by disturbing news from across the Atlantic. Ferdinand de Lesseps, of Suez Canal fame, had consented to assume the leadership of a canal venture in Central America. An international congress, summoned at Paris in May, 1879, to decide upon the most suitable route, voted in favor of a sea-level canal from the Bay of Panama to the Gulf of Limón, which, it was estimated, could be completed in about twelve years at a cost of $240,000,000, including interest charges during the course of construction.[48] A few months later de Lesseps organized the Compagnie Universelle du Canal Interocéanique and purchased the concession obtained

[47] Malloy, *Treaties*, II, 1279 *et seq*. The treaty further provided that Nicaragua should establish a free port at either terminus of the canal, and that the United States should use its influence to obtain the adherence of other nations to a guaranty of protection and neutrality.

[48] Rear-Admiral Daniel Ammen, U.S.N., and A. G. Menocal, a civil engineer employed by the Navy Department, represented the United States Government at the congress. Ammen's instructions and the reports of both men to Secretary Evarts are printed in *Sen. Docs.*, 58th Cong., 2nd Sess., No. 102. According to these reports the membership of the congress included contractors and speculators as well as engineers. It soon became apparent to the Americans that personal interests would have a great deal to do with the ultimate decision. A "technical" committee finally agreed upon a sea-level canal at Panama by a vote of 16 yeas, 11 abstentions, 3 nays, and 7 absentees. A general meeting of the congress adopted this report the following day. Only 98 of the 135 delegates recorded themselves:

from Colombia the previous year by a French engineer, Lucien Napoleon Bonaparte Wyse.[49] Work was to start on the completion of final surveys and efforts were made to raise the necessary capital by international subscription.

Public opinion in the United States was thoroughly aroused. The tone of the press grew increasingly unfriendly, while the Department of State urged upon Colombia the wisdom of discouraging the French undertaking. Burnside of Rhode Island sponsored a resolution in the Senate declaring that any attempt by the European powers "to establish under their protection and domination a ship-canal across the isthmus of Darien . . . could not be regarded in any other light than as a manifestation of an unfriendly disposition towards the United States." [50] Numerous resolutions of similar tenor were introduced in the House. For more than a year the foreign "threat" in Central America—and the applicability of the Monroe Doctrine to it—provided a favorite topic for congressional debate and hearings.[51]

Troubled by this show of resentment and by the difficulty of enlisting American financial support, de Lesseps paid a personal visit to President Hayes early in 1880 in the hope of getting the government's consent to the "European control" of his enterprise. Hayes refused to consider such a proposition. Instead, on March 8, he submitted to the Senate a report signed by Secretary of State Evarts which vigorously expounded the administration's attitude towards all interoceanic canal projects in Central America.[52] In an accompanying message the president added:

> The policy of this country is a canal under American control. The United States cannot consent to the surrender of this control

---

of these, 8 were opposed and 16, including Ammen and Menocal, abstained. The latter noted that only 19 engineers voted in the affirmative, of whom 8 had current or past connections with the Suez Canal, 5 were not practical engineers, and only one, a native Panamanian, had been in Central America.

[49] Signed March 23, 1878; ratified by Law 28 of 1878. Reprinted in *Official Opinions of the Attorneys-General of the United States*, Vol. XXIV (1902).

[50] Perkins, *Monroe Doctrine, 1867–1907*, p. 71; Bemis, *American Secretaries of State*, VII, 236.   [51] Perkins, *Monroe Doctrine, 1867–1907*, pp. 77 et seq.

[52] *Sen. Exec. Docs.*, 46th Cong., 2nd Sess., No. 112.

to any European power or to any combination of European powers. If existing treaties between the United States and other nations . . . stand in the way of this policy . . . suitable steps should be taken by just and liberal negotiations to promote and establish the American policy on this subject consistently with the rights of the nations affected by it.

Since the capital invested in such an enterprise would require protection from one or more great powers, and since European participation in this role would be "wholly inadmissible," the president pointed out that the United States "must exercise such control as will enable this country to protect its national interests and maintain the rights of those whose capital is invested in the work." The most striking statement of the message followed: "An interoceanic canal across the American Isthmus . . . would be the great ocean thoroughfare between our Atlantic and our Pacific shores, and virtually a part of the coast line of the United States." [53]

This declaration to the world went unchallenged. The French government even took pains to assure the Department of State that it had no intention of supporting the de Lesseps project in any way.[54] The resident minister of the United States in Bogotá reported that the French representative there had received instructions to the same effect.[55]

The Garfield and Arthur administrations adhered rigorously to the isthmian policy of Grant and Hayes. Secretary Blaine, in his famous correspondence with the British foreign secretary, Lord Granville, first assumed the attitude that the Clayton-Bulwer treaty did not apply to a canal at Panama, and then, failing to make his point, argued for a modification of that agreement that would give the United States a free hand in the construction and protection of any Central American waterway.[56] The British, with the law on their side, refused to yield their advantage, and

---
[53] Richardson, *Messages and Papers*, VII, 585–586.
[54] *Foreign Relations*, 1880, p. 385, Outrey to Evarts, March 22, 1880.
[55] *Ibid.*, 1881, p. 337, Dichman to Evarts, Nov. 6, 1880.
[56] *Sen. Docs.*, 56th Cong., 1st Sess., No. 237, pp. 380-396.

the controversy fell a legacy to Blaine's successor in office, Frederick T. Frelinghuysen.

Whereas Blaine had worked for a modification of the treaty of 1850, Frelinghuysen set out to secure its total abrogation, on the grounds that the requirements of national safety, the inviolability of the Monroe Doctrine, and the failure of the British to fulfill the terms of the treaty had rendered it an encumbrance, and, in fact, already void. But Downing Street still refused to take any action. Thereupon the disgruntled secretary proceeded in 1884 to negotiate a convention with Nicaragua granting the United States the exclusive right to build and control a canal across that country in open defiance of British claims. This remarkable document included still other precedent-breaking features. Not only did it pledge the United States to protect Nicaragua's territorial integrity, but it provided for a permanent alliance between the two nations. For the first time the neutralization of the transit was completely ignored.[57]

Early in 1885 the Senate rejected the so-called Frelinghuysen-Zavala treaty by a close vote and then promptly agreed to reconsider it. Consequently, the question was still pending when Grover Cleveland entered office in March. The new secretary of state, former Senator Thomas F. Bayard, had been a leading opponent of his predecessor's Central American policy. The pact was soon withdrawn by executive order and never resubmitted.[58] Of the presidents from Grant to Theodore Roosevelt, Cleveland alone favored a return to the internationalization policy of Henry Clay. In his first annual message to Congress he pledged his support to any practicable kind of transit "removed from the chance of domination by any single power." [59] Although no effort was made to reopen the discussion of the Clayton-Bulwer treaty during Cleveland's terms in the White House, Secretary Olney effectively drew the moral from the Blaine-Frelinghuysen-Granville correspondence when he remarked:

[57] *Sen. Docs.*, 58th Cong., 2nd Sess., No. 222, pp. 359 *et seq.;* Bemis, *American Secretaries of State*, VIII, 30–31; Richardson, *Messages and Papers*, VIII, 256.
[58] Nevins, *Grover Cleveland*, p. 205.
[59] Richardson, *Messages and Papers*, VIII, 327.

FROM COLUMBUS TO McKINLEY

If changed conditions now make stipulations, which were once deemed advantageous, either inapplicable or injurious, the true remedy is not in ingenious attempts to deny the existence of the treaty or to explain away its provisions, but in a direct and straightforward application to Great Britain for a reconsideration of the whole matter.[60]

IV

While Republican secretaries of state were searching for a means of escape from the trammels of the Clayton-Bulwer treaty, the Compagnie Universelle was encountering unexpected difficulty in forwarding its gigantic project on the Isthmus. Ferdinand de Lesseps was not an engineer but a diplomat with a marked ability for promoting enterprises requiring publicity and funds. When his undertaking flagged in the months following the adjournment of his "scientific" congress of 1879 and the purchase of the Wyse concession, he personally visited Panama and "inaugurated" the canal in an opera bouffe manner. He then made a tour of important cities in the United States seeking subscriptions. In this he was disappointed, as he was in his interview with President Hayes. His tactics finally fired the imagination of the French public, however, and the stock issue of December, 1880, was greatly oversubscribed at home.

In spite of the optimistic reports of the company's *Bulletin*, excavation did not start on a large scale until 1883. Previous to that, in 1881, the controlling interest in the Panama Railroad had been acquired for an exorbitant sum.[61] Climate and a primi-

---

[60] Moore, *Digest of International Law*, III, 209.

[61] By the terms of a new contract with the United States of Colombia, approved in 1867, the railroad could not prevent the opening of a canal across the Isthmus, but it was entitled to exact an indemnity from the concessioner, which was to be divided with Colombia. Furthermore, it had the right to prevent the construction of a canal along the actual train route. The Compagnie Universelle bought the controlling shares, first, because its plans necessitated cutting through part of the railroad route; second, because it wished to use the wharves, warehouses, etc. of the line; and, third, because by an outright purchase of the company it could avoid paying the indemnity to the Colombian government. The cost of constructing the railroad in the fifties was about $7,000,000; the de Lesseps company paid somewhat over $18,000,000 for 68,863 of the 70,000 outstanding shares. See *Walker Commission Report*, pp. 70, 204, 465.

tive country severely hampered the work but cutting proceeded steadily until some 72,000,000 cubic yards had been removed in 1889.

It was soon apparent, however, that the earlier estimates of the time and cost necessary for the completion of a sea-level canal would have to be considerably revised. A bond issue in 1886 brought a measure of financial relief, while a system of temporary locks was substituted for the sea-level plan the following year in the interest of economy.[62] But reports of incompetence and the intrigues of enemies had already impaired the company's credit, and when, in 1888, two lottery bond sales proved complete failures, the end was in sight. In February, 1889, the French courts appointed a receiver to take over the affairs of the company.[63]

The world-wide sensation caused by this collapse was followed by a series of shocking revelations concerning the conduct of the venture both on the Isthmus and at home. Of more than $260,000,000 received, practically nothing remained. It was shown in subsequent court inquiries that expenses of all sorts had been systematically "padded," that contractors had received millions of francs for services never rendered, and that a part of the French press had been subsidized. The trail of scandal led directly to the doorsteps of deputies and even cabinet ministers. Unfortunately, many aspects of the case were twisted to serve the ends of party faction and the trial of the promoters led to a contest of recrimination that shook France for several years. The aged de Lesseps, possibly the victim of his own folly and certainly the scapegoat of political intrigue, received a five-year prison sentence which was never enforced.[64]

[62] *Ibid.*, pp. 57, 207; Bunau-Varilla, *Panama: The Creation, Destruction, and Resurrection*, pp. 81–82.

[63] *Walker Commission Report*, pp. 57, 208–209; Bunau-Varilla, *Panama: The Creation, Destruction, and Resurrection*, pp. 87–89.

[64] Practically all the literature dealing with the causes of the company's downfall is strongly partisan. Philippe Bunau-Varilla, at one time in charge of the technical work on the Isthmus, is the most ardent of the defenders of the enterprise. For his account of the forces that combined to ruin the de Lesseps company see chaps. ix–xi in the work cited above. A competent and fairly objective treatment of the subject is to be found in Loewel, *Le Canal de Panama*.

The story of events on the Isthmus was likewise made public in all its stirring details. Simultaneously with the disclosures of negligence and extravagance was unfolded a tale of high heroism, of indomitable conflict with the tropic jungle, the heat, and the ravages of malaria and yellow fever.[65] Aside from the railroad there had been no facilities with which to start. Wharves, warehouses, homes, hospitals—everything had to be created in the face of heavy odds before excavation could begin. Nevertheless, approximately two-fifths of the digging had been completed when work was suspended in May, 1889.[66]

In 1887, while the French operations in Panama were at their height, a group of North American capitalists drew up plans for a rival project through Nicaragua. After some maneuvering, Congress incorporated the Maritime Canal Company of Nicaragua in February, 1889, under the terms of the treaty of 1867 and a later Costa Rican concession.[67] The company was formally launched in May with a paper capital of $250,000,000. Actual construction was to be carried on through a subsidiary firm with a paid-in capital of only $6,000,000. Ground was broken in October, 1889, and for over three years the work went forward, though necessarily on a limited scale. Workshops and a breakwater were built and a few miles of track laid. Excavation had scarcely started, however, before the funds gave out. Under ordinary conditions another five or ten millions could have been procured with little difficulty, for the venture was popular in the United States. By misfortune, the need for new financing coincided with the panic of 1893, which cut off further credit advances and sent the company into bankruptcy.[68]

The preliminary work done by the construction company had

[65] The loss of life from disease alone has been conservatively estimated at 16,000 (Bishop, *Panama Gateway*, pp. 97–98).
[66] *Walker Commission Report*, p. 57.
[67] *Ibid.*, pp. 401–402. The company took over the concessions which A. G. Menocal had obtained from Nicaragua and Costa Rica for the Nicaragua Canal Association in 1887–1888 (see *Sen. Reports*, 57th Cong., 1st Sess., No. 1, pp. 439–442).
[68] *Walker Commission Report*, p. 110; Keasbey, *Nicaragua Canal and the Monroe Doctrine*, pp. 437 et seq.

been planned with a view to meeting certain stipulations of the Nicaragua concession. While it was in progress the Maritime promoters had been attempting to cope with the larger problem of raising the quarter of a billion needed for cutting the channel. They thoroughly understood the advantages of retaining the national character of their enterprise and preferred, therefore, to restrict their capital market to the United States insofar as possible. They took pains, however, to emphasize their belief that exclusive North American control would not be possible without government endorsement of a part of their securities. With the help of friendly legislators bills were introduced into both houses of Congress in 1891 and 1892 providing for a guaranty by the United States of the company's bonds to the extent of $100,000,000 in return for control of a portion of the capital stock and the power to appoint a majority of the board of directors. The proposals failed to reach a vote and discussion of the subject was temporarily suspended by the financial disturbances of 1893.[69]

The harassed promoters presently discovered that they possessed an exceptionally able parliamentary spokesman in Senator John T. Morgan of Alabama. A member of the upper house since 1877, the former Confederate cavalry leader had proved his fighting qualities and effectiveness in debate in his struggles to prevent federal interference with the states and to reclaim unearned land grants from the transcontinental railroads. While his interests were not infrequently national in scope, as a Southerner he was vitally concerned with the problem of restoring the economic prosperity of his section. The solid foundation for a commercial and industrial rejuvenation of the Gulf states appeared to him to consist, first, in the development of more efficient transportation facilities within the lower Mississippi basin, and secondly, in the expansion of foreign markets for Southern iron, coal, cotton, and lumber. The first phase of this program had spurred his activity on behalf of local river and harbor improvements. The second

[69] Keasbey, *Nicaragua Canal and the Monroe Doctrine*, pp. 455 *et seq.* President Harrison recommended the passage of legislation guaranteeing the company's bonds in his annual messages to Congress in 1891 and 1892 (Richardson, *Messages and Papers*, IX, 188–189, 317).

had, at least as early as 1888, aroused his interest in the commercial possibilities of an isthmian canal. As between the Panama and the Nicaragua routes, the latter was a natural choice in the early nineties. The northern project was American in conception and held out good promise of success, while the southern was controlled abroad and had already run into serious difficulties. Another weighty consideration from Morgan's viewpoint was the added advantage which the Nicaragua waterway would give the Gulf ports over their Atlantic coast rivals in the matter of distance from points in the north Pacific.[70]

By 1894 the senator from Alabama was the acknowledged leader of the congressional movement to secure official backing for the Maritime Company. For the next nine years not a session passed without his witty and eloquent appeals on behalf of his Nicaragua Canal bills.[71] At first he proposed that the government guarantee the company's bond issues and exercise a close supervision over the undertaking. A more radical policy was embodied in his bill of June, 1896, which provided that the United States

---

[70] For Morgan's views on the canal see his letter to Joseph F. Johnston, Feb. 5, 1899; also Hiram Hitchcock to Morgan, Nov. 7, 1899; and the latter's speech before the Democratic Caucus in 1900, all in the Morgan Papers. The Southern economic argument is well summarized in an article by John L. Williams, of Richmond, Va., in the Chattanooga *Tradesman* of April 1, 1892. Williams quotes extensively from a "thoroughly informed statistician who has long and earnestly studied this question." Certain statements in this extract are worth noting. After pointing out that Galveston, New Orleans, Mobile, and Pensacola are from 750 to 850 miles nearer the proposed Nicaragua canal than New York, Philadelphia, or Boston, the unnamed "authority" continues:

"This advantage is increased by the fact that cotton, the staple product of the South, and iron, of which Alabama and Georgia have lately become such large producers, enter so largely into the manufacture of goods demanded by the markets of the countries thus opened up. The South American and Gulf ports will become the central coaling stations of the world, and the foundries and forges and spinning mills and looms, which during the last decade have become such important factors in the growing prosperity of the South, will hereafter manufacture the product of southern fields and mines, nearly a thousand miles closer to the place where such manufactured goods are to be marketed and consumed . . . The opening of the canal will provide the South with what she lacks today more than anything else, that is, an advantageous market for manufactured goods. With that assured she may confidently expect a growth of population and material prosperity to follow as great if not greater than that which followed the extension of railroads into the great west. . . ."

[71] The first Morgan Nicaragua bill was introduced Jan. 22, 1894 (*Sen. Reports*, 55th Cong., 3rd Sess., No. 1417).

purchase the obligations of the Maritime Company, appoint a majority of the board of directors, and proceed to dig the canal through this agency.[72]

Until 1895 Congress did no more than occasionally discuss the various proposals. In that year, however, it appropriated $50,000 for an investigation of the practicality of the Maritime Company's plans. A commission headed by Lt.-Col. William Ludlow visited the Isthmus during the summer and in October submitted a report endorsing the chief features of the scheme, but suggesting a more elaborate study of the situation.[73] Accordingly, a new commission was provided for in the spring of 1897, with unlimited time and a liberal subsidy at its disposal. President McKinley selected Admiral John G. Walker to head this board with Col. Peter C. Hains and Prof. Lewis Haupt as his associates. After two years of careful examination the Walker Commission reported favorably on the Nicaragua route, although it recommended certain alterations in the plans drawn up by the Maritime engineers.[74]

Further action on the subject was postponed by the rapid sequence of events that resulted in the war with Spain. The nation, weary of Free Silver, the Tariff, and the problems growing out of the recent depression, entered the conflict with enthusiasm. Its outlook expanded within a few brief months to embrace the international scene. Manila Bay and Santiago marked the opening of a new era, in which the world became America's oyster. One incident of the war, particularly, had a direct bearing on the subsequent history of the canal. The record-breaking dash of the *Oregon* dramatized the need for closer intercoastal communication as no number of technical reports could possibly have done. By the end of 1898 chambers of commerce, politicians, and the press, irrespective of their views on other aspects of overseas expansion,

[72] *Cong. Rec.*, 55th Cong., 3rd Sess., pp. 901–902. A convenient collection of all canal bills and amendments introduced in the Senate from 1891 to January, 1899, can be found in *ibid.*, pp. 895–910.

[73] *House Docs.*, 54th Cong., 1st Sess., No. 279.

[74] The report was submitted in May, 1899, and was printed by the Isthmian Canal Commission, the successor of the 1897 board (*Sen. Docs.*, 57th Cong., 1st Sess., No. 357).

were demanding that the government take prompt steps to amend or abrogate the Clayton-Bulwer treaty and subsidize the construction of the isthmian waterway.

Although Congress had made no commitments as to the route, public sentiment in the United States was overwhelmingly in favor of a line through Nicaragua. To the American people, Panama was associated with the French and the scandal that followed their failure, whereas Nicaragua had taken on the character of a "national project." This feeling could be attributed in part to a sense of engineering rivalry with France, for de Lesseps had selected his canal site barely three years after Grant's interoceanic canal commission had recommended Greytown-Brito as the superior route. Every other field survey by United States Army and Navy engineers had also given preference to Nicaragua.[75] Other less technical reasons influenced public opinion as well. Nicaragua was the scene of the Squier-Chatfield skirmishes which had eventually halted the advance of the British in Central America and won the friendship of that republic for the United States. Finally, millions of dollars of American capital were invested there in the dormant Maritime enterprise.

For several years Congress had seemed on the verge of granting financial assistance to the stranded company. Support for such a program began to waver, however, during the summer of

[75] The earliest survey of the Nicaragua route was made by Col. O. H. Childs for the American Atlantic and Pacific Ship Canal Co. in 1850–52. His report was checked and approved by two army engineers appointed by President Fillmore. The suggested route did not vary importantly from that recommended by the Walker Commission of 1897. Grant's commission sent Commanders Hatfield and Lull to Nicaragua in 1872–73 to direct that part of the survey. Maj. Walter McFarland of the Corps of Engineers reported to the War Department in 1874 that the Nicaragua route was practicable and estimated the cost roughly at $140,000,000 for a canal 26 ft. deep. A. G. Menocal, a civil engineer employed by the Navy Department, resurveyed the same region in 1885 and made detailed recommendations. Government surveys were also made of the Tehuantepec, Panama, Atrato, and Darien routes in the seventies. The sole report unfavorable to the Nicaragua line made previous to 1902 appeared in a volume compiled at the request of Congress by Admiral C. H. Davis (*Report on Interoceanic Canals and Railroads between the Atlantic and Pacific Oceans*). This work was based not on direct field tests but upon previous surveys and concluded that in the light of existing knowledge only the Darien route warranted further investigation. See *Walker Commission Report*, pp. 35–43, 75, et seq.

1898 as it became clear that Nicaragua was rapidly losing interest in the Maritime concessioners. The change in the Managua government's attitude was chiefly due to fair promises from another quarter. President Zelaya, mindful of the depleted state of his treasury, was lending an attentive ear to the overtures of a group of United States citizens, generally known as the Grace-Eyre-Cragin syndicate, which was backed, in name at least, by such men as John Jacob Astor, Levi P. Morton, and William R. Grace. After some hesitation, probably induced by pressure from the Department of State, the executive signed a "promise of contract" with Edward Eyre and Edward F. Cragin on October 27, 1898. This agreement declared the existing concession void on October 9, 1899, and authorized the new contracting party to proceed with the construction of a canal after that date. The discomfited Maritime officials protested this as a violation of their privilege of extension and carried the fight to Washington.[76]

The situation was soon further complicated by the appearance in the field of another rival for congressional support—the New Panama Canal Company. Even while the courts were baring to the world the disgrace of de Lesseps and his associates, the receiver of the Compagnie Universelle had been busy knotting again the threads of enterprise. A new plan was adopted involving a lock canal to be completed in eight years at a cost of $180,-000,000. The original Wyse concession expired in 1893, but two extensions were secured from the Colombian government, for considerations, which set October 31, 1904, as the date by which the canal had to be open to traffic. In October, 1894, the New Panama Canal Company was organized to receive the rights and

---

[76] Chester Donaldson, United States consul at Managua, reported confidentially to Hiram Hitchcock, president of the Maritime Company, that he had three times delayed Zelaya's signing of the new agreement by remonstrating in the name of the United States and by personal appeals to him as a friend but that the Cragin party increased their offers, and offered to pay all expenses of an extra session of congress. (Hitchcock sent a copy of this letter to Morgan, apparently in December, 1899; Morgan Papers.) A letter in the same collection, Hitchcock to Morgan, Nov. 7, 1899, gives further indication that the Department of State urged Zelaya not to sign the Cragin contract. For the text of the contract, see *Walker Commission Report*, pp. 403-412.

properties of the "Old Company" and to resume the task of uniting the oceans.[77]

Although the projected undertaking called for an outlay of $180,000,000, there was no such amount on hand. The cash capital of the New Company was about $12,000,000, most of it subscribed by those accused of malefactions connected with the defunct de Lesseps venture on the understanding that the charges against them would be dismissed.[78] Of the 650,000 shares, 50,000 went to the Colombian government in consideration of the extension of time. Sixty per cent of the profits of the New Company were to be turned over to the receiver of its predecessor, in return for the transfer of the latter's assets.[79]

Just when the directors decided to sell out is not certain, though it was very probably their aim from the first. In any case, no attempt was made to raise the remainder of the $180,000,000 called for in the plans. Success would have been unlikely in view of the state of public feeling in France. The company possessed a concession, charts, machinery, a railroad, and almost half the excavation needed for the canal. This property could be utilized either by a private company with sufficient capital or by the United States Government. A deal with the latter would be complicated by a provision in the Wyse concession which forbade its transfer to a foreign government without the consent of Colombia. The Bogotá authorities might very well make their consent conditional upon a substantial share of the sale price. Purchase by a private firm would avoid this contingency, but, although the directors were more than ready to consider offers, nothing definite developed. By the close of the Spanish War it

[77] *Walker Commission Report*, pp. 57–60, 211–213, 488 *et seq.*; Bishop, *Panama Gateway*, pp. 106–107.
[78] *Story of Panama*, pp. 139–140 (Hall testimony).
[79] *Official Opinions of the Attorneys-General of the United States*, XXIV (1902), 379–380. Work on the Culebra cut began once more and continued in desultory fashion until the surrender of the property to the United States in May, 1904. Less than 4,000,000 cubic yards had been cut by the end of 1898 at a cost of about $6,000,000. The working force varied between 1,900 and 3,000 as compared to a 20,000 maximum on the de Lesseps payroll (*Walker Commission Report*, p. 59).

appeared that the United States was the sole prospective customer. That nation, however, had thoughts only for Nicaragua. Unless this partiality were overcome in favor of Panama, the New Company's holdings were worthless. Time and a well-directed propaganda were essential to convert Congress and the public. The chief responsibility for this task devolved upon William Nelson Cromwell, counsel for the company's "interests" in the United States.

Late in November, 1898, a.month after the signing of the Eyre-Cragin contract in Managua, Cromwell brought the French project forward as an open competitor for congressional support. His action precipitated a bitter struggle between the partisans of the rival routes which continued, with scarcely a pause, until the final triumph of Panama in February, 1904. For the first two years of this period the New Company was forced to adopt a defensive strategy. Lacking the necessary authorization to sell its property to the United States, it sought to delay the decision of Congress by blocking every measure favorable to Nicaragua. Towards the end of 1900, however, Colombia yielded to the company's importunities and dispatched a representative to Washington empowered to treat with the Department of State on the subject of an interoceanic canal. From that time on the Bogotá government was a prominent participant in the Battle of the Routes.

II

THE COLOMBIAN BACKGROUND

MANY OF THE CIRCUMSTANCES which shaped the course of the negotiations leading to the Hay-Herrán treaty derived their force from long-standing economic and political problems of the Colombian people. Some account of that nation's history and geographical setting is therefore essential before proceeding with the main narrative. Against the background of these influences Colombia's delays and inconsistencies in dealing with the United States during the years 1901 to 1903 take on fuller significance, while the tactical errors of the two governments are thrown into sharper relief.

The Republic of Colombia is a large, potentially wealthy, and sparsely populated country occupying the northwestern corner of South America where the continent adjoins the Isthmus of Panama. Its exact area was still undefined in 1901 but approximated 480,000 square miles (more than the combined areas of California, Washington, Oregon, and Arizona).[1] In size it ranks fifth among Latin-American nations and is the only country on the southern continent whose shores are washed by both the Atlantic and Pacific oceans.

No physical feature of this land exercises a more pronounced influence over the modes of thought and existence of the inhabitants than the three mighty Andean ranges which extend from the border of Ecuador northeasterly across the country. These chains are known as the Western, Central, and Eastern Cordilleras, and through the two valleys formed by their parallel courses flow Colombia's greatest rivers, the Cauca and the Magdalena.

---

[1] The *Political Handbook of the World* for 1937 gives the present area of Colombia as 447,536 sq. mi. and that of Panama as 32,380 sq. mi. (excluding Canal Zone). Other estimates run considerably higher.

34 THE COLOMBIAN BACKGROUND

The former stream drains the western valley to a point about two hundred miles from the coast, where the subsidence of the Central Cordillera permits it to turn eastward to join the majestic Magdalena in its thousand-mile progress to the Caribbean. Smaller streams, such as the Dagua, Patía, and San Juan, enter the Pacific, while the Eastern Cordillera contributes generously to the headwaters of the Amazon and Orinoco rivers. The Atrato, which rises a few miles from the Pacific and flows due northward into the Caribbean, is interesting because of the recurrent discussion of its practicability as an interoceanic canal route.[2]

Well up on the shoulders of the mountain ranges there are perched a number of broad plateaux, varying in altitude from 6,000 to over 15,000 feet. The loftier of these, known as *páramos*, are desolate, fog-shrouded stretches, whose inhospitality is respected by all but the most adventurous. Those below 9,000 feet, however, are generally temperate in climate and well adapted for agriculture. The most important of the lower tablelands is the *sabana* of Bogotá, about 8,600 feet high, on the eastern edge of which rises the city of that name. Other centers of population and commerce, such as Medellín, are situated in valleys of the Cordilleras, sufficiently elevated to escape the torrid conditions of the coast. Scenically, the crowning grandeur of the country consists in the snow-clad peaks of the central range, most of them inactive volcanoes. Tolima, Mesa de Herveo, and Huila all rise to heights of over 18,000 feet, the glistening summits of the first two being visible from Bogotá, one hundred miles distant.

The mountain range has been mentioned first because it is the home of the greater part of the population and the center of the European culture of the nation. Nearly two-thirds of Colombia's vast area, however, is comparatively lowland, lying eastward and southeastward of Bogotá, and inhabited by aborigines, many of whom have never set eyes upon a white man. The northern part of this district, which drains into the Orinoco,

[2] Good brief descriptions of the geography of Colombia are to be found in Petre, *Republic of Colombia*, Eder, *Colombia*, and Lévine, *Colombia*. Also see *Anales diplomáticos y consulares*, II, 10 footnote, 11–19.

II. THE CONTINENTAL DEPARTMENTS OF COLOMBIA
IN 1902

consists of vast *llanos,* or plains. The part to the south is covered by impenetrable *selvas,* or forests, which have not yet been fully explored. Both sections would be of great value to Colombia had it but the man power and the capital to exploit them.

The *colombianos* are derived from three stocks, white, Indian, and Negro, with numerous degrees of intermixture. As nearly as can be estimated, the population in 1901 numbered somewhat more than four million people, of whom probably half were of mixed blood.[3] The Negroes inhabit the *tierra caliente* along the seacoast and the lowland river valleys. Rarely is one seen in the streets of Bogotá. The whites and *mestizos* (part white, part Indian) live together in the temperate regions of the interior, particularly in the zone between 4,000 and 9,000 feet above sea level. Among the *mestizos,* the lowest economic group consists of domestics and day laborers. Above this is a numerous class of shopkeepers, mechanics, and artisans. The educated *mestizos* are sometimes merchants and traders, but more generally lawyers, physicians, teachers, priests, and politicians. The full-blooded Indians who have adopted the ways of the white man are usually farmers, marketmen, or farm laborers. Race feeling has never been one of Colombia's major social problems, perhaps because of the traditional sanction given to assimilation by the Catholic Church, and the unifying effect of a language and religion common to all types (except, of course, the native tribes).[4] This does not mean that social distinctions based on ancestry are nonexistent, but the effects of such differences seem to be softened by the many degrees of miscegenation and the numerical and economic strength of the mixed groups.

The degree of energy customarily displayed by the inhabitants of the "hot country" is not likely to excite the admiration of North American or European visitors. The traveler whose ac-

---

[3] Petre, *Republic of Colombia,* p. 8; Lévine, *Colombia,* p. 24. In that year the Colombian government placed the population, including savages, at about five million, but the basis for this computation is not given (*Anales diplomáticos y consulares,* II, 19).

[4] Petre, *Republic of Colombia,* pp. 86-91; Scruggs, *Colombian and Venezuelan Republics,* pp. 108-111.

THE COLOMBIAN BACKGROUND 37

quaintance with the Colombian people is limited to a stop-over at Buenaventura or one of the Atlantic ports in many cases departs with an impression that is both unflattering and unjust. With occasional exceptions, the Negroes of the coast appear to exist in a state of perpetual weariness, in spite of their care to avoid undue exertion. Minimum motion has been reduced to a fine art. From the white man's point of view these people often seem sullen and worthless. Yet it is but fair to note that the Negro of the seacoast has his point of view as well, even if inarticulate in form, and that it is the product of equatorial conditions, not of New York or London.

What has been said of the Negro applies in a general way to the various mixed types in the lowlands. Let an actual incident serve as an illustration. A river-steamer on the Magdalena has just commenced its slow journey from La Dorada northward to the Caribbean. An English commercial representative, middle-aged and self-assured, is traveling *en lujo,* which means that his "luxurious" quarters are perched on the top deck where the heat is greatest. He summons the *mestizo* serving-boy and shows him money. That is to be his if he proves himself prompt and willing during the trip. The Englishman wants his tea at four o'clock. It arrives at approximately five-thirty. The exasperated Briton delivers himself of a vigorous discourse on alertness and punctuality. Then, lowering his voice to a coaxing tone, as one who is trying to reason patiently with an obdurate and simple-minded fellow, he adds: "Haven't you any desire to get ahead with your employers?" The boy looks at him in a puzzled way and replies: "No, *señor,* the work is easy and I get my food; as soon as I have a little money I will quit." The interview is brought to an end with a few aphorisms on ambition and a crisp pronouncement on "The Whole Trouble with You People." When the *muchacho* has gone, the Englishman grunts and settles down to his tea with the satisfaction of one who has smitten for the Lord. Outside on the deck the Colombian shrugs his shoulders and tells his companions: "Something happened to make the *señor* angry."

There is no bamboo-hut-to-president legend in Colombia. Those who do the manual work of the hot belt are not lashed by a desire to "get ahead." They work simply to live. With a few *centavos* they feel and act independent, or, to the white man's way of thinking, "impudent." There is a basis of truth to the saying that a man will not cross the street for a *peso* if he has half that sum in his pockets. After all, life is not rigorous in these regions, the necessities are comparatively easy to procure, and, in many communities, the uses for money are limited.

The situation is different in the more temperate altitudes. The population of Bogotá is mostly white and *mestizo*. Here the business of life is more highly organized and social incentives play a greater part. The pace is leisurely but by no means indolent. Black coffee in the middle of the morning is an institution, meals are never rushed, and there is no lack of holidays. As in other Latin-American countries *mañana* is the favorite time for doing anything, unless it be *mañana o pasado* (tomorrow or later). Yet in the end most things get done, and with a courtesy and charm that often atone for the exasperation of delay. The whites are in greatest proportion in the mountainous department of Antioquia, of which Medellín is the capital. It is said that three-fourths of the population in this district is of European descent. In no other part of the nation are the people so enterprising, so thrifty, or so advanced along commercial lines.

Few areas on the earth's surface can boast a more bountiful natural endowment than Colombia. The gold and silver mines of Antioquia and Cauca rivaled those of Peru in the centuries of Spanish dominion and are by no means exhausted today. Platinum, copper, lead, and coal are known to be plentiful. From the quarries of Muzo and Coscuez come the finest emeralds in the world.[5] The forests yield dye-woods, mahogany, medicinal plants, orchids, and vegetable ivory. Soil and climate are well adapted to the growing of coffee, bananas, maize, cacao, cotton, and sugar-cane. A fairly recent estimate places the potential energy of the

[5] Lévine, *Colombia*, chap. xiii; Petre, *Republic of Colombia*, chap. x.

THE COLOMBIAN BACKGROUND

country's streams in the neighborhood of four million horsepower.[6]

In spite of this heritage Colombia was a poor and backward nation in 1900. The reasons for this were partly historical and partly geographical. The frequent and disastrous civil conflicts of the preceding two generations had ruined the country's credit abroad and its industry at home. Lack of capital retarded the introduction of up-to-date methods in mining and agriculture. The available man power was insufficient for the exploitation of the nation's resources, and was constantly subject to depletion by warfare. Owing to these and other causes, the Colombian people had failed utterly in their efforts to overcome the isolation imposed by the great Cordilleras. This fact had been responsible for many of their difficulties and misfortunes during the nineteenth century, and was to play an important role in the events leading up to the separation of Panama.

The effect of the mountains was most immediate upon means of communication. In all Colombia less than four hundred miles of railroad were under operation by 1902.[7] Of the rivers, only the Cauca and the Magdalena were important as inland routes of travel. The mule was as indispensable for conveyance as it had been for the previous four hundred and fifty years. The expense of transportation to the coast discouraged the production of surplus crops of sugar, cotton, and cacao for export, and seriously hampered the increase of the coffee-growing industry. In these and countless other ways the economic life of the nation suffered beneath its mountain yoke. The social and political consequences of this handicap were equally far-reaching. Isolation fostered provincialism and local jealousies. The functions of the central government were performed ineffectively or not at all, while the defiance of authority was rendered correspondingly easy. The

[6] Rippy, *Capitalists and Colombia*, p. 29.
[7] This includes, of course, the 45-mile railroad across the Isthmus of Panama. The longest continuous stretch was the 65-mile line from Cartagena to Calamar on the Magdalena River. See *Anales diplomáticos y consulares*, II, 20–21; Petre, *Republic of Colombia*, pp. 194–196.

Colombian was not lacking in national pride, but the problem of his livelihood appeared to him as sectional rather than national. Nationalism was not economically profitable to any particular class, as it had been in the countries of its origin, and it therefore existed in Colombia chiefly as a sentiment. The intellectuals had introduced it and they were still its guardians. The giant Cordilleras were its foe.

At the beginning of the twentieth century the wealth, social prestige, and political power of the country were concentrated in the hands of a group of families which claimed unmixed descent from the Spanish conquerors. These aristocrats owned the great coffee plantations and cattle ranches of the interior, and shared among themselves the high offices in Church and State. Many of them spent part of the year at least in Bogotá entertaining within their exclusive circle and enjoying the few amusements which the capital afforded. As a class they were well educated and refined, with the sensitiveness and exalted sense of honor of their Castilian forebears. Many of them entered the professions or devoted themselves to literature. Politics was another favorite career, and by no means a dull one, for the vicissitudes of party strife presented recurrent military interludes. This participation in officeholding by the upper classes imparted a marked tone of dignity and good breeding to the government which more progressive nations have sometimes lacked.

One of the most characteristic features of the political scene in Bogotá was the prominence of oratorical display. Lofty sentiment and resounding phrases appealed strongly to the people of all classes. The delight of the crowd is easier to comprehend than the fact that the educated and cultured men responsible for these flights actually believed what they said in certain cases. This is partly accounted for by the genuine regard which many Colombians of the upper classes had, or thought that they had, for elevated ideals, especially those connected with the progress of their country. Also, literary men and academicians were frequently called upon to fill high posts in the government, and they sometimes brought with them exaggerated conceptions of Colombia's

THE COLOMBIAN BACKGROUND 41

place in the family of nations. Yet doubtless a goodly number of the political orators who reminded their hearers that the republic advanced ". . . *en la vanguardia de la civilización*" found in hyperbole a convenient screen for the advancement of interests of a more personal order.

Corruption was, unfortunately, a persistent evil, particularly among the lower classes of officeholders both federal and local. There is no fair basis for comparing the extent of the practice in Colombia with the corresponding situation in the United States. Political graft exacted a heavy toll from the people of both nations, to the distress of high-minded citizens in each. The most significant difference was that the states and municipalities of the United States were often prosperous enough to "carry" a certain amount of peculation, while those of Colombia were not. Incompetence and administrative inefficiency constituted another serious drain on the public funds. Yet these conditions can easily be overstated, for they represent but one part of the political picture. The high officials of the Marroquín government, whatever their limitations, were in most cases men of irreproachable personal character and in no sense meriting Theodore Roosevelt's later characterization of them as "bandits." [8]

Bogotá was founded in 1537 by Gonzalo Jiménez de Quesada, the conqueror of the *sabana* kingdom of the Chibchas, from whose ancient capital the present city takes its name.[9] The location is well suited to white habitation, for, although it lies within five degrees of the equator, the climate is mild and equable. The seasons consist of alternate wet and dry periods, with no extremes of heat or cold. Midday is usually warm, no matter what the time of year, but evenings are often chilly enough to make a fire seem welcome.

[8] In this connection ex-Minister Du Bois wrote: "An impartial investigation at Bogotá, running over a period of two years . . . convinced me that, instead of 'blackmailers' and 'bandits,' the public men of Colombia compare well with the public men of other countries in intelligence and respectability, while the social life is as refined and cultured as can be found in any capital in the world. Bogotá is called the Athens of South America." Quoted from Freehoff, *America and the Canal Title*, p. 43.

[9] The Spanish called the city Santa Fé de Bogotá.

The eastern part of the city rests upon the lower slopes of Guadalupe and Monserrate, twin peaks which rise some 2,000 feet above the *sabana* and offer the climber a magnificent view for scores of miles around. From this vantage point the town below appears to reach out tentatively from the security of the foothills towards the spacious freedom of the plain. The monotony of its red-tiled roofs is broken by occasional plazas and gardens, and by the notable double towers of the Cathedral. Churches are numerous, many of them quaint structures of the sixteenth and seventeenth centuries. Some of the largest buildings were the property of various religious orders until they were seized for the use of the government during the sixties of the last century.

In appearance the Bogotá of 1900 would compare unfavorably with other world capitals. Its streets were poorly paved and, during the rainy seasons, filled with mud. The sidewalks were barely wide enough for two persons to pass, which mattered very little since everyone walked in the streets. From time to time the crowds would part to make way for a file of thoughtful-looking donkeys, heavily loaded with the products of the surrounding countryside. Carriages were used by a few notables, like the president or the archbishop, but more for the sake of dignity than speed. Electric lights and telephones were beginning to appear in the fashionable houses, although the service left a great deal to be desired. Around the Plaza Bolívar were grouped the unfinished government buildings, the Cathedral, and an assortment of shops. Not far away, the Theatre offered accommodation to the occasional operatic or dramatic entertainments, to which Society regularly came for the purpose of seeing and being seen.[10]

While Bogotá lacked many of the conveniences of the larger European and North American cities of the time, it was indisputably a center of culture and refinement. Its poets, novelists, and historians had long been prominent in the Spanish-speaking world. The Colombians prided themselves that their *castellano*

[10] Petre, *Republic of Colombia*, chap. vi; Scruggs, *Colombian and Venezuelan Republics*, pp. 65–66.

THE COLOMBIAN BACKGROUND 43

was the purest in the Western Hemisphere and that their capital was the "Athens of South America." Yet, unlike its classical prototype, Bogotá was very much limited in its contacts with outside people and ideas. The most unfortunate result of this circumstance was a tendency among Colombian intellectual and political leaders to regard the rest of the world as beyond the orbit of their everyday concerns, to be dealt with as an abstraction because of its remoteness.

The reality of this isolation cannot be appreciated without some idea of the "systems" of communication connecting the Colombian capital and the coast. The traveler could choose between two routes of ingress. If he selected to start from the Pacific he would leave Buenaventura by railroad and continue as far as the condition of the line permitted, which by 1903 was not much over seven miles.[11] From that point forward progress was on mule-back. Once across the arid Western Cordillera, the pleasant town of Cali in the Cauca Valley provided a resting place for the more arduous passage over the Quindio Trail. This path, for it was nothing more, scaled the precipitous slopes of the central range to the shoulder of mighty Tolima, and from there down into Ibagué. The remainder of the route traversed the broad valley of the Magdalena, crossed the river, and ascended the abrupt side of the Bogotá plateau. The final twenty-five miles could be made by train, which was a little faster but no more comfortable than the back of the mule. The time consumed in making this trip might vary anywhere from two weeks to a month.

The second method of penetration to the capital was to leave the Atlantic coast at Barranquilla and proceed up the Magdalena to Honda and from there by mule to the *sabana*. This route was less strenuous than the other, but just as incalculable in time. In the rainy seasons the steamers, of the shallow-draught type once common on the Mississippi, could accomplish the five hundred and fifty miles to La Dorada in seven or eight days, barring accidents. When the river was low, however, the trip might re-

[11] Petre, *Republic of Colombia*, p. 203. The line had been laid out as far as Cali, but much of the completed track was unusable owing to lack of repairs.

quire anywhere from ten to twenty days, including the time spent on sandbanks. Navigation was hindered by the stream's shifting load of sediment, which constantly altered the channel of the main current. Yet the possibility of stranding was not serious compared to the danger of collision with submerged snags or other hidden obstructions. The heat, the mosquitoes, and the food constituted the foreign visitor's trinity of tribulation, although the experienced traveler escaped the last of these trials by bringing along his own provisions. From La Dorada it was a few hours' train ride around the Magdalena rapids and sandbars to Honda, starting point for the difficult three-day mule trek to the plateau of Bogotá. A longer but less strenuous alternative route from Honda followed the "upper river" for ninety-three miles to Giradot, from which point the uncompleted Colombian National Railway covered part of the steep ascent to the *sabana*.[12]

The postal and telegraphic services were no more efficient than other means of communication. Mail from the capital to points in the outside world was subject to all the delays of Magdalena traffic. None of the river companies had contracts to carry government dispatches and none seemed to keep any recognizable schedule of departures.[13] At Barranquilla the mail awaited the arrival of some appropriate steamer or was forwarded to Colón for transshipment. Official correspondence between Bogotá and Washington during the urgent months of the Panama Canal negotiations frequently required from eight to ten weeks for delivery. Telegraph lines ran from the capital to Barranquilla and Buenaventura, the latter being generally preferable because it connected directly with the transatlantic and North American cables which touched at Panama City. Unfortunately, these lines had a way of getting out of commission, sometimes when they were needed most, and their messages would then be delayed for a week or more. From every point of view Bogotá was one of the most inaccessible cities in the civilized world during the years with which we are concerned—a circumstance which played an

[12] *Ibid.*, chap. iii; Scruggs, *Colombian and Venezuelan Republics*, p. 27.
[13] See Petre, *Republic of Colombia*, pp. 192–193.

important part in making this period one of unhappy memory for Colombia.

II

Certain aspects of the Colombian people's nine-year struggle for independence and their eventual adoption of republican institutions in 1821 resembled the action of England's North American colonies half a century before. The resemblance was not altogether accidental, but it was in nearly every important respect superficial. The generations of training in self-government which prepared the way for republicanism in the United States had no counterpart in the previous history of New Granada. The leaders who drafted the first constitution of Colombia at Cúcuta were thoroughly imbued with the liberal doctrines of the eighteenth century, yet the mass of the people they represented was unable to discard the burden of its colonial heritage along with the viceroys and captains-general of Spain. By ancient custom the mother country had restricted the high offices of administration to her own sons and, consequently, no experienced group or class among the natives stood ready to assume the tasks of government. Ignorance and suspicion of central authority were widespread, while continued warfare had accustomed the population to disorder and violence. Seven constitutions and seventy civil wars in the years from 1821 to 1901 failed to obliterate the discrepancy between the forms and the facts of political power. Democracy in Colombia during the nineteenth century was a farce, and republicanism was a farce, not because sincere and high-minded leaders were lacking, but because nothing in the tradition of the people fitted them for sovereignty. The mechanics of each successive constitution varied somewhat from its predecessors, but all were based on the assumption that the governed were capable of a large degree of coöperation with their chosen rulers. This fallacy was exposed at every crisis, with the result that the executive power had constant recourse to extra-legal devices to ensure the continuation of any government at all.[14]

[14] The best general account of Colombia in the nineteenth century is to be found in Henao and Arrubla, *History of Colombia*, trans. by J. Fred Rippy (1938).

The first Republic of Colombia, which comprised the present nations of Colombia, Panama, Venezuela, and Ecuador, did not survive the decade of its founding.[15] Civil dissensions and military operations against the Spaniards in Peru absorbed President Bolívar's energies to the exclusion of his plans for a strong, centralized state. A growing sentiment of bitterness between the followers of the Liberator and the partisans of the federalist leader, Vice-President Santander, culminated in an attempt on Bolívar's life in 1828 and his immediate assumption of dictatorial powers over the restive parts of the republic. When he retired to private life in the spring of 1830 the nation he had helped to organize was tottering. Within the next two years Venezuela and Ecuador set themselves up as independent republics.[16]

The remaining fragment, with a territory practically coextensive with that claimed by Colombia in 1901, took the name of the Republic of New Granada and adopted a constitution which theoretically gave considerable power to the national government. Although the centralist principle was retained in the revised constitution of 1843, the difficulties of communication and the ambitions of sectional groups contributed to an increasing demand for a reorganization of the country along federalist lines. The Liberal party, which espoused this cause, secured important constitutional modifications in 1853, and finally forced through a series of acts in 1855–57 erecting the provinces into autonomous states. This arrangement was confirmed by the constitution of 1858 which transmuted the Republic of New Granada into the Granadan Confederation and left the central authority at Bogotá very much weakened.[17]

The most important political changes of the next few years centered about the activities of General Tomás de Mosquera. This gentleman, at first identified with the Conservative party, had served as president of New Granada from 1845 to 1849. Among his noteworthy accomplishments had been the negotiation of the treaty of 1846 with the United States, the inaugura-

---

[15] A constitution was adopted for "Great Colombia" at Cúcuta in 1821.
[16] Robertson, *History of the Latin-American Nations*, pp. 359, 360–362.
[17] *Ibid.*, pp. 362–367.

THE COLOMBIAN BACKGROUND 47

tion of steam navigation on the Magdalena, and the complete reform of the national currency. By 1860 he had become governor of the state of The Cauca and an ardent Liberal. Using for pretext an unpopular law enacted by the national congress in that year, Mosquera led a revolt which culminated in his capture of Bogotá. In May, 1863, after a counter-uprising of the Conservatives had been crushed, a constitution for the "United States of Colombia" was promulgated by a convention consisting chiefly of Liberals. Mosquera's influence was dominant until 1867, when he was exiled for misconduct in office. This second tenure of power was featured by a vigorous attack on the Church; the Jesuits were expelled, religious orders suppressed, and Church property confiscated by the nation. As a result, party lines were more strictly drawn, the Conservatives championing limited suffrage, a powerful central government, and the rights of the Church in opposition to the anticlerical and federalist policies of their antagonists.[18]

In 1880 Dr. Rafael Núñez, a journalist and politician, was chosen president with the support of the Liberals. His accession to office marked the beginning of another period of strong-man control over Colombia's affairs which lasted, with but one brief interruption, until his death in 1894. He soon convinced himself that the most important problems then pressing for solution could not be solved by a particularist form of government or by a conflict with the Church. Defeated for reëlection for the term 1882-84, he turned to the pen once more and lashed out vigorously at the shortcomings of the federal constitution then in force. In a series of newspaper essays he warned that only a return to firm and centralized authority could stay the moral and political disintegration that was overtaking the nation.[19] On the whole Núñez failed to convince the Liberals, but he gained enough strength from other quarters to secure the presidency again in 1884. Shortly after taking office he ordered the dissolution of a convention in the department of Santander dominated by opposition Liberals and thereby forced the issue within his party. Many

[18] *Ibid.*, pp. 365, 367-369.   [19] Núñez, *La reforma política*.

of his former supporters rose in an indignant protest which developed into open civil war in 1885. The Conservatives, moderate Liberals, and a number of university professors and recent graduates, like Carlos Martínez Silva, José Vicente Concha, and Miguel Antonio Caro, flocked to his support.[20] About this nucleus he formed his new Nationalist party, pledged to concerted action for the regeneration of the country. Late in 1885 the dictator-president abolished the constitution of 1863 and summoned a national council, consisting of two delegates from each department, to meet at Bogotá for the purpose of drafting a new set of fundamental laws conformable to his views.[21] The new instrument was proclaimed in August, 1886, and formally ushered in the period of the "Regeneration." [22]

Article 1 declared the nation a centralized republic under the name of "The Republic of Colombia." Succeeding articles defined its territories as precisely as was then possible and described them as belonging "exclusively" to the Colombian people. The executive power was entrusted to a president, chosen by indirect election for a six-year term. His authority was extensive, although he was constrained to act "with the indispensable coöperation of the ministers." Inasmuch as these dignitaries were removable at his pleasure, this provision did not constitute a formidable check upon a strong personality in the presidential chair. The executive power of appointment extended to the judiciary, and, with the additional prerogative of removal as well, to the departmental governors. A council of state, composed of the vice-president and six voting members, served as an advisory body to the government, prepared bills for presentation to con-

[20] Morales, "The Political and Economical Situation of Colombia," *North American Review*, CLXXV (1902), 347–348; Pérez, "The Treacherous Treaty: A Colombian Plea," *ibid.*, CLXXVII (1903), 939–941; Arosemena, *Escritos*, II, 174–175.

[21] Núñez appointed the departmental governors and they were in turn instructed to choose the delegates.

[22] For an account of the events preceding and accompanying the establishment of the Núñez dictatorship as presented by a sympathizer, see Nieto, *Recuerdos de la regeneración*. An attack upon the same regime, chiefly because of its close coöperation with the Catholic Church, is to be found in Cornelio Hispano's *Cesarismo teocrático*.

THE COLOMBIAN BACKGROUND 49

gress, and exercised jurisdiction over controversies of certain kinds. By Article 121 important emergency powers were conferred on the president. In case of foreign war or civil commotion, he might, with the written consent of all the ministers, "declare . . . the whole or a part of the Republic in a state of siege," and proceed to issue legislative decrees of a provisional character carrying the force of law. Such edicts had to bear the signatures of all the ministers and had to be submitted for confirmation or repeal to the first session of the congress to meet after the restoration of normal conditions.

The legislative branch consisted of two houses, meeting at Bogotá biennially for sessions of 120 days, or longer if the administration desired. The president could summon extraordinary meetings, at which only such business could be discussed as he saw fit to place before it. Each department was entitled to three senators in the upper chamber, elected by indirect suffrage for terms of six years. Membership was restricted by income qualifications. The house of representatives was composed of one member for each fifty thousand of the population. Any Colombian citizen of good character over twenty-five was eligible for election to this body, which was chosen every four years by those citizens who could prove literacy or who possessed a specified amount of income or property. Both houses met together at the beginning of each session to name a *Designado,* whose function it was to assume the executive power in case the president and vice-president were unable for any reason to perform their duties. Treaties and bills had to pass three readings in each house and receive the approval of the government to become operative. Members of the council of ministers had the privilege of participating in legislative debates and were responsible individually to congress.

Certain other features of the Núñez constitution are worthy of notice. The imposition of the death penalty for political offenses, including domestic rebellion, was forbidden. Roman Catholicism was recognized as the state religion, but religious toleration was guaranteed and priests were disqualified from holding political office. Public education was required to conform to the dogmas of the Catholic Church, and primary instruction was gratuitous but not compulsory. Freedom of the press was permitted in time of peace. The constitution might be amended by legislative act, adopted after three readings and approved by a two-thirds vote of the succeeding congress.[23]

Núñez was elected first president of the new Republic of Colombia, but, although his control of the government amounted to a dictatorship, he spent very little time at the capital and the actual work of administration generally devolved upon the vice-president or the *Designado*. In 1887, however, he officially resumed his constitutional authority long enough to negotiate a concordat with the Vatican which granted generous privileges to Catholic religious societies in Colombia, provided for compensation for ecclesiastical property seized by the nation, and gave civil sanction to marriages performed by the clergy.[24] This treaty marked the apogee of the clerical-conservative reaction to the era of Mosquera.

Dr. Carlos Holguín exercised the president's functions, as *Designado,* from 1888 until 1892 amid a constantly rising storm of criticism whipped up not only by the die-hard Liberals but also by an influential element within the Nationalist party itself. This latter group, composed for the most part of sincere and high-minded men, was rapidly being alienated by many of the practices of the party leaders.[25] Peculation and inefficiency kept the national treasury in a condition of near-bankruptcy and obliged the government to resort to fresh issues of paper money for routine expenses. Business groups, which had been compelled by a law of 1886 to accept this inconvertible currency as legal tender, were beginning to suffer from its depreciation. Investors in certain types of government securities were being forced to accept payment in *vales,* non-negotiable notes which were redeemable only by the government-controlled *Banco Nacional*

---

[23] *Foreign Relations,* 1886, pp. 179–206.
[24] *Sen. Docs.,* 57th Cong., 2nd Sess., No. 95.
[25] Morales, in *North American Review,* CLXXV (1902), 351; Uribe, *Gobierno Marroquín,* p. iv.

and then at a discount equivalent to seventy percent of their theoretical value in gold.[26] The administration's neglect of its foreign debt obligations had practically ended the inflow of capital and credit from abroad. In addition, the Bogotá authorities were showing a disposition to interfere with local elections for the departmental and national legislatures and to suppress unfavorable comment on its policies. A number of the Nationalist dissenters, disappointed in their high hopes for the "Regeneration," seceded and organized a party known as the Historical Conservatives. They attempted to elect representatives to the assemblies and to create a reform press but soon discovered that those in power had no more intention of tolerating their protests than those of the Liberals.[27]

By 1892 the rift in the Nationalist party was beyond healing. For the presidential campaign of that year the Historicals advanced General Marceliano Vélez as their candidate. The Liberals rallied to his support and coöperated actively in a campaign that Antonio José Uribe later referred to as "the most extensive and impassioned that had been held in Colombia." [28] Núñez had himself placed once more at the head of the National Conservative ticket and succeeded in carrying the election. His total of votes was undoubtedly greatly augmented by a vigorous use of troops to ensure "order" at the polls and his adversaries were quick to raise the cry of fraud.[29]

[26] *Foreign Relations,* 1888, p. 409; State Dept., Dispatches from Colombia, Beaupré to Hay, No. 744, April 6, 1903.
[27] Morales, in *North American Review,* CLXXV (1902), 351–352.
[28] Uribe, *Gobierno Marroquin,* p. iv.
[29] In the article cited above, Eusebio A. Morales gives a Liberal's account of the government's methods of securing a favorable outcome: "Election-day in the cities and towns of importance in the republic was one for the display of power and violence. The troops garrisoned there and the police, from the first hours of the day, headed by their chiefs, surrounded the election tables and proceeded to deposit their votes. In that proceeding they nearly exhausted the time allotted by the law for the purpose to the citizens; for each soldier and each police agent voted under two distinct names and under more if necessary. The free citizen who might venture an effort to break through that barrier of soldiers to approach the urn and deposit his vote, was ill-used, beaten, wounded and threatened with death . . ." Morales claims that as a result the Liberal majority in the republic was represented by only one deputy in the national congress during most of the decade of the nineties. See *North American Review,* CLXXV (1902), 350–351.

Núñez apparently lacked the tact and political sagacity to rebuild his following and win back the disaffected Historicals. Soon after the beginning of the new term in 1892 what remained of the Nationalist party began to melt away and the president was left in control of the agencies of government but without the support of either of the traditional parties. His small officeholding clique, taking the name of *Nacionalismo,* sought to ward off the attacks of the combined opposition by the use of the army, the civil servants, the national funds, and such repressive measures as could be enforced. This state of affairs naturally led to the complete disorganization of the public services and the repeated violation of the personal-liberty provisions of the constitution.[30]

The dictator's death at Cartagena in 1894 advanced Vice-President Miguel Antonio Caro, one of the most prominent and eloquent adherents of the "Regeneration," not only to the highest post in the government but to the leadership of *Nacionalismo* as well. The Liberals, convinced that the new chief magistrate intended to perpetuate the policies of his predecessor under a new "constitutional" despotism, rose in revolt in 1895, but succumbed after a brief struggle.

A feeling of tension pervaded the opening of the presidential campaign of 1897. The Liberals nominated one of their ablest leaders, Miguel Samper, and gave notice that a repetition of the electoral frauds of 1892 would result in another and greater armed rebellion.[31] The Historicals named General Rafael Reyes, a popular explorer and soldier, while the government group put forward Caro's name. The president, however, evidently considered his own chance of victory to be very slight, for after some delay he refused the nomination and proposed Dr. Manuel Antonio Sanclemente as his successor.[32]

Sanclemente was a man of high character and unquestioned patriotism, but he was eighty-five years old and in failing health.

[30] Uribe, *Gobierno Marroquín,* pp. iv–v.
[31] López, "Situación . . . de Colombia," *Cuba Contemporánea,* VIII (1915), 226–227; Samper Brush and Samper Sordo, *Escritos . . . de Miguel Samper,* I, vii–viii.
[32] Uribe, *Gobierno Marroquín,* pp. v–vi.

Moreover, his experience in national politics was limited. He had come to Bogotá in 1894 as senator from the department of The Cauca and had served as minister of state (*gobierno*) in Caro's cabinet for a brief time until illness forced him to resign.[33]

Caro's candidate for the vice-presidency was somewhat younger and more vigorous, but even less practiced in politics. José Manuel Marroquín, an educator and man of letters, was widely known in Colombia and as widely respected. Years before, Caro had studied under him at his private academy, Yerbabuena, located not far from Bogotá. Mutual respect between master and pupil had ripened into friendship in the years that followed and the two men became closely associated in numerous educational and literary activities. A dissimilarity of temperament, which in no way altered their cordial personal relations, had kept Marroquín in the ranks of the Conservative party when the more ardent Caro became a disciple of Núñez. The erstwhile student had plunged eagerly into the hurly-burly of active politics while his former preceptor repeatedly spurned the entreaties of friends who urged that he forsake the study for the rostrum. Marroquín's repugnance for public life was as marked, and as characteristic, as was Caro's zest for it. Apart from a short period of service as member of the council of state in 1888, Marroquín had occupied no important political office previous to his nomination on the ticket with Sanclemente.[34] He accepted reluctantly under pressure from his friends and against his own better judgment. Caro's scheme was clear enough. The candidates would attract general support, particularly from the Conservatives, because of their outstanding respectability and piety. Actually, however, Sanclemente's infirmities would prevent him from fulfilling the duties of his office and the executive power would devolve upon the scholarly and abstracted Marroquín, who would in all prob-

[33] Espinosa, *Manifiestos . . . del presidente de Colombia*, pp. 27–28.

[34] *El Colombiano*, August 8, 19, 22, and 29, 1902—a series of biographical articles on Marroquín by Luis María Mora. Marroquín was prominent in Colombia as an educator, a littérateur, and a Catholic lay leader. He was first rector of the new Catholic University and drew up the statutes for that institution in conjunction with Carlos Martínez Silva. He and Caro were associated in the founding of the Academia Colombiana de la Lengua.

ability be glad to turn to Caro for advice and assistance in matters of importance.[35] The plan worked well at the start, for Sanclemente and his running-mate made heavy inroads on the Reyes vote and secured the election with little difficulty.

The new administration took office on August 7, 1898, although the president was not able to leave his home in the Cauca Valley because of his health. Since Colombian law stipulated that the president could not exercise his functions while away from Bogotá without the express permission of the senate, Marroquín was sworn in as vice-president charged with the executive power. His tenure lasted only until Sanclemente's arrival in November, but in that time he displayed an independence of action which took the leaders of *Nacionalismo* completely by surprise.[36] His policies thrust him into alignment with the Historical faction and precipitated a break with Caro which caused him considerable pain. "My desire to unite my party," he wrote several years later in this connection, "involved me in incessant struggle, not with enemies, but with friends who fought with one another, each of whom tried to obligate me to proceed according to his instructions and favorably to his political interests; so that I could not make a step, of great or little importance, without disconcerting many friends and provoking resistance." [37]

The vigor and high-mindedness of Marroquín's leadership were acclaimed by the Historical Conservatives and even by certain elements among the Liberals, but the Nationalists, chagrined at the flat failure of their strategy, lost no time in putting an end to his authority. The aged Sanclemente was brought up to the capital at the risk of his life to assume the powers of his office—and turn them over to the Caro clique. The change of climate worked such a hardship upon the venerable man that he asked the senate's permission to resign his mandate into the vice-president's hands

---

[35] Casas, *Semblanza de don José Manuel Marroquín*, p. 14; Uribe, *Gobierno Marroquín*, pp. v–vi; Morales, in *North American Review*, CLXXV (1902), p. 353.

[36] Morales, *loc. cit.* Marroquín made public and private statements of his intention to enforce the national suffrage laws. Morales feels that the civil war would have been averted had Marroquín refused to yield his authority to Sanclemente in 1898. See also Nieto Caballero, *Por qué soy liberal?* p. 39.

[37] Casas, *Semblanza de don José Manuel Marroquín*, pp. 15–16.

THE COLOMBIAN BACKGROUND 55

and retire to his native Cauca. This was granted, but his "advisers" had no intention of losing their grip on the government a second time. Instead of permitting him to retire, they moved him from place to place, finally lodging him in a villa outside Bogotá where he was within the letter of the law but out of touch with congress and his ministers.[38]

The year that followed was marked by growing political and economic confusion. The creditor classes were being severely hurt by the continued emissions of paper money. The volume of these bills had risen from 12,000,000 pesos in 1887 to 46,000,000 in October, 1899, while the exchange value of the peso had declined from approximately 100 cents to slightly above fifteen over the same period.[39] Simultaneously, the important coffee-growing industry, for reasons only partly connected with the money question, was facing a serious collapse.[40] Trade and industry were practically at a standstill. This situation, ominous enough for the Sanclemente government, was made critical by the growing demand for political retrenchment and reform. The military budget, which in peacetime had never exceeded $500,000 before 1886, reached $9,500,000 for the two-year period 1897-1898, or more than one-third of the public revenue. The deficit for these years fell little short of $3,500,000.[41] Those Liberals and Conservatives who had voted for Sanclemente in the hope of seeing certain much-needed reforms put through now felt they had been deceived, for with the termination of Marroquín's brief administration the government had fallen once more into the hands of exploiters.

Opposition crystallized rapidly during the summer and early fall of 1899. In August, a junta of delegates representing the Historical Conservative party resolved that "the present government, in its politics and tendencies, does not reflect the ideals, practices, and aspirations of the Conservative Party" and, conse-

[38] Uribe, *Gobierno Marroquín*, pp. vi–vii.
[39] State Dept., Dispatches from Colombia, Beaupré to Hay, No. 744, April 6, 1903; Petre, *Republic of Colombia*, pp. 303–308.
[40] Petre, *Republic of Colombia*, pp. 266–269.
[41] Morales, in *North American Review*, CLXXV (1902), 358–359.

quently, the individual members were under no moral obligation to aid it or share in the responsibility for its acts.[42] The climax came in October when the more impetuous of the Liberal leaders, disregarding the advice of the older heads of the party, raised the standard of revolt in Santander, Cundinamarca, and Tolima, and precipitated the most disastrous civil war of Colombian history.[43] General Rafael Uribe Uribe of the standing army soon deserted to the rebel cause, taking with him practically his entire command.[44] His exploits in the Magdalena Valley quickly won him recognition as the most brilliant of the insurgent chiefs in the field.

For over two years the Liberals held their own under the energetic direction of Vargas Santos, Foción Soto, Uribe Uribe, and Benjamín Herrera. Several departments fell completely under their control and, for a few days in November, 1901, the revolutionary flag floated above Colón. Assistance was expected from the Liberals of Ecuador, Nicaragua, and Venezuela, but nothing materialized from the first of these neighbors and the contribution of the second was disappointing. President Castro of Venezuela, who usurped his office in the spring of 1900, sent secret consignments of arms and munitions to Uribe Uribe, and even permitted insurgent troops to take refuge in his territory without arrest, but he was deterred from his plan of invading Colombia openly on behalf of the Liberals by a sudden revolt in his own political stronghold. In all probability it was only this accident that averted war between the two nations.[45]

Meanwhile the cost of the struggle to Colombia was terrific. Plantations were laid waste by the hundreds, houses and bridges were burned, cattle and hogs requisitioned or scattered. While industry all but disappeared, commerce was kept in a state of confusion by the shifting fortunes of war and the rapid fluctua-

[42] López, "Situación ... de Colombia," *Cuba Contemporánea*, VIII (1915), 228.

[43] Most commentators of Liberal or Historical leanings attribute the outbreak of the civil war primarily to the apparent impossibility of securing monetary and suffrage reform.

[44] Rougier, *Les Récentes Guerres civiles*, p. 5.   [45] *Ibid.*, pp. 4–6.

THE COLOMBIAN BACKGROUND

tion in prices as the treasury printing presses continued to add millions of paper pesos to the currency. In many districts the machinery of government ceased to function, leaving the population at the mercy of wandering bands of "soldiers." The toll in human life has been variously estimated at from 100,000 to 250,000 persons.[46] Never, in Colombia's long experience with civil upheavals, had the nation been called upon to endure such widespread misery.

Sanclemente met the crisis by declaring the country in a "state of siege." Under Article 121 of the constitution he proceeded to issue legislative decrees, signed by his ministers and carrying the force of law, which dispensed with the necessity of consulting the congress. It was one of these decrees that granted the New Company a six-year extension of the construction period provided for in its franchise and thereby dragged the canal question into the arena of party conflict.

The circumstances of this action can be related briefly. When the New Panama Canal Company was organized in 1894 it took over, along with the other assets of the de Lesseps company, the Wyse concession of 1878, which in its amended form stipulated that the canal be opened to traffic by October 31, 1904, at the latest. At no time during the course of the company's operations did this eventuality appear very probable. On November 1, 1898, a few weeks before Cromwell made his first official advances to Secretary Hay, a request was addressed to the Colombian government by Alexander Mancini, the company's representative in Bogotá, asking that the ultimate completion date be advanced to October, 1910, to permit the deepening of the canal cut by another ten meters. This improvement, the note added, was not absolutely necessary, but it was desirable in view of the increased usefulness it would impart to the waterway.[47] The matter was referred to the Colombian congress, but opposition developed and no final action was taken.[48]

---
[46] Rippy, *Capitalists and Colombia*, p. 23; Petre, *Republic of Colombia*, p. 109.
[47] *Sen. Docs.*, 57th Cong., 2nd Sess., No. 34, pp. 6–7.
[48] López, "El Gobierno de Colombia y la Compañía del Canal de Panamá," *Reforma Social*, III (1915), 456.

58 THE COLOMBIAN BACKGROUND

On December 20, 1898, three weeks after the adjournment of the legislature, Sanclemente and his advisers drew up a decree conceding the desired extension, subject to the ratification of the next congress. The order was approved by the cabinet and communicated to Mancini, but not promulgated.[49] The following February the administration dispatched a well-known Liberal, Dr. Nicolás Esguerra, to Paris to report on the practicability of the proposed grant and the conditions which ought properly to constitute its basis.[50] After a visit to the Isthmus and a brief stop in New York, the envoy crossed the Atlantic in company with the director-general of the New Company, reaching the French capital in May, 1899. He was soon joined by General Reyes, minister to France and Switzerland, and Dr. Clímaco Calderón, minister to Washington. The three men quickly learned that their mission did not meet with the company's favor and that they could expect little coöperation from that quarter. In spite of this, Esguerra appears to have informed Bogotá in September that the continued existence of the canal corporation depended upon an extension of time and that he approved it in principle.[51]

The New Company officials remained unresponsive to the commissioners, probably because they suspected them of having sizable financial conditions in mind. The board of directors protracted the negotiations while intimating to the Colombian government that the business would move more swiftly if the discussions were conducted through Mancini at Bogotá.[52] In Febru-

[49] Terán, *Tratado Herrán-Hay*, I, 52.

[50] In his instructions to Esguerra, Carlos Calderón, minister of hacienda, emphasized the advantages to Colombia of a canal built by a private company with capital subscribed by citizens of various nations. Not only would such an enterprise be under the jurisdiction of Colombian laws, but its nature would make an international guaranty of neutrality easier to secure. See López, "El Gobierno de Colombia . . . ," *Reforma Social*, III (1915), 456.

[51] Cám. de Rep., *Investigación sobre la rebelión del Istmo de Panamá*, p. 11; *El Correo Nacional*, letter from Dr. Carlos Calderón printed Jan. 14 and 15, 1903; Terán, *Tratado Herrán-Hay*, I, 59–60. Reyes and Clímaco Calderón endorsed Esguerra's opinion in a cable to Bogotá dated Nov. 18, 1899: "We have agreed that Dr. Esguerra proceed to contract for extension. Mail brought notes, reports that show absolute desirability of negotiations" (Terán, *op. cit.*, I, 62).

[52] Cám. de Rep., *Investigación sobre la rebelión del Istmo de Panamá*, p. 11.

THE COLOMBIAN BACKGROUND 59

ary, 1900, the minister of hacienda cabled Esguerra to suspend activities and let him know how much the canal concern would be able to pay for an extension. The latter replied that he could obtain thirty million francs if he were given full authorization to proceed. On February 16, however, before Esguerra's wire reached the Colombian capital, the administration prepared a legislative decree fixing the compensation at five million francs, to be paid within four months. Delays followed, during which the commissioners in Paris insisted they could drive a better bargain. The company meanwhile steadfastly refused to consider any payment higher than that proposed at Bogotá.[53]

By the early spring of 1900 the Sanclemente government had its own reasons for wishing to arrive at a speedy agreement. The civil war was in full swing, military expenses were rapidly mounting, and the treasury was empty of gold and silver. The president and his ministers no longer regarded the New Company's request as a simple matter of canal policy but rather as an opportunity for financial succor in a time of crisis.[54] With the legislative authority lodged in executive hands, congressional objections were no longer relevant. Each week that passed increased the administration's need and the company's hope. Finally, on April 23, 1900, the cabinet took action. By Legislative Decree 721 the New Company was granted an additional six-year period of grace for completing the canal, commencing October 31, 1904, in consideration of a payment of five million francs in gold. The order was countersigned by the ministers in accordance with the constitution. Two days later, the minister of hacienda, Carlos Calderón, entered into a definite contract with Mancini to carry out the provisions of the decree.[55]

[53] Terán, *Tratado Herrán-Hay*, I, 72–77, 91.

[54] Cám. de Rep., *Investigación sobre la rebelión del Istmo de Panamá*, pp. 12–13. Likewise, the government was very probably watching the rapid progress of the Nicaragua bill in the United States Congress at this time. An extension would strengthen the New Company's position in Washington. See *infra*, chap. iii.

[55] Cám. de Rep., *op. cit.*, p. 11. The text of the decree is printed in *Libro azul*, Appendix, pp. 156–158; the text of the contract with Mancini appears in the *Walker Commission Report*, pp. 483–484. Subsequently Dr. Esguerra attacked

The Liberals were thoroughly angered. Generals Vargas Santos and Foción Soto, president and vice-president respectively of the provisional Liberal government, warned the New Company and the world in general that their party, if successful, would refuse to ratify the decree on the grounds that it was permanent, rather than provisional, in character.[56] Even the Historicals, most of whom were either neutral or very halfhearted in their support of the *Nacionalismo,* privately questioned the legality of the grant.[57]

By early summer the groups backing the administration were torn by dissension. The little control that Sanclemente had once exercised now slipped from his fingers. It was reported that the rubber stamp bearing his signature had been copied and was being used by the inner clique of officials for its own purposes.[58] Disgusted by this lack of leadership and by what appeared to them an unnecessary prolongation of the war, thirty-one well-known Conservatives organized a movement to place the chief executive's functions once more in Marroquín's hands. When a plea to oust the president constitutionally on the basis of non-residence at the capital was disallowed by the supreme court, the conspirators determined to use force. Negotiations were secretly opened with Dr. Aquileo Parra, foremost political leader of the Liberals, with the object of ending the rebellion and ensuring the coöperation of the "reform" element in both parties. An understanding was reached between Parra and Luis Martínez Silva, spokesman for the "Thirty-One," that the proposed administra-

---

the contract as a "bad bargain" and generally sought to give the impression that he had opposed an extension of the New Company's franchise—a fact which was played up by the opponents of the Sanclemente regime. Dr. Carlos Martínez Silva, while on mission in Washington in 1901, wrote Foreign Minister Uribe that he had seen Esguerra's original documents and that they had expressed opposition to a further time-grant (*Libro azul,* pp. 9, 57). The facts seem to be that the commissioner turned against the extension only after the negotiation was taken from his hands. His hostility was increased by the low price obtained and by Sanclemente's use of a legislative decree, which he considered insufficient authority for a permanent grant. Dr. Calderón defended the administration in a long letter to *El Correo Nacional,* cited above. See also López, "El Gobierno de Colombia . . . ," *Reforma Social,* III (1915), 260–261 and footnote.

[56] *Cong. Rec.,* 57th Cong., 2nd Sess., pp. 2260–2261.
[57] *Libro azul,* pp. 8–9, 57–58, 121–122.
[58] *Anales diplomáticos y consulares,* I, 21.

tion would release political prisoners, unmuzzle the press, and summon a new congress under a guaranty of free suffrage. Marroquín acquiesced in the terms, although he voiced strong objections to a provision specifically barring Aristides Fernández, chief of the Bogotá police, from any post in the reconstituted government.[59]

The *coup d'état* occurred on the night of July 31, 1900, when a band of Historicals, aided by soldiers of the Bogotá garrison, imprisoned Sanclemente in his villa at Anapoima, outside the city. The conspirators then proclaimed the vice-president chief of the executive power as a result of the president's "absence." The move was completely successful. The populace of Bogotá greeted the change with apparent enthusiasm and most of the departmental governors and field commanders hastened to declare their loyalty to the new regime. Those Liberal leaders who knew of the preliminary conferences with Parra waited hopefully for signs of the early restoration of peace.[60]

In public justification of their action Marroquín's followers asserted that Sanclemente had voluntarily surrendered his office. This was indignantly and eloquently denied by the aged president in a series of protests addressed to the Colombian people during the month of August.[61] The Historicals replied variously that he had entered into a secret understanding with the Liberals [!] and that he was mentally and physically incapacitated for his duties. On September 13 General Pinzón visited the prisoner and offered to set him free on condition that he agree not to attempt to exercise the functions of his office—terms which the old man promptly rejected.[62] Before the end of the month the

[59] Martínez Delgado and Otero Muñoz, *Obras completas del doctor Carlos Martínez Silva*, IX, 168 *et seq.*

[60] The new government's official version of the overturn was sent by Silva to the Colombian diplomatic officers abroad and appears in *Anales diplomáticos y consulares*, I, 17–25. See also Nieto Caballero, *Por qué soy liberal?* pp. 38–39; Morales in *North American Review*, CLXXV (1902), 355; López, "Situación ... de Colombia," *Cuba Contemporánea*, VIII (1915), 229 footnote. "There is no record in our annals," A. J. Uribe wrote, "of an event more sincerely and spontaneously applauded by national opinion" (*Gobierno Marroquín*, p. viii).

[61] Espinosa, *Manifiestos ... del presidente de Colombia, passim.*

[62] *Ibid.*, pp. 5–11, 24.

practically-minded supreme court, by a four-to-three vote, had sustained Marroquín's accession to power.[63]

Carlos Martínez Silva, the brother of Luis and one of the principal organizers of the coup, was rewarded with the portfolio of foreign relations.[64] He was an able lawyer and a former Nationalist who appears to have joined the conspiracy in the belief that the elimination of Sanclemente and the "ring" surrounding him would hasten the end of the civil struggle. Other prominent citizens, many of whom had not been actively identified with either side until then, were appointed to important posts in the administration.

For a time the fighting lagged as the Liberals waited to see what action the new government would take. The moment was auspicious. During his short term of office in 1898 Marroquín had publicly announced his determination to secure an honest enforcement of the suffrage laws—one of those alarming utterances which caused Caro's followers to bring Sanclemente up from The Cauca in haste. A sincere effort to reëstablish a truly representative system, thus permitting the Liberals to bring strong parliamentary backing to their reform program, would very likely have broken the backbone of the rebellion. But, in spite of the understanding with Parra, no such proposal was made. The new executive offered amnesty to all those willing to lay down their arms, but no political concessions were held out.[65] After a few weeks of pause the insurgents resumed hostilities. Marroquín turned the prosecution of the war over to the military men and devoted himself to the reorganization of the governmental departments.[66] The destruction of the nation's manhood and economic resources recommenced and the flood of paper money continued unabated. The great opportunity had been allowed to pass.

[63] Uribe, *Gobierno Marroquín*, pp. 1–5. The United States formally recognized the Marroquín government in September (*Foreign Relations*, 1900, p. 410).
[64] *Anales diplomáticos y consulares*, I, 9.
[65] Morales, in *North American Review*, CLXXV (1902), 356; Rougier, *Les Récentes Guerres civiles*, pp. 11–14; López, "Situación . . . de Colombia," *Cuba Contemporánea*, VIII (1915), 235–236.
[66] Uribe, *Gobierno Marroquín*, pp. x–xiv.

III

This was the general nature of the internal situation in Colombia late in 1900 when the New Company suddenly introduced another train of complications by calling the government's attention to the advanced position of the Nicaragua Canal bills in the congressional session just opening in Washington and pointing out the desirability of having a Colombian diplomatic representative on the spot. None of Colombia's international concerns rivaled the isthmian canal problem in importance, nor were any likely to have such far-reaching repercussions. Marroquín was fully aware that his compliance with the company's request would be tantamount to approval of the purchase of the Wyse concession by the United States. At the moment, with public opinion wavering between the contending parties at home, a misstep by the government in the matter of the canal might prove fatal. On the other hand, a successful negotiation would strengthen the administration's hand and provide the country with a much-needed revenue for use in stabilizing the national currency and in the coming work of reconstruction. The vice-president would have preferred to postpone his decision until peace had been restored, but no choice of time existed.[67] Dr. Silva was selected to undertake the mission under the imposing title of envoy extraordinary and minister plenipotentiary to the Government of the United States—a distinction destined to be even more imposed upon than imposing.[68] To understand the difficulties of

---

[67] *Anales diplomáticos y consulares*, IV, 805.

[68] Carlos Martínez Silva was born of good family in the city of San Gil, Santander, in 1847. He was brought to Bogotá eleven years later upon his father's appointment to the presidency of the supreme court. After taking his doctorate in political science at the national university in 1872 he entered politics and soon won distinction not only in public office but in the fields of journalism and education as well. As a member of the departmental assemblies of Santander and Cundinamarca, and as representative from Tolima in the national legislature, he achieved a reputation as a debater and authority on constitutional questions. He served as secretary to the convention which drafted the constitution of 1886 and twice held cabinet posts during the period of the "Regeneration." In 1889 he represented Colombia at the first Pan-American Congress in Washington. When the civil war broke out in 1899 he attempted for a time to bring about a pacific settlement of the points at issue. Failing in this, he joined the conspiracy

64 THE COLOMBIAN BACKGROUND

Silva's task in Washington it is necessary to summarize the principal problems connected with the canal from the Colombian point of view.

During the first six decades of its independence Colombia granted numerous concessions to private individuals and syndicates for the opening of a waterway across the Isthmus. Each of these arrangements provided for the reversion of all the property and improvements after a term of years, usually ninety-nine, and specified that the government should meanwhile participate financially according to the business handled by the company, either through a percentage of the profits or through a fixed impost on the tonnage using the canal. In addition, every contract contained the stipulation that the concessionary corporation could not transfer its holdings to any foreign state under penalty of forfeiture. Such matters as policing, the administration of justice, and defense were left to the Bogotá authorities without question.[69] The concession in force in 1901 was that granted to Lucien Napoleon Bonaparte Wyse in 1878 and transferred by him the next year to the Compagnie Universelle. This privilege was to run for ninety-nine years after the opening of the enterprise to commerce. The national treasury was to receive five percent of the gross profits for the first quarter-century of operation, six percent for the second, seven for the third, and eight for the remaining twenty-four years. The time allowance for construction and a few other details were modified by the laws of 1890 and 1892, by the contract of April 4, 1893, and by the legislative decree of April 23, 1900.[70]

While the Colombian government generally preferred to award canal concessions to groups of private capitalists there were three separate occasions prior to 1878 when it took steps toward

---

to displace Sanclemente in the apparently sincere belief that Marroquín would be willing and able to promote a just and enduring peace. See Martínez Delgado and Otero Muñoz, *Obras completas del doctor Carlos Martínez Silva*, I, 11 *et seq.*

[69] *Anales diplomáticos y consulares*, II, 950–954; *Foreign Relations*, 1879, pp. 297–303.

[70] *Walker Commission Report*, pp. 473–483. The Wyse concession provided that under no circumstances should the annual payments to the Colombian government be less than $250,000.

THE COLOMBIAN BACKGROUND 65

having other nations superintend the work.[71] In 1843 the minister of foreign relations instructed the Granadan envoy in London to sound out the governments of Great Britain, France, the United States, Holland, and Spain on the proposal that they assume joint charge of the project. The representative was ordered to point out, however, that any such undertaking would have to be conducted without prejudice to New Granada's sovereignty and jurisdiction.[72] In 1869, and again in 1870, conventions were signed between Colombia and the United States providing for the construction of an isthmian canal by the latter nation or its citizens. In neither instance were ratifications exchanged. Both documents limited the duration of United States operation to one hundred years. By the first treaty, twelve years after the canal was put into service Colombia was to begin to receive ten percent of the net profits, this to continue until the United States had reimbursed itself for its investment, after which Colombia was to receive twenty-five percent. By the second treaty, Colombia was to receive three percent of the tolls for twenty years and two percent thereafter, plus $250,000 annually for the railroad. In neither case did the United States secure any judicial privileges, while its right to maintain troops in the zone was strictly limited.[73]

Not only did Colombian statesmen have to look abroad for financial assistance in realizing their dream of a canal but they also had to consider the problem of defense. A passage at Panama would figure prominently in the naval strategy of all maritime powers and Colombia might find it extremely difficult to protect the work from seizure or destruction in time of war. For this reason successive ministers of state endeavored to obtain international acknowledgment of the neutrality of any means of transit that might be constructed across the Isthmus of Panama. The Granadan note of 1843 referred to above specified that the con-

---

[71] In addition the Colombian government cordially welcomed a proposition advanced by Peru in 1873 that a canal be built by a combination of American states (*Foreign Relations*, 1873, II, 760–761).

[72] *Libro azul*, Uribe Report, June 1, 1902, Appendix, pp. 47, 59–60; Rivas, *Relaciones internacionales entre Colombia y los Estados Unidos*, p. 107.

[73] *Sen. Docs.*, 56th Cong., 1st Sess., No. 237, pp. 45–61.

tracting governments should "guarantee by force the neutrality of the route." [74] When this proposition came to nothing New Granada signed a treaty with the United States in December, 1846, whereby it guaranteed "that the right of way or transit across the Isthmus of Panama upon any modes of communication that now exist, or that may hereafter be constructed, shall be open and free to the Government and citizens of the United States" and their commerce. The United States, in return, guaranteed "the perfect neutrality of the before-mentioned isthmus, with the view that the free transit from the one to the other sea may not be interrupted or embarrassed . . . and, in consequence, the United States also guarantee, in the same manner, the rights of sovereignty and property which New Granada has and possesses over the said territory." [75] In concluding this treaty New Granada had no intention of making the United States the sole protector of the Isthmus. Rather this agreement was designed to be the first of a series with the chief commercial nations granting trade concessions in consideration of a guaranty of New Granada's sovereignty over the province of Panama. President Polk took the same view in a special message to the Senate on February 10, 1847:

. . . there does not appear to be any other effectual means of securing to all nations the advantages of this important passage but [through] the guaranty of great commercial powers that the Isthmus shall be neutral territory. . . .

The guaranty of the sovereignty of New Granada over the Isthmus is a natural consequence of the guaranty of its neutrality . . .[76]

As it turned out, no other treaty of this character was made and the United States thus acquired special privileges in connection with Panama which it later came to regard, without any justification whatever, as exclusively its own.

The treaties of 1869 and 1870 both included neutrality provisions. The contracting parties obligated themselves to work for an international guaranty of Colombia's sovereignty over Pan-

[74] *Libro azul*, Uribe Report, 1902, Appendix, p. 60.
[75] Malloy, *Treaties*, I, 312.
[76] Richardson, *Messages and Papers*, IV, 513.

THE COLOMBIAN BACKGROUND 67

ama and Darien. By the convention of 1869 the canal was to be closed to countries at war. That of the year following was modified so as to close the canal to the flags of all nations at war with the signatories. The latter article met with severe criticism in the Bogotá congress as being likely to involve Colombia in future conflicts of the United States. An amendment was therefore added which stated that the canal was to be open to such belligerents as guaranteed Colombia's sovereignty but that no act of hostility was to be committed in or near the zone.[77] Since these pacts were not consummated the pledges they contemplated were neither sought nor given.

The increasing aggressiveness of Washington's Central American policy under Grant and Hayes caused some uneasiness in the southern republic concerning the sufficiency of the 1846 guaranty. As soon as the de Lesseps company started active work the Colombian government began to consider the practicability of abrogating the understanding with the United States in favor of a joint guaranty by the powers of Europe. News of this plan reached the Department of State and elicited a note in Blaine's best manner to all United States diplomatic officers declaring that "In the judgment of the President this guarantee [of 1846] . . . does not require re-enforcement, or accession, or assent from any other power." [78] This was notice to the world that politically the Isthmus was to be regarded as lying within the North American sphere of influence. As the European chancelleries hastened to indicate their lack of interest in the matter the scheme for neutralizing the canal by international accord was temporarily abandoned.

These repeated failures of Colombian diplomacy would have left that nation's interests at Panama wholly dependent upon the doubtful security of the treaty of 1846 had it not been for the welcome and unsolicited protection afforded them from 1850 to 1901 by the Clayton-Bulwer treaty. This understanding, it will be remembered, was drawn up to allay the bitter Anglo-American

[77] Moore, *Digest of International Law*, III, 21–22.
[78] *Foreign Relations*, 1881, p. 537.

rivalry in Central America which for a time had threatened to lead to war. It was agreed by this instrument to substitute cooperation for competition and harmonize the conflicting interests of both parties by the joint protection of any interoceanic canal in Central America. With reference to the Nicaragua route it was stipulated that neither government would "ever obtain or maintain for itself any exclusive control" over any ship canal there or "erect or maintain any fortifications commanding the same, or in the vicinity thereof . . ." The two nations also contracted to extend their protection "to any other practicable communications, whether by canal or railway, across the isthmus . . . especially . . . by the way of Tehuantepec or Panama." But it was declared that neither would occupy, fortify, colonize, or exercise dominion over "any part of Central America." [79] To Colombian statesmen and students of international law it was the Clayton-Bulwer treaty and not the convention of 1846 that constituted the real safeguard of their country's sovereignty over any canal within its territory. A full international guaranty was still preferable, but at the turn of the century this did not appear very close to attainment.

The great merit of the Clayton-Bulwer treaty from the Colombian point of view consisted precisely in the check it exerted upon the political ambitions of the "Colossus of the North." During the decades that followed its ratification the United States had rapidly displaced Great Britain as the most active power in Central America and the Caribbean. While relations between Washington and Bogotá were continuously friendly down to 1901, many influential Colombians came to share the growing apprehension of other Latin-American peoples regarding the possible future activities of their powerful neighbor. Indications were not lacking that the United States was developing a possessive rather than a strictly protective attitude toward the Isthmus. As early as 1849 Secretary of State Clayton instructed his minister to New Granada that "The obligations we have assumed give us a right to offer, unasked, such advice to the New Grana-

[79] Malloy, *Treaties*, I, 660–662.

THE COLOMBIAN BACKGROUND 69

dian Government, in regard to its relations with other powers, as might tend to avert from that Republic a rupture with any nation which might covet the Isthmus of Panama." [80]

In 1856, after a riot had interfered with the operation of the Panama Railroad, President Pierce commissioned Isaac Morse to join Minister Bowlin at Bogotá in urging upon the government of New Granada the creation of an autonomous zone twenty miles wide across the Isthmus which would be under the protection of United States troops in case of serious trouble. New Granada was also asked to transfer its interest in the railroad and cede the islands in Panama harbor to the United States for about one and a half million dollars. The Bogotá government declined "to even negotiate upon the questions at issue." [81] Two years later Secretary Cass warned the republic that no Latin-American state would "be permitted, in a spirit of Eastern isolation, to close these gates of intercourse on the great highways of the world, and justify the act by the pretension that these avenues of trade and travel belong to them, and that they choose to shut them...." [82] About the same time he commented that the United States preferred to have the transit route under the control of its own nationals.[83]

In a note to Minister Dichman on April 19, 1880, Secretary Evarts declared that the United States expected to receive notice of any concession for building the Panama Canal in advance for consideration and approval and that it had the right to exercise, if necessary, "a positive supervision and interposition in the execution of any project" which would affect its commercial and political interests.[84] President Hayes repeated these views in his congressional message that December.[85] The following February representatives of the United States and Colombia signed a protocol in New York providing for the selection of strategic sites

[80] Quoted from Moore, *Digest of International Law*, III, 24.
[81] *Ibid.*, pp. 19–20.
[82] *Correspondence in Relation to the Proposed Interoceanic Canal*, p. 281.
[83] Moore, *Digest of International Law*, III, 256.
[84] *Ibid.*, p. 15.
[85] Richardson, *Messages and Papers*, VII, 610–611.

for the military and naval defense of the Isthmus. These were to be occupied by Colombia in time of peace and to be used by the United States forces if called upon to enforce the treaty of 1846. Evarts approved the protocol but Bogotá did not.[86]

Quite aside from these direct diplomatic assertions of special privilege Colombian officials could hardly have failed to be impressed by the ease with which North American naval detachments recurrently established their authority along the line of the railroad, incidentally crushing insurrections which the local troops were powerless to handle. While in each case previous to 1901 intervention had come only at the request or with the consent of the Colombian government, yet the disparity in the military efficiency of the two nations was so obvious as to raise the question in some quarters whether it was possible for Colombia really to retain control of a canal built at Panama. This consciousness of weakness, combined with the failure of all efforts to supplement the neutrality provisions of the treaty of 1846 by an international agreement, heightened the suspicion with which many Colombians viewed the southward trend of Yankee trade and political interests.

The Spanish War and its aftermath still further increased these feelings of distrust. Whatever appeal the liberation of Cuba from Spain made to the Latin Americans was largely outweighed by the imposition of the Platt Amendment, by the annexation of Puerto Rico and the Pacific islands, and by the vigorous pronouncements of men like Henry Cabot Lodge and Theodore Roosevelt.[87] Even those Colombians who were well disposed towards their northern neighbor were inclined to regard its growing taste for imperialistic expansion as an ominous sign for the future, particularly with the canal project so much to the fore in both countries.[88] The hostility with which the press and Senate

[86] *Foreign Relations*, 1881, pp. 361–388.

[87] *Libro azul*, p. 53, Appendix, pp. 33–34; for a clear statement of this attitude see Mendoza, *El canal interoceánico y los tratados*.

[88] In an analysis of the effect of the Spanish-American War upon international politics, written in August, 1899, Dr. Antonio José Uribe remarked: "The negotiations between the English and North American diplomats concerning the abrogation of the Clayton-Bulwer Treaty, the sole guaranty of our sovereignty in the Isth-

THE COLOMBIAN BACKGROUND 71

in the United States pounced upon the neutrality and nonfortification provisions of the first Hay-Pauncefote treaty and the aggressive tenor of the amendments proposed during the spring and fall of 1900 quite naturally added to this uneasiness.[89]

Despite uncertainties such as these there is no record of any serious movement among the Colombian people for the abandonment of the canal project. On the contrary, the idea of linking the oceans at Panama had completely captured the popular imagination by the beginning of 1901. The majority of the educated classes looked upon the Isthmus as their country's richest possession, a heritage from the heroic founders of the republic, and the touchstone of its future wealth and prestige. An artificial waterway there would place Colombia upon one of the great highways of the world's trade, it would bring the fertile Cauca Valley of the west coast into direct communication with Europe and eastern United States, it would attract the foreign capital so badly needed for building the nation's railroads, for opening up its mines, and for financing its agriculture. The prospect not only appealed to Colombian national pride, but held out promise of a roseate financial future. At the same time it furnished a superb topic for endless debate.[90]

This optimism is traceable in good part to the efforts of numerous orators and publicists, both in and out of public life, who had long availed themselves of the opportunity the theme presented for the display of their own talents and patriotism. In addition, leading businessmen and planters from Panama and The Cauca were constantly endeavoring to identify their local advantage with the march of national progress in the eyes of the

---

mus of Panama, and, in general, the tendencies of the imperialist party in the United States, now in charge of the Government, justify the fears which we manifested at the beginning of the Spanish-American War, in the sense that, after Spain, those principally threatened will be ourselves, because of the exceptional situation of our territory." Uribe, *Colombia y los Estados Unidos*, p. xxvii.

[89] *Infra*, pp. 97–98, 105–106.

[90] *Libro azul*, pp. 54–55; report of the majority of the San Carlos Commission, Feb. 20, 1902 (*ibid.*, Appendix, p. 4); report of Francisco Groot, May 20, 1902 (*ibid.*, Appendix, p. 43); *Diario oficial*, 1903, p. 3; *Foreign Relations*, 1876, pp. 76 *et seq*.

electorate. It should be noted, however, that the agitation for the canal was not confined to the demagogues and the sectional spokesmen. Disinterested scholars and jurists contributed much effective support in the form of articles and addresses dealing with the historical, economic, and legal angles of the question.

Over one aspect of the great national scheme there had never been much argument. It was generally recognized that the work of finance and construction would have to be carried out by foreigners. Colombia had neither the credit nor the technical means to execute so vast a design. The isthmian project was one from which the Bogotá government hoped to receive handsome profits for national development and over which it intended to retain strict political control. Yet should the New Company fail to discharge its contract successfully, as seemed probable to many influential citizens in 1900, the task of completion and management would have to be entrusted to some other gigantic economic agency, either a nation or a syndicate, powerful enough to superintend an enterprise admittedly too big for Colombia to handle. The situation had its potential dangers. An aggressive concessioner might conceivably attempt to become master as well as agent. Or, in pursuit of its own interests, it might succeed in involving the republic in foreign war. It was partly because of this possibility that certain Colombians vigorously opposed any arrangement that would place the United States in sole charge of the work. Nevertheless, as it became increasingly apparent during and after 1900 that Great Britain did not intend to insist upon the continuance of the Clayton-Bulwer treaty, provided its commercial interests were adequately protected by other means, and that neither the New Company nor any other purely private corporation was likely to muster resources sufficient to complete the enterprise, the active objection to a pact with the Washington government temporarily subsided. A few prominent irreconcilables persisted in their criticism even after the opening of the discussions in Washington, but they were unable to produce any fundamental change in the administration's policy.

It seems to be a fair conclusion from the published correspond-

THE COLOMBIAN BACKGROUND 73

ence of leading Colombians that disappointment over the progress made by the French on the Isthmus was not the only consideration which led many of them to favor a canal convention with the United States. The chaotic state of the republic's currency and credit, which had been greatly aggravated by the expenses of the war, helped to place the financial advantages of a partnership with the Yankees in a very attractive light.[91] A private corporation would have been more amenable to Colombian control, it is true, but the treasury would have derived no revenue from such a concessioner until 1910 and then only at the rate of five percent of the receipts (during the first quarter-century). On the other hand, a substantial indemnity in gold might reasonably be anticipated from an agreement with the United States, payable upon the exchange of ratifications. This was a circumstance which could hardly be viewed with indifference by businessmen whose affairs had been thrown into disorder as the result of inflation, by holders of depreciated government securities, or by public officials who were already looking ahead to the costly work of postwar reconstruction.

In sending Silva northward to campaign for the adoption of the Panama route by the United States, therefore, Marroquín was acting in accordance with the views of powerful political and economic groups in his own country. While not sharing the extremely high hopes of some of his compatriots as to the terms the nation was in a position to exact, he recognized that he was in effect obligating himself to secure substantial benefits from the United States without permitting that power to extend its authority over any phase of Colombia's affairs. He was aware that his future reputation would be largely based upon his handling of this negotiation. Yet the situation offered no opportunity for experiment, for the methods of trial and error. Once ratified, a canal treaty would be the law of the land for generations, no matter how unsatisfactory its provisions might prove.

The Liberal leaders, whether friendly or opposed to the idea

[91] *Libro azul*, p. 55, Appendix, p. 18; *Anales diplomáticos y consulares*, II, 944–945, 954, and IV, 816–817.

of a canal convention with the United States, joined in condemning the vice-president for initiating discussions of such far-reaching national importance at a time when only one of the parties was represented in the government and that not by popular election. Uribe Uribe voiced his suspicion that the Silva mission was a "petition for money" to wipe out the Liberal party.[92] It is doubtful that there was any sound basis for such a charge. As has been said, Marroquín was not at all anxious to enter into diplomatic exchanges on the canal question in December, 1900. His hand was forced by the approaching vote in Washington on the Nicaragua bills.[93] Had one of these been approved without any effort on his part to make known Colombia's desire for consideration he would have had to shoulder the responsibility for his country's fallen hopes (and most certainly face the bitter denunciations of the Liberals). There were no two ways open to him. Success naturally would have placed a big feather in the cap of the administration but the evidence hardly warrants the conclusion that the Silva mission was created primarily as a war measure to promote the triumph of the Conservative cause.

In tracing the background of Colombia's participation in the canal negotiations of 1901 to 1903 we have of necessity carried our story past certain important developments in the United States. Before following Silva northward on his diplomatic errand, therefore, let us pause to note the progress of the fight for the Panama route in Washington during the closing years of the nineteenth century.

[92] Urueta, *Documentos* . . . *del General Rafael Uribe Uribe,* p. 175.
[93] *Infra,* p. 105.

III

THE BATTLE OF THE ROUTES

The "lobby" was a familiar feature of national politics to every veteran congressman of the McKinley era. Yet it is improbable that its pressure had ever been applied with greater skill or more fateful consequence than during the "Battle of the Routes" which preceded the enactment of the Spooner bill in June, 1902. The publicity given to Mark Hanna's "spontaneous" triumph on this measure in the Senate added handsomely to his personal prestige while it drew attention from a long series of intrigues which had set the stage for his success.

Although the final vote in favor of the Panama route was largely the result of Hanna's efforts, the New Company "lobby" was fundamentally the decisive influence. It provided the initiative and painstakingly built up a case which won the fighting support of the Ohio senator. The significant point is that the Panama route was not adopted because of its obvious merits as a canal site. The energy and resourcefulness of a few men served to reverse the "deliberate judgment" of both houses of Congress in the face of an overwhelming partiality for Nicaragua. Similar maneuvers had been executed many times on a smaller scale, but judged by the magnitude and audacity of the design and the far-reaching character of its results, the Spooner Act of June 28, 1902, deserves to rank with the masterpieces of the lobbyist's art.

Aside from Senator Hanna, the principals in this coup were William Nelson Cromwell and Philippe Bunau-Varilla. The participation of all three men has frequently been ascribed to venal motives, as the disposition of forty million dollars hung upon the outcome of their efforts. This interpretation has a dual advantage in that it requires no qualification and is sufficiently plausible to satisfy the uncritical. In the light of available evidence, however, the only member of the trio whose leading motive was unquestionably hope of material gain was Mr. Cromwell.

The New York attorney was admirably fitted for the type of "representation" which the New Panama Canal Company needed in the United States. As counsel, director, and stockholder of the subsidiary Panama Railroad Company from 1893, he was conversant with the general condition of the isthmian enterprise.[1] A man of remarkable energy and winning personality, he pursued his aims with a resourcefulness and boldness that drew no fine distinctions over method. The story of Panama, replete as it is with intrigue, fails to reveal his peer in contrivance. Congressman Rainey termed him the "most dangerous man the country has produced since the days of Aaron Burr."[2] In testifying before the House Committee on Foreign Affairs in 1912, Henry N. Hall of the New York *World* described him as "the man whose masterful mind, whetted on the grindstone of corporation cunning, conceived and carried out the rape of the Isthmus."[3] The exaggerated tone of these characterizations illustrates the state of mind produced in many who came into contact with his activities.

By 1900 Cromwell had achieved considerable prominence in his profession, particularly through his skill in launching and reorganizing large corporate enterprises. His appearance was distinguished and his manner affable and disarming. Although only forty-eight at the time of the passage of the Spooner Act, his hair and mustaches were snow white. He wore his hair longer than most men and customarily crowned it with a glistening silk hat. A reporter on the New York *World* recorded his impressions of the lawyer in 1908:

Mr. Cromwell is about 5 feet 8 inches high, and medium in build. . . . His eyes are a brilliant light blue, as clear as a baby's, and as

---

[1] *Sen. Docs.*, 59th Cong., 1st Sess., No. 457, p. 4. Cromwell had purchased some of the 1,137 shares of Panama Railroad stock which had not been acquired by the Compagnie Universelle in 1881. His salary as counsel for the line was $3,500 a year. At no time, so far as is known, was he a stockholder in the de Lesseps venture or its successor (*ibid.*, pp. 8–9).

[2] *Story of Panama*, p. 61 (Rainey testimony). [3] *Ibid.*, p. 140.

THE BATTLE OF THE ROUTES 77

innocent looking as a girl's. His complexion also would not shame a maiden. He can smile as sweetly as a society belle and at the same time deal a blow at a business foe that ties him in a hopeless tangle of financial knots. . . . He is a wizard with figures and a shorthand writer of wonderful skill. . . . He is one of the readiest talkers in town. . . . He talks fast, and when he wishes to, never to the point. . . . [He] has an intellect that works like a flash of lightning, and it swings about with the agility of an acrobat. . . .[4]

Bunau-Varilla, although a stockholder in the New Company, was primarily a zealot and a propagandist. With him a conviction soon became a Crusade for Truth. He prosecuted his campaign for Panama with an almost religious fervor. His right to a hearing was undoubted. As a student in the military École polytechnique his imagination had been fired by the canal project. He had procured assignment under the de Lesseps company and at twenty-six found himself in charge of the engineering work on the Isthmus. His subsequent resignation to join a contracting firm which held a valuable excavating concession led to charges that he had used his official position to advance his own interests. It was never proved, however, that he had been involved in the wholesale corruption which ruined the undertaking. In the years that followed, disgusted with the dilatory tactics of the New Company, and convinced of the hopelessness of reawakening French interest in the canal, he turned to the United States as the agency most likely to succeed in completing the work. He wished it to adopt the Panama site in preference to Nicaragua, partly because it would vindicate the engineering genius of his countrymen, and

[4] N. Y. *World*, Oct. 4, 1908. Cromwell was born in Brooklyn, N. Y., in 1854. After finishing his law course at Columbia, he became associated with the partnership of Sullivan, Kobbe & Fowler, headed by Algernon S. Sullivan. Kobbe and Fowler dropped out and the firm was reorganized as Sullivan & Cromwell. In 1888 Sullivan died, and although his place was taken by his son, Cromwell quickly became the dominating spirit of the organization. When Decker, Howell & Co. failed in 1891, with debts of $10,000,000, Cromwell was made assignee. Within six weeks the affairs of the firm were adjusted, the creditors paid in full, and operations resumed. The $260,000 fee awarded by the courts was the largest of its kind up to that time. Subsequently, Cromwell reorganized the Northern Pacific and other railroads, coöperated in the launching of the National Tube Co., and was one of the founders of the U. S. Steel Co. See *ibid.*, and *Who's Who in America*, XVIII (1934), 637.

partly because he had long been an exponent of a sea-level canal, which was practicable only at Panama.[5]

In contrast to Cromwell and Bunau-Varilla, Marcus Alonzo Hanna was a nationally-known figure at the turn of the century. Chairman of the Republican National Committee and chief architect of his party's triumphs in 1896 and 1900, he had entered the Senate early in 1897 as an ad interim appointee of the governor of Ohio. His interest in man-made waterways was not new. "The operation of canals," he told his Senate colleagues, "was one of the few subjects with which in my business life I had become acquainted in all directions."[6] He had been attracted by the possibilities of an interoceanic canal for many years. For reasons to be set forth below, Cromwell's alleged $60,000 contribution to the Republican campaign funds does not offer an altogether satisfactory explanation of Hanna's decisive stand on Panama in 1902.[7]

In spite of their singleness of purpose, these three men did not work as an intimate and harmonious group, as some commentators have implied. This is made clear by the separate versions of the affair recorded by Cromwell and Bunau-Varilla. Each has sought, with some ingenuity, to demonstrate that he was the exclusive source of the inspiration and energy that defeated the Nicaragua bills and brought about the adoption of the Panama route. In addition, the Frenchman appropriates the principal credit for engineering the revolution of November, 1903. Both men gratefully acknowledge the invaluable assistance of Hanna in the congressional battle, and of Roosevelt and Hay in the subsequent dealings with Colombia, but for each other they manifest only contempt. On the rare occasions when they worked together it was under the impulsion of necessity and not of goodwill.[8]

[5] Bunau-Varilla, *Panama: The Creation, Destruction, and Resurrection*, pp. 2–3, 35–37, 48, 72–75.
[6] *Cong. Rec.*, 57th Cong., 1st Sess., p. 7000.   [7] *Infra*, pp. 102–104.
[8] Bunau-Varilla, *Panama: The Creation, Destruction, and Resurrection*, pp. 214–215, 221–222, 428; *Story of Panama*, pp. 193–298 *passim*, and also the "Statement on Behalf of Historical Truth" by Bunau-Varilla, pp. 10–14.

THE BATTLE OF THE ROUTES 79

From the welter of conflicting testimony concerning the activities of these men a few facts stand out. In the first place, Cromwell was the inaugurator, and for some years the principal promoter, of the active campaign for the adoption of the Panama route by the United States. Secondly, this route did not figure seriously as an alternative to the Nicaragua one until after Hanna's conversion to it some time between the spring of 1900 and April, 1901 (for which both Cromwell and Bunau-Varilla claim the credit). Thirdly, although Bunau-Varilla advocated the purchase of the New Company's properties by the United States as early as 1899, he did not cross the Atlantic in pursuance of that end until January, 1901, and then entirely in an individual capacity, without any connection with Cromwell or the New Company. From that time on, all three made substantial contributions to the propaganda for Panama, Hanna by his influence in the Senate, Cromwell by his indefatigable "contact" work, and Bunau-Varilla by his personal charm and effective lecture methods.

The firm of Sullivan & Cromwell undertook its advisory duties on behalf of the New Company in January, 1896. Agitation for an isthmian canal, under government control, was then greater than ever. Owing to the existence of the French concessions at Panama, and to the American character of the enterprise in Nicaragua, most of the public assumed that as far as the United States was concerned an isthmian canal meant a Nicaraguan canal. Bills designed to bolster the faltering Maritime Company with funds from the national treasury were awaiting action in both houses of Congress. The report of the Ludlow Commission in the preceding October gave grounds for hope of early legislation.[9]

Cromwell was fully aware of the consequences to his clients should Congress adopt any of the pending bills. "No company," he later wrote in reviewing the situation, "would ever be able to raise the capital necessary to build the canal in competition with a Government whose resources are . . . unlimited and which would exploit it not as a source of profit, but to further its na-

[9] *Supra*, p. 28.

tional interests." [10] His plan was to bring Panama promptly into the field as an open rival to Nicaragua and, if possible, to procure an official comparison between the two routes. Unfortunately, the directors in Paris shared neither the anxiety nor the energy of their New York counsel, and for approximately three years strictly enjoined him from overtly pressing the case of the New Company.[11]

This interval Cromwell employed in obstructing all Nicaragua legislation presented to Congress, utilizing every plausible pretext for objection, while keeping his own connections well in the background. In this work, as later, he relied largely upon his talent for making and using "contacts." His Brief states that

in the course of . . . more than 30 years, the firm of Sullivan & Cromwell had . . . come to know, and be in a position to influence, a considerable number of public men in political life, in financial circles, and on the press, and all these influences and relations were of great and sometimes decisive utility, and of valuable assistance in the performance of their professional duties in the Panama matter.[12]

At this time all canal bills were handled through Morgan's Select Committee on the Construction of the Nicaragua Canal in the Democratic Senate and Hepburn's Committee on Interstate and Foreign Commerce in the Republican House. Both chairmen were strong advocates of a Nicaragua waterway, but each, assuming that the route was beyond question, was maneuvering to capture the honors of the final enactment for his own party. In the spring of 1896 the Perkins and Mahon bills were being pushed towards a vote in the upper and lower houses respectively. Sullivan & Cromwell bent to the task:

[10] *Story of Panama*, p. 206 (Cromwell Brief). The principal single source dealing with Cromwell's activities is his Brief, or Plea for Fees (to the amount of $800,000), written in 1907 for presentation to a Board of Arbitration in France charged with evaluating his services to the New Company. His account is graphic, but often exaggerated. Important incidents, if unfavorable to him, are omitted or rapidly dismissed. If used with caution, however, and in the light of other sources, the Brief contains much valuable information. It was translated from the French by Henry N. Hall of the N. Y. *World,* and is printed as Exhibit A in *The Story of Panama.*
[11] *Ibid.,* p. 210.   [12] *Ibid.,* p. 207.

We studied each of these bills; we prepared comments and arguments in regard to them; we studied the constitutional, diplomatic, or international questions bearing on them, in connection with the power of Congress to pass such legislation and to lend credit to an enterprise of this kind; we had personal interviews with Members of Congress; we employed as assistants Washington lawyers instructed to follow, day by day, the evidence then being taken by a House committee on the subject of the Nicaragua Canal, and we were in daily communication with them on this subject, studying the reports and giving instructions.[13]

On June 1 Morgan introduced a new measure, providing that the United States purchase the controlling interest in the Maritime Company, but the rush of last-minute business forced it over into the winter session.[14] It fared no better there. A few days before discussion on it began, Señor Rodríguez, representative of the Greater Republic of Central America, of which Nicaragua had recently become a part,[15] called the Department of State's attention to a clause in the Maritime Company's concession forbidding it to transfer its rights to any foreign power under penalty of forfeiture.[16] Opposition developed on other grounds as well, and on February 10 Morgan withdrew his bill from immediate consideration to speed the regular order of business.[17] The special session which convened after McKinley's inauguration in March, 1897, was principally interested in framing a new Republican tariff. Canal legislation was limited to provision for a new commission to continue the study of the Nicaraguan route.[18]

There was no let-up in Cromwell's activity. Throughout the

[13] *Ibid.*, p. 210.
[14] *Sen. Reports*, 55th Cong., 3rd Sess., No. 1417, p. 9.
[15] Although the consolidation did not take place formally until 1898, the Greater Republic was represented in Washington from December, 1896 (Robertson, *History of the Latin-American Nations*, pp. 457-458).
[16] *Sen. Reports*, 55th Cong., 3rd Sess., No. 1418, p. 71.
[17] *Cong. Rec.*, 54th Cong., 2nd Sess., p. 1703. Cromwell's comment was: "We can say in all justice that our constant care, our serious opposition, and our varied efforts had contributed in a somewhat considerable degree to this result" (*Story of Panama*, p. 213).
[18] This was the Walker-Hains-Haupt Nicaragua Canal Commission. *Cong. Rec.*, 55th Cong., 1st Sess., p. 1398; *Sen. Docs.*, 57th Cong., 1st Sess., No. 54, p. 59. Its report is dated May 9, 1899, and was published by the second Walker Commission (*Sen. Docs.*, 57th Cong., 1st Sess., No. 357).

year he corresponded with the directors of the New Company, pointing out the imminence of victory for Nicaragua. The company's only hope, he predicted, lay in an "open, audacious, and aggressive" campaign of publicity and opposition, planned with "Napoleonic strategy." He particularly wished authority for "an energetic demonstration" before the commission's return from the Isthmus.[19] Whatever the private attitude of the directors towards these importunities, they remained outwardly unresponsive.

In April, 1898, the United States declared war on Spain. No conflict could have done more to emphasize the strategic advantages of an isthmian canal. Both combatants were forced to split their naval power between the Pacific and the Caribbean. With a well-fortified canal at the Isthmus, the tactical advantage of the United States would have been greatly increased. The lesson was not lost on the nation. While hostilities lasted, however, emergency legislation brushed canal proposals aside as summarily as tariff schedules had done the previous spring.

Before the war was many weeks old, public opinion in the United States had reacted so sharply against the pro-Spanish tone of the French press that Cromwell suspended his agitation for an "audacious campaign" until the feeling had blown over. He visited Paris during the summer and subjected the directors of the company to his forceful persuasion. After more than six weeks he carried his point. It was agreed that the New Company should take the offensive and, by vigorous propaganda, attempt to interest the United States Government in the Panama route.[20] Cromwell is not definite as to what form the directors hoped this "interest" might take. An outright sale to a foreign government was forbidden by Article 21 of the Wyse concession unless Colombia gave its consent. The company knew from experience that Colombia gave away nothing. On the other hand, very handsome profits might accrue to the stockholders if the United States could be induced to take shares in, or otherwise financially support, the New Company.

[19] *Story of Panama*, pp. 214–218.   [20] *Ibid.*, pp. 219–220.

THE BATTLE OF THE ROUTES 83

The basis of the campaign was to be the report of the International Technical Commission. This body, consisting of fourteen well-known engineers from France, Germany, the United States, Russia, Belgium, and Colombia, had been appointed by the company in February, 1896, to make a survey of work done on the Isthmus and recommend a plan of procedure.[21] Its findings were to be published the following November and it was known that they would be favorable to the company.

Cromwell did not propose to wait until November. His greatest obstacle was the complacency in the United States over the Nicaraguan route. The ignorance in regard to Panama was immense, and comparatively few people had even heard of the New Panama Canal Company. The soil had to be broken for the seed to follow. Hurriedly returning to New York, he organized a press bureau to disseminate popular and technical information dealing with the work of the company and the advantages of its route. Lecturers, magazine writers, and even scientists were engaged to make the nation "Panama-conscious." [22]

As the opening of Congress drew near, the canal sentiment gained in momentum with the public and the press. The peace negotiations in Paris during the fall had caused much debate on the wisdom of acquiring overseas possessions. The foes of the administration cried "Imperialism!" while its defenders hurled back lines from Kipling. But on the subject of the canal there was remarkable unanimity. Its benefits would be not only strategic but commercial, and Bryan was not attacking the expansion of overseas commerce. Petitions poured in upon congressmen from boards of trade and shipping associations, from civic and patriotic societies. The country was prosperous and confident, it had acquired new authority in international affairs. It was in a mood to link the oceans.[23]

[21] Bishop, *Panama Gateway*, p. 108; *Sen. Docs.*, 57th Cong., 2nd Sess., No. 34, p. 3.
[22] *Story of Panama*, pp. 220–221.
[23] For citations of resolutions favoring the construction of an isthmian canal adopted by various boards of trade in the United States in 1898, see Julius W. Pratt, "American Business and the Spanish-American War," *Hispanic American Historical Review*, XIV (1934), 180 footnote.

While this enthusiasm was sweet to Morgan, it cut no thorns from Cromwell's path. It was one thing to obstruct a senator's "hobby," it was quite another to thwart the wishes of an aroused nation. The fact that Cromwell was attempting to sell the country a "foreign" route in substitution for the "national" one was certain to lay him open to the patriots' attack as soon as his purpose was disclosed. Several bills sponsoring the Nicaragua Canal were to be introduced in the coming session; there would be none for Panama. Difficulties had still to be cleared away, but the *locus operandi* appeared settled. Under the circumstances Cromwell could only delay and divide his opponents by "Napoleonic strategy" until his propaganda should weave its spell.

The International Technical Commission completed its task on November 16. Its report to the directors of the New Panama Company praised the achievements of the French engineers on the Isthmus and endorsed their general plan of future work.[24] The director-general and chief engineer hastened to the United States, where Cromwell had made arrangements through Secretary Hay for an interview with the president. At this meeting, on December 2, McKinley was presented with a copy of the commission's report and a memorial, prepared by Cromwell, setting forth the history and intentions of the company.[25]

This move was checkmated two days later when the Department of State officially announced that the Colombian government had refused to grant the New Company an extension of its concession.[26] The statement was not strictly accurate, as the matter was still unsettled, but the Colombian minister did not issue a denial for several days.[27] By then the damage had been done, for McKinley's annual message went to Congress on the 5th. It contained no mention of the Panama route. It reviewed the situation

---

[24] The text of the report is reproduced in *Sen. Reports*, 56th Cong., 1st Sess., No. 1337, Appendix II.

[25] *Story of Panama*, p. 221; *Sen. Docs.*, 57th Cong., 2nd Sess., No. 34, pp. 1–5.

[26] N. Y. *World*, Dec. 5, 1898. The article added that the "news from Colombia has cheered the various groups of Nicaraguists greatly."

[27] *Sen. Docs.*, 57th Cong., 2nd Sess., No. 34, pp. 5, 7–8, Cromwell to Hay, Dec. 5 and 21, 1898.

THE BATTLE OF THE ROUTES 85

in Nicaragua at some length, however, and recommended prompt provision for the construction of a canal there.[28]

Having flung its banners to the breeze, the New Company quickly drew the enemy's fire. A former president of the Maritime Company branded the audience of the 2d "an astounding piece of effrontery." [29] Ten days later, in the Senate, Morgan denounced the Panama interests for conspiring with the transcontinental railroads to deprive the people of a Nicaragua canal.[30] The Battle of the Routes was joined.

Morgan's bill provided for a canal to be built, owned, and fortified by the United States.[31] Such a plan was clearly in contravention of the terms of the Clayton-Bulwer treaty. The British ambassador pointed this out to the Department of State while Cromwell was busy pointing it out to various senators and representatives. Nevertheless, the bill was placed on the Senate calendar and discussion began early in January. The prospect could hardly have been more auspicious. Within Congress and without, sentiment for a Nicaragua canal was overwhelming. The Maritime stockholders were willing to sell. The only considerable opposition in the Senate came from a group which protested against the inclusion of "control" clauses until the Clayton-Bulwer treaty had been abrogated or amended. Even these men professed sympathy with the purpose of the measure.[32] The possibility of an alternative route was not suggested. On January 21 the Morgan bill was adopted by a vote of 48 to 6.[33]

[28] Richardson, *Messages and Papers*, X, 101–102.
[29] N. Y. *Tribune*, Dec. 4, 1898.   [30] *Cong. Rec.*, 55th Cong., 3rd Sess., p. 107.
[31] This bill had been introduced on June 21, 1898. In May the Senate had adopted a resolution inviting the Maritime Company to make a proposal for the transfer of its capital stock, concessions, and indebtedness to the United States. The company offered to sell for $5,500,000. This offer formed the basis of Morgan's June bill. See *Cong. Rec.*, 55th Cong., 2nd Sess., pp. 4923–4924; for text of bill see *Cong. Rec.*, 55th Cong., 3rd Sess., pp. 97–98.
[32] See *Cong. Rec.*, 55th Cong., 3rd Sess., Dec. 12, 1898, to Jan. 21, 1899 (particularly the debates of Jan. 17).
[33] *Ibid.*, p. 911. Morgan was pleased with his victory, as far as it went, but frankly expressed his fears concerning the House in a letter to Governor Joseph F. Johnston of Alabama: ". . . The bill that passed the Senate, by a vote of eight to one, may be defeated in the House, through the combined influence of all the trans-continental Railroads, including the Panama Railroad, and the Canadian

The final decision now rested with the House. It was in this branch that Cromwell had concentrated his efforts, for, according to his statement, the Senate's action had been fully anticipated. After some difficulty he secured an audience before Hepburn's committee and for three days regaled it with what he later described as a "most profound study of the technical sides of the question." This exposition, profound though it may have been, left the prejudices of most of the members quite unshaken. Cromwell admitted that "an enthusiastic and large majority of the House was openly pledged to Nicaragua. . . . If [a vote] could not be deferred, the fate of Panama was sealed." To compass this postponement

> we conceived the plan of obtaining the appointment of a new canal commission, for the examination of the Panama route as well as of all the other routes, which would prevent the United States from deciding in favor of Nicaragua before the presentation to Congress of an official report on Panama, with the certainty that we should be able to prove the superiority of Panama. This idea was met almost everywhere with energetic opposition; but Mr. Cromwell and his partners succeeded, by personal interviews and arguments, in convincing several important members of the House—in particular its Speaker, Mr. Reed; the chairman of the Committee on Ways and Means, Mr. Cannon, who was also leader of the Republican Party in the House; and the chairman of the Committee on Rivers and Harbors, Mr. Burton—of the wisdom, the justice, and the advantages of this plan.[34]

By his own admission, in short, Mr. Cromwell had the wizard's touch. However, he fails to mention other influences that were at work. The most important of these was the old Morgan-Hepburn

---

Pacific Railroad, they being determined that, if they can prevent it, no waterway, not owned or controlled by them, shall be opened for ships through the Isthmus. . . . Their purpose is to put their own rates of taxation upon all the commerce that shall pass across the Hemisphere between the Atlantic and Pacific Oceans . . ." (Morgan Papers, Feb. 5, 1899). Prof. Lewis Haupt, of the Walker Nicaragua Canal Commission, knowing less of politics, was more hopeful. "Croakers," he told Morgan, "think it will not pass the House. I made an urgent plea before the Interstate Com. on Thursday and I trust it was not without effect . . ." (*ibid.*, Jan. 21, 1899). The hearings are printed in *Sen. Docs.*, 56th Cong., 1st Sess., No. 50.

[34] *Story of Panama*, pp. 224–225.

THE BATTLE OF THE ROUTES 87

rivalry over the authorship of the canal act. Had these gentlemen been coöperating as closely as Cromwell suggests it is difficult to see how the "personal interviews and arguments" of the Panama "lobby" could have stemmed the Nicaragua tide at that session. The Hepburn Committee report on the Morgan bill, submitted to the House on February 13, reveals something of the actual situation. It reads in part:

The Senate bill, for which your committee recommended a substitute, proposes to amend the charter of the Maritime Canal Company, and then reorganize the Company by the appointment of a majority of the board of directors by the President of the United States, and then use that corporation as its agent for constructing and operating the canal. This corporation is created by the United States. . . . It is to bear all of the responsibilities and burdens. Yet it shares the pecuniary benefits with other stockholders, to whose stock it alone gives value, by advancing all of the money to be used. In this behalf the Government descends from the character of a sovereign to become a majority stockholder in a corporation it had created. . . .

If the Government should initiate its effort to secure this canal by payment of $5,000,000 to the Maritime Company, $6,000,000 in stock to Nicaragua, and $1,500,000 in stock to Costa Rica, as provided by the Senate bill, do we not thereby open the door to the demands of the Cragin-Grace syndicate, the Atlas Company, the Atlantic and Pacific Navigation Company, and all of the other enterprising and speculative persons, artificial and natural, that have been toying with canal concessions with more or less activity during the last half century?

The better course would seem to be for the United States to deal with Nicaragua and Costa Rica direct; and if any of the corporations referred to suffer from an invasion of rights let these Governments deal with them and remedy their wrongs.[35]

With less than three weeks of the session remaining, Hepburn's committee had deadlocked the canal issue. This was no surprise to some of the veterans. When Congress opened in December Cannon had declared the chance for canal legislation in the session "exceedingly doubtful."[36] Yet party considerations de-

[35] *House Reports*, 55th Cong., 3rd Sess., No. 2104, pp. 3-4, 6-7.
[36] N. Y. *World*, Dec. 4, 1898.

manded an outward show of activity. A new commission, to conduct an impartial investigation of all proposed isthmian routes, would resolve the difficulty in a politic manner. It would save the party's face before the electorate without deserting Mr. Hepburn, and provide time to determine more precisely Nicaragua's attitude toward the Maritime concessions.[37]

A question naturally arises as to the authorship of the commission idea. Although the White House was closely in touch with the situation, there is no indication that the scheme originated with McKinley. He had been a consistent supporter of the Nicaragua route, until, according to a statement made by Hanna in 1902, the hearings before the Hepburn Committee convinced him of the necessity of studying both routes with care. The senator did not maintain, however, that the president influenced the action of the House in any way.[38] It is possible that Cannon or Reed conceived the scheme. On the other hand, Cromwell had been working for months on ways and means to block the Morgan bill, and it is very likely that he is correct in assuming credit for the commission idea. Such a plan would be practicable if a split occurred between the houses, and apparently Cromwell had reason to believe this would be the case. It will be remembered that in the face of large Nicaragua majorities in both branches, he felt justified in concentrating his whole attention on the House.[39]

[37] It will be recalled that Nicaragua had declared the Maritime concessions null and void the previous autumn and had signed a "promise of contract" with the Grace-Eyre-Cragin syndicate, to take effect on Oct. 9, 1899 (*supra*, p. 30). The Maritime Company had appealed to the Department of State, which had taken the matter up with the Zelaya government. Should the cancellation stand, the Morgan bill would be eliminated automatically. *Sen. Reports,* 55th Cong., 3rd Sess., No. 1417, p. 10.

[38] *Cong. Rec.,* 57th Cong., 1st Sess., pp. 6997–6998.

[39] Bunau-Varilla claims that he inspired the creation of the commission. According to his account, the idea was propagated at Washington during the winter of 1898–99 by the Hon. John Bigelow and Lt.-Comdr. Asher Baker, U.S.N., both of whom had been converted to the Varilla doctrine in Paris. Baker, especially, had connections with Speaker Reed and Mr. Cannon and he "enlightened" them as to the "real situation of the Panama Canal." Bigelow communicated with his friend Hay. In this way "light fell on the Government itself through the intermediary of Mr. Hay. Thanks to Lieutenant Baker it penetrated to the two recog-

THE BATTLE OF THE ROUTES

Morgan was too astute a parliamentarian to accept as final the action of the Hepburn Committee. He would ride the Eagle. Certain party measures were then being considered, whose passage the Republicans earnestly desired. One was the Rivers and Harbors bill which the House had recently sent to the Senate for its concurrence. Morgan attached his canal bill to it with a $10,000,000 appropriation for commencing work. On February 25 the amended bill passed by 50 votes to 3 and went to conference.[40]

To block this sudden flanking movement Cromwell had to convince the House conferees of the desirability of substituting a canal commission amendment for Morgan's "rider." This required a demonstration that a real choice of routes existed. The New Company must match the offer of the Maritime Company by granting the United States the opportunity of controlling its enterprise. With the permission of the director-general, who had just arrived in New York, Cromwell submitted to the House Committee on Rivers and Harbors a proposition to reincorporate his company under the laws of one of the states and extend to the national government as much representation and control as the Colombian concession would permit. At the same time he sent a letter to President McKinley repeating this offer, with the explanation that "while the New Panama Canal Company does not seek any financial aid from the Government, it recognizes the national sentiment in favor of acquiring some pecuniary interest in any canal connecting the Atlantic and Pacific oceans."[41]

---

nised heads of the House." Bunau-Varilla, *Panama: The Creation, Destruction, and Resurrection,* p. 161.

[40] The Morgan amendment had been adopted the previous day (*Cong. Rec.,* 55th Cong., 3rd Sess., pp. 2295-2296; *Story of Panama,* p. 225). The suggestion for the "rider" may have originated with members of the House. Hitchcock wrote Morgan from New York on Feb. 11 that he had talked with several representatives on the train. Ex-Speaker Grow was very positive, he said, that the only way to get the Canal was by attaching the Morgan bill to the Rivers and Harbors bill in the Senate. The letter added that Senator Sherman felt that the Hepburn bill with his amendment (authorizing the president to deal with the Maritime Co.) should be put on the Rivers and Harbors bill by the Senate. Morgan Papers.

[41] *Sen. Reports,* 56th Cong., 1st Sess., No. 1337, p. 7; *Story of Panama,* pp. 225-226.

The House conferees, appointed by Reed, accepted the Cromwell plan as sufficient grounds for the examination of all the isthmian routes, but the Senate's spokesmen stood firm for the Morgan amendment. After several days of deadlock the Republican leaders grew anxious over the approach of the date set for adjournment. Their forces, as a result of the election of 1896, controlled both houses of Congress, and the responsibility for canal legislation lay directly upon them. At the crack of the party whip, therefore, the Republican Senate conferees abandoned the Democrat Morgan to save the bill. Consequently, the conference report, embodying the House amendment, became law in the final hours of the Fifty-fifth Congress.[42] "We think," Cromwell subsequently declared, "we are justified in stating that without our efforts the new commission would not have been created." [43]

II

The law of March 3, 1899, required the president to name a commission "to determine the most feasible and practicable route" for a canal across the Isthmus "under the control, management and ownership of the United States." One million dollars was appropriated for its use.[44] Cromwell set to work immediately to prevent the appointment of any of the members of the boards of 1895 and 1897. He wrote McKinley on March 11 explaining his objections and then journeyed to the capital for an interview with him and the secretary of state. He records in his Brief that he "refused" to propose anyone for the commission but "at the President's request we furnished him the list of prominent engineers which we had prepared." [45] His efforts were

[42] *Cong. Rec.*, 55th Cong., 3rd Sess., p. 2843 (March 3, 1899).
[43] *Story of Panama*, p. 227. Hitchcock, the president of the Maritime Company, considered Speaker Reed responsible for side-tracking the Morgan "rider" (Morgan Papers, Hitchcock to Morgan, April 21, 1899).
[44] *U. S. Statutes at Large*, XXX, 1150.
[45] *Sen. Reports*, 56th Cong., 1st Sess., No. 1337, p. 8; *Story of Panama*, p. 227. Cromwell was probably particularly anxious to bar the selection of Professor Haupt, an ardent champion of the Nicaragua route. About this time Haupt was confiding his own fears to Morgan: ". . . Permit me to suggest that any engineers whose chief clientage has been on RRs and especially Southern Pacific

THE BATTLE OF THE ROUTES 91

fruitless, for the Isthmian Canal Commission, as constituted in June, 1899, included Admiral Walker, U.S.N., Colonel Hains, U.S.A., and Professor Haupt of the 1897 commission, as well as Col. Oswald Ernst, U.S.A., Samuel Pasco, a lawyer, Professor Emory Johnson, an economist, and George S. Morison, Alfred Noble, and William Burr, civil engineers.[46]

The commission divided its labors into two parts. It planned a visit to the Isthmus to gain a first-hand knowledge of the several possible routes and a trip to Europe to inspect the Kiel and Manchester canals and the records of the French company. Cromwell asserts that he induced Walker and his associates to defer the isthmian trip (where at least two routes would have been under discussion) until after the visit to France (where Panama alone would be considered).[47]

On the commission's arrival in Paris about the middle of August, Mr. Cromwell, already there, assumed the role of master of ceremonies. The company had made its preparations with care. For the next five weeks the Americans listened to expositions by members of the International Technical Commission, illustrated by an array of maps, charts, plans, and graphs.[48] "The hearings," wrote Cromwell, "were conducted with very formal and elaborate procedure . . . as before a court of highest jurisdiction." [49] Walker, while still in Paris, approached Maurice Hutin, the director-general of the New Company, on the sale price of the Wyse concession. Hutin explained that so important a matter required careful study and that he was not then in a position to make a definite reply.[50]

Meanwhile, Bunau-Varilla, working entirely independently of the company, of whose policies he was openly critical, secured an introduction to the members of the subcommittee designated to

---

may be in position to repeat the experience of this winter's legislation by retarding reports. I am also advised that the report of this Com'n must be unanimous if it is to be continued but I expect to express my convictions concerning certain features of the work if it can be done." Morgan Papers, March 15, 1899.
[46] *Walker Commission Report*, p. 12.   [47] *Story of Panama*, p. 228.
[48] *Walker Commission Report*, p. 14.   [49] *Story of Panama*, p. 228.
[50] *Sen. Reports*, 56th Cong., 1st Sess., No. 1337, pp. 24, 67.

study the Panama route. It happened that none of these men—Morison, Burr, and Ernst—had served on any previous canal commission and they were, therefore, entirely uncommitted. The Frenchman brought the full power of his contagious enthusiasm to bear on these engineers. His methods were not retiring. It had long been his custom to endeavor to meet any influential Americans who visited Paris. Frequently he would invite them to his home for dinner, and hold them with his graphic discourse until far into the night. With the commissioners his tactics were similar. "Our conferences," he recounts, "were long and frequent. I was gradually able to impress their minds with facts showing at the same time the inferiority of Nicaragua and the admirable superiority of Panama. . . . When the Commission left Paris I was certain that the scales had fallen from the eyes of at least three of its members." [51]

While the Walker party was preparing for its field researches on the Isthmus, Cromwell turned to the details of his scheme to Americanize the New Company's property. By this ruse he hoped to remove the stigma of "foreign enterprise" without depriving the French investors of control.[52] With the approval of the directors, the attorney incorporated the Panama Company of America on December 27, 1899, under the laws of New Jersey. Of the thirty million dollars capital, five thousand was subscribed in cash.[53] The next step was to persuade the shareholders to transfer the New Company's assets to the American firm in return for a majority of the stock. At this point there was a vigorous protest from the legal representatives of the Old Company, and the New Company shareholders refused to ratify the transaction.[54] Thereupon the directors resigned in a body. Hutin, the

[51] Bunau-Varilla, *Panama: The Creation, Destruction, and Resurrection*, p. 166.
[52] *Story of Panama*, pp. 229–230.
[53] *Sen. Docs.*, 59th Cong., 1st Sess., No. 457, pp. 22–23, 28 *et seq.*
[54] Bunau-Varilla, *Panama: The Creation, Destruction, and Resurrection*, pp. 169–171. Bunau-Varilla points out that since only a majority of the stock was to go to the New Company, which would get only a similar proportion of the profits from the sale of its property by the American company, whoever held the rest of the stock would get money properly belonging to the French stockholders. The insinuation seems clear that Cromwell's purpose in organizing his American corporation was to defraud his clients.

THE BATTLE OF THE ROUTES 93

director-general, was shortly afterward elected president of the board.[55] Cromwell had once again been checked by his clients.

Diplomatically, the year 1899 was marked by an energetic but futile attempt to clear the ground for canal legislation by eliminating the Clayton-Bulwer obstacle. In December, 1898, almost simultaneously with the conclusion of the treaty of Paris, Secretary Hay had instructed Henry White, temporarily in charge of the London embassy, to sound out Lord Salisbury on the possibility of a revision of the 1850 convention.

> . . . There has been [he wrote] . . . a great deal of discussion as to whether the provisions of the Clayton-Bulwer treaty actually stand in the way of any practical action by the Government of the United States in the construction and control of the canal. It is even held by many of our public men that the treaty is already obsolete and that it has been so treated and regarded by the action of both the British and American Governments. I do not wish at this moment to revive or to entertain any controversy upon these points. The President thinks it is more judicious to approach the British Government in a frank and friendly spirit of mutual accommodation, and to ask whether it may not be possible to secure such modification of the provisions of the Clayton-Bulwer treaty as to admit such action by the Government of the United States as may render possible the accomplishment of a work which will be for the benefit of the entire civilized world. . . .[56]

The move was nicely timed. The undisguised sympathy of the British government and press for the United States during the recent war had created a cordial bond between the two nations which statesmen on both sides of the water were ready to turn to advantage. On receiving White's assurance that Salisbury viewed the proposed negotiations with favor and was willing to conduct them through his Washington envoy, Hay promptly

---

[55] *Sen. Reports,* 56th Cong., 1st Sess., No. 1337, p. 144.

[56] *Dip. Hist. of the Panama Canal,* pp. 1–2, Hay to White, Dec. 7, 1898. In his annual message on Dec. 5 McKinley had recommended prompt congressional action on the canal so strongly that Ambassador Pauncefote called on Hay to inquire as to the president's attitude towards the Clayton-Bulwer pact. He was assured that while the United States was ready to undertake the task of construction it did not intend to disregard its treaty obligations to Great Britain but rather to seek a modification of them. Mowat, *Lord Pauncefote,* pp. 272–273.

opened parleys with Ambassador Pauncefote. By January 11, 1899, the two men had completed the preliminary draft of a new treaty, releasing the United States from the most irksome of the existing restrictions.[57] The hopes born of this rapid progress were quickly dashed, however, by Downing Street's sudden insistence upon a *quid pro quo* in the northwest. Intimations were conveyed to the Department of State that Great Britain's consent to the surrender of certain of its treaty rights on the Isthmus would depend largely upon the readiness of the United States to settle the long-standing dispute over the Alaskan boundary to Canada's satisfaction.[58] Hay flatly refused to sanction a "trade." Although he and Pauncefote resumed informal talks on the subject after the latter's return from a summer assignment to the Peace Conference at The Hague, nothing significant was accomplished. At the end of the year the January convention still lay unconsidered in the files of the Foreign Office.

Hepburn introduced a bill into the Congress that met in December, 1899, empowering the Executive to construct and fortify a Nicaragua canal at once in open disregard of British treaty claims.[59] In reply to the objections of more cautious legislators that the findings of the Walker investigation would not be known for many months to come, the adherents of the "national route" professed to see no reason to await another report on a project

[57] *Dip. Hist. of the Panama Canal*, pp. 2–3, 12; Mowat, *Lord Pauncefote*, p. 273; Dennett, *John Hay*, p. 250.

[58] This suggestion was prompted by the collapse, at about this time, of an unrelated negotiation. On Feb. 20, 1899, the Anglo-American Joint High Commission, appointed the preceding summer in an effort to remove sources of friction between the United States and Canada, brought its contentious and fruitless sessions to an end. Its demise left several important questions, including the Alaskan boundary difficulty, in complete deadlock. Apparently, the British cabinet had no serious objection to modifying the Clayton-Bulwer treaty along the lines desired by Hay, but hoped to turn its act of yielding to account by extracting a concession in return which would strengthen its prestige at home and with the Empire. See *Dip. Hist. of the Panama Canal*, pp. 12–13; Nevins, *Henry White*, pp. 145–147, 186 *et seq.*

[59] *Cong. Rec.*, 56th Cong., 1st Sess., p. 151 (Dec. 7). The bill was reported favorably with minor amendments by the House Committee on Interstate and Foreign Commerce, Feb. 17, 1900 (*House Reports*, 56th Cong., 1st Sess., No. 351). The Walker Commission had meanwhile left for the Isthmus on Jan. 6 (*Walker Commission Report*, p. 14).

THE BATTLE OF THE ROUTES 95

which had received such repeated official endorsement in the past. They pointed out, furthermore, that Costa Rica and Nicaragua were prepared to discuss necessary diplomatic arrangements while Colombia had not as yet indicated the slightest disposition to coöperate with the United States.

Hay watched the growth of the "immediate action" sentiment in Congress with uneasiness. The possibility that the commission's studies might be scrapped by legislative caprice appeared to him much less important, however, than the increasing danger that Hepburn's proposal would be enacted before a revision of the Clayton-Bulwer convention could be pushed through. About the 21st of January he dispatched a private letter to Ambassador Choate in London summarizing his views. It read in part:

. . . You will remember that last year, the Congress, in apparent despair of an agreement between the two Houses on the comparative merits of the Hepburn and the Morgan bills, passed all at once, with very little deliberation I am bound to say, the bill for the creation of a commission to examine and report upon all possible routes across the Isthmus. To do thoroughly the work assigned to them, this Commission will require at least a year, and probably two. Now, both Houses seem to have grown impatient at this prospect of delay which was rendered necessary by their own act. Mr. Hepburn has introduced a bill . . . which, if it passes the House, Mr. Morgan is quite sanguine he can carry through the Senate. . . . I think we should be in a most unenviable attitude before the world if that bill should pass in its present form. My own position would be one of especial awkwardness, and would raise very serious questions as to what would personally be required of me. I think we ought to make an effort to arrange the matter through diplomatic channels, so that at least the administration would have its skirts clear of any complicity in a violent and one-sided abrogation of the Clayton-Bulwer Treaty.

. . . As soon as Congress is convinced that the people of the country demand the construction of the canal, it will be done. . . . It is hard to say whether we or England will profit by it most. It would be a deplorable result of all our labor and thought on the subject, if, by persisting in postponing the consideration of this matter until all the Canadian questions are closed up, England should be made to appear in the attitude of attempting to veto a work of such world-wide importance; and the worst of all for international relations is that the veto would not be effective.[60]

By design this communication reached London simultaneously with an official report from Pauncefote covering much the same ground.[61] Results followed swiftly. The Canadian government was informed that the interests of the Empire required a prompt settlement of the isthmian question, even at the sacrifice of reciprocal advantages for the Dominion.[62] Late in the evening of February 3 Choate wired the Department of State that the British cabinet had decided to accept the pact drawn up in Washington twelve months before. On the 5th Hay and Pauncefote affixed their signatures to the document, which the president immediately transmitted to the Senate.

The first Hay-Pauncefote treaty consisted of four articles. The first conceded to the United States the right to construct a canal across the Isthmus as well as "the exclusive right of providing for the regulation and management" of the waterway. The second laid down seven rules, similar to those embodied in the Suez Canal convention of 1888, as the basis for preserving the "general principle" of neutralization established in Article VIII of the Clayton-Bulwer treaty. These included provision that the canal was to be "free and open, in time of war as in time of peace, to the vessels of commerce and of war of all nations, on terms of entire equality . . ."; that the canal was never to be blockaded

[60] Quoted from Dennett, *John Hay*, p. 252.

[61] *Ibid.*, p. 251. Pauncefote stated his reasons for recommending the prompt modification of the Clayton-Bulwer treaty and added: "Mr. Hay assures me that such a Convention [as the Hay-Pauncefote] would pass the Senate, and that the situation would thus be saved. Even Senator Morgan, he tells me, would vote in favour of it." Quoted from Mowat, *Lord Pauncefote*, pp. 276-277, Pauncefote to Salisbury, Jan. 21, 1900.

[62] The colonial secretary, in seeking Canada's concurrence in the plan for a separate canal treaty, explained to the governor-general that a refusal to conclude negotiations with the United States "would tend to shake the position of the President, whose friendly attitude is in the present condition of public affairs of great importance" (quoted from Mowat, *Lord Pauncefote*, p. 279, Chamberlain to Lord Minto, Jan. 30, 1900). The Ottawa government raised no objections to the step. It should be noted that a *modus vivendi* on the Alaskan boundary had been arranged the previous fall.

THE BATTLE OF THE ROUTES 97

or subjected to other acts of war; and that while the United States was privileged to maintain military police to keep order along the route, no fortifications were to be erected commanding the canal "or the waters adjacent." Article III stipulated that the signatories were to invite other powers to adhere to the pact when ratified. The final article set a six months' time limit on the exchange of ratifications.[63]

Despite the Senate's refusal to waive the customary injunction of secrecy, an obliging member of the upper house supplied a copy of the convention to the press. Within a week an intensive journalistic debate was in progress. Criticism was directed principally against the ban on fortifications and the inability of the United States to close the canal to the warships of its own foes. The Boston *Post* asked its readers whether it was not an "astounding" treaty which permitted the armed vessels "of all our possible enemies to pass through a canal built on the American continent with American money, to attack our coasts and our fleets?" The Chicago *Post* predicted that it would be "overwhelmingly rejected by the people if submitted as a political issue by any party" and warned the nation that it "must choose between a fortified and exclusive waterway and the abandonment of the whole project." The Detroit *News* felt that "another of the administration's 'great diplomatic victories' has been won—by the British government." The New York papers, with the notable exceptions of the *Sun* and the *Journal,* were inclined to take a more favorable view of Hay's accomplishment and to minimize the dangers of an unfortified canal. Typical of this attitude was the *World's* comment that "we would lose far more than we would gain if we sought to make the canal our private property, to be closed at our pleasure." In the Mid-west the Chicago *Record* came to the support of the State Department.

A neutral canal [it observed] would require no defenses. Moreover, our neighbors in this hemisphere are likely to regard us with

---

[63] *Dip. Hist. of the Panama Canal,* pp. 289–291. The time limit was later extended by mutual agreement.

98 THE BATTLE OF THE ROUTES

less suspicion if we do not insist on making a military fortress out of the waterway which is of so much importance to the development of both the western continents.[64]

Little coaxing was required to draw certain public figures into the fray. Hepburn denounced the administration's folly in reviving the Clayton-Bulwer treaty at a time when "every authority on international law, every man posted on international treaties" regarded it as obsolete.[65] Governor Roosevelt of New York, eager to be "on record" in the matter, issued a statement of vigorous protest to the New York *Sun* and followed it a few days later with a letter to Hay expounding the thesis that an unfortified canal "strengthens against us every nation whose fleet is larger than ours." [66]

Hay's initial confidence that the Senate would speedily ratify his treaty soon waned. Unaccustomed to the rough-and-tumble side of public life, he was deeply hurt by the criticism of the press.[67] When, on March 9, the Committee on Foreign Relations reported the convention favorably, but amended in such a way as to render the provisions of Article II inapplicable to "measures which the United States may find it necessary to take for securing . . . the defense of the United States and the maintenance of public order," the secretary was exasperated to the point of handing in his resignation.[68] Fortunately for the future of the

---

[64] *Public Opinion*, XXVIII, No. 7, 198–199. The Washington *Post*, the Baltimore *American*, and the Brooklyn *Eagle* also attacked the treaty editorially, while the *Times*, the *Press*, and the *Tribune* of New York and the *Inquirer* and the *Ledger* of Philadelphia advocated ratification. On March 4 the N. Y. *Times* published an article by John Bassett Moore in which he examined the precedents relating to the neutralization of an isthmian canal. He concluded that the policy of a neutralized canal was the historic one of the United States, that the Clayton-Bulwer treaty was still in force, and that, even if abrogated in the future, the neutralization of the canal was "guaranteed by various other treaties."

[65] N. Y. *World*, Feb. 13, 1900.

[66] N. Y. *Sun*, Feb. 12, 1900; Thayer, *John Hay*, II, 340.

[67] "I am horribly busy," he wrote his son on March 17, "and am having, now in my old age, my first experience of filthy newspaper abuse" (Thayer, *John Hay*, II, 229).

[68] The committee's report is printed in *Sen. Docs.*, 56th Cong., 1st Sess., No. 268. The majority report, presented by Chairman Cushman K. Davis, strongly supported Hay's contention that the Clayton-Bulwer treaty was still in effect.

THE BATTLE OF THE ROUTES 99

negotiations, McKinley returned it immediately with a cordial and reassuring note.[69] With a presidential election in the offing the Senate was unwilling to commit itself on an issue which had started so many repercussions throughout the country. The committee amendment was discussed in secret session on April 5 but no further action was taken until the following winter.[70]

As yet there was no active movement in either branch of Congress for the Panama route. The accomplishments of the Cromwell "lobby" had been entirely those of delay. Every indication pointed to a decisive victory for the Nicaragua Canal in the event of a vote in the House. The attorney and his associates applied themselves, therefore, to the task of postponing all legislative action until the Walker Commission had made its report. To this end they supported the growing opposition to the Hay-Pauncefote treaty, particularly stressing the disadvantages of the neutrality and nonfortification provisions. This was a very temporary line of resistance and Cromwell acknowledged that "few Members of Congress . . . could be brought to offer open opposition to the Nicaragua bills." [71]

Morgan, in a minority report, joined in this view but opposed the committee's amendment to the new convention.

[69] Thayer, *John Hay*, II, 226-228. Hay felt that the newspaper attacks upon the treaty had strongly influenced the Senate's attitude towards it. He wrote to Henry White on March 18: ". . . Nearly every member of the Foreign Relations Committee approved the treaty and promised his support—but the *Sun* and the *Journal* began their furious attack which met with so much response from the papers in Chicago, who are cross with the President for personal reasons, that it frightened the weak sisters out of their wits. Lodge was the first to flop—then Cullom, who is a candidate for reëlection, and in great danger of failing. They have worked on Davis, who is too indolent to make a strong fight. Wolcott, who is all right, is most of the time in New York, and was of no use. So they hit on the idiotic expedient of working into the treaty the utterably inapplicable and futile tenth article of the Suez Act. They thought that they would save the treaty by placating the howling fools in the Senate, and that England, seeing how silly and ineffective the amendment is, might contemptuously accept it. . . ." Quoted from Nevins, *Henry White*, p. 152.

[70] *Dip. Hist. of the Panama Canal*, p. 14. Henry White gathered, from talking with Arthur Balfour in April, that both he and Salisbury were inclined to accept the Senate committee's alteration (Nevins, *Henry White*, p. 153).

[71] *Story of Panama*, pp. 231–232. Cromwell asserts that "we retained and had several consultations with Prof. Woolsey, the eminent author of works on inter-

THE BATTLE OF THE ROUTES

Throughout the winter and early spring months of 1900 the law-making machinery of the House ground slowly ahead, moving Hepburn's bill towards the top of the calendar. It arrived on May 2, and passed by a vote of 224 to 36.[72] The prospects for concurrence by the Senate were greatly improved by indications that Morgan intended to coöperate with Hepburn at last. His reorganization scheme had been ended by Nicaragua's cancellation of the Maritime concessions.[73] In addition, Cromwell's growing influence and the rumors regarding the activities of the transcontinental railroads had much alarmed the senator. The time for quibbling had passed.

In an attempt to commit Walker and his colleagues to the practicability, if not the preferability, of the Nicaragua route in advance of the official report, the members of the commission were closely examined on May 11 by Morgan's Committee on Interoceanic Canals. Beyond admitting that a good lock canal was possible by either route, and a sea-level canal possible only at Panama, the commissioners refused to venture any opinions without more study of their material.[74]

On May 16 Morgan reported the Hepburn bill favorably to the Senate. His recommendation was accompanied by a vigorous denunciation of Cromwell's "interference." As evidence the senator cited the attorney's letters to McKinley of February 28,

---

national law, professor at Yale University, and obtained from him a formal professional opinion, of which we made use in support of the arguments we were putting forward among the Senators who recognized in him an eminent authority on this subject" (*ibid.,* p. 232).

[72] *Cong. Rec.,* 56th Cong., 1st Sess., pp. 5014–5015. Cannon led the opposition to the bill. Hepburn challenged his sincerity and accused him of having tried to block legislation for a Nicaragua canal for the past five years. Cannon replied: "I know no man connected with the Panama Canal, officially or unofficially, and never have known one of them" (*ibid.,* pp. 4998–4999).

[73] *Sen. Reports,* 55th Cong., 3rd Sess., No. 1417, p. 10. Although Hitchcock's company was attempting to secure redress through arbitration proceedings, the Nicaraguan government's insistence that the board be composed exclusively of its own citizens foreshadowed an unfavorable decision (Morgan Papers, Hitchcock to Hay, Feb. 3, 1900). As for the Grace-Eyre-Cragin syndicate, Minister William L. Merry wrote Hitchcock confidentially from Managua that he was certain Zelaya would gladly "throw over" their promised concession in favor of the United States (*ibid.,* Hitchcock to Morgan, Feb. 9, 1900).

[74] *Sen. Reports,* 56th Cong., 1st Sess., No. 1337, pp. 23 *et seq.*

1899, offering to sell an interest in the New Company to the United States, and March 11, 1899, suggesting that "impartial" men be selected for the recently created canal board. Still more objectionable, in the opinion of the chairman, was a communication to the president from the same source, dated April 30, which protested against the pending action on the Hepburn measure in the House in view of the fact that the Walker Commission had not completed its investigation. The note concluded with the request that the chief executive "advise the Congress of the facts in the case." Such a demand, Morgan declared, constituted "an insult to the intelligence of Congress." The rest of the Morgan report was taken up with a detailed demonstration that the treaty of 1846 prevented the United States from acquiring sovereignty over a Colombian canal and a charge that the opposition represented the transcontinental railroad pool.[75]

With success imminent, Morgan's hopes were shattered once more by the press of other business. In a desperate effort to precipitate a debate and vote on the Hepburn bill he offered a resolution on June 4 declaring the Clayton-Bulwer treaty abrogated.[76] No action had been taken on either measure when Congress adjourned three days later. The disappointed senator was forced to content himself with a resolution making his bill a special order of business for the second Monday in December.

Within a fortnight the Republicans gathered at Philadelphia for their national convention. The platform as adopted contained a paragraph announcing that "We favor the construction, ownership, control, and protection of an isthmian canal by the Government of the United States. . . ."[77] This wording contrasts significantly with the corresponding declaration in the 1896 platform that "the Nicaragua Canal should be built, owned, and operated by the United States . . ."[78] The several possible interpretations of this change have given rise to a lengthy and inconclusive discussion. Cromwell states in his Brief that the first draft of the "plank" recommended Nicaragua as in 1896,

[75] *Ibid.*, pp. 1-21.
[77] N. Y. *Times*, June 21, 1900.
[76] *Cong. Rec.*, 56th Cong., 1st Sess., p. 6506.
[78] *Ibid.*, June 19, 1896.

but that he argued insistently for the substitution of a "neutral" expression and "the justice of our views was at last recognized." [79] Representative Rainey charged during the congressional investigation in 1912 that the alteration was the result of Cromwell's contribution of $60,000 to Hanna's campaign fund.[80]

The evidence of this donation rests solely upon a statement made by Bunau-Varilla to Don C. Seitz of the New York *World* that such an item was included in the lawyer's expense account.[81] Hanna was then dead. Cromwell, however, had apparently been using money so freely in his propaganda that at the time of his reinstatement by the New Company early in 1902 he was warned "expressly that no donations be made now or later." [82] Yet more than the factual substantiation of Bunau-Varilla's remark would be necessary to explain the motive behind Hanna's subsequent championship of the Panama route or even to explain the phraseology of the 1900 platform. Many organizations contributed to Hanna's war chest, but there is nothing to indicate that his vote or his influence was ever purchasable. It was his belief that government should operate in the interests of property, and property was expected to pay for the general protection it received. Whatever money was required for party purposes he secured without recourse to petty bargains. According to Croly, the total sum collected by Hanna's National Committee in 1900 amounted to approximately $2,500,000. "If he did not raise any more . . ." writes his biographer, "it was because the expenditure of a larger sum would have contributed nothing to the chances of Republican success." [83] As a matter of fact, $50,000 of the Standard Oil's $250,000 subscription was refunded after the election, and "a cheque for $10,000 was returned to a firm of bankers in Wall Street because a definite service was by implication demanded in return . . ." [84] If Hanna accepted $60,000 from Cromwell it is probable that he had reasons of his own for adopting a course which coincided with the attorney's wishes. Had his actions been

[79] *Story of Panama*, p. 234.
[80] *Ibid.*, pp. 71–72.
[81] *Ibid.*, p. 158 (Hall testimony).
[82] *Ibid.*, p. 168, Bô to Cromwell, Jan. 27, 1902.
[83] Croly, *Hanna*, pp. 322–323.
[84] *Ibid.*, pp. 325–326.

THE BATTLE OF THE ROUTES 103

governed by a bribe rather than by conviction it is difficult to understand the vigor with which he later threw his failing strength into the fight for the Spooner bill.

What were Hanna's personal reasons for accepting a noncommittal statement on the canal routes? Beer maintains that the senator was worried by Bryan's issue of imperialism. Might he not link the Nicaragua Canal to Puerto Rico and the Philippines as evidence of a Republican scheme to create an American empire?[85] It is certain that Hanna was not particularly interested in imperialism, and wished to make sound money and the party record the basis of the campaign.[86] For several reasons, however, Beer's explanation of the change in the canal plank seems inadequate. The Nicaragua project long antedated the colonial policies which Bryan was attacking. For Bryan to oppose the canal would be to play into the hands of one of his pet aversions, the transcontinental railroads. Moreover, if the Nicaragua Canal could be considered a party issue at all, its sponsorship belonged to the Democrats. Their 1900 platform, adopted on July 6, confirmed this by declaring in favor of the "immediate construction, ownership, and control of the Nicaragua Canal by the United States" and by denouncing Republican "insincerity . . . in face of the failure of the Republican majority to pass the bill pending in Congress."[87]

It is more likely that Hanna was beginning to comprehend that a real choice of routes did exist. He had entered the Senate Committee on Interoceanic Canals at the request of McKinley.[88] During the examination of the Walker Commission on May 11, he displayed a strong interest in the Panama route, and by his questions appeared favorably disposed towards it.[89] As a matter of fact, had the Republicans in 1900 recommended a Nicaragua canal, they could very properly have been asked why they had

[85] Beer, *Hanna*, pp. 262–263.   [86] Croly, *Hanna*, pp. 304–305.
[87] N. Y. *Times*, July 6, 1900.   [88] *Cong. Rec.*, 57th Cong., 1st Sess., p. 7000.
[89] *Sen. Reports*, 56th Cong., 1st Sess., No. 1337, pp. 51–54. Beer quotes a letter which Hanna wrote to Senator Allison in the fall of 1897 in which he said: "I have recently heard a lot about the Panama route which impresses me favorably" (*Hanna*, p. 261).

created a million-dollar commission, only the year before, to investigate other routes as well.[90] The party had, in effect, committed itself to impartiality by the act of March 3, 1899, and there was no harm, and much expediency, in preserving that attitude.

While the presidential campaign engaged public attention during the late summer and fall, the Walker Commission busied itself with the results of its travels and the reports which continued to arrive from the technical parties still at work in the field. On April 10 it had again requested the New Panama Canal Company to submit a price on its property. Cromwell's repeated arguments during the months that followed failed to bring the directors to a decision. Not until November 26 did Walker receive the company's reply, which declined to make an absolute offer, adhering rather to "the principle of the proposal of February 27, 1899." [91] Four days later the commission filed a preliminary report. Many of its technical conclusions were favorable to Panama, but the Nicaragua route was recommended as the most feasible because of the unwillingness of the French interests to state definite terms of sale.[92]

[90] In the course of a speech in the Senate in June, 1902, Hanna stated that "just before the Philadelphia convention President McKinley said to me, 'It will not be wise to do as we have done in our platforms heretofore, to announce ourselves in favor of a Nicaragua Canal, because I am just now appointing a Commission to investigate the subject of all the routes . . .'" (*Cong. Rec.*, 57th Cong., 1st Sess., p. 6998).

[91] *Walker Commission Report*, pp. 141–142; *Story of Panama*, pp. 235–236. This was the proposal to reincorporate the New Company under the laws of New York or some other state and extend to the United States such representation on its board of directors and such opportunity to acquire an interest in its securities as its concession permitted.

[92] *Sen. Docs.*, 56th Cong., 2nd Sess., No. 5, pp. 43–44. Editorial comment on the report revealed the growing popularity of the Panama route among influential eastern journals. In New York the *World* and the *Evening Post* voiced hope that the difficulties with the French concessioners would eventually be overcome. The Philadelphia *Times* remarked: "The preference for the Nicaragua route is determined by other than purely scientific considerations, and it leaves a doubt in the unprejudiced mind whether the commerce of the world might not be better served, after all, by encouraging the completion of the Panama canal than by undertaking a competitive canal by a less advantageous route. . . . Of course, if American control is essential and we can not control the Panama route, we must take the other, as the commission points out. At the same time it is disappointing . . . to feel that we are actually put off with the second choice." *Public Opinion*, XXIX, No. 24, 743–744. This trend was probably influ-

THE BATTLE OF THE ROUTES

On December 1 Secretary Hay signed protocols with the ministers of Nicaragua and Costa Rica by which those governments undertook to negotiate canal treaties with the United States as soon as the president should be authorized by Congress to acquire the route traversing their territories. The treaties thus provided for were to settle the details of construction and to specify as to the "ownership and control" of the waterway.[93]

III

The friends of the Nicaragua Canal had ample cause for rejoicing as the second session of the Fifty-sixth Congress opened. The Hepburn bill had passed the House and held a position of privilege in the Senate. The Walker Commission had approved the site and outlined a tentative plan of operations. Costa Rica and Nicaragua stood ready to grant the necessary measure of control. Most encouraging of all, the rising clamor against the Clayton-Bulwer treaty in both houses had reached proportions which made it extremely unlikely that remedial action could be postponed for long.

In an effort to head off the growing sentiment for unilateral abrogation the Senate leaders promptly ordered the Hay-Pauncefote pact up for consideration. It was ratified on December 20 with three amendments sponsored by the foreign relations committee.[94] The first stated expressly that the new convention "su-

---

enced in part by the increasing advocacy of the Panama route by technical writers in the leading engineering and geographical publications. See Parks, *Colombia and the United States*, p. 384.

[93] Malloy, *Treaties*, I, 351; II, 1290.

[94] "Our friends were persistently misled," Hay wrote to Choate on Dec. 21. "They were sure that the Davis Amendment would satisfy everybody—but the moment it was adopted, a swarm of new ones came up—from which the Republican leaders adopted two, which they thought relatively innocent. They submitted them to the President, who asked me to meet a committee consisting of Lodge, Aldrich, and Foraker, at the White House. They told their story—that the treaty would be rejected if these additional amendments were not adopted; that with these amendments, they could not only carry the treaty through, but could prevent any hostile legislation pending further negotiations with England. The President said the treaty was right as originally drawn, ought to be ratified without amendment; but as this seemed impossible we were willing to do our best to persuade the British government to accept the Davis Amendment; but

perseded" that of 1850. The second was the so-called "Davis Amendment" of the preceding spring, relating to measures which the United States might take in its own defense. The third eliminated the provision inviting other powers to adhere to the treaty.[95] The discomfited secretary of state forwarded his revised handiwork to London with a private letter to Choate which reflected the bitterness of his feelings. The alterations, he felt, disfigured the treaty, although from a practical point of view they were of "little moment." [96] The neutral character of the canal was unaffected as was the ban on fortifications. He admitted that if Great Britain chose to reject the changes "the general opinion of mankind would justify her in it" but hoped that Downing Street would accept them with indulgence as a harmless exhibition of Brother Jonathan's bad manners.[97]

By a Senate resolution of the previous June the Hepburn bill was to be considered upon the completion of unfinished business December 10.[98] As it happened, so many important items had been carried over that Morgan made no effort to push the measure until after the Christmas recess. In the interval a disposition developed among the administration senators to await Great Britain's decision on the treaty amendments before proceeding with any canal legislation.[99] Cromwell not only worked to strengthen this feeling but took the offensive by calling attention

---

that he did not think they could accept the other two. Upon which Lodge said 'That puts the onus of rejecting the treaty on England!' But they all agreed that if the treaty were rejected now, it would be impossible to prevent the violent repudiation of the Clayton-Bulwer Treaty by act of Congress." Quoted from Dennett, *John Hay*, p. 258.

[95] *Dip. Hist. of the Panama Canal*, pp. 289–291.

[96] Hay's estimate of the importance of the amendments did not correspond with the views of the foreign office as Lansdowne's note of Feb. 22, 1901, was to make clear (*infra*, p. 108).

[97] Dennett, *John Hay*, pp. 258–259.

[98] *Cong. Rec.*, 56th Cong., 1st Sess., p. 6441.

[99] Morgan's papers include a letter from Senator McBride of Oregon, dated Jan. 1, 1901, informing his colleague that "a considerable number of the real friends of the bill wish to allow Great Britain a reasonable time in which to ratify the amended Hay-Pauncefote treaty, before attempting to push forward the Hepburn bill."

to the tangled condition of the Nicaragua concessions and the fact that the exclusive rights to steam navigation of the San Juan River had been granted to an English firm until 1920.[100]

As the adjournment of the "short session" approached, Morgan made several eloquent pleas to have his bill placed upon the calendar for immediate consideration. The Republican leaders were determined to block it, however. Spooner declared the time inappropriate, while the president *pro tem* ruled that the unfinished business of the previous session was still before the house.[101] The Alabaman then resorted to his strategy of 1899 and proposed a "rider" to the Sundry Civil Appropriations bill authorizing the president to acquire the necessary land from Nicaragua and Costa Rica.[102] This motion was lost shortly before Congress dissolved for McKinley's second inauguration.

[100] *Story of Panama*, pp. 237-238. Cromwell's argument based on the navigation monopoly was highly misleading. It referred to the contract drawn between Nicaragua and the Atlas Steamship Co. in 1897. The concession was to expire in 1927 but included explicit provision that it should never constitute an obstacle to any government contract for the opening of an interoceanic canal. *Walker Commission Report*, pp. 413-415.

[101] *Cong. Rec.*, 56th Cong., 2nd Sess., pp. 2884, 2886-2887, 2949, 3517-3519. In a carefully-worded letter to Allison on Jan. 12, 1901, Morgan charged the Republican "steering committee" with delaying the vote on the Hepburn bill and requested a definite statement of the party's attitude. "If the republican party," he added, "prefers to assume the responsibility that rests so heavily and awkwardly upon me, and will so advise me, I will cheerfully resign the chairmanship of the committee on Interoceanic canals, and state my reasons to the country. Then I will have the right of a senator to urge the canal bill without incurring the censure of holding a position of influence under the courtesy of the Republican party and using it to antagonize their party policy. I am thus deeply concerned about this matter, because a delay in passing the bill, beyond this congress, will put the canal in extreme peril." Allison replied on the 18th that the committee on the order of business believed it unwise to fix a day for debate on the canal bill until Great Britain had been given a reasonable time to consider the Hay-Pauncefote amendments. Morgan Papers.

The same position was adopted by the foreign relations committee in an adverse report on a resolution urging the passage of the Hepburn bill regardless of British action. Morgan submitted a lengthy minority opinion on Feb. 21, 1901. *Sen. Reports*, 56th Cong., 2nd Sess., No. 2402.

Spooner declared in the Senate, in answer to a question from Morgan, that if Great Britain ratified the amendments he would vote for the Hepburn measure at that session (*Cong. Rec.*, 56th Cong., 2nd Sess., p. 2886).

[102] *Ibid.*, p. 3297.

On March 11 Hay received a note from Lord Lansdowne, who had taken over Prime Minister Salisbury's duties at the foreign office, rejecting the Senate's amendments to the canal treaty. The implications of the proposed changes were examined in detail. Attention was called to the fact that the first, which declared the Clayton-Bulwer treaty "superseded," canceled certain provisions of the latter which would otherwise have continued in force under the new convention. The most important of these was the undertaking that neither power would fortify, colonize, or assume dominion over any part of Central America. The abrogation of this article, the note observed, "would certainly be of advantage to the United States, and might be of substantial importance." The second and third amendments were held to be even more objectionable. Their effect, if adopted, would be to strike at the very root of the "general principle" of neutralization upon which the Clayton-Bulwer treaty was based. In addition, Great Britain would find itself in a particularly unfavorable position.

It would follow . . . that while the United States would have a treaty right to interfere with the canal in time of war, or apprehended war, and while other powers could with a clear conscience disregard any of the restrictions imposed by the convention, Great Britain alone, in spite of her enormous possessions on the American continent, in spite of the extent of her Australasian colonies and her interests in the East, would be absolutely precluded from resorting to any such action, or from taking measures to secure her interests in and near the canal.

Under the circumstances, Lansdowne concluded, the British government, while regretting the failure of the negotiations, preferred "to retain unmodified the provisions of the Clayton-Bulwer treaty." [103]

As the situation stood in the winter of 1900–1901 two principal difficulties threatened to wreck Cromwell's plans. The first was the adverse preliminary report of the Walker Commission. Yet the attorney was convinced by a study of the document that

[103] *Dip. Hist. of the Panama Canal,* pp. 11–17, Lansdowne to Pauncefote, Feb. 22, 1901.

THE BATTLE OF THE ROUTES 109

this obstacle could be eliminated if the company offered to sell its holdings at a reasonable figure.[104] The second involved Colombia's attitude toward the 21st and 22d articles of the Salgar-Wyse contract. Would it permit a transfer of the concession, and would it seek to exact a financial consideration? Cromwell had advanced as far as he dared; it was now necessary to bring Colombia directly into the negotiations.

At this time the ranking representative of the Marroquín administration in the United States was Arturo de Brigard, consul-general at New York.[105] Cromwell called upon him and explained the nature of the emergency. De Brigard at once cabled the vice-president requesting that a minister be dispatched with all speed to Washington empowered to treat on matters relating to the canal. The Bogotá agent of the New Company added his solicitation.[106] Despite its absorption in the task of fighting the civil war, the Colombian government had its own reasons, as we have seen, for coöperating closely with its concessioner on this point. It selected its envoy with a minimum of delay. Shortly after the beginning of the new year, the widely-respected and kindly Carlos Martínez Silva set out upon his memorable mission to the United States.

Dr. Silva reached Washington towards the middle of February and remained about a year, but failed to accomplish anything definite. His correspondence with his superiors, however, throws much light on the attitude of the Colombian government towards the canal project. Upon disembarking in New York he visited the offices of Sullivan & Cromwell. This, Cromwell writes, was the first of "a series of conferences between the minister and ourselves which lasted several months." [107] The lawyer soon discovered that Colombia had no expectation that the New Company would complete the canal by 1910, and that it consequently regarded its own interest as paramount. He was given to understand that the Marroquín administration was willing to consider

[104] *Story of Panama*, p. 238.
[105] Clímaco Calderón had lost his ministerial post with the coup of July, 1900. Since then the Colombian legation in Washington had been closed.
[106] *Ibid.*, pp. 238–239.   [107] *Ibid.*, p. 239.

a transfer of the concession to the United States, in spite of much adverse opinion at home, provided the terms were sufficiently advantageous.

After presenting his credentials, Silva had a preliminary conference with Secretary Hay in which he expressed Colombia's willingness to coöperate in the construction of a Panama canal by the United States on conditions compatible with his country's sovereignty. Hay asked him to draft a memorandum to serve as a basis for future negotiations.[108]

As a matter of fact, Silva had very little actual authority. His instructions were to secure the best terms possible for Colombia, but on all questions of import to consult his government by cable, "because of the serious nature of a promise, even when made *ad referendum.*" [109] This note of caution, repeated in later dispatches, combined with the irregularities of the cable service and the distractions caused by the conflict raging at home, deprived Silva's mission of its effectiveness and kept the minister himself in a state of constant helplessness and embarrassment.

Silva's correspondence leaves no doubt of his desire to place the construction of the Panama Canal under the supervision of the United States, but his first reports on American public feeling toward the rival routes caused the authorities in Bogotá to overestimate their power to bargain with Washington. The minister somehow convinced himself that the technical advantages of Panama were obvious to Congress, and that Nicaragua was preferred only because the United States felt it could establish its control more easily there. The realization of this plan hinged upon Great Britain's consent to the abrogation of the Clayton-Bulwer treaty.[110] When the British rejection of the Hay-Pauncefote amendments was announced in March, Silva wrote his government: "By this action the Clayton-Bulwer treaty remains in force, which absolutely prevents the United States from acquiring and building the Nicaragua Canal. . . . There remains on foot at present only the Panama route." [111] Even after

[108] *Libro azul*, p. 12.
[110] *Ibid.*, pp. 37 et seq.
[109] *Ibid.*, pp. 3-4.
[111] *Ibid.*, pp. 11-12.

Hay renewed negotiations with Lord Pauncefote in April, Silva was certain that "if Great Britain and the United States finally come to an understanding it will necessarily be on the principle of a free and neutral canal; and in this case the Nicaragua undertaking would be *out of the question,* being, in a technical sense, inferior to that of Panama. . . ." Colombia, in his opinion, "held the trump cards." [112] In the summer of 1903 this attitude was still widespread among influential Colombians. Talk about the Nicaragua route was commonly dismissed as a Yankee attempt to drive a sharp bargain.

On March 20 Hutin inquired of Silva what interpretation the Colombian government would place on Articles 21 and 22 of the Wyse concession in case the company negotiated a sale to the United States. Silva replied that his government would insist on its right of previous consent.[113] A month later he asked the director-general for the bases on which the company would be willing to transfer its rights to the United States "with the necessary authorization, of course, from the Government of Colombia." [114] Hutin's reply was indefinite. The company, he said, was ready to come to an agreement with the United States independently of any convention between that country and Colombia. The price could be fixed by amicable arrangement, or, failing that, by arbitration. The company would expect compensation for the profits it would have been in a position to make had it completed the canal.[115]

While this exchange was in progress, the Walker Commission, then engaged in preparing its final report, sounded out Silva on the diplomatic questions involved in the acquisition of the Panama route. On May 9 it submitted for his comments and additions a series of general points which should properly be included in a treaty.[116] Silva forwarded the note to Bogotá, and, after waiting several weeks in vain for a reply, drew up a paper

---

[112] *Ibid.,* p. 16. [113] *Ibid.,* pp. 19–20.
[114] *Ibid.,* p. 21.
[115] *Ibid.,* pp. 22–23. A letter to this effect was sent to the Walker Commission on May 15 (*Walker Commission Report,* p. 146).
[116] *Libro azul,* pp. 25–27.

discussing certain of the proposed topics.[117] He added nothing to the commission's draft but objected to the principle of a lease in perpetuity, to the inclusion of the cities of Panama and Colón in the canal zone, and to the provision for a fixed indemnity instead of a percentage of the tolls. He also insisted that the sovereignty of Colombia be cited explicitly.

Toward the end of June, 1901, both Silva and Cromwell appear to have lost the confidence of their superiors. The attorney, after a visit from Walker on the 25th, cabled to the directors of the company:

> Admiral Walker came to see us today. Declares that commission will finish advance report to President first part July. Declares Pananova proposal to arbitrate inacceptable. . . . He promises me to delay his report until July 20 if you come here before then ready to discuss estimate and fix definite sum. Am convinced that if Pananova fixes sum in keeping with views commission it will have very favorable influence on the report. Cable if you accede to admiral's request or if you can come and when you can come. . . .[118]

The company made no proposal. Instead, it informed Cromwell that after July 1 it would take the negotiations with the United States into its own hands.[119] What motives prompted this action the lawyer professes not to know. The company's later correspondence would seem to indicate that Cromwell's use of money in his campaign had something to do with it.[120] It is also possible that the directors were irritated by his importunities for a definite offer of sale and his failure to obtain a settlement by arbitration.

On the same day that Cromwell sent his cable, Dr. Silva wrote a long letter to his government.[121] His views had undergone a remarkable change since the early spring when he had confidently declared the Nicaragua route to be "out of the question." He no

---

[117] *Ibid.*, pp. 59–61. "Junio 5 de 1901" at the head of the note is probably intended to be "Julio 5 de 1901."

[118] *Story of Panama*, p. 241.

[119] *Ibid.*, p. 242. Cromwell's euphemistic description of this incident in his Brief runs: "July 1, 1901–January 27, 1902—Our instructions are to cease all activity."

[120] *Infra*, p. 122.   [121] *Libro azul*, pp. 37–59.

longer pictured Great Britain as the champion of the neutral and unfortified canal which Colombia wished to have built at Panama. The trend of Hay's renewed negotiations with Lord Pauncefote had convinced him that the British government would not prevent the United States from controlling any canal it built on the Isthmus. This meant that the latter had, in actual fact, a choice of routes. Consequently, Silva now urged that Colombia grant the United States whatever "control" was necessary to assure a canal through its territory. Should Nicaragua be selected, who could be found to build at Panama? Neutrality the minister belittled as unnecessary, since the United States was already pledged to maintain Colombia's sovereignty over the Isthmus. He felt that his country's interest lay in coöperating with the Yankees, not in attempting to resist them. In conclusion he suggested an investigation of the validity of the New Company's extended concession, as its cancellation would greatly strengthen the hand of the Colombian government.

Silva received no direct answer to this memorandum, nor further instructions of any kind from Bogotá on the canal question until early the following year. Although the negotiation had reached a decisive stage, his superiors showed no anxiety to press the issue. Orders were already on the way to Silva from Foreign Minister Uribe to proceed to Mexico City in the fall as one of the Colombian delegates to the Second Pan-American Congress, scheduled to commence its sessions in October.[122] With Cromwell dismissed, and the Colombian minister's communications ignored by his own government, Admiral Walker's effort to secure a basis for a convention seemed to have broken down completely.

Bunau-Varilla, meanwhile, had been continuing his personal campaign on behalf of Panama. His carefully nurtured contacts with prominent Americans had borne fruit. He arrived in the United States in January, 1901, to deliver a lecture on the Panama route before the Commercial Club of Cincinnati at the invitation of some of its members whom he had met in Paris. He was enthusiastic over the result. "While I was speaking and devel-

[122] *Anales diplomáticos y consulares*, II, 213.

oping my argument," he writes, "the expression on their faces gradually changed: astonishment took the place of scepticism. Before I had finished the opinion of my audience had totally changed." [123] After addressing the Society of Civil Engineers of the same city, he went to Cleveland to meet Col. Myron Herrick, one of Hanna's most powerful supporters in Ohio. At luncheon with "twenty of the most distinguished men of Cleveland" he expounded his theories until half-past five. By that time he had assured himself that "not an atom of doubt" remained in the minds of his hearers.[124] He spoke in Boston and Chicago, and, in spite of some opposition, before the Chamber of Commerce of the State of New York.[125] He was everywhere satisfied with the impression he made. His most important achievement, however, was his interview with Senator Hanna in Washington.

The meeting was effected through the influence of Colonel Herrick. The senator listened attentively to the Frenchman's discourse and is reported to have replied:

M. Bunau-Varilla, you have convinced me. My friends at Cleveland had told me what an echo your words had had in their minds. You have already provoked an intense movement in favour of Panama. But I must say I was still doubtful, though very much impressed, by the atmosphere you had created. I thought, formerly, that Panama was a demonstrated impossibility. . . . The only information I ever saw about Panama was a kind of prospectus distributed some time ago by the lawyers of the Company, but I did not attach much importance to it. . . . Naturally, it will be necessary that what you say should be ratified by men like Morison, Burr, or

---

[123] Bunau-Varilla, *Panama: The Creation, Destruction, and Resurrection*, p. 179; *Story of Panama*, p. 7 (Pavey Testimony).

[124] Bunau-Varilla, *Panama: The Creation, Destruction, and Resurrection*, pp. 180–181. "It would be a mistake," Alfred Noble of the Canal Commission wrote to Morgan, "to underrate Mr. Bunau-Varilla's ability. He is doubtless here to promote the Panama project as far as he can, and he has prepared a very skillful and adroit lecture" (Morgan Papers, April 8, 1901).

[125] Bunau-Varilla, *Panama: The Creation, Destruction, and Resurrection*, pp. 181–182. Senator Platt wrote to Morris K. Jesup, president of the New York Chamber, calling attention to the importance of the pending Nicaragua legislation and urging his "coöperation" (Morgan Papers, Platt to Morgan, April 2, 1901). Jesup opposed the extension of an invitation to the Frenchman, but was outmaneuvered by the latter's friends during the president's absence from the city.

Ernst. If, as you assert, they think as you do, I shall go over to your side.[126]

Bunau-Varilla paid his respects to McKinley, and even had an interview with Senator Morgan, which terminated abruptly when the gentleman from Alabama referred to Panama as a "rotten project." [127] After a correspondence with members of the Walker Commission, he left for France on April 11, 1901.

This was the situation when, on September 5, the nation was stunned by news of the shooting of McKinley at Buffalo. After a few days of improvement, the president's condition turned for the worse, and on September 14 Theodore Roosevelt succeeded to the office of chief executive. This change in magistracy assured a vigorous canal policy, for Roosevelt's interest in the subject was well known.

Toward the middle of October, Hutin arrived in New York in answer to an ultimatum from the Walker Commission. He brought with him a statement of the company's views which repeated the proposal of the preceding May to settle the purchase price by arbitration. The only concession offered was the elimination of the demand for a future-profits indemnity. The holdings of the company were valued at $109,141,500, not as a figure of sale, but simply for the information of the commission.[128] As Hutin could not suggest how much less the directors would accept, Admiral Walker ended the negotiations.

The commission filed its final report on November 16, 1901.[129]

[126] Bunau-Varilla, *Panama: The Creation, Destruction, and Resurrection*, pp. 186–187. This version of Hanna's remarks reflects Bunau-Varilla's animosity towards Cromwell. If it is literally accurate, the senator was deliberately misrepresenting the facts in saying that his previous knowledge of Panama was limited to a Sullivan & Cromwell prospectus. As a member of the Committee on Interoceanic Canals he had taken a prominent part in the examination of the Walker Commission on the Panama route in May, 1900, and it is to be presumed that he was acquainted with the preliminary report of the Walker Commission submitted in November, 1900. Considering the French engineer's rich imagination and fondness for graphic narrative, his frequent use of the direct quotation should be accepted with reservations as to detail.

[127] *Ibid.*, pp. 187–188.

[128] *Walker Commission Report*, pp. 149–160 (Walker-Hutin correspondence).

[129] This report was first published as *Senate Document* 54, 57th Congress, 1st Session, and later, with a volume of maps and charts, as *Senate Document* 222, 58th Congress, 2nd Session (citations herein refer to latter edition).

Much of it consisted of a survey of the technical problems encountered in each of the routes studied. The relative merits of Nicaragua and Panama were set forth in detail. The engineering expense of the former was estimated at $189,864,062, compared to $144,233,358 for the latter. To the cost of Panama, however, would have to be added the purchase price of the New Company's property and concessions, which the commission considered worth $40,000,000 to the United States.[130] Inasmuch as the owners had persistently refused to submit a definite offer, no authoritative computation could be made for Panama. Therefore, the commission unanimously recommended that the "most practicable and feasible route" for a canal "under the control, management, and ownership of the United States" was that by way of Nicaragua.[131]

[130] *Walker Commission Report*, p. 174.
[131] *Ibid.*, p. 175. Without more evidence than at present available, it is impossible to do more than surmise at the motives which actuated Hutin and his colleagues. The most reasonable guess is that the directors wished to sell to the United States, but feared that any offer which would suit the United States would fail to satisfy the stockholders, whose approval was necessary. They possibly expected that the Walker Commission would make them a definite offer before submitting its report. In a letter to Hay dated Nov. 22, 1901, Hutin attempted to explain and justify the company's failure to set a price on its properties but his statement is not convincing (*Sen. Docs.*, 57th Cong., 2nd Sess., No. 34, pp. 16–21). On Dec. 7 Silva sent the secretary of state a letter which emphasized the fact that the figure of $109,141,500 was intended to be no more than a basis of discussion and "is very far from being the value that may be definitely fixed." It added the significant point that "the position of the President of the New Canal Company was extremely embarrassing as any price fixed by him would have been binding upon the Company, while the other contracting party would preserve perfect liberty of action." State Dept., Notes, Colombia, Vol. 10.

IV

THE PASSAGE OF THE SPOONER ACT

Two days after the Walker Commission submitted its report the second Hay-Pauncefote treaty was signed. The Department of State had started work early in April on a substitute for the 1900 convention which would incorporate the Senate's views and at the same time meet with the approval of Great Britain. Upon the basis of suggestions drawn up by Assistant Secretary Adee, Hay had prepared a new draft after extended conversations with the British ambassador and leading members of the upper house. On April 25 the results were forwarded to London, where, upon his arrival in June, Lord Pauncefote took them up with his superiors. Throughout August and September the task of ironing out differences went slowly forward. The chief burden of negotiation fell upon Choate and Lansdowne, ably seconded by White and Pauncefote.[1] By the end of September Hay was able to write President Roosevelt from New Hampshire that "Our Canal Treaty is past the breakers. Even if we get no further improvement, it is a great success as it stands."[2] On October 26 Henry White dispatched the confidential news to Hay that the British cabinet had accepted the treaty. Final touches were added in Washington upon Pauncefote's return and the formalities of signing carried out on November 18.[3]

By the terms of the new convention the Clayton-Bulwer treaty was explicitly abrogated and provision made for the construction

---

[1] *Dip. Hist. of the Panama Canal*, pp. 19 et seq.; Dennett, *John Hay*, pp. 262–263.

[2] Roosevelt Papers, Sept. 30, 1901. The secretary sketched in some of the details a few days later: "So far as Lord Lansdowne is concerned, the work is done; and we have gained every point we started out for. Salisbury, I am sure, will approve. . . . In this matter and in the Alaska boundary question, Choate has shown great ability and tact. Harry White, too, has been very valuable." Roosevelt Papers, Hay to Roosevelt, Oct. 4, 1901.

[3] *Dip. Hist. of the Panama Canal*, pp. 51–52.

and operation of the canal under the auspices of the United States. Use of the waterway was to be open to the vessels of commerce and war of all nations without discrimination upon payment of "just and equitable" tolls. Neutralization, based upon a modification of the rules included in the abortive 1900 agreement, was preserved, but under the sole guaranty of the United States. The thorny question of defense was disposed of by the simple expedient of omitting all reference to fortifications, while sanctioning the maintenance of "such military police along the canal as may be necessary to protect it against lawlessness and disorder." [4]

With a wisdom born of bitter experience, Hay had made certain of his senatorial support in advance. Roosevelt, enthusiastic over the first diplomatic success of his administration, helped to corral the recalcitrants. Under the skillful guidance of Cullom and Lodge the treaty encountered no serious obstacle and was ratified on December 16 by a vote of 72 to 6.[5] By this action the uncomfortable possibility of a one-sided abrogation of the Clayton-Bulwer pact was removed. The United States had gained substantially everything asked for. So far as the Old World was concerned, the way was clear for "an American canal under American control." The doctrine of Grant and Hayes had finally triumphed.

Meanwhile, on December 6, Hepburn had introduced a measure in the House appropriating $180,000,000 for the construction of the Nicaragua Canal, of which $10,000,000 was to be made immediately available.[6] His own committee promptly sent in a favorable report and the bill was made a special order of business for January 7.[7]

The predicament of the New Company was serious. Hutin had resigned as director-general on learning of the commission's report and had been succeeded by Marius Bô. At a meeting on December 21, the shareholders authorized the board of directors

[4] Malloy, *Treaties*, I, 782–784.   [5] Nevins, *Henry White*, p. 159.
[6] *Cong. Rec.*, 57th Cong., 1st Sess., p. 184.
[7] *House Reports*, 57th Cong., 1st Sess., No. 15; *Cong. Rec.*, 57th Cong., 1st Sess., pp. 447–448.

THE PASSAGE OF THE SPOONER ACT 119

to make a fixed offer to the United States Government subject to their ratification.⁸ The decision to sell was approved by the directors on the 23d and the secretary-general, Edouard Lampré, left for Washington to reopen negotiations. At both meetings the representatives of the Colombian government voted in favor of the move.⁹

The news of the approaching debate on the Hepburn bill spurred Bunau-Varilla to swift action. He had hurried to the United States in November only to find that Walker had already submitted his report. The friends of Panama, including Hanna, had seemed discouraged. Returning to Paris the engineer had watched with chagrin the slow deliberations of the New Company in its hour of peril. Further negotiations on its part meant the certain passage of the Hepburn bill and the destruction of his dream of a Panama canal. Through the columns of *Le Matin,* therefore, he vigorously attacked the company for neglecting its own interest and the honor of France.¹⁰ To arouse public opinion he inserted a large advertisement in the principal Paris papers describing the situation and demanding that the directors of the New Company offer to sell at the commission's own valuation. "It is necessary to act," he concluded, "and to act immediately; the duty of the Board is strictly defined by facts. If they have not accomplished it between to-day and the 7th of January next their responsibility will be also definitely defined before the people and before the law." ¹¹

The directors suddenly bestirred themselves. Without waiting for Secretary Lampré to reach Washington, Bô cabled the Canal Commission on January 4 offering to sell the New Company's entire property for $40,000,000.¹² By additional cables on the

---

⁸ *Sen. Docs.,* 57th Cong., 1st Sess., No. 123, p. 2.

⁹ Olarte Camacho, *Tratado de 6 de abril 1914,* pp. 101, 107; *Dip. Hist. of the Panama Canal,* p. 385.

¹⁰ *Le Matin* was owned by Philippe Bunau-Varilla's brother, Maurice (*Story of Panama,* p. 465).

¹¹ Bunau-Varilla, *Panama: The Creation, Destruction, and Resurrection,* pp. 210–211.

¹² *Sen. Docs.,* 57th Cong., 1st Sess., No. 123, p. 3. This offer included 68,863 of the 70,000 shares of the Panama Railroad.

9th and 11th the archives and plans in Paris and on the Isthmus were specifically included.[13] These communications were officially transmitted to Roosevelt and Hay and to the press.[14] Nevertheless, on the 9th the Hepburn bill came to a vote in the House and was adopted by the overwhelming majority of 308 to 2.[15]

No one was more eager than Roosevelt to set the steam shovels to work on the Isthmus. The quickest and simplest course would have been to ignore the tardy overtures of the French and permit Morgan to guide the Hepburn bill through the Senate. Had the president been thoroughly convinced of the superiority of Nicaragua this would have been the natural procedure.[16] Instead, he ordered Walker to confer with the New Company's emissary and on January 16 called the commission together once

[13] *Ibid.* The wire of the 9th set March 4, 1903, as the expiration date of the option.

[14] The newspaper reaction to this announcement indicates a continuance of the editorial trend away from uncritical adherence to the Nicaragua route. By January, 1902, most important eastern journals favored an open-minded weighing of the relative merits of the two sites. The opinion that "the Panama canal is not to be opposed simply because it is the Panama canal" was expressed by the N. Y. *Tribune* and echoed by the *Times*, the *Evening Post*, and the *Commercial Advertiser* of the same city. In Chicago, the *Evening Post* remarked: "We are told that public sentiment is committed to Nicaragua, but this is sheer nonsense. The people are enthusiastic in their support of the isthmian-canal proposal, but they are practical and level-headed enough to recognize that the question of routes must be settled without reference to caprice, sentiment, or prejudice." The Detroit *Tribune* felt that the "Nicaragua crowd have been driven from the last line of entrenchments, and they are now seeking shelter behind sentimental shams . . ." Other dailies which recommended a careful consideration of the New Company's offer included the Philadelphia *Record*, the Syracuse *Post-Standard*, the Baltimore *American*, and the Louisville *Courier-Journal*. The Memphis *Scimitar* stood doggedly by its belief in the superiority of Nicaragua, while the N. Y. *Sun* was at this period non-committal. *Public Opinion*, XXXII, No. 2, 36.

[15] *Cong. Rec.*, 57th Cong., 1st Sess., pp. 557–558. Cannon's amendment leaving the selection of the canal route to the president was defeated 206 to 41. Both he and Burton supported the bill on the final vote.

[16] In 1894 Roosevelt favored the construction of a canal at Nicaragua; see McCaleb, *Theodore Roosevelt*, p. 155; Cowles, *Letters from Theodore Roosevelt to Anna Roosevelt Cowles*, p. 143. In April, 1901, Henry White wrote his wife concerning a visit with Roosevelt: "He . . . seems to favor the Panama rather than the Nicaragua route." (Quoted in Nevins, *Henry White*, p. 156.) During the spring of 1902 he made no public statement of opinion, preferring "that the question of the route should be decided by Congress" (Hay to Morgan, May 12, 1902, from Thayer, *John Hay*, II, 302).

THE PASSAGE OF THE SPOONER ACT 121

more to consider the new development. Two days later, on the motion of George S. Morison, this body unanimously adopted a supplementary report which concluded:

> After considering the changed conditions that now exist and all the facts and circumstances upon which its present judgment must be based, the Commission is of the opinion that "the most practicable and feasible route" for an isthmian canal . . . is that known as the Panama route.[17]

Roosevelt forwarded this important document to Congress on January 20.

On the 27th William Nelson Cromwell was reinstated as counsel for the New Company. His version of the incident is characteristic. A despairing company cabled him "to resume his former connection and activity." The firm of Sullivan & Cromwell could not abandon its one-time clients in their distress, so "leaving aside all our other business we acceded to this request." [18]

This account of the attorney's generosity of spirit was ridiculed by Bunau-Varilla in a statement written several years later for the House Committee on Foreign Affairs.[19] According to the engineer, Senator Hanna asked him to use his influence with the company to procure Cromwell's reinstatement, adding,

---

[17] *Sen. Docs.*, 57th Cong., 1st Sess., No. 123, pp. 2, 10. The day after this action was taken, Professor Haupt, Morgan's confidential ally on the commission, wrote to the disappointed Alabaman:
"When the proper time comes I will see you and explain the situation. In the mean time please withhold your judgment. I have not betrayed my trust to my country nor evaded my solemn duty.
"Permit me to suggest that it may be better to secure enabling legislation of some kind (even if for Panama) from the Senate & get the matter into conference where the question of the *best route* may be rapidly settled.
"I have been *greatly* surprised & disappointed, but felt that a divided report would be fatal to any legislation." Morgan Papers.
Haupt later stated in *The North American Review* that he signed under protest and against his convictions because he was confronted with the argument "that if a divided opinion were presented to Congress the opposition to an Isthmian Canal was so influential as to be able to defeat legislation entirely on that ground" (CLXXV, 129).

[18] *Story of Panama*, pp. 244–246.

[19] "Statement on Behalf of Historical Truth," printed in *The Story of Panama*, pp. 10–43.

It is not because I care at all for him, but my old banker, Edward Simmons, presses me to obtain that for his old friend. You know it is difficult to refuse something to a man who has been your banker for 30 years. At any rate the company wants a lawyer to discuss the legal questions of Panama. Why not Cromwell? He is one of the best lawyers in New York and knows the question when another would have much to learn.

Bunau-Varilla's influence with the company was slight, and he had never met Cromwell. The latter soon called and "engaged in a conversation of terrible length rather in the form of a monologue"—a form of exclusion always painful to the Frenchman. The reinstatement was finally accomplished after considerable difficulty, through friends in Paris.[20]

The cable from Bô confirming this action contains some comments which may have had reference to Cromwell's previous methods. It reads in part:

You to be reinstated in your position as general counsel of Compagnie Nouvelle de Panama, rely on your coöperation to conclude matter sale property; . . . But it must be clearly understood, and on this point we shall surely be in accord with you, that the result must be sought only by the most legitimate means; that is to say, that in no case could we recourse to methods as dangerous as they are unlawful which consist principally in gifts or promises, of whatever nature they may be, and that the same reserve must be scrupulously observed by every person acting for us or in our name. . . .[21]

Cromwell was twice reminded that the board of directors would determine all questions relating to his remuneration.

To Bunau-Varilla, Cromwell's return to the combat was "but a slight incident in the great struggle which was going on in January 1902." [22] Nevertheless, after ample allowance is made for the lawyer's gift of exaggeration, his activity in the succeeding five months made possible the adoption of the Panama route in that session of Congress. His principal achievement was his success in securing assurances from the company and the Co-

[20] *Ibid.*, p. 22. Edward Simmons was president of the Panama Railroad Company.
[21] *Story of Panama*, pp. 168–169 (Cromwell Brief). This may refer in part to Cromwell's alleged $60,000 donation to the Republican party.
[22] Bunau-Varilla, *Panama: The Creation, Destruction, and Resurrection,* p. 215.

THE PASSAGE OF THE SPOONER ACT 123

lombian government sufficient to warrant Hanna's carrying the Panama fight to the floor of the Senate.

On the basis of the commission's supplementary report, Senator Spooner on January 28 proposed his famous amendment to the Hepburn bill, which was then in the hands of the Committee on Interoceanic Canals. It authorized the president to purchase the property and concessions of the New Company for $40,000,000, provided valid titles could be obtained; to acquire from Colombia perpetual control of a zone at least six miles wide across the Isthmus of Panama; and to construct an interoceanic canal there through the agency of an Isthmian Canal Commission. Should the president be unable to procure valid titles from the New Company or a satisfactory treaty with Colombia within a "reasonable time," the amendment directed him to proceed with arrangements for a canal through Nicaragua.[23]

Three days later the company received word from Cromwell that he had drawn up "a general plan of campaign" and had "inspired" a new "bill." [24] In answer to an insinuation made by Morgan to this effect in the debates of the following June, Spooner declared that he himself not only wrote the amendment but devised it.[25] By 1907 Cromwell's claim was more moderate: "we . . . had long conferences with Senator Hanna and Senator Spooner . . . and these conferences resulted in Senator Spooner preparing and introducing in the Senate a bill for the adoption of the Panama route project and the acquisition . . . of the Panama Canal Co." [26]

With respect to these "long conferences," it should be noted that Cromwell was reinstated only the day before the Spooner amendment was introduced. In all probability, Cromwell had little connection with the launching of the new proposal, although he certainly knew something about it in advance.[27]

[23] *Cong. Rec.*, 57th Cong., 1st Sess., p. 1048.
[24] *Story of Panama*, p. 246.
[25] *Cong. Rec.*, 57th Cong., 1st Sess., p. 6657.
[26] *Story of Panama*, p. 248.
[27] The attorney was in New York when word of his reinstatement by the company reached him through Bunau-Varilla about noon on the 27th. He immediately telegraphed back to his informant in Washington that he was prepared to act at

Taken as a whole, the evidence supports the conclusion that Spooner brought forward his substitute plan at the instigation of the White House. The senator from Wisconsin had not hitherto been conspicuous as an advocate of the Panama route. He was, however, conspicuous as one of the four or five Republican leaders who dominated the upper house and who were steering its course at this time in general conformity with the president's policies. Roosevelt appears to have definitely made up his mind in favor of Panama after receiving the Walker Commission's supplementary report. His decision raised serious tactical problems for his supporters on Capitol Hill, for it meant overriding the pro-Nicaragua majority of the Senate canal committee and the scrapping of the Hepburn bill. To do this would necessitate carrying the fight to the Senate floor and vanquishing the redoubtable Morgan in open debate. Spooner was the logical choice of leader to direct a difficult maneuver of this kind. There were other experienced and forceful men among the senator's party colleagues, men far less heavily burdened with legislative tasks than he, but there were none who excelled him in the technique of piloting administration measures past the shoals of parliamentary debate. Spooner was one of the busiest men in Congress and his letters show that he was feeling the strain. He was floor manager for some of the most important administration bills of the session. It is very unlikely that he would have accepted overnight the added responsibility of guiding the strategy of the Panama fight principally to accommodate a newly reëstablished lobbyist. It is even more unlikely that a man in his party role would have sponsored any far-reaching legislation that did not bear the positive stamp of approval of the president. It does not seem to be stretching facts too far to interpret Spooner's action in offering his amendment as tanta-

---

once. His message concluded: "Expect important movement in our favor this morning and will give you details." *Story of Panama*, pp. 167–168. It so happened that Spooner was in conference with the president at almost precisely the time that Cromwell sent his wire. Spooner Papers, Cortelyou to Spooner, Jan. 26, 1902.

mount to an unofficial White House endorsement of the Panama route.

The question of the authorship of the amendment need not detain us long. Spooner was an eminent constitutional lawyer and quite capable of writing the document himself. He may very possibly, and properly, have had the assistance of some of the members of the Walker Commission. Several of the provisions, indeed, reflect a special concern for the powers and privileges of the proposed Isthmian Canal Commission which suggests such a coöperation. The characteristic Cromwell phrasing is absent from the original draft presented to the canals committee on January 28, but it can be detected in the final version which was adopted by the Senate in June. If the New York attorney may be properly said to have "inspired" the Spooner amendment at all, it is in the sense that he had in the preceding years contributed very materially to bringing the Panama route to official notice as a serious rival to Nicaragua.

Although a clear majority of Morgan's committee favored the Hepburn bill, Hanna insisted that no report should be made to the Senate until the members of the Walker Commission had been questioned. At a series of hearings all but Mr. Pasco and Professor Haupt were examined and all admitted frankly that they had favored Panama from the technical point of view in November, but had been compelled to recommend Nicaragua because of the company's refusal to state a definite price.[28] In reference to these hearings Cromwell writes:

We had conferred with the members of the commission, we had informed ourselves in detail as to their individual opinions, . . . and we prepared for the use of Senator Hanna and his colleague, Senator Kittredge, a series of questions which were necessary to bring out the facts during the deposition of each of the members of the commission.

These depositions answered their purpose admirably, not only in enlightening the commission [sic] and the Senate as to the facts, but also in gaining time to obtain, if possible, the necessary proposal of

---

[28] *Sen. Docs.*, 57th Cong., 1st Sess., No. 253.

a treaty with Colombia and her consent to a transfer by the company.[29]

II

The work of securing a treaty draft from Colombia acceptable to the Senate was blocked during these weeks by Dr. Silva's continued failure to procure definite instructions from his government. He had hastened back from Mexico City on receiving news of the Canal Commission's final report only to discover that his long-promised instructions from Bogotá had not arrived and that he was still bound by Dr. Uribe's admonition not to contract any obligations whatever pending their arrival.[30] In consequence, the minister had been left without the means of formulating a positive course of action during the critical session of Congress then about to open.

Three times in December—on the 6th, 13th, and 23d—Silva called the attention of his superiors to the acute state of affairs in Washington and the need for prompt and precise treaty proposals. The confident tone of the dispatches of the preceding spring is missing from these notes. The unfavorable recommendation of the Walker Commission, the ratification (on De-

[29] *Story of Panama*, p. 249.
[30] *Libro azul*, pp. 68–69. Silva's increasing irritation over Marroquín's refusal to push the canal negotiations is reflected in a letter written to his friend Uribe from Mexico City on Nov. 4 on learning of the latter's resignation from the Marroquín cabinet. It read in part: "With your departure from the ministry the final hope that remained of reaching a settlement of the canal question is lost. I see that in Colombia they neither understand this question nor wish to understand it, basing their opinions upon deplorable illusions and on an absolute disregard of the facts related to the problem; and the most serious thing about it is that there is not going to be opportunity to correct the error which is being committed. It is already known officially that the treaty between England and the United States has been concluded on the basis of leaving to the latter country the *control* of the canal and the guaranty of its neutrality . . . If Colombia . . . does not acquiesce in acceptable conditions, Congress will adopt the Nicaragua route, even though it costs more, and we will be left out in the cold . . . Then will come the complaints and lamentations and the consequent recriminations. I have done as much as has been within my power—as you know—to prevent this evil; but my zeal has been unfavorably interpreted and has only served to bring down insults and diatribes upon me . . ." Uribe, *Colombia y los Estados Unidos*, pp. xxxi–xxxii.

THE PASSAGE OF THE SPOONER ACT   127

cember 16) of the second Hay-Pauncefote treaty, and the reported negotiation by the Department of State of new protocols with Nicaragua and Costa Rica all confirmed the minister's belief that a choice of routes did, in fact, exist for the United States and that the "trump cards" were now in its hand.[31] "Consequently," he wrote, "if the Government of Colombia feels that it is of great importance for the present and the future of the Republic that the canal be opened by the Panama route, it should be prompt to make reasonable concessions, in the certainty that once the Nicaragua Canal is opened, all hope of another maritime passage at Panama is lost." [32]

Silva was too frank to conceal the exasperation he felt at his position. He referred to it as "false" and later added that "it would be highly irregular and dishonorable for the Government of Colombia to take steps for the purpose of hindering or delaying the adoption of the Nicaragua route, only to have it appear in the end that Colombia has nothing to offer." Suspecting that Bogotá had lost confidence in him, he suggested resigning so that his presence in Washington might not continue to injure his country's vital interests there. At length, on December 23, he informed the minister of foreign relations of his determination to drop negotiations until instructions should arrive, and specifically declined responsibility for any loss of opportunity to Colombia.[33]

In his last official letter to Bogotá, on January 8, 1902, the disgruntled envoy reported that a representative of the New Company had formally requested Colombia's permission to transfer its franchise and property to the United States. The representative had been informed that such consent was dependent upon a previous canal convention between Colombia and the United States. Silva therefore asked his government for specific instructions on five essential topics: the feasibility of granting a six-mile zone; the desirable duration period of the

---

[31] *Libro azul*, pp. 68–74.
[32] *Ibid.*, pp. 69–70.   [33] *Ibid.*, p. 74.

lease; the propriety of renting the Panama Bay Islands as coaling stations; the extent of the policing rights in the zone to be accorded the United States; and the form and amount of indemnity.[34]

Had Silva abided strictly by his decision to withdraw from the contest in Washington pending the receipt of adequate instructions, his successor might have had the advantage of greater freedom of negotiation than proved to be the case. But the increasingly critical situation in Congress and the importunities of Cromwell caused him to waver. The impending misfortune to his country began to outweigh the self-assigned duty of doing nothing for lack of official orders. At length he determined to submit a treaty draft on his own authority in the hope of postponing Senate action on the Hepburn bill. He explained his change of course some weeks later in a personal letter to Marroquín:

The past six months have been virtual torture for me; pressed and harried day after day at various critical moments to express categorically the propositions of the Government of Colombia, I have had to resort to every manner of delay without compromising the outcome of the negotiations. To maintain this equilibrium, this indefinite procrastination, was no longer possible when the House of Representatives voted, almost unanimously, the bill in favor of Nicaragua; when the French Company, threatened with death, made its offer of sale for 40 millions; when, in view of this proposal, the Canal Commission definitely recommended the Panama route, and when the Senate Committee prepared to render its report, which should be considered as almost decisive. In these circumstances, realizing that I had not a moment to lose, I resolved to prepare a complete project of a Treaty, dealing with all the points in question and taking advice on the matter with a special commissioner, whom I sought of the Governor of Panama, Dr. Facundo Mutis Durán, and with Enrique Cortés, who happened to be here in Washington and whose assistance as a distinguished Liberal I considered of so much importance for the future fate of the Treaty. . . . On the very day on which I intended to present the project to the Secretary of State I received your telegram in which I was ordered to await instructions before contracting commitments and to refrain from giving out an

---

[34] *Ibid.*, pp. 78–81.

THE PASSAGE OF THE SPOONER ACT 129

opinion on the proposition which the French Canal Company had made to the Government of the United States.[35]

Elsewhere Silva mentions another reason for his sudden decision. Disturbing reports were reaching him from the Isthmus that the citizens of substance there were not disposed to accept the sacrifice of their well-being by Bogotá in a spirit of philosophical patriotism, and that, if the United States should decide to construct a canal at Panama in defiance of the Colombian government's refusal to treat, ready assistance might be expected from the Panamanians.[36]

Silva's treaty project of January, 1902, embodied the results of a year's close study of the problems of joint control over an isthmian canal zone and the effects on the bargaining power of Colombia of the Hay-Pauncefote negotiations and the Nicaragua-Costa Rica protocols. It provided that Colombia was to authorize the New Company to transfer its concessions and property to the United States, and that the latter was to construct a suitable canal across the Isthmus of Panama within a zone ten kilometers in width, under a lease for a hundred years, renewable for equal periods at the option of the United States. The lessee received the right to build free ports at either end of the canal, to police the zone, and to determine the toll rates—provided that these were equal for ships of all nations. Sanitary and police regulations were to be agreed upon by the two governments, while criminal and civil cases were to be under the jurisdiction of mixed tribunals. The United States was to guarantee the perpetual neutrality of the canal and the sovereignty of Colombia over the zone and the cities of Panama and Colón. Colombia was to be responsible for the military defense of the work, but it reserved the right to call upon the United States for assistance when necessary and, in extreme emergency, the latter might use its forces to defend the canal without secur-

[35] *Anales diplomáticos y consulares,* IV, 815–816. Silva apparently did not see fit to mention the fact that Cromwell had assisted in drawing up the treaty draft. The lawyer's participation in this work came to the knowledge of Bogotá indirectly some months later (*Libro azul,* p. 238).
[36] *Anales diplomáticos y consulares,* IV, 816.

ing previous consent. In return for these concessions, the United States was to pay Colombia an annuity of $600,000, plus an increment of three percent for each renewal of the lease.[37]

Although this proposal was never formally presented to Secretary Hay because of the cable from Bogotá, its general tenor was communicated to the Department of State by Cromwell and Colombia's later emissaries were never fully able to free themselves from its influence.[38] Silva remained in Washington several weeks longer but no treaty instructions came. Instead, on February 26, Dr. Vicente Concha, Marroquín's former secretary of war, disembarked at New York with orders to take over the negotiations.[39]

Concha was highly respected in Colombia for his intellectual attainments and disinterested patriotism, but he was inexperienced as a diplomat. This trip was his first outside his native land and he spoke no English. To Silva's dismay, he tarried in New York, ostensibly to await further orders and permit Silva to take formal leave.[40] Inasmuch as his government's communications to him were addressed to the legation and Silva was persistently urging him to continue on to the capital, it is more likely that he wished to stop in New York to go over the current situation with Dr. Mutis Durán, a former governor of Panama residing there.[41]

While the new minister's conferences with Mutis Durán doubtless opened his eyes to some of the unsuspected difficulties confronting him in the United States, his greatest worries were to develop from the conditions existing at home. Colombia's

---

[37] *Libro azul*, pp. 90–102.

[38] *Anales diplomáticos y consulares*, IV, 807. Marroquín later wrote that "It compromised the attitude of the Government, which ought to be prudent and reserved, and in addition rendered extremely difficult the succeeding efforts of the Legation."

[39] *Libro azul*, pp. 82–84; *Story of Panama*, p. 252.

[40] *Story of Panama*, p. 252.

[41] *Libro azul*, p. 86. Other undisclosed business may have prolonged Concha's stay in New York, for it would seem that Mutis Durán could have explained the principal questions relating to the canal in a few days at most.

apparent apathy towards the canal negotiations during the preceding eight months was the result, not of indifference to opportunity, but of an all-absorbing domestic crisis. Throughout the fall and winter of 1901 Marroquín's hold on power had been steadily undermined by the tenacity of the Liberal opposition and the spread of disaffection among his own followers. The withdrawal of Antonio José Uribe from the cabinet in September had been symptomatic of the growing resentment of many original supporters of the coup of July, 1900, against the government's methods of dealing with the insurrectionists. Silva's recall, as we shall presently see, was more closely related to this political rift than to his official conduct in Washington.[42] By February, 1902, the vice-presidential faction was in a precarious position. The rebels had rallied and were making conspicuous progress in the field. A series of successful engagements had brought their forces to the very gates of Bogotá. The administration, faced with military disaster and torn by internal disputes, was beginning to show signs of confusion. Minister Hart informed Hay on February 3 that governmental unity had disappeared and that the executive departments appeared to be acting independently of one another. Foreign affairs, he reported, were particularly neglected.[43] Although the tension with Venezuela had resulted in the severance of diplomatic relations in December and war with that country was still a strong possibility, no one had so far been appointed to fill the vacancy left by Uribe. The portfolio was temporarily under the care of Dr. Miguel Abadía Méndez, the minister of hacienda, whom Hart characterized as "the least satisfactory of all those who have held the office since I have been at this capital." [44]

Matters improved somewhat in this latter respect shortly after Concha's landing in New York with the appointment of Felipe Paúl to this post on March 1. A member of the Nationalist party

---

[42] These circumstances are explored in greater detail in chap. vi.
[43] State Dept., Dispatches from Colombia, Vol. 58, No. 559.
[44] *Ibid.*

and briefly minister of foreign relations under Sanclemente, Paúl ignored the bitter alignments of the time to place his services at the disposal of the state.[45] A question might well be raised as to whether his subsequent undistinguished handling of the canal negotiation provides an entirely satisfactory basis for judging his abilities as a statesman. The task that faced him was by no means easy. His government's aim was to secure a canal at Panama without subordinating Colombian sovereignty in the slightest degree to United States "control." This might appear somewhat of an academic point, for Bogotá's authority on the Isthmus had been frequently interrupted by local rebellions, several of which owed their failure principally to the presence of United States sailors and marines along the line of the railroad. For many Colombians, however, the concept of *soberanía* was closely associated with the struggles and aspirations of their countrymen during the preceding century, and, no matter how nominal its exercise might sometimes prove in fact, its legal integrity was worth preserving at all costs. Besides, it was one thing to permit a group of private individuals to construct and operate a canal at Panama under the jurisdiction of the nation's laws, it was quite another to surrender the perpetual control of an important strip of territory to an aggressive world power whose expansionist tendencies had been recently demonstrated in the Caribbean and the Pacific.

Colombia's situation was likened to that of a little boy taking a lion for a walk around the block—a few precautions would seem wholly justifiable. Unfortunately for Paúl, he entered office too late to apply precautions. The march of events in Washington was rapidly depriving him of all effective freedom of maneuver. The little boy was about to discover how it feels to be taken around the block by a lion.

[45] Paúl had resigned from Sanclemente's cabinet in January, 1899, with three other ministers in protest against the use of certain repressive measures decided upon by the government. The Nationalists took pains to emphasize the fact that Paúl's acceptance of a place in the Marroquín administration did not mean that the party endorsed the policies of the vice-president. *Ibid.*, Hart to Hay, No. 569, Feb. 19, 1902.

THE PASSAGE OF THE SPOONER ACT

III

Shortly before Concha's arrival Hanna informed Cromwell that while he and several of his colleagues on the isthmian canals committee were in favor of the Panama route they would not be willing to submit a minority report on the Hepburn bill recommending the acceptance of the New Company's offer unless they had substantial assurance that the shareholders would ratify the sale and that a satisfactory treaty was possible with Colombia. Silva was called into conference but was unable to make any promises regarding a treaty.[46]

In order to secure the required ratification of the directors' offer a meeting of the shareholders of the New Company was called for February 28. The Republic of Colombia, as owner of fifty thousand shares, was of course notified. On the day before the meeting the Colombian consul-general in Paris apprised the company officials that his government forbade the transfer of the canal concession to the United States without its previous consent, under pain of forfeiture. Consequently, the meeting merely adopted resolutions postponing ratification until the difficulties with Colombia had been adjusted.[47]

Naturally the Nicaragua party greeted the incident with open satisfaction and gave it wide publicity. Cromwell admits that "this action on the part of Colombia was a grave blow to the cause of Panama. It furnished official proof that the necessary consent of Colombia had not yet been given."[48] He was aware that Silva's consent of the previous spring had been conditional upon a definite arrangement with Bogotá. This had not been consummated. The attorney was anxious not to press the point, as he felt certain that the Marroquín government intended to demand a sizable portion of the sale price in return. It was to forestall this assessment, as well as to fulfill the conditions of Hanna's support, that he wished to bind Colombia to the United States by a treaty project. Such a convention would necessarily include permission for the transfer of the New Company's rights

[46] *Story of Panama,* p. 252.   [47] *Ibid.,* pp. 252–253.   [48] *Ibid.,* p. 253.

and property and thereby place the sale on the plane of international diplomacy. Once this was effected the company could plausibly refuse any subsequent demand for indemnity as an attempt at extortion.[49]

The instructions issued to Concha by Abadía Méndez (before Paúl took over the office) show how poorly the Colombian government comprehended the international situation and the recent developments in Washington.[50] Concha was directed to ensure by every means at his disposal the construction of a Panama canal on terms as advantageous as possible for his country. The only condition was that Colombia's sovereignty must not be diminished. All questions of importance were to be communicated to Bogotá for decision. He was to sound Great Britain, France, and other powers on a proposal for "international control of the Panama Canal and its neutrality, guaranteed by all countries." If this was found practicable, he was to denounce the treaty of 1846 with the United States. In view of the position of the Hepburn bill in Congress, such nonchalance in approaching what Abadía himself described as the "most serious, delicate, and transcendental" of Colombia's external problems is understandable only in terms of the administrative disorganization to which Hart's dispatches had referred.

In supplementary instructions of January 27 Abadía Méndez declared that Colombia was entitled to "no less than twenty million dollars" from the New Company for its assent to the transfer of the concessions.[51] He gave three reasons for this claim: the properties of the company were valueless without the permission; Colombia would be obliged to sacrifice her reversionary interest in the railroad; and Colombia would very likely receive a fixed sum from the United States instead of a percentage of the canal tolls, a change which he estimated would deprive the former of at least a million dollars of annual income.

[49] Cromwell's suspicions were justified. In January, 1902, Silva suggested to his government that the company be asked to pay two million dollars as the price of Colombia's consent to the proposed transaction (*Libro azul*, p. 80). As it turned out, the government at Bogotá intended to ask a much larger sum.
[50] *Ibid.*, pp. 82–83.   [51] *Ibid.*, p. 84.

THE PASSAGE OF THE SPOONER ACT 135

While Colombia was completely within its rights in making these demands, exception might be taken to Abadía's attempt to justify them on the grounds of the financial loss entailed by a transfer of the concession to the United States. Had there been any reasonable prospect that the New Company could complete the canal, these arguments might have had some cogency. However, at this time very few Colombian leaders still seriously believed that the New Company, or any other private group, possessed sufficient resources to carry the project through. The properties of the concessioner were, therefore, as valueless to Colombia as to the French if the United States chose to go elsewhere. The consent to the sale of the concession merely enabled both parties to salvage something from the fiasco at Panama. Naturally, if the Bogotá government could be sure that the United States would wait patiently until 1910, as some Colombians apparently thought it would do, a possible profit might be lost by permitting the New Company to sell out before its rights expired. But this was a gamble which at best would result in the postponement of the opening of the canal and, consequently, of the beginning of the annual rental payments.

Furthermore, Abadía was not entirely candid in stating that Colombia would lose its reversionary interest in the railroad. The administration was determined, at the time this dispatch was written, to restrict the tenure of the United States on the Isthmus to ninety-nine years if that could possibly be done. Colombia's sacrifice, then, would consist solely in a postponement of the reversion, not in a surrender of it. Finally, Abadía estimated that his country would be deprived of at least a million a year in revenues. How he arrived at this figure is not at all clear. Such a calculation, to have any validity, would require a knowledge of the amount of the canal traffic, the toll rates which the New Company would have imposed, and the rental to be paid by the United States—factors which Abadía was not in a position to judge with any degree of accuracy. It is noteworthy in this regard that the treaty bases drawn up in Bogotá a few weeks later called for a percentage of the tolls greater than that stipulated in the contract with the French corporation. Actually, Colombia's demand for a share of the purchase price of the company's property was prompted primarily by the nation's desperate financial situation. The company urgently desired a favor which only Colombia could grant and the latter felt justified in charging for it. The question of "damages" had little or nothing to do with the matter at this stage of the negotiations.

While Concha was still in New York he received two cables from Bogotá by way of Washington which clearly indicated his government's fear of being rushed into a premature treaty with the United States. The first, dated February 13, warned the minister not to commit himself on the company's offer to sell. The second, sent on the 22d, following the adjournment of a council of prominent Colombians, stated that "the Canal Company cannot transfer its rights to a foreign nation or government without first modifying the original contract, in agreement with the Government of Colombia." [52]

Cromwell's task was increasing in difficulty. Concha continued to ignore Silva's pleas that he take over the legation. The attorney finally went up from Washington himself and called on the minister. In two long conferences he "convinced him that the Nicaragua project would inevitably be adopted if Colombia did not change her attitude and show a willingness to coöperate . . ." [53] On March 7 Concha signed a letter, drafted by Cromwell and addressed to himself as counsel for the New Company, stating that Colombia's warning to the company on February 27 did not imply opposition to the transfer if mutually satisfactory arrangements could be made between the United States and Colombia, and that the latter looked with favor on the construction of the Panama Canal by the United States. Copies of this letter were sent to Secretary Hay, the press, and members of the minority of the Morgan Committee.[54]

Cromwell's touch is also discernible in Concha's cable to Bogotá of March 5: "The cablegram of the Minister of Foreign Relations relative to the Panama Canal Company inexplicable.

[52] *Ibid.*, pp. 84–85.   [53] *Story of Panama*, p. 253.   [54] *Ibid.*, pp. 253–254.

THE PASSAGE OF THE SPOONER ACT 137

Has produced a disastrous effect here. In official circles something serious impends concerning Panama. I will not be responsible. Send me instructions immediately." [55] The envoy's apprehension over the intentions of "official circles" was not based on firsthand observation, for at that time he knew no one connected with the government. His informant was either Silva or Cromwell—probably the latter.

The hearings before the Morgan Committee came to a close on March 10, and three days later the Hepburn bill was reported favorably to the Senate by a seven-to-four vote. The Spooner amendment was simultaneously returned with an unfavorable report. The committee gave no detailed explanation of its decision. And, in spite of Cromwell's solicitation, Hanna and his dissenting colleagues failed to submit a statement of their views. On March 19 Morgan transmitted a subcommittee report which pronounced the titles of the New Company to its Panama property defective.[56]

As matters stood on March 19, with the Hepburn bill approved by the House and favorably reported to the Senate, the chances for a Panama victory had all but disappeared. The Colombian government alone remained unperturbed. On March 17 it wired Concha:

In such business of the greatest importance we ought not to allow ourselves to be hurried by threats, intrigues; the Panama Canal will be made in any case, the Nicaragua way being more difficult and costly. . . . You can explain in satisfactory terms our attitude and also obtain possible aid from the United States for a previous arrangement with the Canal Company [!] if you believe it convenient.[57]

Elsewhere in the body of this cable was casually inserted the information Silva had pleaded for so long in vain: "The United States Minister in Bogotá carries unofficially the bases of an

[55] *Libro azul*, p. 35.
[56] *Sen. Reports*, 57th Cong., 1st Sess., No. 783, pt. 1. Accompanying this was a minority opinion, signed by Senators Kittredge and Pritchard, but chiefly the work of Sullivan & Cromwell. This was circulated judiciously and had "a great effect," according to Cromwell (*Story of Panama*, p. 250).
[57] *Libro azul*, pp. 85–86.

understanding with the United States. Sending them to you by the next mail." This news, which might have altered the entire course of the negotiation, was not to reach the legation for more than a fortnight, and then in so mutilated a form as to lead to a serious misunderstanding.

A whole week after sending this cablegram Felipe Paúl, the new minister of foreign relations, dispatched the promised memorandum embodying his government's proposals.[58] It began with the statement that "The Government of Colombia ought not to advance any negotiation with the United States until after having reached an understanding with the Canal Company over the different points which constitute the rights and obligations between them." That done, the Colombian government would be willing to discuss a treaty based on the following considerations: a guaranty by the United States of Colombian sovereignty over the entire Isthmus; a guaranty of the neutrality of the canal, to be open to all nations in peace and war; a ninety-nine-year concession, reverting to Colombia with all appurtenances; a zone six miles wide; a zone police corps with Colombian personnel, paid by the United States; compensation by the same for private property condemned; coaling rights on the Bay Islands; a percentage of the tolls greater than that established in the French Company contract; ratification of the convention by the Colombian congress. In conclusion, Concha was instructed to inform Cromwell of the necessity for a previous understanding.

This important communication was drafted so tardily and forwarded by such slow mails that it had no direct influence upon the negotiations with Washington. The dilatory methods used in acquainting Concha with these instructions afford one of the clearest evidences of Bogotá's diplomatic inefficiency during this period. By contrast, Hart had acted with creditable promptness. He had been officially informed of the nature of the Colombian proposals on March 6 and had immediately wired his

[58] *Ibid.*, pp. 116–117.

THE PASSAGE OF THE SPOONER ACT 139

information to the Department of State.[59] The delivery of his message had been delayed until the 17th by the irregularities of the telegraph service, but on the 18th Hay had cabled back curtly that "the terms are entirely inadmissible." [60] Thus it was not until six days after Hart had learned his department's reaction to the Colombian terms that Paúl's memorandum to Concha commenced its slow journey northward by mail.

Meanwhile, Concha sent his credentials to the Department of State on March 8 and was promptly received by Roosevelt.[61] For more than two weeks he waited for the instructions requested in his cable of the 5th. Finally, on the 20th, with the situation in the Senate at its worst (and probably under pressure from Cromwell) he wrote his superiors, informing them of certain "circumstances not precisely understood in the capital [Bogotá] and in Government circles." [62] The first was that the European governments proposed to "abstain entirely from intervening in the matter of the canal." He had interviewed the French ambassador in particular and learned that his government did not intend to interfere with the plans of the United States. The second was the reality of the Nicaragua danger. The Hepburn bill was soon to come up in the Senate and "it is very probable that, without an offer by Colombia, it will secure a majority of votes." Thirdly, he mentioned the importance of a canal to the Panamanians and the feeling among prominent people there that the failure of negotiations would cause a rebellion. He concluded:

> In my estimation, then, it is not convenient, opportune or practical, to assume at this moment . . . an attitude of open resistance to the pretensions of the United States, under penalty of involving the

---

[59] State Dept.: Dispatches from Colombia, Vol. 58, telegram, March 6, 1902.
[60] *Ibid.*: Instructions to Colombia, Vol. 19, telegram, March 18, 1902.
[61] *Libro azul*, p. 86.
[62] *Ibid.*, pp. 86–89. Concha enclosed the treaty draft which Silva was preparing to submit to Hay at the time of his recall. He emphasized the fact that on various important points the convention differed materially from his own verbal and written instructions. These points included particularly the duration of the concession, the establishment of North American police and law courts in the zone, the provision for the use of United States troops to preserve order in territory adjacent to the zone, and the size of the indemnity.

Republic in a most serious conflict, in which it would certainly not preserve its integrity. . . . In such circumstances the lack of reply to the telegrams which I have sent to the Ministry throughout the course of the present month has served to increase my doubts and perplexities; but, in spite of everything, I find myself under the necessity . . . of adopting a course of action for the reasons expressed.[63]

This "course of action" consisted in the preparation of a treaty memorandum for presentation to the Department of State before the Hepburn bill came up for discussion in the Senate. Cromwell states that he had daily conferences with the minister, giving him advice on questions of international law and attempting to make the terms as acceptable as possible to the United States.[64] The points of greatest difficulty were the duration of the concession and the amount of the indemnity. Until March 24, according to the attorney, Concha held out for a fixed-period lease and a cash payment of $7,500,000, with an annuity of $600,000 commencing fifteen years after the completion of the canal. After much persuasion he agreed to Cromwell's compromise scheme of a lease for one hundred years renewable at the option of the United States upon revaluation. The compensation was to be a fixed sum plus an annuity, the latter to be determined by arbitration before the opening of the canal.[65]

Concha handed his draft convention to Secretary Hay on March 31. At the same time, at the minister's "request," Cromwell presented a long statement of his own explaining that the proposals were not final, but were open to further negotiation on points unsatisfactory to the United States.[66]

The Colombian government's ambiguous cable of March 17 informing Concha that Hart was on his way to Washington bearing a copy of its instructions was not delivered until April 2. Even then the text was so garbled in transmission that for several days its meaning was in doubt.[67] Concha made the understand-

[63] *Ibid.*, p. 89. [64] *Story of Panama*, pp. 257–258.
[65] *Ibid.* On March 22, Bunau-Varilla had written a lengthy letter to Concha, suggesting a fixed indemnity of $12,500,000 (*Libro azul*, pp. 183–190). For the Frenchman's account of his further correspondence with the Colombian minister, see *Panama: The Creation, Destruction, and Resurrection*, pp. 220–225.
[66] *Dip. Hist. of the Panama Canal*, pp. 551–556. [67] *Libro azul*, p. 137.

THE PASSAGE OF THE SPOONER ACT 141

able error of interpreting it as a notice that the United States minister was to deliver the instructions in question to the legation upon his arrival. He occupied himself meanwhile with a consideration of Hay's suggestions for modifying the Memorandum of March 31. Cromwell acted as intermediary between the legation and the Department of State.[68]

Hart reached the United States on April 14 or 15, but did not continue at once to the capital. Several days later Concha is complaining to his government: "I have not received the instructions you announced in the cable of March 17, nor has Señor Hart . . . gotten in touch with the undersigned, as it would appear he should, in conformity with the version given here in the same telegraphic dispatch." [69]

Cromwell, anxious to commit Concha thoroughly before the arrival of the instructions from Bogotá, was urging the minister to submit the amended convention to Hay. His efforts were unwittingly seconded by the Nicaragua faction in the Senate, which tried to bring the Hepburn bill up for immediate discussion and vote.[70] Unwilling to assume the responsibility for the possible effects of further delay, Concha called upon Hay on April 18 and presented his treaty project of March 31 with certain changes of a minor character.

Article I authorized the New Company to transfer its rights and property, including the Panama Railroad, to the United States. Succeeding articles granted the United States a zone ten kilometers wide, excluding the cities of Panama and Colón, for one hundred years renewable at the option of the United States for similar periods; specifically acknowledged the sovereignty of Colombia over the zone and continued the provisions of Article 35 of the treaty of 1846-48; declared the canal neutral in perpetuity and open to the vessels of all nations upon equal terms; provided for future agreement between the two governments for the administration of civil and criminal justice in the zone; placed the responsibility for defense upon Colombia, with right

[68] *Ibid.*, p. 153; *Dip. Hist. of the Panama Canal*, p. 556.
[69] *Libro azul*, p. 153.   [70] *Ibid.*

of appeal to the United States, excepting that in case of emergency the latter might act directly to defend the canal. In return for these privileges the United States agreed to pay Colombia $7,000,000 on exchange of ratifications and, after fourteen years, a "fair and reasonable annuity." Three years before the expiration of each hundred-year term the rental for the succeeding term would be similarly fixed. In case of disagreement as to what constituted a "reasonable annuity" both parties were to accept the decision of a high commission of five members, two appointed by each nation and the fifth to be, "for the time being," the president of the International Peace Tribunal of The Hague.[71]

Two days later Hart reached Washington and delivered the complete text of the Bogotá proposals to his superiors. Concha, on discovering that the returning minister bore no dispatches for him, was embarrassed and confused. He realized that the Department of State now possessed a copy of his instructions while he himself was in complete ignorance regarding them. What he did not realize was that the department had enjoyed this advantage (as the result of Hart's cable of March 6) throughout the parleys of the preceding month. There is good reason to believe that Cromwell had acquired a pretty accurate idea of the nature of these orders during his conferences with Hay while he was playing confidant to the Colombian minister. If so, the lawyer had a more impelling motive than the situation in Congress for his haste to get the Memorandum of April 18 into the hands of the secretary of state. Had Concha been aware of the terms outlined by his government as the bases for negotiation his proposals could not have been offered. As it was, the blunders of his superiors made possible the fulfillment of the first of Hanna's two conditions of open support.

The day following Hart's arrival Hay addressed a note to Concha signifying his readiness to sign the draft convention of the 18th as soon as Congress authorized the president to enter into such an arrangement, and as soon as the United States had satisfied itself that the New Company's title to the isthmian prop-

[71] *Infra,* Appendix A.

THE PASSAGE OF THE SPOONER ACT 143

erty was valid. This communication was handed to Cromwell on the 23d for transmission to the minister.⁷²

The climax came on the 26th with the receipt of the long overdue instructions of March 24. Concha cabled immediately to Bogotá:

> Previously presented to the United States Government Colombia's bases for the Panama Canal concession, everything referable to our Congress. This is no time to negotiate with the Canal Company, which was authorized by my predecessor to begin the negotiation with the United States Government. . . . The Minister of Foreign Relations would not have been able to break the negotiation commenced last year without offending the United States, precipitating the Isthmian situation, forcing the selection of the Nicaragua canal. I cannot withdraw the project without producing incalculable complications. . . . The United States Government would consider me *persona non grata* for having submitted a petition of withdrawal to the Department of State. I believe I ought to retire. Please inform me by cable.⁷³

The Colombian government's reply made it clear that Hart had been entrusted with a copy of the proposed treaty bases for Hay's use and was under no obligation to communicate with Concha.⁷⁴ Presumably the March 24 copy was expected to reach Washington about the same time. The cable contained no comment on Concha's actions, but merely instructed him to remain at his post.⁷⁵

Hay now set about the task of obtaining tentative conventions from Nicaragua and Costa Rica for presentation to Congress. Negotiations with these countries had been beset with difficulties for some months past. Early in November, 1901, when it was certain that the second Hay-Pauncefote treaty would be signed, the

---

⁷² *Dip. Hist. of the Panama Canal*, p. 565; *Story of Panama*, p. 259.

⁷³ *Libro azul*, pp. 175–176. In a lengthy letter of self-defense to Paúl, dated May 2, Concha repeated that Silva had specifically authorized the opening of the negotiations between the New Company and the United States and that it was diplomatically impossible to withdraw that permission (*ibid.*, p. 179).

⁷⁴ Hart had been recalled to Washington to answer certain complaints which had been lodged with the Colombian government. Concha did not learn this until after Hart's arrival (*ibid.*, p. 180).

⁷⁵ *Ibid.*, p. 176.

Department of State requested its minister to Central America, William L. Merry, to ascertain whether the protocols signed in Washington the previous December had been accepted by the Nicaraguan and Costa Rican governments. The envoy, whose diplomatic experience was limited, presently exceeded his instructions and became involved in what amounted to a full treaty discussion with the Managua authorities. Hay accepted President Zelaya's suggestion that the indemnity take the form of a capitalized lump sum, without rentals, and the figure of $6,000,000 was finally agreed upon. Merry then plunged confidently ahead into difficult questions of sovereignty and judicial control. Hay grew uneasy but waited for more complete details. On December 9 a strange diplomatic mixture, part protocol and part treaty, was signed at Managua and forwarded to the department for approval. A month later the secretary sent his minister a long, critical analysis of the document. He ended on a note which left little doubt as to his feelings:

> The result of my examination of the Protocol of December 9, 1901, is to satisfy me that it is as a whole entirely inadmissible. The President instructs me to inform you that the said protocol is not approved; and I am instructed by him to resume the negotiation at the point where it was left by my presentation of the draft convention of December 1900.[76]

On February 12, 1902, Hay submitted his own version of a treaty to the Nicaraguan legation. This was several times amended during March and April. Meanwhile, in Costa Rica, President Iglesias had decided that he lacked authority to conclude a canal convention and was considering either a constitutional amendment or a constituent convention to meet the situation.[77]

The secretary of state described his troubles to Morgan in a letter of April 22:

---

[76] State Dept., Dispatches from Central America: Vol. 69, Merry to Hay, No. 652, Nov. 29, 1901; Vol. 70, same to same, No. 654, Dec. 6, 1901, and same to same, telegram, Dec. 9, 1901. State Dept., Instructions to Nicaragua, Vol. 22: Hay to Merry, telegram, Dec. 7, 1901; same to same, telegram, Jan. 4, 1902; same to same, No. 435, Jan. 10, 1902. Roosevelt Papers, Hay to Roosevelt, Dec. 5, 1901.

[77] *Dip. Hist. of the Panama Canal,* pp. 566, 573–574.

THE PASSAGE OF THE SPOONER ACT 145

It is true that the Panama people have at last made their proposition. . . .

I regret to say that I have not yet been able to get a firm offer from the Government of Nicaragua. . . . Let me assure you in strictest confidence that I was unwilling to send in the Panama proposition until I was able also to send in the Nicaragua proposals. . . . The principal difficulty in the case is this, that both in Colombia and in Nicaragua great ignorance exists as to the attitude of the United States. In both countries it is believed that their route is the only one possible or practicable and that the Government of the United States in the last resort will accept any terms they choose to demand. The ministers here of both Powers know perfectly well that this is untrue, and they are doing all they can to convince their people at home that no unreasonable proposition will be considered . . . but it is slow work convincing them.[78]

The next day he informed the senator: "I do not consider myself justified in advocating either route, as this matter rests within the discretion of Congress." [79]

After several weeks of futile correspondence, Hay informed Señor Corea, the Nicaraguan minister, that unless a formal proposition were submitted by May 13 the Colombian treaty draft would be sent to the Senate with a statement that "it has been impossible to get anything definite from the Government of Nicaragua." [80] On the 14th Corea presented the required proposal with a note explaining that it was "not to be taken as final," but was still subject to possible amendments.[81] The following day Hay sent this and the Concha convention, together with copies of the Nicaragua and Costa Rica protocols of 1900, to the appropriate committees of the two houses of Congress.[82]

Cromwell, meanwhile, was endeavoring to satisfy the second

[78] Thayer, *John Hay*, II, 300–301.
[79] *Ibid.*, p. 301. Tyler Dennett concludes from his own study of the Hay Papers that the secretary had a personal preference for the Nicaraguan route (*John Hay*, pp. 367–369).
[80] State Dept., Notes to Nicaraguan Legation, Vol. 2, Unnumbered, May 10, 1902.
[81] *Dip. Hist. of the Panama Canal*, pp. 565–572.
[82] About the middle of June, Hay submitted the draft of a treaty with Costa Rica to J. B. Calvo, minister from that republic in Washington. The proposed compensation was $1,000,000 together with a rental of $10,000 or $1,500,000 and no rental. The passage of the Spooner bill a few days later suspended further action in the matter. Morgan Papers, Calvo to Morgan, June 19, 1902.

condition required for Hanna's support, namely, definite assurance that the company shareholders would ratify their directors' offer of sale to the United States in case it were accepted. M. Bô, president of the board, was disinclined to call another general meeting until after the vote in the Senate for fear that Colombia would again interpose a demand for a previous settlement with the company and thereby ruin whatever chances of victory Panama possessed.[83] The date for the commencement of debate was drawing near. Without a minority report disaster was inevitable. Cromwell contrived a scheme to circumvent the danger from Bogotá:

> We gave our consent to the conclusion that it would be dangerous for the company at this juncture to risk a conflict with Colombia in the course of a general meeting. It was imperatively necessary, however, to show to the satisfaction of the Senators, and above all to the members of the minority of the committee, that they could rely upon this ratification. In the face of this difficulty we devised a plan which we explained to the Senators . . . and which we induced them to accept, to wit: That the company should at once obtain from at least a majority of the shareholders of the company the signatures of formal written consents to the sale, with the undertaking to ratify this sale at any future general meeting called for this purpose.[84]

The directors adopted this stratagem and the necessary signatures were obtained and forwarded to Cromwell through William J. Curtis, one of his partners then in Paris on business.

Hanna and his colleagues appear to have accepted this as final evidence that the case for Panama was sufficiently plausible to warrant a dissenting opinion to the Morgan report on the Hepburn bill. Cromwell asserts that he himself wrote a complete draft of a report which "after full consideration . . . was corrected, adopted, and signed by the minority, and became famous under the name of the 'Hanna Minority Report.' "[85] In addition,

---

[83] *Story of Panama*, pp. 259–260.   [84] *Ibid.*, p. 261.

[85] Cromwell's statement is supported by letters from Cromwell and his partner, Edward B. Hill, to Spooner, dated May 26 and 29 respectively. Spooner Papers. While Hanna's membership on the Senate canals committee and his personal prestige placed him naturally in the forefront of the campaign for Panama, no tactical move was made without careful consultation with Spooner.

THE PASSAGE OF THE SPOONER ACT 147

the legal opinion of Sullivan & Cromwell on the validity of the New Company's titles, concessions, power to transfer, and similar matters was accepted "word for word" by the minority and transmitted to the Senate.[86]

IV

Debate on the Hepburn bill commenced on June 4 and continued with interruptions until the 19th. Morgan, as commander-in-chief of the Nicaragua forces, opened the battle with a general attack on the Panama route on the ground of seismic instability, political unrest, unhealthful conditions, and the unsatisfactory character of the Colombian convention. He pointed out that the majority of his committee was convinced that the New Company could not show clear title. He also called attention to the fact that the Spooner amendment did not place the choice of routes in the president's hands, but directed him to negotiate with Colombia first.[87]

The champions of Panama met the earthquake argument with the charge that the northern route was itself subject to physiographical disturbances, not only seismic, but volcanic as well. Reports of danger from the latter source were not new. Cromwell's propaganda had emphasized this peril for many months.[88] By a whim of Fate, certain incidents occurred shortly before the canal debate began which centered public attention on the unpleasant characteristics of the active volcano. Early in May, Mont Pelée, on the Caribbean island of Martinique, broke into violent eruption with the loss of many lives.[89] St. Vincent's La Soufrière exploded soon afterwards, and on May 29 the New York *Sun* reported that Mt. Momotombo, situated on Lake Managua about one hundred miles from the proposed line of the canal, erupted to the accompaniment of earthquake shocks. Presi-

---

[86] *Story of Panama*, p. 261. The text of the report appears in *Sen. Reports*, 57th Cong., 1st Sess., No. 783, pt. 2. Appended to it there is the legal opinion referred to above and a historical account of the canal project, both signed by Sullivan & Cromwell.

[87] *Cong. Rec.*, 57th Cong., 1st Sess., p. 6277.

[88] *Story of Panama*, p. 262; Heilprin, *Defense of the Panama Route*, pp. 6–7.

[89] N. Y. *Times*, May 9, 1902.

dent Zelaya promptly denied this in a message to Corea. The minister forwarded this information to Morgan with the added comment that his country had experienced no volcanic outbreak since the unimportant one of 1835.[90]

Morgan read this correspondence to the Senate and also a letter from Minister William L. Merry at Managua declaring that the line of the Nicaragua canal was free from shocks, but that according to reports which had leaked through the strict censorship at Panama tremors had been felt there.[91] Hanna countered on June 6 by showing that Merry was a stockholder in the Maritime Company and by reading clippings from Central American papers describing the disturbances in Nicaragua.[92] Before long both sides were discounting the dangers from earthquakes, partly because technical experts did not consider them particularly important, and partly because the two zones were alike susceptible. Volcanic activity, however, was more serious, and on that point the Panama forces lost no opportunity to harass their opponents.

Bunau-Varilla, operating independently of Cromwell as usual, supplied an effective climax to the debate. He procured ninety Nicaraguan stamps of an issue of 1900 which depicted Mt. Momotombo rising above Lake Managua, the steam curling from its summit. He attached them severally to sheets of paper inscribed "An official witness of the volcanic activity of Nicaragua" and had them placed on the senators' desks on June 16. This did not, of course, prove anything that had not been set forth many times in scientific and pseudo-scientific articles, but the stamps conveyed a graphic and conclusive impression which no monograph could approach. Bunau-Varilla asserts that this bit of propaganda was one of the principal factors in winning the Senate over to Panama.[93]

[90] *Cong. Rec.*, 57th Cong., 1st Sess., p. 6269.
[91] *Ibid.* [92] *Ibid.*, pp. 6379–6380.
[93] Bunau-Varilla, *Panama: The Creation, Destruction, and Resurrection*, p. 247. While the eruptions of May, 1902, attracted wide attention and undoubtedly influenced many persons against the Nicaragua route, it is important to note that

THE PASSAGE OF THE SPOONER ACT 149

In his second speech, on the 12th, Morgan argued the political advantages of dealing with Nicaragua and Costa Rica rather than Colombia. The rights of the Maritime Company, he declared, had expired by their own limitations, and Nicaragua's proposal for a treaty with the United States had already arrived. Costa Rica was about to submit hers. No third parties entered into the negotiations. In Colombia everything was uncertain and confused. The senator read into the *Record* correspondence which had been in the Department of State archives since 1900, proving that the Colombian Liberals had then warned Secretary Hay that if successful in the civil war, they would not ratify the extension of time granted by President Sanclemente to the New Company.[94] He insisted that even if the Spooner amendment were adopted, several of its provisions varied widely from the terms of the Concha convention.

Morgan's most telling shots were directed at Cromwell. In his opening speech he had referred to the New Company as "the star performer in the drama, and when we have provided its compensation all other considerations become matters of minor concern."[95] He did not hide his suspicions as to the origin of the Spooner amendment. On June 11, he referred to it in passing as "the amendment accredited to the Senator from Wisconsin."[96]

---

certain well-informed engineers tended to minimize the extent of the danger. W. H. Burr, of the Walker Commission, for example, in an article published after the passage of the Spooner bill, commented on the fact that Mt. Ometepe rose from Lake Nicaragua only ten miles from the proposed line of the canal. "That there is some danger," he wrote, "is beyond question, but it is very remote. There is no evidence to show that a canal or canal structure ten miles distant from Mount Pelee would have been injured by its recent eruptions, although navigation might have been interrupted for a short time. It is an open question, therefore, whether Ometepe in most violent eruption, even, would injure the Nicaragua Canal, although danger would exist. On the other hand, as there is no volcano within about 175 miles of the Panama route, that route would be free from all danger of volcanic eruption." *Popular Science Monthly*, LXI (1902), 316.

[94] *Cong. Rec.*, 57th Cong., 1st Sess., pp. 6653–6656. Morgan quoted an interview granted by Silva to the *Commercial Advertiser* of New York on March 20, 1902, to prove that the former minister did not believe the extension of the concession valid. This, of course, was immaterial as long as arrangements for the transfer were completed before October, 1904, when the previous concession expired.

[95] *Ibid.*, p. 6278.   [96] *Ibid.*, p. 6609.

The next day he mentioned "the amendment that has been offered here in his [Spooner's] name." Spooner at once asked if Morgan implied that he was not the author of it. The latter answered that he was "satisfied the Senator wrote it." [97]

The Alabaman's heavy artillery was trained full upon Cromwell on the 17th. After tracing McKinley's early negotiations for the abrogation of the Clayton-Bulwer treaty he continued:

> There were still other embarrassments that he encountered. The chief of these was the artful, persistent, and intrusive overtures and supplications of the Panama Canal Company, assisted by its powerful allies, the transcontinental railroads. The entire group, in one solid agreement, which included all the railroads from the Canadian Pacific to the Panama Railroad, brought all their power to bear upon the President, and have never ceased their opposition to these agreements.[98]

Step by step Morgan followed the history of the Panama "lobby" beginning with November, 1898. At the hearings before the Hepburn Committee in January, 1899, "Mr. William Nelson Cromwell was the first witness to be examined, and he took charge of the French forces as general in chief, legal counsel, diplomatic functionary, orator, and witness for the Panama Canal Company." [99] The senator quoted his own canal committee's report of May 16, 1900, which had condemned the attorney's tactics.[100] He described as "humiliating" and "repulsive"

> the direct, constant, and offensive intrusion of the Panama Canal Company into the legislation of Congress, the hearings of committees, the deliberations of canal commissions, and the frequent presentation of letters of advice and remonstrance to the Secretary of State, and to the President, rebuking the conduct of the House of Representatives, and its ignorance.[101]

Concerning Cromwell's part in the Concha-Hay negotiations Morgan remarked that he referred "only to what the record discloses of his action" for he would not "dare to follow him when he is not on the surface." [102]

[97] *Ibid.*, p. 6657. [98] *Ibid.*, p. 6922.
[99] *Ibid.*, p. 6932. [100] *Supra*, pp. 100–101.
[101] *Cong. Rec.*, 57th Cong., 1st Sess., p. 6927. [102] *Ibid.*, p. 6932.

THE PASSAGE OF THE SPOONER ACT 151

In his closing appeal just before the vote on the 19th Morgan delivered a final thrust:

> ... I can not neglect Mr. Cromwell, because he will not permit it. ...
>
> I trace this man back ... to the beginning of this whole business. He has not failed to appear anywhere in this whole affair; and after this convention was submitted here, he finds his way to the rear end of the report of the minority of the committee, and they quote his letter. Of course he wrote it; and, Mr. President, there is so much in the balance of that minority report of the committee that is just like it that I have dreadful fears that Mr. Cromwell wrote pretty nigh the whole report.[103]

Hanna, Fairbanks, Cullom, Kittredge, Gallinger, Spooner, Teller, and Allison spoke for the minority report. The senator from Ohio was unquestionably the most effective. Croly regards his speech of the 5th and 6th of June as the high-point of his senatorial career.[104] It did more than attract attention, it changed votes.[105] His arguments borrowed impressiveness from his own great personal prestige. Whether the Panama route eventually would have prevailed on its merits in any case is, of course, conjectural, but its adoption in the summer of 1902 was very largely the result of Hanna's forceful exertions on its behalf. Ten years later, during a meeting of the House Committee on Foreign Affairs, Representative Cooper of Wisconsin remarked:

> I want to say that the thing that defeated the Nicaragua Canal was a speech I heard Mark Hanna make in the Senate. He had his charts up on the wall, and he had the earthquake territory marked, showing that there had been frequent earthquakes and shocks along the line of that proposed canal ... In my judgment, that was one of the things more than any other that influenced the passage of the Spooner bill through the Senate for the Panama Canal.

---

[103] *Ibid.*, pp. 7064–7065. Morgan not only planned and directed the fight for the adoption of the majority report, but bore the principal speaking burden. Speeches in favor of Nicaragua were also made by Mitchell, Harris, Turner, Perkins, Stewart, and Pettus.

[104] Croly, *Hanna*, p. 376. Beer maintains that Hanna exerted party pressure to line up support for Panama (Beer, *Hanna*, pp. 266–267).

[105] Croly quotes Senator Orville Platt as saying that this was the most effective speech made in the Senate during his career (*Hanna*, p. 384). Senator Frye stated that Hanna converted him from a life-long advocacy of Nicaragua (*ibid.*, p. 384).

Representative Rainey of Illinois replied that "the gentleman is absolutely correct." [106]

The speech on June 5 lasted between one and two hours and was delivered in a quiet, almost conversational tone. Hanna's secretary, seated behind him, from time to time handed him references and figures.[107] His attitude throughout was that he wished to consider the subject as a business enterprise, and that he as a businessman had arrived at certain conclusions. "I was once," he admitted, "in favor . . . of the Nicaragua Canal, and I would have been satisfied, perhaps, two years ago if we had made the experiment; but looking at this business from a practical standpoint . . . I have been forced by stubborn facts and conditions to change my mind." [108]

In the two days over which, due to his failing strength, he spread his remarks Hanna outlined the minority's reasons for preferring Panama. First, the Panama route was 49.09 miles long compared to the 183.66 miles through Nicaragua. Second, there was considerably more curvature by the northern route. Third, the time of transit would be twelve hours by Panama and thirty-three by Nicaragua. Fourth, the number of locks necessary favored Panama by five to eight, with the possibility of converting Panama into a sea-level canal against the impossibility of such an improvement in Nicaragua. Fifth, the Panama route was already provided with good harbors, whereas these would have to be constructed at Greytown and Brito. Sixth, the Panama route followed an ancient path of civilization, while the Nicaragua route traversed an undeveloped wilderness. Seventh, the railroad

---

[106] *Story of Panama*, p. 69. In commenting in July, 1902, on the passage of the Spooner bill the *Review of Reviews* remarked editorially: "If the Nicaragua route should finally be defeated, it may, perhaps, be said that the scale was turned by the recent terrible eruption of volcanoes in the West Indies. More than once, in years past and gone, arguments have been made against the Nicaragua route on the ground of its lying in a dangerously volcanic region. But the argument made no impression on the public mind until Senator Hanna advanced it again, with great maps and charts, in the Senate chamber, while Mont Pelée and La Soufrière were still in active eruption, and the newspapers were full of the terrors of volcanoes and earthquakes." (XXVI, 12–13.)

[107] Beer, *Hanna*, pp. 264–266; Croly, *Hanna*, p. 383.

[108] *Cong. Rec.*, 57th Cong., 1st Sess., p. 6319.

THE PASSAGE OF THE SPOONER ACT 153

at Panama was an advantage. Eighth, there would be an annual difference in maintenance of $1,300,000 in favor of Panama. Finally, the problems of engineering at Panama were known and assured, while no one could predict what might arise along the other line.[109]

So far Hanna was following the findings of the Walker Commission, but when he introduced new material he quickly laid himself open to attack. He produced a volume of testimony from eighty-three shipowners, captains, and navigating officers of ocean-going vessels purporting to show that the men who would use the canal preferred the conditions which they would encounter at Panama to those inherent in any canal through Nicaragua. The information presented was in reply to questions sent to these individuals dealing with weather conditions, towing, night navigation, trade winds, transit time, canal curvature, and similar problems.[110] Cromwell later divulged the source of this material:

... At our suggestion Senator Hanna authorized us to obtain this evidence. ... The replies to this series of questions ... fully confirmed our arguments and justified our attitude; they were given to Senator Hanna who presented them in extenso to the Senate in the course of the debate that followed.[111]

Hanna's replies to a succession of queries from Senator Perkins made it evident that the senator from Ohio did not fully comprehend the meaning of all the questions himself. Senator Mitchell urged him to state the source of the testimony. Hanna tried unsuccessfully to change the subject and finally declared: "I ought not to be questioned as to how, when, or where I obtained the

[109] *Ibid.*, p. 6380.   [110] *Ibid.*, p. 6382.
[111] *Story of Panama*, p. 263. There can be little doubt but that Cromwell furnished Hanna with most of the data for his speeches. In May, while preparations for the debate were in progress, Bunau-Varilla urged Hanna to present in person a series of clever diagrams he had drawn up setting forth the advantages of Panama over Nicaragua. The senator, who doubtless was aware of the coolness between Cromwell and the Frenchman, extricated himself adroitly on the grounds that he could not assume, even indirectly, the credit for so important a document. Bunau-Varilla thereupon published the material under his own name in pamphlet form and Hanna had it distributed to his colleagues. Bunau-Varilla, *Panama: The Creation, Destruction, and Resurrection*, pp. 229, 239.

facts and the information." When Senator Harris took up the scent and began to press for the author of the questionnaire Hanna flatly refused to answer further.[112]

On June 18 Hanna addressed the Senate again, this time presenting the replies to eleven questions submitted to the individual members of the Walker Commission. One of the most significant queries was whether the commission's supplementary report of January 18, 1902, which reversed the November recommendation, was based principally on the fact that the New Company's offer to sell at $40,000,000 made the Panama Canal cheaper than the Nicaraguan. Every reply was to the effect that price was a minor consideration, that every member but Haupt considered Panama the better route and that Nicaragua was recommended in November only because no fair price could be secured from the Paris directors. In a separate letter Pasco wrote that an examination of the November report "makes it manifest that the Commission regarded the Panama route as the most feasible and practicable" and needed only a reasonable offer from the New Company to alter its decision.[113]

Hanna then disposed of Morgan's contention that the Nicaragua route was McKinley's choice by recounting his conversations with the former president on the subject. According to these, McKinley was uncommitted to either route, but realized the necessity for thorough investigation. It was at his request that Hanna consented to take a place on the Committee on Interoceanic Canals.[114]

The real test came the afternoon of the 19th on a motion to substitute the minority report for that of the majority. The poll showed forty-two in favor and thirty-four opposed, with twelve not voting.[115] Fourteen senators who had voted for the Nicaragua bill of January 21, 1899, now voted for Panama. These included Cullom, Hanna, Hoar, Lodge, and Spooner.

The Morgan group promptly attempted to limit the period of negotiation with Colombia to six months. This motion, which

[112] *Cong. Rec.*, 57th Cong., 1st Sess., p. 6385. [113] *Ibid.*, pp. 6994–6996, 7000–7003. [114] *Ibid.*, pp. 6997–6998, 7000. [115] *Ibid.*, pp. 7072–7073.

THE PASSAGE OF THE SPOONER ACT 155

would almost certainly have doomed the project, was rejected 44 to 31, as was a similar proposal to confine the parleys to a year.[116] On the final roll call on the Spooner bill itself the measure was approved 67 to 6.[117]

In discussing the Senate vote the New York *Tribune* remarked that "there can be no doubt that sentiment—and not unreasoning sentiment, either—has been overwhelmingly upon the side of Nicaragua, and not only thus negatively but positively and aggressively against Panama." The editors therefore hoped to see "the friends of Panama prove by their works that they are in earnest in desiring the construction of a canal, and that they are not mere marplots." The New York *Press,* bitterly opposed to the choice, declared:

This victory for the Panama ditch lobby is a smarting defeat for the isthmian canal plan. For the senate's action on the Spooner measure does not mean that an isthmian waterway . . . is assured. Rather does it mean that there will be no isthmian canal at all, or that the completion of such a project is so indefinitely delayed that the railroad interests need have no concern about it for a long, long time.

The New York *Sun* replied:

The partisans of the Nicaragua route have been declaring that the sole purpose of the Panama advocates is to prevent the construction of a canal by either route. If they are sincere in that opinion, they can defeat the supposed plot of the transcontinental railroads and their agents, tools, and dupes, by turning to in the house and passing the canal bill as it comes from the senate. Then there will be an isthmian canal in short order.

Among recent converts to the Panama cause, the Springfield *Republican* felt that the favorable action of the upper house "vindicates one's faith that the more this simple business question were studied the surer would be the adoption of the policy now determined upon." Another convert, the Philadelphia *Press,* stated that "as the house has a better understanding of the relative merits of the two routes than it had when it declared for Nica-

---

[116] *Ibid.,* p. 7071. An amendment to leave the route to the president's discretion was defeated 42 to 32 (*ibid.,* p. 7072).
[117] *Ibid.,* p. 7074.

ragua there is a fair prospect of its accepting the senate proposition in lieu of its own." [118]

At first the House refused to abandon the Hepburn bill and the dispute was referred to a conference committee consisting of Senators Hanna, Morgan, and Kittredge, and Representatives Hepburn, Fletcher, and Davey.[119] After several days of discussion the House conferees yielded on June 25, preferring the Spooner bill to no canal legislation at all.[120] The House accepted the conference report by a vote of 260 to 8.[121] This unanimity was in part attributable to a general feeling among the Nicaragua supporters that the New Company could not show a good title and that Colombia would not grant a satisfactory treaty, in either of which events the president would be obliged to proceed with the Nicaragua route. Roosevelt affixed his signature on June 28 and for the time being Panama had triumphed.

By the terms of the Spooner Act the president was authorized to acquire for and in behalf of the United States, at a cost not exceeding forty million dollars, all the rights, privileges, franchises, concessions, and property on the Isthmus of Panama owned by the New Panama Canal Company; to acquire from the Republic of Colombia, on such terms as he might deem reasonable, control of a strip of land, not less than six miles in width, between the two oceans, in which to construct and operate a canal; to acquire such additional territory and rights from Colombia as in his judgment would facilitate the general purpose; and when a satisfactory title had been secured from the New Panama Canal Company, to proceed to construct a canal of sufficient capacity and depth to afford "convenient passage for vessels of the largest tonnage and greatest draft now in use, and such as may be reasonably anticipated." If these terms were found impossible of fulfillment within a "reasonable time" the president was directed to proceed with steps to build the Nicaragua Canal.[122]

[118] *Public Opinion*, XXXII, No. 26, 805–806.
[119] *Cong. Rec.*, 57th Cong., 1st Sess., pp. 7074, 7416.
[120] *Story of Panama*, p. 264.
[121] *Cong. Rec.*, 57th Cong., 1st Sess., pp. 7441–7442.
[122] *U. S. Statutes at Large*, XXXII, Part I, 481–484; see also *infra*, Appendix B.

V

THE NEGOTIATION OF THE HAY-HERRÁN TREATY

NOT EVEN the most enthusiastic supporters of the Panama route could hail the signing of the Spooner Act as more than a temporary victory for their cause. Morgan's Nicaragua forces were checked, but still confident that their rivals would fail to procure a valid title from the New Company and a satisfactory treaty from Colombia. The Battle of the Routes was not over, it had merely entered another phase.

The investigation into the New Company's power to transfer its property was undertaken promptly and brought to completion before the end of October. For over two months a special assistant attorney-general toiled through the intricacies of the company's legal history in the Paris archives. Cromwell, arriving at the beginning of August, contributed a series of detailed diagrams and constant advice. Questions involving the interpretation of French law were submitted to a group of eminent jurists of the country, including Maître Waldeck-Rousseau. Their opinions endorsed the pretensions of the New Company in every respect.[1]

Attorney-General Knox went to Paris for the last few weeks of the examination, but reserved his decision until after his return to the United States. On October 25 he presented his final report to the president, setting forth his opinion that the company's titles and concessions were valid and could be legally transferred to the United States.[2]

This piece of technical research was simple compared to the task which confronted Hay in dealing with the Bogotá government. To draft a treaty which would not merely conform to the

---

[1] *Official Opinions of the Attorneys-General*, XXIV (1902), 504-530; *Story of Panama*, pp. 265-267.
[2] *Official Opinions of the Attorneys-General*, XXIV (1902), 148 *et seq.* (Panama Canal Title).

provisions of the Spooner Act but also satisfy two-thirds of the Senate required important changes in the April 18 agreement with Concha. The very points on which Congress demanded concessions were those on which Colombia was most unwilling to yield.

The difficulty centered on the degree of control to be accorded to the United States, particularly in the regulation of police and sanitary affairs and the establishment of tribunals within the zone. The April Memorandum provided that both governments should "agree upon" ordinances to govern these matters; the Spooner Act stipulated that these powers should rest exclusively with the United States. Furthermore, while the act included in the inventory of items to be transferred to the United States certain areas of unsettled land on the Isthmus which were to have become the property of the New Company upon the completion of the waterway, the Memorandum specifically excluded these except as they might fall within the canal strip. Finally, the act called for a perpetual lease, whereas the Memorandum conceded the use of a zone "for the term of one hundred years, renewable at the option of the United States for periods of similar duration."[3] The issue between Colombian sovereignty and North American "control" was clearly joined.

Even while the canal bill was under debate in the Senate attempts were made to alter the provisions of the Memorandum. Walker and Spooner called upon the Colombian minister and asked him unofficially whether he would consent to a lease in perpetuity and the establishment of United States tribunals in the proposed zone. They explained that these concessions would materially assist the passage of the bill in the upper house. Concha gave formal and definite refusals to both suggestions.[4]

The measure as finally adopted did not meet with the minister's full approval, because of "fundamental differences" be-

[3] For the texts of the Hay-Concha Memorandum and the Spooner Act see Appendices A and B.

[4] *Libro azul*, p. 199. These proposals had been incorporated in the memorandum drawn up by Silva the previous winter, but were never officially presented.

tween its terms and those of the April convention. He informed his government that the Department of State would soon start negotiations for a treaty conformable to the Spooner Act and, as "conditions will be demanded in that treaty not included in the Colombian *Memorandum*, it is indispensable that Your Excellency instruct this Legation, by cable, whether it should or should not accept the conditions of the American law, bearing in mind that the government of this country . . . will not submit to the delays of our postal service." [5]

In the ensuing diplomatic exchanges between Hay and Concha, Cromwell appears to have resumed his old role of intermediary and general confidential adviser. He later asserted that he drew up a draft of the revised convention at Hay's request and discussed it with the secretary until an understanding was reached as to what would be acceptable to the Senate. A copy of these modifications was submitted to Concha unofficially on July 9, and Cromwell entered upon a series of conversations with that official. On the 12th Hay wrote to Roosevelt:

> I have been at work for the last ten days trying to get the Colombian treaty in the shape desired by our friends of the Senate, particularly Spooner and Lodge. I have got at last a draft embodying all things which are at present possible, and which, if accepted by the other side, will make a very good treaty. As I anticipated, General Concha does not feel strong enough in his instructions or his personal influence, to accept this *en bloc*, without consulting his government. He has sent several long telegrams to Bogotá, and is awaiting an answer. I have no idea that the thing can be done in a moment. It will require a good deal of correspondence between him and Mr. Marroquín to determine how far they will yield on questions of jurisdiction and other details. I have no doubt that we shall get finally a very good treaty, even if it may be necessary for the Senate to make some slight amendments in it; but, as it looks now, this cannot be accomplished in a few days. I shall, therefore, if nothing further turns up to keep me here, go to my place in New Hampshire the end of next week.[6]

---

[5] *Ibid.*, pp. 203–204.

[6] Roosevelt Papers. In a letter to Senator Spooner three days later the secretary remarked: "I embodied in a draft of the treaty with Colombia all the ideas you set forth in our recent conversations . . ." A postscript read: "Gen. Morgan says

Finally, on July 18, at a formal meeting, Hay handed Concha the amendments proposed by the Department of State to the Memorandum of April 18. In an accompanying note the secretary acknowledged the original provisions as binding "until some other agreement be reached." [7]

Most of the seventeen changes proposed were technical in nature and presented no serious obstacles to an eventual adjustment. Even the financial terms, while falling far short of Colombia's expectations, left opportunity for negotiation. It was the amendments concerned with the nature and extent of United States control which were destined to create the real difficulty.[8]

The proposed changes revived Hay's previous suggestion that the lease be in perpetuity. A new clause provided that the zone be enlarged to include such canal accessories as lay within fifteen miles of the line of the waterway. Within the zone Hay proposed that the United States be granted the right "to establish and execute sanitary and police regulations which it shall consider necessary for the preservation of order and the public health."

For the administration of justice within the concession area the United States advanced a scheme comprising three types of courts. The first would be Colombian, with jurisdiction over all cases between citizens of Colombia or between citizens of Colombia and those of foreign countries other than the United States. The second type would consist of United States courts, with jurisdiction over suits between United States citizens or between citizens of that nation and foreigners other than Colombians. These latter courts would dispense justice according to the laws of the United States "without diminution of the general sover-

---

we ought to acquire Panama—the entire state—from Colombia. I told him I would consult, as occasion offered, some of the leading members of the Senate on that subject." Thayer, "John Hay and the Panama Republic," *Harper's Magazine*, CXXXI (1915), 168. A few weeks later, while Hay was vacationing in New Hampshire, the president wrote him: "Why cannot we buy the Panama isthmus outright instead of leasing it from Colombia? It seems to me to be a good thing. I think they would change their constitution if we offered enough." Roosevelt Papers, Oyster Bay, Aug. 21, 1902.

[7] *Libro azul*, pp. 204–216, 221; *Story of Panama*, p. 265.
[8] For text of the Hay amendments see *Libro azul*, pp. 222–231.

NEGOTIATION OF THE TREATY

eignty of Colombia over the said zone." [9] Finally, a series of mixed tribunals, whose members would be appointed by the two nations, would be instituted to handle cases arising between citizens of the United States and Colombia or between citizens of countries other than the treaty powers. These courts would also administer criminal and maritime law within the zone in accordance with such codes as the two governments should draw up.

With the object of winning support for the treaty in the Senate Hay also sought to alter the article dealing with the armed defense of the zone. By the terms of the April agreement this duty was entrusted to Colombia, with the stipulation that the United States should lend assistance in case of need, and, when the occasion had passed, withdraw its forces. The proposed substitute read:

> If it should come to be necessary at any time, . . . in order to make effective, promptly and efficaciously, the security and protection of the canal and its dependencies . . . the United States shall have the right to employ for this object such portion of its armed force as it shall require, according to the circumstances of the case, but it shall withdraw such forces wholly or partially as soon as the necessity for their presence shall have ceased. The Government of the United States shall give immediate notice to Colombia of the measures adopted for the said ends.

The financial provision of the April Memorandum had the great merit, from Cromwell's point of view, of postponing the delicate topic of indemnity until after the exchange of ratifications, when the transfer of the New Company's property to the United States would be assured. There were those in the Senate, however, who did not look with favor on the prospect of having the amount of the annuity determined by the president of the Hague Tribunal, or by any other agency beyond its control. To meet this objection Hay now offered the Colombian government alternative methods of compensation. By selecting the first, Co-

[9] These courts would also have jurisdiction over "all controversies growing out of or related to the construction, maintenance, or operation of the canal, railroad, and other properties and works."

lombia would receive $7,000,000 on the exchange of ratifications, and, after fourteen years, a perpetual annuity of $100,000. By the other, a cash payment of $10,000,000 would be supplemented, after fourteen years, by a $10,000 annual rental.[10]

Concha, having no authority to discuss these amendments, merely acknowledged their receipt, and sent them on to Bogotá with a request for instructions.[11] A lull in the progress of the negotiations followed, as Hay had predicted to Roosevelt, and partly for the reasons the secretary had suggested, i.e., the inefficiency of the cable service and the extreme difficulty of corresponding with the Bogotá authorities by mail. Concha's standing orders required him to consult his government on all matters of importance, yet an exchange of notes frequently took from three to four months to complete. On the other hand, such communications as did reach him at intervals were either vague about the points on which he asked for specific orders or else omitted mention of them entirely. The government praised the minister's work, hinted at detailed instructions about to be sent, and told him to "continue the negotiations." As the summer wore on Concha's irritation grew.

Some extenuating circumstances could be advanced to explain a delay on Colombia's part even if it be assumed that the Marroquín administration wished to hasten the conclusion of the treaty. The precise terms of the Spooner Act were not known in Bogotá until nearly the middle of August. Furthermore, in transmitting a summary of the unofficial revision draft of July 9, Concha made the inexplicable error of stating that the United States wished to include the cities of Panama and Colón in the zone. This was a clear contradiction of the text of the articles which accompanied his letter. Then, strangely enough, he repeated this mistake in a cable of July 26 reading: "It is required that Colón and Panama remain included in the zone of the concession to the United States." As the Department of State had dropped this demand during the preliminary exchange of proj-

[10] *Ibid.*, pp. 222–231.
[11] *Ibid.*, p. 222; State Dept., Notes, Colombia, Vol. 10, July 19, 1902.

NEGOTIATION OF THE TREATY 163

ects the preceding March, the basis for this misconception remains a mystery.[12]

While this unpromising example of long-range diplomacy probably contributed to the confusion of the Bogotá authorities, the vice-president and his advisers had other and weightier reasons for refusing to hurry the negotiations in Washington. The scattered embers of civil war, which had been burning low for several months past, blazed up anew on the Isthmus during the early summer. Revolt in this quarter had first broken out in the spring of 1900, when Belisario Porras, Carlos A. Mendoza, and Eusebio Morales took the field at the head of a considerable body of Liberals. Although local separatists undoubtedly lent their support, the uprising was not to any important degree an independence movement. It was primarily a phase of the bitter, nation-wide struggle between Liberals and Conservatives for control of the political machinery of the state. Many isthmians evidently believed at this time that their grievances would be satisfactorily adjusted by a victorious Liberal regime. Porras' campaign had ended abruptly in July, following an unsuccessful assault on Panama City. After a year of guerilla warfare the insurgents had assembled and equipped another force, probably with secret assistance from the Nicaraguan authorities.[13] The operations which ensued had culminated in the temporary capture of Colón by the rebels in November, 1901, and a hurried request from Colombian officials for United States naval units to protect the transit. The passage of the Spooner Act in June, 1902, stirred the Liberals to new exertions in Panama. Possession of the Isthmus would not only revive their waning military fortunes but would make their party an important factor in the canal negotiations. By mid-summer General Benjamín Herrera

[12] *Libro azul*, pp. 205, 209, 220, 235.
[13] In December, 1901, Foreign Secretary Sanchez of Nicaragua informed Minister Merry that "President Zelaya has decided to immediately withdraw from the alliance he has maintained with the Colombian 'Liberal' Revolutionists, as he considers it inconsistent with the position he has now assumed . . . [with respect to the canal treaty under discussion between Nicaragua and the United States]." State Dept., Dispatches from Central America, Vol. 70, No. 654, Merry to Hay, Dec. 6, 1901.

had taken the offensive with a well-organized insurgent army. His force quickly won a series of notable successes and at the beginning of August was seriously threatening the government's hold on the department.[14]

As the Liberals had anticipated, Marroquín's bargaining power with respect to the canal was sharply curtailed by these reverses. It was becoming apparent to the Bogotá cabinet that only military or diplomatic intervention by the United States could save the cities of Panama and Colón from falling into insurgent hands and thereby destroying the administration's hopes of a treaty. Under these circumstances Marroquín decided to cut short the Concha negotiations and conclude an agreement on the best financial terms possible. Then, with the fair certainty of North American military aid in case of need, he could restore order, summon the national congress, and permit that body to amend the Hay convention to its satisfaction. Unfortunately, he did not take Concha fully into his confidence, an error which had far-reaching effects upon the subsequent course of the treaty discussions.

In accordance with his plan Marroquín wired the Washington legation on August 9: "To make the amendments to the *Memorandum* presentable to the Congress, we require ten millions indemnity and six hundred thousand annuity after fourteen years." Concha cabled back that he would not proceed until he had fuller instructions.[15] This reply crossed a letter from Paúl, minister of foreign relations, which set forth the government's attitude in more detail.[16] Paúl stated that he recognized the need for promptness, but considered the cable unsuitable for communications "with the precision required in the delicate matter of the canal." He therefore proposed that the Hay amendments

---

[14] To the newspaper-reading public in the United States these operations seemed remote and unimportant. The general attitude of the press was summarized by the *Review of Reviews* in September, 1902: "Until something very decisive occurs in the course of the civil combats that have been running along so obscurely in . . . Colombia, it is not expected that the outside world will try to follow the meager and contradictory details of the marching, countermarching, and occasional fighting . . ." (XXVI, 275).

[15] *Libro azul*, p. 235, Aug. 13, 1902.   [16] *Ibid.*, pp. 235–237, Aug. 13, 1902.

NEGOTIATION OF THE TREATY 165

be submitted to the judgment of the Colombian congress, excepting that dealing with compensation, which should be discussed further with the United States. In stressing the importance of ratification he wrote:

> Your Excellency will endeavor to have it clearly understood that this is not a mere formality, and that our National Representation has ample right to accept or not the pact in its entirety and in each of its parts, and that it may, in consequence, introduce into it any modifications it may deem fitting. This reservation is very necessary since Your Excellency cannot subscribe to the treaty, nor is Your Excellency hereby authorized to do it, except *ad referendum,* so that it shall not be understood or pretended later that it is being presented to the Congress of the United States in definite form . . .

In other words, Paúl and Marroquín intended to shift the duties of negotiation to the ratifying body, and, incidentally, the scene of parley from Washington to their capital. While this strategy was applicable enough to the domestic situation, Concha felt that it had nothing to recommend it as a principle of diplomacy.

The minister never acted upon these instructions, for negotiations with Hay were at a complete standstill when the letter arrived, on October 22. He knew the tenor of the plan, however, from a cable, sent August 25, which read: "Say to the American Government, that the Colombian Government accepts in principle the recent suggested amendments . . . Ratifications of Congress necessary; the assembling of which awaits only the pacification of Panama." [17] He did not inform Hay of this communication, but wrote to Paúl that he was "perplexed." Later on, when he was about to leave Washington in disgust, he was more explicit with the minister of foreign relations:

> I have not believed that just because the Colombian Congress has the right to approve or disapprove the treaty under consideration, an agent of the Executive Power can sign it in any form, exempting himself and his superiors from all moral and legal responsibility. The Executive Power, according to the existing Constitution of Colombia, is a co-legislator; by presenting a project of law it antici-

---
[17] *Ibid.,* p. 253.

pates the sanction to be given it; guarantees its constitutionality and its convenience for the country; voluntarily deprives itself of the right to make objections, and, in this way, places a weight in the scale of debate, a weight which may be considered decisive in most cases, whereby it assumes a moral responsibility as great as that of the Chambers themselves.[18]

On September 9, Paúl sent Concha special powers to sign a treaty *ad referendum* and instructions to preserve the principle of national sovereignty "as far as it might be compatible with the jurisdiction which the United States demands in the canal zone." But if the Department of State refused to accept all of Colombia's views, the treaty was to be signed anyway. The wording of Article I was to be altered "in order that it be not understood, or pretended later, that due to the signing or approval of the treaty, the Canal Company may consider itself authorized to execute the transfer of its concession to the United States without a previous arrangement with Colombia." [19]

II

The negotiations reached a crisis about the middle of September when Concha, thoroughly annoyed at the policy of his superiors, received news that detachments from United States warships were interfering with the operations of Colombian troops against the insurrectionists at Panama. The circumstances surrounding this action appeared to him a violation of the 1846–48 treaty, on which several of the most important provisions of the Hay negotiation rested. He therefore refused to continue the general discussions until the conditions and manner of future interventions should be precisely determined.

The use of the United States naval forces on the Isthmus was by no means a novelty in 1902. On the contrary, the practice dated back nearly fifty years. It derived its legal basis from

[18] *Ibid.*, pp. 292–293.
[19] *Ibid.*, pp. 246–249. This is interesting in view of Roosevelt's later insistence that the idea of exacting a payment from the company was an afterthought and a piece of "blackmail."

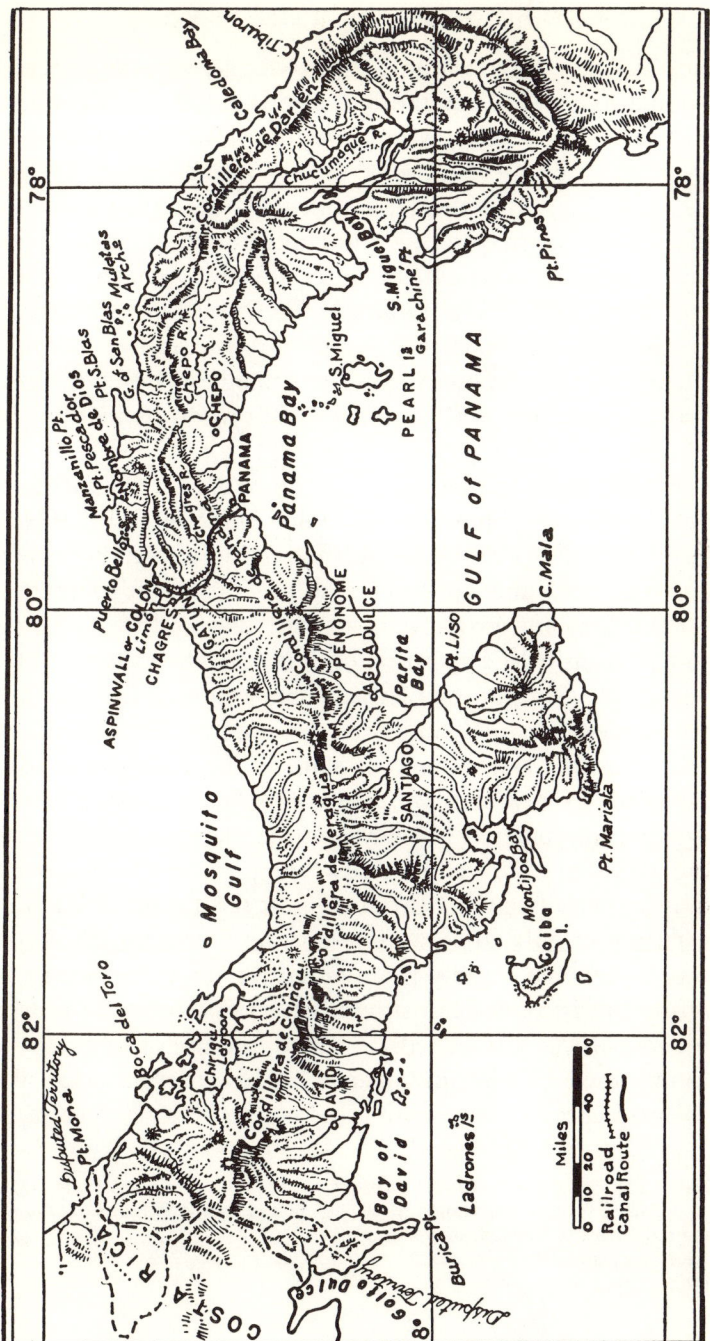

III. THE ISTHMUS OF PANAMA IN 1903

Article XXXV of the treaty of 1846–48 with New Granada, which guaranteed free and uninterrupted transit across the Isthmus of Panama to the United States and its citizens. In return, the latter nation guaranteed the neutrality of the region, "positively and efficaciously, . . . with the view that the free transit from the one to the other sea may not be interrupted or embarrassed," and it likewise guaranteed the sovereignty of New Granada over the same territory.[20] By these stipulations the United States obligated itself to lend military assistance to New Granada in two eventualities: when that government could not maintain free and uninterrupted transit between the oceans, and when its sovereignty over the Isthmus was imperiled.

Of the fifty-three outbreaks in the department of Panama in the years from 1850 to 1902, all but seven were successfully handled without North American intervention.[21] In 1856, 1860, 1865, 1873, 1885, and 1901 the United States landed men to protect the lives and property of its nationals and to assure the freedom of transit. In each instance, however, the consent of the legation at Washington or of the Panama authorities was previously secured.[22] In 1865 an official request for aid from Bogotá was refused by the Department of State on the ground that compliance would involve the United States in factional strife. Secretary Seward summarized his views on the matter in his instructions to Minister Allan A. Burton: "The purpose of the stipulation was to guarantee the Isthmus against seizure or invasion by a foreign power only. It could not have been contemplated that we were to become a party to any civil war in that country by defending the Isthmus against another party." In case the freedom of transit was threatened, he added, the use of force would be "determined by circumstances." [23] This interpretation was generally accepted by succeeding secretaries of state, including

[20] Malloy, *Treaties*, I, 312.
[21] Offutt, *The Protection of Citizens Abroad, passim*. On several occasions during this period naval forces were landed at various points on the Isthmus for reasons unconnected with the freedom of the transit.
[22] *Use . . . of a Military Force in . . . Colombia*, pp. 2–3.
[23] *Ibid.*, p. 27, Nov. 9, 1865.

NEGOTIATION OF THE TREATY 169

Hay. The difficulty was that the distinction between merely protecting the railroad in a time of disturbance and aiding one side or the other was very tenuous in a wilderness region where the railroad constituted the sole means of communication. The "neutrality" of the transportation system was certain to affect the fortunes of war. Six of the seven interventions prior to 1902 had, by chance or design, worked to the advantage of the established regime in Colombia.

During August, 1902, Herrera's insurgents had continued their victorious advance on the Isthmus, driving the demoralized government troops back upon the coastal towns. Their greatest triumph came on the 30th with the capture of two thousand federals at Aguadulce on the Gulf of Parita. Their forces then began to close in upon Panama City.[24] Up until this time the Colombian government had maintained guards on all trains crossing the Isthmus and no interruption of the transit had occurred. After the Aguadulce disaster, however, this protection was withdrawn and all civil officials were called in from the towns along the line. Military details stopped trains before they entered Panama or Colón and searched them for members of the Liberal party. At first these inspections entailed only a few minutes' wait but gradually the delays lengthened to as much as half an hour before the trains were permitted to proceed.[25]

Commander Potter, of the U. S. S. *Ranger,* observing the progress of events from Panama harbor, cabled the Navy Department on September 11 that the city was daily expecting attack, and that he had insufficient men to protect American interests. The railroad line was still open, he added, but insurgent bands were near it.[26] The department immediately ordered the *Cincinnati* to Colón and the *Wisconsin* to Panama City.[27] The next day Potter asked for instructions regarding the transportation of belligerent troops if he found it necessary to land his men for the protection of the line.[28] The reply from Washington came promptly:

[24] *Ibid.,* p. 282.   [25] *Ibid.,* pp. 289–290.   [26] *Ibid.,* pp. 282, 335.
[27] *Ibid.,* p. 326.   [28] *Ibid.,* p. 335.

United States guarantee perfect neutrality of Isthmus and that a free transit from sea to sea be not interrupted or embarrassed. United States of Colombia guarantee right of way or transit across Isthmus open and free to Government and citizens of United States and their property. Any transportation of troops which might contravene these provisions of treaty should not be sanctioned by you, nor should use of road be permitted which might convert the line of transit into theater of hostility.[29]

On the 13th a delayed cable from Hart in Bogotá reached the Department of State:

Minister of foreign affairs desires me to inform you that his Government would appreciate your good offices to bring about peace in the country, especially on the Isthmus, where the revolution is strong. This Government has no new terms to offer, but thinks your good offices may avail to induce revolutionists to accept terms heretofore offered, and thus prevent otherwise inevitable heavy loss of life. Minister for foreign affairs added: Not only is the question of humanity involved, but so long as the war lasts Congress will not be convened, and therefore the continuance of war will delay submission of the canal matter to the Congress.

Minister for foreign affairs emphasized this last point as being well to present to your consideration.[30]

Roosevelt, acting through the State and Navy Departments, entrusted this peace mission to Commander McLean of the *Cincinnati* at Colón by cable on the 18th. Two days later another cable to this officer repeated the orders previously sent to Potter defining the attitude of the United States towards the revolution. It added, however, that the "transportation of Government troops not in violation of treaty, and which will not endanger transit or provoke hostilities, may not be objectionable." [31]

McLean had already acted before the receipt of this message. On the 17th he had directed that a naval detachment accompany every train across the Isthmus. He had then sent identical notes to the commanders of the government and rebel forces apprising them of his action and notifying them that "no armed men except

[29] *Ibid.*, p. 332, Moody to Potter, Sept. 12, 1902.
[30] State Dept., Dispatches from Colombia, Vol. 58, Sept. 6, 1902. Adee forwarded the telegram to the Navy Department on the 16th.
[31] *Use of . . . a Military Force in . . . Colombia*, pp. 284–285.

NEGOTIATION OF THE TREATY 171

forces of the United States will be allowed to come on or use the line." When Governor Salazar pointed out that the railroad company was obliged by contract to transport Colombian troops, McLean replied, through Vice-Consul-General Ehrman, that such a provision did not appear to cover the carriage of armed troops, especially in time of hostilities, and that no one was competent "to make agreements in diminution of the rights of the United States Government." On the 20th he permitted about one thousand Colombian soldiers to travel each way under American guard, their arms being shipped as freight in separate trains.[32]

On the last day of September Rear-Admiral Silas Casey arrived at Panama on the *Wisconsin* and took over the command. After a tour of inspection he informed the governor of the department, on October 2, that the railroad could not be used for the transportation of "any combatant or any ammunition and arms . . . which might cause an interruption of traffic or convert the line of transit into a theater of hostility."[33] Governor Salazar protested vigorously and insisted that stores of ammunition and rifles recently landed at Colón for the suppression of the rebellion be transported to Panama. Casey refused permission to move the supplies and referred the governor to Washington on the question of interference with the rights of Colombia.[34]

The admiral's reports to the Navy Department indicate he felt that the situation on the Isthmus had gotten beyond the control of the Colombian authorities. He had been unable to learn, he said, of any effort on the government's part to crush the insurrection prior to or since his arrival. "It is my opinion," he wrote on October 13, "that if it were not for the restraining influence of our naval force here Panama would fall an easy victim to the combined land forces and gunboats of the insurgents." In a later

---

[32] *Ibid.*, pp. 73-75, 286-287, 335-336. In his messages to the opposing leaders McLean stated that his action was "without prejudice or any desire to interfere in domestic contentions of the Colombians."

[33] *Ibid.*, pp. 289-290, 292.

[34] *Ibid.*, pp. 291, 304. Part of these supplies were later shipped to Panama City without Casey's knowledge through a "mistake" of the railroad company.

dispatch he described Panama and Colón as "practically besieged." [35]

If the Liberals had any intention of attacking these cities they waited until too late. The arrival of General Nicolás Perdomo at Colón on the 16th marked the beginning of an energetic attempt by the government to restore its authority in the department. Reinforcements were sent over from Barranquilla as fast as they could be spared from service in other parts of the republic. The new commander established friendly relations with Admiral Casey and the American consular officials. He was tactful and polite. In a press interview he flattered the United States and praised the marines.[36] By the 22d of the month he had Casey's permission to march his troops along the line of the railroad on condition that the transit was not thereby impeded; by the 31st he had been informed that it would not "inconvenience" the United States if his men crossed the Isthmus by train, under arms and without naval guards.[37] Before the middle of November over six thousand Colombian troops were ready to take the offensive against the insurgents. On the 15th Casey began to reëmbark his men.[38]

Meanwhile arrangements were being completed for a conference between Governor Salazar and representatives of the Liberal party to discuss terms of peace. The surrender of Uribe Uribe's

[35] *Ibid.,* pp. 300, 305. On Oct. 20 Casey wrote: "I firmly believe if our men were removed from shore the insurgents would be in Panama in forty-eight hours. I think the Government, therefore, is very willing that they should remain, making occasional mild objections, which really it does not mean shall be taken seriously."

[36] *Ibid.,* pp. 304, 311, 315–316. If Governor Salazar was indignant at the occupation of the railroad line by the United States, General Perdomo was, apparently, much better informed as to the national government's attitude. In the interview mentioned above he said: "I have been agreeably impressed with the American forces on the Isthmus. . . . I think the landing of the United States marines has been effective in maintaining free transit over the Isthmus. I expect soon to have a powerful army here, and . . . shall then be able to relieve the American forces doing shore duty on the Isthmus. I am a great friend of the United States, and I admire that country. . . . My principal object in pacifying the Isthmus is to make possible a meeting of the Colombian Congress to consider the canal bill."

[37] *Ibid.,* pp. 306, 310–311, 313. It was agreed that the troops would be moved at hours other than those of the regular trains.

[38] *Ibid.,* p. 317. By Nov. 22 about 10,000 Colombian soldiers were assembled on the Isthmus.

NEGOTIATION OF THE TREATY

army in the department of Magdalena late in October had rendered the revolutionary cause all but hopeless. The possibility of a counterstroke on the Isthmus had been thwarted by the concentration of a superior federal force there, backed by the moral (and naval) support of the United States.[39]

On November 19 General Herrera, "director of the war" in the departments of Panama and The Cauca for the Liberal party, reached the city of Panama with two associates, Lucas Caballero and Eusebio Morales.[40] The delegation was escorted on board the *Wisconsin*, where a meeting was effected with Salazar and General Vásquez Cobo, representing the government. After two days of conference a treaty of peace was signed providing for the cessation of hostilities and a general amnesty to all accepting the treaty, and pledging Marroquín to summon a special session of congress to deal with the Panama Canal question, the currency, and necessary reforms.[41] Admiral Casey sailed soon afterwards for San Francisco.

III

Considered from the standpoint of Concha's negotiations in Washington, the events on the Isthmus could hardly have been more untimely. They caused a virtual cessation of the minister's efforts to harmonize the interests of his country with the treaty requirements of the United States. From then on he was inflexibly hostile to the Department of State and all its works. Yet

---

[39] While the United States violated the precedents of enforcement of the 1846-48 treaty in disarming Colombian troops using the railroad it nevertheless performed an inestimable service to the Bogotá government by insisting on the neutrality of the line and preventing the possibility of its capture by the rebels during the two months that it took the Marroquín party to collect a force of adequate size to handle the situation. For no matter what the outcome of an insurgent attack on Panama and Colón might have been, the railroad had already been abandoned to the Liberals when Potter landed his men.

[40] *Ibid.*, p. 319. Caballero and Morales were the Liberal secretaries of war and treasury, respectively, in the departments of Panama and The Cauca.

[41] *Ibid.*, pp. 319-321. General Caballero later stated that certain of the American naval officers openly threatened future intervention by the United States Government to assist the Panamanians in winning their independence if the conflict was not ended (*Story of Panama*, p. 184). The text of the treaty is printed in *Consular Reports*, LXXI (1903), No. 269, 198-199.

there is convincing evidence that his superiors not only concurred in the intervention at Panama, but actually proposed that such a step be taken.

The vice-president frankly admitted in his message to the Colombian congress in July, 1904, that he had requested military aid:

> Triumphant at Aguadulce, the revolutionary army overran the whole Isthmus, invaded the line of the railroad and threatened Colón and Panama in a most serious manner. The forces on which the Government depended to oppose the revolution were much reduced, particularly because of sickness. The negotiations which were afoot, the sad spectacle which was submitted to the gaze of the world, the supreme necessity of terminating the war as soon as possible . . . obliged my Government to take an extreme resolution, which was to call upon the United States, through its Minister in Bogotá and the Legation in Washington, for American forces to reëstablish the freedom of the transit of the Panama Railroad. This proceeding was not new, and although exceedingly painful, it had not up until then produced results which might arouse the fears of Colombian patriotism.[42]

Henry N. Hall testified before the House Committee on Foreign Affairs in 1912 that during the summer of 1902 Minister Hart was approached by Lorenzo Marroquín, son of the vice-president, and Aristides Fernández, the minister of war. These men suggested, according to the witness, that if the United States would interfere on the Isthmus so as to ensure the defeat of the rebels the Colombian government would be in a better position to forward the canal convention.[43] The credibility of this statement is considerably lessened by the fact that no record of such

[42] *Anales diplomáticos y consulares*, IV, 824.

[43] *Story of Panama*, pp. 184, 655. Hall asserted that Lorenzo Marroquín declared under oath in October, 1909, that he and Fernández conferred with Hart to bring about intervention by the United States in 1902. There is no suggestion in his testimony that the Colombian government promised to accept any specific treaty terms in return for aid. This material was part of the evidence gathered by the N. Y. *World* in 1909 for use in the case of the United States *v.* the Press Publishing Company (see *ibid.*, Exhibit K, pp. 630 *et seq.*). It was accepted without objection by the committee appointed by the Colombian house of representatives to investigate the circumstances surrounding the revolution of 1903 (Cám. de Rep., *Investigación sobre la rebelión del Istmo de Panamá*, pp. 64–65).

an interview is to be found among Hart's reports to the Department of State. Whether this conference actually took place or not, the incident related by Hall is in close accord with the disposition then prevailing in Bogotá.

It has been mentioned above that Washington kept a close watch on developments at Panama during the first weeks of September when the insurgent bands began to gather along the railroad. A week after the Department of State received Paúl's request that the United States use its good offices in the interests of peace, Commander Potter was ordered to deny the use of the line to the rebels, though the "transportation of Government troops ... which will not endanger the transit ... may not be objectionable." [44]

On the 20th, three days after naval guards had been installed on all transisthmian trains, Marroquín cabled Concha that Perdomo was on his way to Panama with a strong force and that it was time "to demand of the United States the execution of the Convention of 1846 to assure the transit from Panama to Colón." [45] That was the day, it happened, on which McLean's marines acted as escort for the disarmed Colombian soldiery in order not "to endanger the transit." Concha apparently lodged a protest with his superiors, for on the 22d Marroquín and Paúl dispatched another cable reading: "We are not aware of the form of the intervention of the United States. We only ask the execution of article thirty-five of the Treaty of forty-six, as has already been done in analogous circumstances." [46]

Before this second message arrived, the minister, thoroughly aroused by the news from the Isthmus, wired Governor Salazar to protest and use force if necessary to prevent intervention by the United States. He also sent Hay a memorandum stating that no interruption of the transit had occurred and that the Colom-

[44] *Supra*, p. 170.
[45] *Libro azul*, p. 253. The action of the United States in landing forces on the Isthmus three days before the formal request for such aid left Bogotá does not alter the fact that the Colombian government, unaware of the proceedings of the 17th, asked for intervention on its own initiative and not merely in compliance with pressure from Washington.
[46] *Ibid.*, p. 254.

bian officials had not failed, in any particular, to carry out their obligations under the treaty of 1846.⁴⁷ This reaction, which was quite understandable in view of Concha's ignorance of his government's plans, created some apprehension when it became known in Bogotá. To forestall any diplomatic indiscretion, the Washington legation was instructed, by a cable of the 25th, to "abstain from treating the question of American intervention at Panama; the Minister of Foreign Relations will handle it here." When, on top of this reproof, Concha learned of Admiral Casey's edict of October 3, he wired his resignation. Marroquín refused it as "unpatriotic and inadmissible." ⁴⁸

The minister's position was wholly anomalous. Outraged by the actions of the United States, and entirely out of sympathy with the attitude of his own government, he found himself forbidden either to protest or to resign. He made no attempt to conceal his bitterness in his letters to Paúl. Writing on October 2 he declared that the entire basis of the treaty negotiation had been altered by the events at Panama. Admiral Casey

> had assumed in fact the superior authority over the Isthmian region not in the possession of the rebels; the Colombian troops are disarmed by those of the United States, and travel under guard of the latter; the Governor himself submits to be escorted like a Khedive; the American commander gives identical notification to the officials of the government and to the rebels as to what he will permit and what he will not permit in the territory he occupies; and, to cap the climax, when the minister of the Republic in Washington announces that he has sought the information necessary to formulate the protest which international law and the most elementary national dignity require, peremptory silence is imposed upon him by the Chief of the Executive Power in Colombia and by the Minister of Foreign Relations. Between a Power which thus imposes its force, and a Government which cannot or will not defend the national sovereignty, treaties cannot be made.⁴⁹

---

[47] *Dip. Hist. of the Panama Canal,* pp. 254–255. As Concha had no authority to present a formal protest, this communication to Hay merely "rectified" various reports of the situation on the Isthmus, leaving Bogotá free to make whatever objection it might wish.

[48] *Libro azul,* pp. 254–255. [49] *Ibid.,* pp. 256–257.

NEGOTIATION OF THE TREATY

A few days later he cabled Paúl: "General Reyes telegraphs me as follows: 'The attitude of the American admiral at Panama will hinder Congress' approval of the canal treaty. It obligates you to protest and seek your passports.' Like Reyes we feel that all Colombians will not forget the Fatherland." The government immediately ordered him not to demand his passports. The question of the admiral, the dispatch continued, would be taken up directly with Hart.[50]

As a matter of fact, Marroquín and Paúl had been protesting vigorously to Hart for more than a fortnight. The kind of intervention they had expected in response to their request of September 20 would have kept the railroad open to the government and closed to the insurgents. It was certainly not anticipated that the United States would guarantee the "freedom of transit" with such impartiality as to place restrictions upon the transportation of Colombian armed troops in their own territory. Bogotá had looked for coöperation rather than interference. Furthermore, there had been a suggestion of contempt in McLean's action in excluding federals and rebels alike from the use of the line which did not escape the sensitive Colombian officials. Hart was called to the foreign office as soon as word of the American commander's order reached the capital on the 24th. He cabled his report of the interview the same day:

. . . Minister for Foreign Affairs requests me to advise you that this [interference] is regarded by the Colombian people as an unnecessary humiliation, and may provoke, if not on the Isthmus, then here in the interior, popular demonstrations resulting from wounded national pride, which demonstrations Colombian Government would regret and would probably be unable to prevent.

In view of this, and of further fact that if armed Government forces cannot proceed to Panama Colombian Government will be practically powerless to deal with the revolution on the Isthmus, and the war may therefore continue indefinitely . . . Minister for Foreign Affairs asks that our commander on the Isthmus be instructed

---

[50] *Ibid.*, p. 257, Concha to Paúl, Oct. 8, 1902; Marroquín-Paúl to Concha, Oct. 9, 1902.

to allow Government forces to pass freely from place to place as occasion may require.⁵¹

The next day Paúl sent Hart a copy of Salazar's telegram, dispatched from Panama on the 23d. It complained that the commander of the *Cincinnati* had "assured" the governor that he would land troops to protect North American lives and property in spite of the latter's insistence that he had sufficient men for the purpose and that foreigners were in no danger, inasmuch as the insurgents had retired "a hundred miles." To this protest Paúl added a note of his own, pointing out that the presence of the landing parties was not only unnecessary but dangerous, as it might occasion clashes with the local soldiery which it "would be better to prevent now." He therefore requested the American minister to

say to the Department of State that the landing of troops of the United States or any other measures for making effective freedom and securing of the traffic, be not carried into effect except at the request of the Governor, or with his consent.⁵²

The remonstrances did not end there. Disturbing reports continued to arrive from the Isthmus which increased the cabinet's anxiety over the possible results of the intervention. The plan to turn the transit guaranty to its own advantage was in serious danger of miscarrying. The conduct of the naval officers may have given rise to a suspicion that the United States was preparing to aid the Liberals or even encourage the formation of a separate state. On the 26th, for the third successive day, the administration lodged a protest with the legation. This time Hart was summoned to the presidential palace, where he was received by Marroquín, Paúl, and Minister of War Fernández. The meeting went over the ground covered in Paúl's note of the previous day and ended with the request that Colombia's sentiments be telegraphed to Washington.⁵³ Hart had another interview with Marroquín on October 6 concerning Admiral Casey's refusal to

⁵¹ State Dept., Dispatches from Colombia, Vol. 58, Hart to Hay (received Oct. 3).
⁵² *Ibid.*, same to same, telegram, Sept. 25 (received Oct. 2).
⁵³ *Ibid.*, same to same, telegram, Sept. 26 (received Oct. 2).

NEGOTIATION OF THE TREATY

permit the shipment of government munitions across the Isthmus. The vice-president stated that unless troops and supplies were allowed to use the line the suppression of the rebellion would be seriously hampered. He therefore requested that Casey be instructed to permit the railroad company to comply with its contract in this respect.[54] In Washington on the same day Governor Salazar's protest was forwarded to Hay by the secretary of the navy.[55]

It was apparent that the military efficiency of the intervention was beginning to overreach itself. Hay accordingly suggested to the Navy Department that "Admiral Casey should be instructed to refrain from any restriction of the right of Colombia to use the road for military transportation up to the point where such use may occasion actual or imminent hostilities on the line . . ." On the 16th the secretary wired Hart: "This Government regrets misunderstanding which has apparently arisen in Panama. No intention to infringe sovereignty or wound dignity of Colombia. American commander was instructed in that sense October 10." [56]

Paúl's notes of August 13 and September 9 reached the Washington legation during the fourth week of October, and elicited from Concha a full exposition of his stand on the negotiations.[57] The guaranties of Colombian sovereignty in the proposed canal zone, he wrote, were derived from the treaty of 1846 and formed the most vital part of the new convention. These rights had been specifically defined and developed in certain articles of the April Memorandum. Article XVII provided that

> The Government of Colombia shall have the right to transport over the canal its vessels, troops and munitions of war at all times without paying charges of any kind. This exemption is to be extended

---

[54] *Ibid.*, same to same, telegram, Oct. 6 (received Oct. 9). On the 1st Hart informed the department that Colombia wanted to purchase two small war vessels from the United States. "With these," the minister added, "it says it could bring about peace quickly, assemble the Congress, and close canal matter with little delay." Hay replied that he had no authority to make such a sale. *Ibid.*, same to same, telegram; State Dept., Instructions to Colombia, Vol. 19, Hay to Hart, telegram, Oct. 7.

[55] *Use . . . of a Military Force in . . . Colombia,* pp. 75–76.

[56] State Dept., Instructions to Colombia, Vol. 19, Hay to Hart, telegram.

[57] *Libro azul,* pp. 259–267, Oct. 23, 1902.

to the auxiliary railway for the transportation of persons in the service of the Republic of Colombia or of the Department of Panama, or of the police force charged with the preservation of public order, as well as to their baggage, munitions of war, and supplies.

Article XXIII, concerning the defense of the zone, stipulated that the United States should land its forces only in case the Colombian troops were unable to handle the situation, and then only at the request of, or with the consent of, the Colombian authorities, except in the event of extreme emergency. Finally, in Article IV the United States disavowed any intention of impairing Colombia's sovereignty "in any way whatever."

These three provisions taken together comprised Concha's interpretation of the proper relations between the two nations during any disturbance on the Isthmus. In other words, the April Memorandum introduced no new principle in this regard, but simply confirmed in detail certain rights which pertained inherently to Colombia's sovereignty. From this viewpoint the United States had violated the treaty by landing armed forces without consent, by preventing the railroad company from executing its contract to transport government munitions, and by disarming Colombian troops engaged in quelling the insurrection. Concha reasoned that the only alternative to this conclusion was that the Department of State had placed a new interpretation on the privileges granted the United States by the 1846 treaty. In that case the right of future intervention would have to be settled to Colombia's satisfaction before the discussion of other phases of the canal treaty could be resumed. Concha had his instructions of September 9 to complete the negotiations, but inasmuch as he had been forbidden to touch upon the affair of Admiral Casey, he informed his superiors that he would do nothing further until he had learned the result of the conversations with Hart in Bogotá, as he considered the two matters inseparable.

For the purpose of formally complying with his orders Concha wrote Hay on October 26 that he had received "supplementary and full instructions" to conclude the treaty, but that as these

NEGOTIATION OF THE TREATY

were dispatched previous to the incidents at Panama he did not feel at liberty to act in accordance with them until he had more explicit authorization to do so. He expressed regret that "a new interpretation, on the part of Your Excellency's Government, of the treaty in force between the two countries" made delay unavoidable. Hay replied that he did not recognize that the United States had done anything on the Isthmus to which the Colombian government "could justly take exception," and that no new interpretation had been placed upon the treaty referred to by Concha. He warned the minister that the president would be obliged to open negotiations for the Nicaragua route if the prospect for an arrangement with Colombia was no better when Congress convened in December. "I need not point out to your excellency," he concluded, "how grave a responsibility will be assumed by anyone who, by positive or negative action, may make it necessary for this Government to resort to the alternative mentioned." [58]

Hay requested Hart, by cable on the 27th, to repeat this warning to Paúl.[59] At the same time he sought to lessen the friction at Panama. As the result of a conference with Secretary of the Navy Moody, the latter ordered the following wire sent to Admiral Casey:

While approving your attitude, the Department wishes to impress upon you that the relations of the United States with Colombia are much strained. You must adopt measures as conciliatory as is consistent with dignity United States, overlooking matter of minor importance. Negotiations for ship canal are at present at a standstill on account of a feeling of irritation on part of Colombian representative.[60]

Meanwhile the Bogotá authorities continued to show concern over the attitude of their colleague in Washington. They cabled him on the 30th:

Continue the Panama Canal negotiation. It is the best occasion for settling the interpretation of the 1846 treaty, concerning tem-

---

[58] *Ibid.*, p. 267; *Dip. Hist. of the Panama Canal*, pp. 255-256.
[59] State Dept., Instructions to Colombia, Vol. 19, p. 209.
[60] *Use . . . of a Military Force in . . . Colombia*, p. 333, Oct. 29, 1902.

porary occupation, as you have proposed in article 23 of the *Memorandum*. Direction as to what you should avoid has no relation to the canal negotiation. If you lose heart all is lost.[61]

Hart had evidently been taken into Paúl's confidence concerning the difficulties with Concha. He informed the department early in November that the Colombian government appreciated the situation which Hay complained of in his telegram of October 27:

. . . Concha, having been much exercised about the interpretation of Article XXXV the treaty of 46, is instructed, for his consolation, that this is the opportunity to make clear the interpretation of that article.

Confidential. Minister for Foreign Affairs reminded me that Concha is subject to great nervous excitement, but that this will not be permitted to defeat the treaty. Minister for Foreign Affairs added that if Concha will not proceed with the negotiation he will be recalled.[62]

Reluctantly Concha arranged for an audience with Hay. His distaste for his mission had become so strong that, as he told Paúl later, he acted "solely in obedience to official orders." On November 4 he called at the Department of State accompanied by Dr. Herrán, secretary of the legation. After an exchange of civilities Concha stated that, as a preliminary to advancing the negotiation, he had instructions to clarify that part of Article XXXV of the treaty of 1846 which sanctioned intervention by the United States. To that end he asked that the text of Article XXIII of the April agreement be retained in the final draft of the canal treaty in place of the substitute suggested by Hay on July 18, and that it be linked by reference to Articles III, IV, and XVII. The secretary replied that President Roosevelt would be absent from the capital until November 7, but that he would consult him immediately upon his return. He then assured Concha of the friendly disposition entertained by the United States for Colombia and expressed his desire to avoid any incident

[61] *Libro azul*, p. 269.
[62] State Dept., Dispatches from Colombia, Vol. 58, Hart to Hay, telegram, Nov. 3 (received Nov. 9).

NEGOTIATION OF THE TREATY 183

which might injure the cordial relations then existing. In order to expedite the discussions Hay suggested that Concha draw up an unofficial statement of the observations which he intended to lay before the Department of State when the question concerning Article XXIII had been determined.[63]

Concha complied with this request in a note on November 11.[64] He renewed Colombia's former demand that the permission to be accorded the canal and railroad companies to transfer their property be regulated by a special previous arrangement between Colombia and those corporations. He refused to accept the phrase "in perpetuity" in reference to the term of the concession on the grounds that it would necessitate an amendment to the Colombian constitution. The details of the financial compensation the minister was willing to defer until the rest of the convention had been settled, but he noted that his government expected to receive an increased indemnity for the new concessions demanded by the United States. He also requested an additional article specifying the mode of composing differences in regard to the interpretation of the treaty.

While awaiting a reply from the Department of State Concha inscribed a personal letter to Paúl which discloses the strain and worry under which he had been laboring during these weeks.[65] His former bitterness seemed to have given place to weariness and a sense of hopelessness, relieved only by the feeling that he had scored over the distinguished secretary. In this connection he wrote:

> However clever Mr. Hay may be, the dilemma in which he has been placed cannot fail to mortify him somewhat: either he accepts article XXIII of the *Memorandum* of April as the correct interpretation of the Treaty of 46, and thus admits implicitly that the acts perpetrated at Panama are a violation of that treaty; or he will have to pretend that article XXIII is not the interpretation of the treaty and thus disavow his note of April in which he accepted the *Memorandum*.

---
[63] *Libro azul*, pp. 272–280.
[64] *Ibid.*, pp. 280–282; State Dept., Notes, Colombia, Vol. 10.
[65] *Libro azul*, pp. 283–287, Nov. 15, 1902.

He considered that Hay and Cromwell were responsible for the "more or less disguised threats" constantly appearing in the papers. Both these gentlemen, he suspected, would prefer to deal with another minister and might even force him out as *persona non grata* if he did not leave voluntarily. Such a dismissal he would regard as an honor. "I understand," he continued,

> that the condition which surprised them most, after the matter of article XXIII, is the observation that the canal and railroad companies cannot transfer their rights without a previous arrangement with the Government of Colombia. As a result, Cromwell has had many conferences with the Department of State, and although before this he hardly ever left me, he now avoids me, and publishes editorials in the newspapers saying that the United States can buy the rights of the Canal Company, undertake the work, and postpone *until later* the treaty with Colombia.

Although Concha did not expect that the United States would build through Nicaragua and very much doubted that forcible measures against Colombia were being seriously considered, he felt that a treaty agreement was remote. Apart from Article XXIII the other July amendments were extensive in nature and "their unconditional adoption would be equivalent to the cession of Panama." His own distaste for continuing the negotiation, he wrote, amounted to a "neurosis" which only death could eradicate. It seemed as if a steel wall had arisen between Hay and himself. His sense of loneliness was intense and painful. The representatives of other nations, especially Cambon of France, avoided him, or, if that was impossible, were as brief and formal as etiquette permitted in their contacts with him. His greatest wish was to depart from a post where he no longer served any useful purpose.

On the morning of the 18th a cable from Paúl, dated four days previously, reached the legation. It instructed Concha to obtain all possible advantages for Colombia, but in any case to sign the treaty "to save our responsibility." The final decision would rest with the congress.[66] The minister replied that he could not sign a treaty such as the United States wished, which would sacrifice

[66] *Ibid.*, p. 291.

his country's interests without even the excuse of a financial compensation equal to that derived from the railroad. He announced his unalterable decision to place Herrán in charge of the legation as soon as the latter should return to Washington.[67]

Later in the day there arrived Hay's reply to Concha's note of the 11th. It was sharp and captious in tone. The secretary first considered the subject of his interview with the Colombian minister on November 4. He expressed confidence that, if any questions relating to the treaty of 1846 really existed, the pending convention would cover them satisfactorily. Nevertheless, in order to manifest the nation's good-will towards Colombia, the president had authorized him to permit the substitution of Article XXIII of the April Memorandum for that proposed by the United States in July, on condition that all other points of difference be settled "to the satisfaction of the United States." Otherwise, the acquiescence was not to be operative.

Hay then turned to the observations on other articles submitted by Concha on the 11th, although they had not been offered officially. He termed Colombia's demand for a previous understanding with the railroad and canal companies "wholly inadmissible." He professed inability to understand the objection made to the phrase "in perpetuity," but offered to replace it with the circumlocution ". . . for the term of 100 years, renewable at the sole and absolute option of the United States for periods of similar duration so long as the United States may desire." The remaining observations, which included a forfeiture clause, the provision for interpretation, and a number of technical matters, were dismissed with a few brief remarks as unacceptable. A clean copy of the revised draft, ready for signature, was enclosed.[68]

In writing this note Hay was aware, from Hart's telegram of November 9, that Concha's observations were not to be taken too seriously. He knew that Paúl had authorized the minister to discuss the interpretation of Article XXXV of the treaty of 1846–1848 "for his consolation." It was on this point that the secretary

[67] *Ibid.*, p. 287.
[68] *Ibid.*, pp. 293–297; *Dip. Hist. of the Panama Canal*, pp. 260–263.

made his only important concession. For the rest, he had received assurances from Bogotá that Concha's "great nervous excitement" would not be allowed to stand in the way of the treaty. This fact probably explains the brusqueness with which most of the other objections included in the envoy's memorandum of November 11 were swept aside. One is left to speculate as to what further conciliatory steps Hay and Roosevelt might have taken had Paúl been more reserved about discussing his subordinate's temperamental mannerisms with Hart. As it turned out, the indiscreet remarks of the minister of foreign affairs had the effect of discrediting Concha in Washington.

Concha immediately advised his government that the answer of the Department of State was in the nature of an ultimatum, but that the form of the treaty was still unsatisfactory. He asked that Herrán be supplied with credentials for continuing the negotiations, as he was preparing to take his leave.[69]

On November 22, the minister sent his last communication from the legation to the Department of State, an able point-by-point commentary on Hay's note. It called attention to the fact that the observations of the 11th were made unofficially for Hay's information and consequently were unaccompanied by the statements necessary to explain and support them. Nevertheless, Concha agreed to the secretary's method of procedure in order to avoid further delay, but insisted on submitting his arguments. He rejected the condition attached to the department's concession on Article XXIII on the ground that he could not surrender every other point to secure one which his instructions made peremptory. Besides, Hay had acknowledged when he presented the July amendments that the provisions of the April Memorandum were valid until altered by mutual arrangement. He then presented his reasons for each of the objections offered on the 11th, withdrawing only the proposal for arbitration of differences, which he agreed to postpone. Respecting the refusal of the United States to admit Colombia's right to exact conditions from the canal and railroad companies, he said, in part:

[69] *Libro azul*, pp. 287–289.

Limited as is the time during which the companies will enjoy the usufruct from these properties, it is clear that if these have a great price, it pertains to Colombia, and there is no reason or motive for its being paid to the companies or that its owner shall cede it gratuitously. Already Colombia has exercised an act of exceptional liberality in extending the period for the construction of the works, the only effect of which has been that the canal company is now in a position possibly to recover a part of its capital, which, without this circumstance would have passed to Colombia within a few months . . .

The treaty between Colombia and the United States cannot have the judicial effect of adjusting or cancelling the bonds which exist between the Republic of Colombia and those companies, bonds arising from perfect contracts which cannot be undone . . . because one of the parties celebrates a pact concerning the same material with a third party, which in this case would be the United States.[70]

The Department of State did not see fit to answer (or even acknowledge) this note, which it probably regarded as no longer pertinent to the negotiation. Instead, it dispatched the following cable to Hart:

One. Congratulate Colombian Government on cessation of civil war in Colombia and the beginning of what we hope will be a long period of peace and prosperity.

Two. We have made all possible concessions to Colombia in canal matter; have ceded article twenty-three, also question of perpetuity and several minor concessions, but can go no farther. It is incumbent on Colombia now to say promptly whether they want the canal or not. Nicaragua offers perfectly satisfactory treaty.[71]

This message reached the Colombian capital on the 25th. Hart quickly arranged for an interview with Paúl and wired the results to Washington the same day:

. . . Minister of Foreign Affairs wishes you to be informed that Colombia wants canal and in view of the attitude of Colombian Minister, Secretary of Legation has been telegraphed as follows:

First. If Minister refuses to sign treaty Secretary of Legation is to take charge the Legation and to sign.

Second. The Legation is to require in writing your ultimatum declining to make further concessions to Colombia.

---
[70] *Ibid.*, pp. 297–305; *Dip. Hist. of the Panama Canal*, pp. 263–269.
[71] State Dept., Instructions to Colombia, Vol. 19, Hay to Hart, Nov. 22, 1902.

Third. The Legation to ask increase in sum to be paid Colombia. Note. This in order to satisfy the views Congress is expected to entertain, and to show that the effort was made.

Fourth. It must be distinctly understood that the whole treaty is to be submitted for consideration congress. Note. This because of disturbing newspaper publications sent by Colombian Minister.

Minister for Foreign Affairs says Government hopes to convene Congress next April, and that the ratification of the treaty would be more probable if price increased, but notwithstanding, Government will exert itself to secure ratification.[72]

Broken in health and discouraged, Concha turned the affairs of the legation over to Herrán upon the arrival of the telegram to which Hart referred. He left Washington on the 28th without paying his respects to the secretary of state and sailed for Barranquilla from New York on December 13 in the company of his brother-in-law, González Valencia.[73] The day preceding their departure the latter cabled Marroquín: "I follow with Concha; he agrees that the Panama Canal negotiation should be delayed." [74]

IV

The orders which Herrán received on November 28 placed him in charge of the negotiations in the event that the minister left. He was instructed to continue the parleys and to "exact from the United States Government a written *ultimatum:* make efforts

[72] State Dept.: Dispatches from Colombia, Vol. 58, Hart to Hay, No. 690, Nov. 25, 1902, confirming telegram of date. This crossed a wire from the department saying that Concha still refused to accept its proposals and that "unless Colombian Government instruct him to sign, the President will be compelled to consider seriously what is next to be done" (*ibid.:* Instructions to Colombia, Vol. 19, Nov. 25, 1902). Hart acknowledged this on Dec. 3 and added that Paúl had told him he was expecting to hear at any time that Herrán had taken charge of the legation and signed the treaty (*ibid.:* Dispatches from Colombia, Vol. 58, No. 697).

[73] *Libro azul,* pp. 323, 326, 328. On Dec. 1 he wrote Hay from New York that reasons of health prevented his return to the capital before taking his departure (State Dept., Notes, Colombia, Vol. 10).

[74] *Libro azul,* p. 325. The latter part of this message reads in the *Libro azul:* "*el conviene en reanudar negociación Canal de Panamá.*" González Valencia explained in the Colombian senate in July, 1904, that *reanudar* ("renew") should have been translated (from the cable code) as *retarder* ("delay") thus completely altering its meaning. It is not impossible that the "error" was inserted deliberately for purposes of publication. See *Anales del senado,* July 21, 1904.

NEGOTIATION OF THE TREATY 189

to secure pecuniary advantages, but in any case sign contract conformable to *ultimatum*." [75]

The new Colombian representative was confronted with a task which carried great responsibility and little prospect of honor. He was not only under the necessity of counteracting the unfortunate impression made by his predecessor's departure, but of wringing sufficient concessions from the stubborn and impatient Hay to make the treaty presentable at the forthcoming session of the national congress. His equipment for this work was limited by the incomplete condition of the legation archives and his own lack of acquaintance with many details of the negotiation. On the other hand, these handicaps were partially offset by a familiarity with the language and customs of the North Americans greatly superior to that possessed by his immediate predecessors. He had spent the years 1847–1849 and 1855–1863 in the United States while his politically prominent father was employed on diplomatic missions in Washington for the government of New Granada. He had been educated in the schools of the capital and at Georgetown University. His own diplomatic career had carried him to posts in London, Paris, Lima, and Hamburg. He was master of four languages and highly regarded in his own country for his classical learning and intellectual refinement.[76]

One of Herrán's first difficulties concerned the renewed activity of the supporters of the Nicaragua route. Several weeks before, when rumors of Concha's strained relations with Hay became current, Senator Morgan began to press the Department of State to conclude treaties with Costa Rica and Nicaragua. The ministers from these countries were now prepared to sign practically any terms demanded by the United States. Concha's departure was the signal for an outburst of agitation for the abandonment of the futile discussions with Colombia. Newspapers like the

---

[75] *Libro azul*, p. 325.

[76] International Union of American Republics, *Monthly Bulletin*, XVII (1902), pp. 619–620. The canal negotiation was Herrán's last public service. The strain of his labors aggravated a pulmonary affection and he died at Liberty, N. Y., Aug. 31, 1904.

New York *Times* and New York *Herald,* which had reluctantly forsaken the cause of Nicaragua, now protested that the "reasonable time" stipulated by the Spooner Act had elapsed.[77]

Herrán's pleasant manner and his knowledge of English were distinct assets to him. If he shared his predecessor's feelings towards the United States he concealed the fact sufficiently to make a good impression. Between December 1 and 19 he had five conferences with the secretary—more than Concha had during the entire nine months of his incumbency—and one with Senators Hanna and Spooner. The discussions were confined to the question of compensation, for Hay insisted that his note of November 18 was final in every other respect.[78] The alternative form in which the indemnity article had been offered left that subject alone open to further negotiation. Herrán's supplementary instructions, received on December 12, ordered him to hold out for $10,000,000 indemnity and $600,000 annuity with all other possible advantages. He was not to sign the treaty until he had obtained a written statement from the United States that no better terms were obtainable, and he was to include a provision for ratification by the Colombian congress. He reported to his government the next day that the greatest concession the Department of State would make was an initial payment of $10,000,000 and rental of $100,000 after ten years. This he considered altogether unsatisfactory.[79]

Hay took the position that the interest on $10,000,000 at five percent amounted to $500,000, which added to the $100,000 annuity made up the $600,000 yearly income demanded by Colombia. Herrán contended that his government asked no more than it needed in order to compensate it for sacrificing the $250,000 Panama railroad rental, its reversionary interest in the line, lighthouse fees, and other sources of revenue which he estimated at $100,000 annually. He argued that, as the United States offered Nicaragua $7,000,000 cash and $35,000 per year for the use of an unproductive zone, Colombia, in effect, was being offered only

[77] N. Y. *Times,* Dec. 1, 1902; N. Y. *Herald,* Nov. 26 and 27, 1902.
[78] *Libro azul,* pp. 336–337.   [79] *Ibid.,* pp. 326–327.

NEGOTIATION OF THE TREATY

$3,000,000 cash and $65,000 per year for the several valuable considerations which were included in the Panama route. If the difference in rentals were capitalized at five percent and added to the difference in initial payments, it would represent a total of only $4,300,000. This sum was proposed by the United States as reimbursement for a yearly yield of $350,000, or a capitalization of $7,000,000.

If Hay was impressed with the force of Herrán's argument, he gave no outward sign of it. His weather eye was fixed upon the Senate. He had not forgotten the battle in the upper house six months before nor the slim margin of eight votes which had decided the issue for Panama. Thirty-four "nays" had not been enough to defeat the Spooner Act but they were more than sufficient to defeat a treaty.[80] Under such circumstances every concession to Colombia had to be weighed in terms of senatorial opinion. While the compensation offered by Hay was meeting with strong opposition from Herrán, an increased compensation would meet with still stronger opposition on Capitol Hill. Whatever the secretary's personal estimate of a fair payment may have been, he was confronted by the practical problem of getting his treaty through the Senate. Expediency called for the greater firmness towards the lesser point of resistance.

The most that Hay would venture to the Colombian chargé d'affaires was the suggestion that, if conditions warranted after the opening of the canal, a new convention might be made increasing Colombia's payments. Unofficially he informed him that Roosevelt had originally set January 5 as the deadline for Colombia's acceptance of the treaty in the first draft of his recent message to Congress, but that he had substituted the colorless references which appeared, at the instance of several senators and members of the cabinet.[81]

It is evident from Herrán's cables during the latter part of

---

[80] The final 67 to 6 vote on the Spooner Act was a formality. The vital test had occurred earlier in the afternoon of June 19 on a motion to substitute the Hanna minority report for the Hepburn bill. This motion had been carried 42 to 34 with 12 senators not voting.

[81] *Ibid.*, pp. 327, 330–332.

December that he considered Hay's remark a warning that an ultimatum would be presented on the date mentioned. On the 30th the secretary began to apply pressure: "I regret appearing to importune you, but today it is absolutely necessary that I report to the President regarding the condition of our negotiations. Will you have the kindness to let me know as briefly as possible what I should say to him?" The Colombian replied that he had no new instructions from his government that would authorize him to resolve the difficulty concerning the annuity. He added:

> The discrepancy between the sum offered and the sum demanded is so great that it does not appear as if we can arrive at any advantageous agreement; but, as several years must elapse before the payments shall begin, possibly the present difficulty can be overcome by deferring the determination of the annuity for a future contract between the two Governments.[82]

Meanwhile rumors of various sorts were afloat. Certain papers reported that Colombia was deliberately delaying the negotiations because a German syndicate was ready to buy out the New Company's rights on March 4, the day the United States option expired. Senator Shelby Cullom of Illinois, chairman of the Committee on Foreign Affairs, expressed the opinion that in case no satisfactory treaty could be arranged with Colombia, the United States could deal directly with the company and proceed to build the canal on the justification of "universal public utility," leaving the settlement with Colombia until later. Herrán commented to Paúl that Hay had not even hinted at such a possibility, but "President Roosevelt is a decided partisan of the Panama route, and in view of his impetuous and energetic character, it is to be feared that the suggestion of Senator Cullom is not offensive to him." [83]

The seeming hopelessness of his task amid these perplexities

[82] *Ibid.*, p. 333. At a conference held on January 3 Hay renewed his proposition that if, when the canal was finished, circumstances appeared to justify an increase in the annuity, either government might open the question for diplomatic discussion. This did not satisfy Herrán, but he agreed to transmit the suggestion to his government. Bogotá took no action on it (*ibid.*, p. 330).

[83] *Ibid.*, pp. 328, 332. This is precisely what Roosevelt later planned to suggest to Congress in the fall of 1903.

NEGOTIATION OF THE TREATY 193

greatly depressed the chargé d'affaires. "I am left alone," he wrote Paúl, "in indefinite status, without coöperators or advisers . . . and with small hope of being able to achieve the desires of the Government in this struggle." [84] Bunau-Varilla, who had cabled Marroquín on December 19 that $250,000 a year would be a fair rental for the zone, he considered "officious" and "working for his own interests." [85] Even Cromwell was no longer fully trusted. Respecting this gentleman, Herrán wrote his superiors on January 9:

> In the initial period of our work here, when it was necessary to gain adherents to the Panama route, in competition to that of Nicaragua, the agents of the Panama Canal Company were very useful allies, especially Mr. William Nelson Cromwell, the clever lawyer of the company, a man of indefatigable activity and great influence. So long as the interests of Colombia and the canal company were identical, this powerful coöperation was most useful, but now these interests are no longer common, and I am working independently of our former allies. Now that the Panama route has been preferred, the agents of the company . . . are doing all they can to have the treaty signed, no matter what the cost to Colombia.[86]

Notwithstanding the truth of these remarks, Herrán could not dispense with Cromwell's assistance, even if the latter had been willing to let him, and the attorney was a frequent visitor at the legation until the negotiations ended. One of his greatest services was to persuade Hay, in the course of the conferences on January 2 and 3, to postpone the ultimatum to Colombia for a short period. The secretary, in acceding, warned that the president would send the Nicaragua and Costa Rica treaties to Congress for ratification unless Bogotá quickly took some action.[87]

On the 13th, with the negotiations rapidly nearing a crisis, the

[84] *Ibid.*, p. 328, Dec. 19, 1902.
[85] *Ibid.*, p. 334; Bunau-Varilla, *Panama: The Creation, Destruction, and Resurrection*, pp. 256–257.
[86] *Libro azul*, p. 334.
[87] *Story of Panama*, pp. 270–271. One of the reasons for the department's delay in submitting an ultimatum concerned the confusion over Herrán's credentials. On Dec. 10, Hay telegraphed Hart: "Please let me know whether or not Herrán is to receive his full powers. Time is critical." The minister replied on the 12th that Paúl had just furnished him with a copy of Herrán's official authorization to sign

department was startled by news from its minister in Bogotá that Herrán was being instructed to insist upon the changes suggested in Concha's note of November 22! Hart's wire continued:

> He must report result and wait for further instructions before signing the treaty; especially he is to insist upon ten millions down and six hundred thousand annually, to begin immediately . . . Minister for Foreign Affairs says his Government is of opinion that before Colombia can conclude the matter with the United States it is necessary that canal and railroad companies send here representative authorized to cancel existing contracts.[88]

Hay snapped back: "If Colombian Government persists in present attitude it renders further negotiations impossible." [89]

Owing to one of those strange delays so characteristic of Colombian diplomacy at this period Herrán remained in ignorance of these new orders while the Department of State was discussing them. They finally reached him on the 16th, the day that Hay sent his reply to Bogotá. Their contents varied somewhat from Hart's version. Marroquín and Paúl stated that they "trusted" the United States had accepted the Concha amendments. The chargé was instructed to work for better pecuniary terms, but "if this is not possible and you see that everything may be lost by delay, sign the treaty." [90]

Impressed with the need for immediate action, Herrán disregarded the puzzling references to the Concha amendments and adopted a suggestion advanced by the ever-present Cromwell for ending the impasse. He authorized the attorney that same day,

---

the treaty. This cable did not reach Washington until Jan. 9, having been twenty-eight days in transit. State Dept., Instructions to Colombia, Vol. 19, Hay to Hart: telegram, Dec. 10, 1902; No. 445, Jan. 13, 1903.

[88] State Dept.: Dispatches from Colombia, Vol. 59, Hart to Hay, telegram, Jan. 5, 1903.

[89] *Ibid.*: Instructions to Colombia, Vol. 19, telegram, Jan. 16, 1903.

[90] *Libro azul*, p. 335, telegram, Jan. 10, 1903. Just as this message was being dispatched Hart cabled home: "Am advised by Minister of Foreign Affairs that instructions will be telegraphed immediately to Herrán to sign the treaty if he can secure 'slight modifications which it is thought will be accepted by the Government of the United States'" (State Dept., Dispatches from Colombia, Vol. 59 [received Jan. 16]).

NEGOTIATION OF THE TREATY

the 16th, to notify the Department of State that he was prepared to sign the treaty if the indemnity question were referred to a board of three men, presided over by the president of the Hague Tribunal. The sum fixed was to be within the maximum and minimum limits proposed by the two nations. Hay concurred in this solution as a final resort in case no definite amount could be agreed upon by the plenipotentiaries.[91]

The chargé soon learned, as the discussions progressed, that his efforts to increase the remuneration were hampered by reports from Hart that the Colombian government had ordered its representative to sign for $100,000 a year. This he energetically denied as erroneous, and declared flatly that he would not subscribe to such a figure.[92]

On January 21 Hay delivered the long-awaited ultimatum, which read:

I am commanded by the President to inform you that the reasonable time provided in the statute for the conclusion of the negotiations with Colombia for the excavation of an Isthmian Canal has expired, and he has authorized me to sign the treaty of which I had the honor to give you a draft, with the modification that the sum of $100,000, fixed therein as the annual payment, be increased to $250,000. I am not authorized to consider or discuss any other change.[93]

Cromwell asserts in his Brief for Fees that he was responsible for this compromise, and for bringing both parties to accept it. During the afternoon of the following day Herrán and the attorney called at Hay's residence and at 5:15 o'clock the two principals affixed their signatures.[94] In token of Cromwell's contribution to the event the secretary presented him with the pen.

[91] *Story of Panama*, pp. 271-272.
[92] *Libro azul*, pp. 337-338. The *Libro azul* does not reproduce a cable sent by Herrán to Bogotá on Jan. 20. In it he states that the Washington authorities regarded the project of Nov. 18 as an ultimatum and that although he had made no further progress with the indemnity provisions of the treaty he would sign, if it became imperative, in accordance with his government's cable of Jan. 10 (Cám. de Rep., *Investigación sobre la rebelión del Istmo de Panamá*, p. 22).
[93] State Dept., Notes to Colombian Legation, Vol. 7, p. 354.
[94] Roosevelt Papers, Hay to Roosevelt, Jan. 22, 1903; *Story of Panama*, p. 272; *Libro azul*, p. 339. The text of the treaty is reprinted in Appendix B.

The anticlimax occurred three days later. On the 25th a cable from Marroquín reached the legation ordering the chargé not to sign the treaty but to await new instructions.[95]

Roosevelt sent the Hay-Herrán treaty to the Senate on the 24th. It was referred to the Committee on Foreign Relations after Morgan had failed to secure it for the committee on canals. The veteran Alabaman's enthusiasm for the Nicaragua route was as strong as ever, and he soon gave evidence that ratification was not to be achieved without a struggle. As a member of the Foreign Relations Committee, he submitted to that body ten resolutions addressed to the president ostensibly asking for information on various aspects of the negotiation but actually implying that Herrán had signed without the proper credentials, that Marroquín had no constitutional authority to enter into a convention, and that Colombia was politically in hopeless chaos. Upon the committee's refusal to endorse these resolutions he took them to the floor of the Senate, possibly not so much with the hope of seeing them adopted as to spread a feeling among his colleagues that even if the United States ratified the treaty the Colombian congress, when it met, would very likely reject it.[96]

Debate on the treaty began in the middle of February, but the slow progress of pending appropriation bills and Morgan's addiction to lengthy speeches quickly convinced administration leaders that an extra session was unavoidable.[97] This decision

[95] *Anales diplomáticos y consulares*, IV, 840–841. These instructions were sent from Bogotá on Jan. 24—the day the cable was sent (see *infra*, pp. 239–240). The text of the cable was not included in the *Libro azul*, but it was offered as part of Mr. Hall's testimony before the House Committee on Foreign Affairs in 1912. The cable is also mentioned in the report of the committee of investigation for the Colombian house of representatives made the same year (Cám. de Rep., *Investigación sobre la rebelión del Istmo de Panamá*, p. 71).

[96] *Cong. Rec.*, 58th Cong., 1st Sess., p. 21.

[97] On Feb. 16 Morgan made a bitter attack on Colombia occasioned by the publication in the Washington *Post* of Feb. 14 of a cable from Rafael Reyes, Colombian minister to Mexico, taking the Alabama senator to task for statements which he had made in executive session of the Senate two days before. At the same time an article had appeared in the Philadelphia *Inquirer* assailing Morgan on almost identical grounds. Morgan insinuated that Cromwell had prepared both of the attacks and that he had somehow obtained access to the confidential proceedings of the Senate in executive session (*Cong. Rec.*, 57th Cong., 2d Sess., pp. 2257–2264).

NEGOTIATION OF THE TREATY

introduced another complication. The option granted the United States by the New Company on its properties was to expire March 4, and, although Hay had requested Cromwell early in February to take the steps necessary to procure an extension of time, the Department of State was unable to give a pledge that the government would buy, since at that time neither nation had approved the treaty.[98] The New Company, on the other hand, did not wish to extend the option indefinitely for reasons that concerned its opponents in France. Cromwell takes to himself the credit for working out a formula, whereby the United States was to accept the purchase offer on condition that the treaty was properly ratified. Attorney-General Knox made such a proposal to the company on February 17, but it was not agreed to by the board of directors until after the call for a special session had been issued (i. e. after March 2).[99]

The first session of the Fifty-eighth Congress convened on March 5 and promptly undertook the consideration of the canal treaty. Morgan roused himself to a last mighty effort in leading the assault. In a series of speeches delivered between March 9 and 14, the report of which fills nearly ninety pages of the *Congressional Record*, the aged senator attacked almost every article of the convention and then went on in vituperative fashion to condemn the Colombian people, their religion, and their government.[100] Even the Panamanians were characterized as "degraded, dissatisfied, turbulent, mixed, and filthy." [101] Repeatedly he cited the Concordat of 1888, entered into between the Colombian government and Pope Leo XIII, pursuant to which a marriage contracted in conformity with the rites of the Catholic Church *ipso jure* annulled a purely civil marriage entered into with another person.[102] To sum up Morgan's picture of the situation in a sentence, a crowd of French jailbirds (the New Company), cleverly

---
[98] *Story of Panama*, p. 275.   [99] *Ibid.*, pp. 275–277.
[100] *Cong. Rec.*, 58th Cong., 1st Sess., pp. 13–105. On March 17 Morgan summed up the argument against the treaty in a speech filling six and a half pages of the *Record*.
[101] *Ibid.*, p. 16.
[102] The text of this concordat appears in *Sen. Docs.*, 57th Cong., 2nd Sess., No. 95.

advised by a "New York railroad wrecker" (Cromwell), had fraudulently secured an extension of its franchise by bribing a Colombian president so that they might unload an otherwise worthless property on the United States for an exorbitant sum, thereby leaving this country to attempt to build a canal over a poor route, infested with disease, in conjunction with a depraved, priest-ridden people whose constitutional government was a "myth."

In spite of this, Morgan expressed himself as willing to vote for a Panama Canal treaty provided it was actually in conformity with the Spooner Act. He therefore submitted a revised text of the Hay-Herrán document containing about sixty amendments. The most important of these called for the abolition of the joint tribunals, the inclusion of the cities of Panama and Colón in the proposed zone, the reduction of the lump indemnity from $10,-000,000 to $7,000,000, and the cessation of the $250,000 annuity after sixty-two years. As to the provision for defense, the United States was to secure the right "at all times and in its discretion, to use its police and its land and naval forces for these purposes." At the end were appended two additional amendments, the second of which stated that

> It is agreed by the high contracting powers that [out of] respect for the rights of the citizens of the United States under their Constitution and for the present humane state of the Christian religion, in which the ordinances and prescriptions of the Spanish Inquisition have no place or tolerance, that the provisions of the concordat of 1888 . . . and the laws enacted by Colombia . . . in furtherance . . . of said concordat, shall not apply to any citizen of the United States in Colombia . . .[103]

Cromwell and his law partners worked constantly to refute the charges of the senator and to assure the defeat of all amendments. This was not an easy matter as some of the best friends of the route, such as Spooner, Hanna, and Foraker, believed that certain changes were desirable. Particularly was there insistent demand that the United States receive specific permission to fortify and

[103] *Cong. Rec.*, 58th Cong., 1st Sess., pp. 14–16.

NEGOTIATION OF THE TREATY

defend the canal and exercise absolute sovereignty over it.[104] Cromwell pointed out that any amendment would be tantamount to a rejection by Colombia as every possible concession had already been made. He even had Herrán write him a letter to this effect which he showed to those senators who were sponsoring amendments.[105]

In view of Roosevelt's subsequent assertion to Congress that it was a question whether the United States "had not gone too far in [Colombia's] interest" in drafting the treaty, the arguments used at this time by the chairman of the Foreign Relations Committee are particularly interesting. In summing up his reasons for opposing amendments, Senator Cullom remarked:

> Colombia's concessions are not unimportant. They amount to at least half a million dollars annually, and in addition, the right to have the railroad property, which is one of the greatest paying enterprises perhaps in the Western world, in 1966 revert to Colombia as her own property; and in ninety-nine years from the completion of the canal to have the canal revert to her as her property—all without one cent of compensation. For these important concessions we pay Colombia in cash $10,000,000, and at the end of nine years we commence paying her an annuity of $250,000, which is not changed during the life of the present treaty, and this treaty is a perpetual one.[106]

As the day set for the vote approached both sides labored strenuously for converts. Every senator was solicited. The leaders of the Panama forces gradually withdrew from their insistence on amendments and brought pressure to bear on the rank and file.[107] On March 17 the treaty was ratified without amendment by a count of 73 to 5.[108]

---

[104] *Ibid.*, pp. 109–111. In discussing the last clause of Article XXIII, which gives the United States the right to use its armed forces for the defense of the canal without Colombia's prior consent "under exceptional circumstances," Senator Cullom remarked: "The United States will determine what are exceptional circumstances and unforeseen or imminent danger. Those terms are susceptible of a very broad construction. I think I am safe in saying that if it ever becomes necessary to fortify or protect the canal by armed forces, it will be a case of unforeseen or imminent danger, or an exceptional circumstance."

[105] *Story of Panama*, p. 274. [106] *Cong. Rec.*, 58th Cong., 1st Sess., p. 110.
[107] *Story of Panama*, p. 274. [108] N. Y. *Sun*, March 18 and 19, 1903.

VI

THE COLOMBIAN DOCTOR'S DILEMMA

THERE IS NO RECORD that Herrán ever informed Hay of the contents of Marroquín's cable of January 24. He was too keenly aware of the impossibility of reopening the discussion of the "control" clauses not to have experienced some private feeling of relief that the signing of the treaty made it unnecessary to disclose the nature of his new instructions. In view of the correspondence of the preceding months, the Department of State would undoubtedly have interpreted this sudden reversal of policy as substantial evidence of Colombian duplicity. It would have taxed the powers of a far more resourceful diplomat than Herrán to have reconciled his government's suspension of the negotiation with its repeated assurances that it stood ready to accept all Hay's proposals except the one on compensation. As late as January 10, the vice-president had wired Herrán to work for better terms but under no circumstances to risk losing the canal. The orders of the 24th took the chargé completely by surprise and, since they were no longer applicable to the situation, they were judiciously filed away in the legation archives.

At first glance Marroquín's behavior in a matter of such national importance appears capricious in the extreme. A closer examination of the forces at work in Colombia during the preceding two years indicates, however, that this and other inconsistencies of the administration were dictated by the pressure of circumstances imperfectly known to Herrán and almost wholly beyond the cognizance of the Department of State. It is to the nature and effect of these circumstances, and to the pattern which appears behind the inconsistencies they produced, that we now turn our attention.

It will be recalled that Marroquín embarked with considerable

THE COLOMBIAN DOCTOR'S DILEMMA

reluctance upon his canal negotiations with the United States in January, 1901. That feeling was only strengthened by subsequent events. Instead of improving, the domestic situation in Colombia grew worse during the year and reached a series of crises in the winter and late summer of 1902 at the very time when the Colombian legation in Washington was most in need of support and guidance from home. Time and again the stability of the Conservative regime had been seriously threatened by rebel successes in the field or the prospect of Venezuelan invasion. Not until the greater part of the Liberal army had capitulated in the autumn of 1902 was there any marked lessening of the tension in the capital. It is hardly surprising, therefore, that the Bogotá authorities concentrated their energies upon the emergency before them to the neglect of other important public business. Much of the inefficiency which hampered the foreign office's handling of the canal affair in 1902 can be traced to this preoccupation.

Personally, the vice-president was wholeheartedly in favor of an isthmian canal and, apparently, quite ready to entrust the execution of the work to the United States, provided a satisfactory treaty could be arranged. Mindful, however, of the delicate nature of the problems involved in such a partnership, he preferred to do no more than go through the motions necessary to keep the discussions open until order had been reëstablished at home.[1] Once that had been accomplished (and the cherished Conservative doctrines of political centralization and coöperation with the Church made secure) he and his advisers would be in a position to give the canal negotiation the close study and supervision its importance merited.

Another reason for Marroquín's desire to avoid conclusive treaty conversations during the course of the civil war concerned the somewhat precarious nature of his power. The venerable doctor was far from being the complete master of Colombia's affairs that Roosevelt seems to have imagined him to be. His "dictatorship" depended upon the active and continuing support of a number of political, military, and religious leaders and upon

[1] *Anales diplomáticos y consulares*, IV, 805.

the acquiescence, at least, of a substantial part of the property-holding classes. The alienation of any important group of his adherents might easily prove disastrous. Although the Panama Canal question had only an indirect bearing upon the issues of the civil war it carried much political high explosive. A serious blunder in managing the negotiation might widen the existing split between the Nationalist and the Historical branches of the Conservative party and open the way for a military triumph of the Liberals.

In addition to these considerations, the vice-president lacked the legal authority to ratify a treaty with a foreign state. Strictly speaking, there was nothing to prevent his issuing a legislative decree of ratification, but such action would have been clearly unconstitutional and contrary to his repeated claim that he exercised only such powers as the constitution assigned to the executive in times of emergency. Inasmuch as these powers were confined to matters of a provisional character, a treaty with the United States would require the approval of the congress. This body had not met since 1898 and there was no prospect of holding an election until the insurrection had been crushed. It followed logically, therefore, that the pacification of the country was the essential preliminary to a definitive consideration of the canal problem. With order restored, the government's attention would be freed from the distractions of prosecuting an internal war, the results of disaffection within the ranks of the party would be less consequential, and the legal machinery of ratification could be speedily reconstituted.

An examination of the correspondence which passed between Bogotá and the legation in Washington from the beginning of 1901 to the end of January, 1903, reveals how assiduously the Colombian government played for time.[2] Hay's subsequent statement that the treaty discussions were "energetically pressed" upon the United States by Colombia for several years appears in the light of these notes to be little less than a bald misrepresentation of fact.[3] The only thing that Marroquín pressed for during

[2] *Libro azul*, pp. 3–340.   [3] *Dip. Hist. of the Panama Canal*, p. 392.

THE COLOMBIAN DOCTOR'S DILEMMA 203

this period was delay. The Colombian tactics throughout were defensive. Silva was sent north in response to Cromwell's warning that the adoption of the Nicaragua route by the United States would mean the collapse of the Panama project. His title was dignified, but his instructions were vague and his power limited. He was authorized to do little more in his own discretion than conduct a propaganda campaign on behalf of Panama. All matters of importance, including possible treaty terms, had to be submitted to Bogotá for decision.[4] Five months after his arrival he was told to await detailed instructions which never came.[5] Concha had similar experiences. The official Colombian treaty proposals failed to reach him until after the pressure of events in Washington had obliged him to subscribe to the Hay-Concha protocol on his own authority. It was not until the late summer of 1902, when the victorious insurgent forces seemed on the point of taking Panama City, that the authorities at home were finally driven to act. Yet even then their move turned out to be no more than a somewhat disingenuous device for postponing the real negotiations. As we have seen, Concha was ordered to accept without further discussion all the Hay proposals except the one concerning compensation, subject only to the express understanding that the resulting convention could be amended by the Colombian congress whenever it met.[6] In thus attempting to link the treaty interests of the United States with the need for the speedy restoration of civil order in Colombia, Marroquín and Paúl evidently hoped to gain valuable time—and possibly military aid—without the necessity of making hasty commitments.

This policy of procrastination continued throughout the fall and into the winter. The record of Herrán's pathetic notes to his superiors during the first two months of his incumbency presents incontrovertible evidence as to which party was being "energetically pressed" in the parleys. His orders were to withhold his signature from the convention until the United States had presented an official ultimatum. He obeyed these orders implicitly. Yet even as he was affixing his signature to the Hay-

[4] *Libro azul,* pp. 3-4.   [5] *Ibid.,* p. 35.   [6] *Supra,* p. 164-165.

Herrán treaty Marroquín and Paúl were preparing to cable instructions for further delay. There is no question but that Colombia entered into the treaty with the greatest reluctance and only when all the possibilities of prolonging the conversations had been exhausted.

II

Inasmuch as the Bogotá government had been maneuvered into a position where the only alternative to the acceptance of an unfavorable treaty was the complete abandonment of the negotiations, it may be wondered why the latter course was not adopted as the lesser of two evils. The answer is to be found chiefly in the political exigencies confronting Marroquín at this time. Unfortunately for him and for Colombia, the Panama project had come to have a bearing on domestic affairs during the course of the preceding two years which had not been foreseen and which, once manifested, could not be disregarded. As a result, the administration's original tone of exalted statesmanship in canal matters had slowly given way to a policy of undisguised expediency growing out of the fiscal situation, the separatist threat in Panama, the unexpected prolongation of the rebellion, and the vice-president's declining prestige. These considerations in the main may be said to have dominated the latter part of the parleys from the Colombian angle and eventually to have forced the signing of the treaty. It is our purpose now to examine the general nature of these domestic pressures.

One of the most powerful arguments in favor of a canal agreement with the United States was that only in such a manner could Colombia hope to meet the enormous costs of the war, retire the hundreds of millions in outstanding paper money, and ultimately develop the rich resources of the nation. This point carried a wide appeal with prominent men in all parties. Only rarely does any Colombian discussion of the canal question written during the years 1901 to 1903 neglect to touch in some way upon this aspect of the proposed treaty.

In summarizing the problems facing the Colombian people

at the opening of 1901, Dr. Antonio José Uribe, then undersecretary of foreign relations, placed the necessity for retiring the paper money first, although he made no direct allusion at that time to the interoceanic canal as a possible solution.[7] A few months later, however, he wrote:

> If one takes into account, furthermore, the development which the vast, rich and uninhabited regions nearby will undergo with the opening of the canal, no less than the Department of The Cauca, the emphatic opinion among the inhabitants of the Isthmus in favor of the negotiations and the pecuniary profit which can be obtained from the concessionary, not only in the form of a stipulated lump payment, but also in the form of an annual rental; if these circumstances are taken into consideration, we repeat, nobody will hesitate to admit that the government is under the imperious obligation to make every kind of effort, and even sacrifices of another sort, to procure the opening of the canal on the best possible terms for the republic.[8]

In the penetrating analysis of the canal situation which Silva prepared for Uribe's use in June, 1901, he presented his view of the intimate connection between the Panama Canal and Colombia's financial future:

> With this question of the canal . . . is closely linked our problem of paper money. With its present resources Colombia cannot think of redeeming or amortizing it for many years. With the high rate of exchange an increase in taxes will be intolerable and productive of very little; the Government will not be able to increase its receipts sufficiently to pay for the services which good public administration requires; foreign capital will not flow to promote the enterprises we most need, such as the construction of railroads, because with depreciated paper money interest will not be paid in gold; the national credit will have no standing abroad for the same reason; and thus with bad government, with general maladjustment, with business depression, with permanent obstruction of all work other than that of a merely speculative character, it is not very difficult to foresee that a new war looms, a thousand times worse in character than that just passed. Then—it may be the end.[9]

---

[7] *Diario oficial*, Jan. 25, 1901.
[8] *Anales diplomáticos y consulares*, II, 944–945. [9] *Libro azul*, p. 55.

This state of affairs was one of the principal arguments advanced by the envoy in Washington to support his contention that Colombia could not afford to take an uncompromising stand on technical points of sovereignty and thereby risk the adoption of the rival route and the loss of the needed indemnity. He repeated this plea in a personal letter to Marroquín on March 11, 1902, shortly after he had been relieved by Concha.[10] Almost despairingly he warned that

if we do not assure ourselves now, in some negotiation on the canal, of a fixed annuity with which to care for the amortization of the paper money, this awful problem holds no possible solution. With five or six hundred millions of notes in circulation . . . all means of stabilizing the paper will be fruitless.

Inasmuch as the leading advocates of a treaty with the United States were making great capital of the fact that whatever political concessions Colombia might be obliged to make would be more than compensated for by generous financial terms that would smooth the road to future economic prosperity, it is not difficult to comprehend the general note of disapproval with which the news of the indemnity clause of the Hay-Concha protocol of 1902 was received in Bogotá.[11] Francisco Groot and Clímaco Iriarte both asserted that $7,000,000 was far too small a return for what the nation was contributing.[12] To Uribe the proposal to leave the amount of the annuity to a commission was "absolutely inacceptable"—if Colombia was entitled to a rental it was also entitled to know definitely what the amount would be before ratifying the convention. He suggested to Marroquín that since the disparity of the construction costs between the Panama and Nicaragua canals was estimated to be $58,000,000 in favor of

[10] *Anales diplomáticos y consulares,* IV, 815–817. Francisco Groot prophesied that a treaty with the United States would permit the immediate amortization of the paper money, the payment of the entire external debt, and the restoration of the gold standard. See *Libro azul,* Appendix, pp. 26, 30; also *Anales diplomáticos y consulares,* II, 949.

[11] It will be recalled that this provided for a payment of $7,000,000 on exchange of ratifications and a "fair and reasonable annuity" after fourteen years. In case of disagreement the latter was to be determined by a commission of five, to be presided over by the president of the Hague Tribunal. See *supra,* p. 142.

[12] *Libro azul,* Appendix, pp. 41, 70.

the former, and since the United States would have to pay $40,000,000 for the New Company's property, it would be proper to ask for the $18,000,000 difference, plus $2,000,000 for the surrender of the railroad annuities and reversionary rights, or a total of $20,000,000. The annuity, he thought, should be computed to meet the charges of servicing the external debt. Starting at $1,000,000, it might be augmented by $100,000 a year.[13] Rudolfo Samper, the Colombian representative on the board of directors of the New Company, wrote from Paris that in his opinion Concha should be instructed to demand $20,000,000 on the exchange of ratifications and an annual payment that would begin with $2,000,000 and increase at the rate of $100,000 a year.[14]

While there is no record of Silva's reaction to the specific form of compensation proposed in the Hay-Concha agreement, his conclusions on this general subject are worth quoting. In his dispatch to Bogotá of January 8, 1902, he set forth his belief that a fixed annuity

is preferable to assure this benefit to future generations; to prevent the malversation or the squandering of an indemnity received at one time; to calm the susceptibilities of the political parties and to fix a firm basis for gradually amortizing the paper money and funding the foreign debt of the Republic, taking care of the punctual payment of the interest on the debt.[15]

Such payments as the United States might be prevailed upon to make for the use of the canal zone did not, however, constitute the sum total of Colombian monetary expectations. While the negotiation was still in its early stages the Marroquín government was considering the possibility of levying a contribution on the New Company in return for the cancellation of Articles 21 and 22 of the concession. If Colombia refused to sanction the transfer, it was argued, the company's property would be worth nothing and uncompensated forfeiture would almost inevitably follow in 1910; therefore, it would be entirely ethical for the

[13] *Anales diplomáticos y consulares*, II, 954. The difference in the construction costs of the two canals was officially estimated by the Walker Commission at $45,630,704, not $58,000,000 (*Walker Commission Report*, p. 173).
[14] *Libro azul*, Appendix, p. 44. [15] *Ibid.*, pp. 80–81.

nation to participate in any salvage money which its acquiescence would place the company in a position to obtain. Cromwell's shrewd circumvention of this scheme was among the bitterest fruits of Bogotá's dilatory diplomacy and an important contributive to the rejection of the Hay-Herrán treaty.

Pitiful mismanagement characterized Colombia's dealings with the canal company throughout the years 1901 to 1903. Silva was responsible for the first misstep in accepting Hutin's clever letter of May 1, 1901, without comment or qualification. In this note the director-general of the French enterprise informed the minister that his company would "consent" to sell its property to the United States "if permission should be given in effect by the Colombian Government" and on the understanding that "the conditions of transfer will be determined for the Company apart from and independently of the special arrangements which may be made between the Governments of Colombia and the United States." [16] The possible implications of this latter statement evidently escaped Silva and his tacit approval of the principle of a private understanding cleared the way for one of Cromwell's boldest stratagems. In brief, his plan, as it developed, was to avoid any settlement with Bogotá by opportune pretexts until Colombia had committed itself to the transfer of the company's holdings in a convention with the United States and then to resist subsequent financial demands by raising the cry of "blackmail" and broadly hinting at a "breach of faith" with Washington.

It was essential to the success of this maneuver that the Department of State be kept in ignorance of Colombia's intention to collect from the company until the two governments had signed an agreement covering the basic terms of a treaty. Silva unwittingly coöperated to the full. He said nothing about the necessity for a "previous arrangement" with the New Company to either Secretary Hay or Admiral Walker. He wrote Hay that his government would consent to a transfer of the French property pro-

---

[16] *Ibid.*, p. 22. See also López, "El Gobierno de Colombia . . . ," *Reforma Social*, III (1915), 463.

THE COLOMBIAN DOCTOR'S DILEMMA

vided a satisfactory treaty could be made with the United States.[17] He left Walker with the distinct impression that the company had been officially authorized to sell.[18] The minister was very naturally anxious to make the Panama route appear as attractive as possible to the Canal Commission, which was then completing its final report, and he possibly felt it was good policy not to introduce a phase of the situation which did not directly affect the United States. If this was the case, his wisdom was of the moment only, for his reticence about the actual conditional nature of Colombia's consent was later to prove one of the most unfortunate of that nation's tactical blunders. Silva was afterwards severely criticized by certain of his countrymen for his error in this matter, but it must be borne in mind that his correspondence was forwarded promptly to his superiors in Bogotá and that their failure to make their intentions clear to the United States places a share of the blame upon them as the responsible agents.

The canal negotiation lagged during the latter half of 1901 and the Marroquín government, dogged by troubles at home, made no effort to reach a "previous understanding" with Hutin. Then, in November, came the Canal Commission's final report favoring the Nicaragua route, followed a month later by the Senate's ratification of the Hay-Pauncefote treaty. The directors of the New Company, in desperation, cabled their offer to sell for $40,000,000 early in January, 1902. These events shifted Colombian attention perforce to the canal question once more and aroused new interest in the prospects for assessing the corporation. Four days after the arrival of the famous cable from Paris, Silva was writing to Bogotá:

I have not told the representative of the French Company on what conditions the permission to transfer the concession will be granted; but it seems to me in strict justice that they should give a good sum to the Government of Colombia, since if consent is denied them, they will lose everything. Moreover, **inasmuch as the Company took** advantage of the straitened circumstances of the Government to

---

[17] *Libro azul*, p. 20, March 27, 1901. [18] **Walker Commission Report**, p. 145.

obtain an extension of six years, which is in reality what they are going to sell for forty millions, I do not believe that it would be unfair to exact at least two million pesos from them in addition to the million which they have paid [in 1900].[19]

Among the matters laid before the special conference of officials and distinguished citizens which Marroquín summoned to the presidential palace on February 13, 1902, was the question of the conditions to be imposed upon the company in the event that permission for the transfer of its property seemed advisable. Such a wide discrepancy of opinion developed, however, that a commission of five was appointed to examine the problem and submit its conclusions in writing.[20] The majority report of this body was surprisingly inimical toward any treaty whatever with the United States and recommended that the company be required to complete its contract as it stood.[21] Francisco Groot, in dissent, argued ably for a treaty and suggested that the government approve the sale of the Wyse concession in return for the ownership of the stock of the Panama Railroad or, alternatively, for $10,000,000 in gold.[22] Uribe, in a letter to the vice-president dated about the same time, expressed his conviction that the company ought to give something but that the amount should be kept moderate.[23]

Interestingly enough, the only advocates of a canal partnership with the United States openly to oppose the assessment of the company were Pablo Arosemena, José de Obaldía, Federico Boyd, Tomás Arias, and Oscar Terán, all inhabitants of the Isthmus and, all but the last, future supporters of the Panama separation. They were unanimous in urging that the French be allowed to effect an agreement with Washington without financial impositions of any kind from Colombia.[24] An illuminating side-light on the government's method of procedure at this time is afforded by the fact that, while the executive was thus outwardly soliciting

[19] *Libro azul*, p. 80. [20] *Ibid.*, p. 103. [21] *Ibid.*, Appendix, pp. 3–9.
[22] *Ibid.*, pp. 38–39. [23] *Anales diplomáticos y consulares*, II, 7–8.
[24] *Libro azul*, Appendix, pp. 75, 79–80. These men did not attend the February meeting, but were selected at Marroquín's request by Governor Albán of Panama to present the Isthmian viewpoint.

THE COLOMBIAN DOCTOR'S DILEMMA 211

advice on the proper attitude to assume towards the New Company, official instructions were nearly three weeks on their way northward to Concha with word that the price of the transfer was to be at least $20,000,000.[25]

Evidently the administration found nothing sufficiently convincing in the majority report of the presidential commission when it was submitted on February 20 to cause it to abandon the course of action it had already quietly adopted. Indeed, hardly had the document been filed when the Colombian consul-general in Paris was ordered to advise the company that its property would be subject to forfeiture should it permit the stockholders to ratify the offer of sale to the United States without first reaching an agreement with Bogotá. As a result the meeting called for this purpose on February 28 took no action. In Washington Cromwell interpreted this warning as "official proof that the necessary consent . . . had not yet been given" and as evidence of "the intention of Colombia to demand pecuniary tribute." [26] Almost simultaneously with the Paris message, a cable was dispatched to Concha stressing the indispensability of a previous understanding.[27]

This sudden determination on Colombia's part to force the issue alarmed the lawyer. He hurried to New York in an effort to impress Concha with the precarious nature of the situation in which Colombia's interests (and his own) then stood.[28] His success

[25] *Ibid.,* p. 84.
[26] *Story of Panama,* pp. 252–253. On Feb. 22 the agent of the New Company in Bogotá cabled the Paris office as follows: "My opinion is that if the Company address itself directly to the Colombian Government to ask authority to sell its concession to the Government of the United States, this ought to be done with much prudence, for this request would be granted only with very onerous conditions. The only easy and immediate way to a favorable solution would be to sell property and concessions to an American company, which could at once and easily arrange with the Government of the United States and with the Colombian Government. All other solutions would be dangerous. I do not wish to insist more." Hart secured a copy of this message and forwarded it to Washington by cable. It reached the capital on March 1. See State Dept., Dispatches from Colombia, Vol. 58, Feb. 21, 1902.
[27] *Libro azul,* p. 85. Cromwell was very probably informed of this cable by Silva who was still in charge of the legation and awaiting Concha's arrival from New York.
[28] *Supra,* p. 136.

was strikingly complete. Not only did Concha indite a formal letter to Cromwell for the benefit of Hay and the press emphasizing his government's willingness to approve the purchase of the company's holdings by the United States, but he wired home that the cable he had recently received was "inexplicable," that it had "produced a disastrous effect," and that "something grave" was pending in official quarters concerning Panama.[29] The attorney's achievement was all the more remarkable when it is considered that Concha could have had no direct knowledge of what was going forward in "official quarters" and that the message which had produced such a "disastrous effect" had been given no publicity. Except for a cabled promise of instructions to come and a reiteration of the necessity for an arrangement with the company the minister received no further word from his capital until April 26.

With Concha won over to the need for haste, Cromwell now turned his ingenuity to the task of securing a signed draft convention incorporating the all-important permission to transfer. Not only was there danger that the pro-Panama senators might become discouraged and abandon the fight but there was also the possibility that the promised instructions for Concha might arrive and precipitate the complete breakdown of the negotiations.[30]

Since we have had occasion in an earlier chapter to trace the development of the Hay-Concha negotiations insofar as they directly concerned the Department of State in Washington we are at present concerned only with the tactics employed by the counsel of the New Company to evade a cash payment by his clients to Colombia. The completion of the protocols of March 31 and April 18 marked an important step towards this goal. Article I of both conventions provided that "the Government of

---

[29] *Libro azul*, p. 85.
[30] It has been mentioned above that Cromwell had probably learned the nature of these instructions from the Department of State on or shortly after March 17. Hay had characterized the proposed terms as "inadmissible," while the attorney was doubtless particularly interested in the stipulation that an agreement with the New Company was a condition necessarily precedent to any further negotiation with the United States. See *supra*, pp. 138–139.

Colombia authorizes the New Panama Canal Company to sell and transfer to the United States its rights, privileges, properties, and concessions, as well as the Panama Railroad . . ." [31] In thanking Cromwell for this achievement, Bô, the president of the board of directors, wrote from Paris:

> We have especially appreciated Article I . . . which, in fact, abrogates articles 21 and 22 of our contracts of concession . . . and will permit us to resist the pecuniary pretensions of Colombia, as we are absolutely determined to do.[32]

Concha's failure to insist upon an understanding between his government and the New Company before entering into a treaty protocol with the United States was not based upon any sympathy for Cromwell's clients or any objection to the principle of an assessment. It was rather the result of his conviction that until Congress had accepted the Panama route the interests of the company and Colombia were inseparable. Disagreement or delay in the face of the Nicaragua threat might easily lead to the destruction of Colombian hopes and to incalculable domestic difficulties.[33] The minister therefore permitted the question of sharing the $40,000,000 to recede temporarily into the background while he coöperated with Cromwell in the fight for the adoption of the Spooner amendment.

It was during the supplementary negotiations with Hay in July that Concha missed his best opportunity to inform the

---

[31] *Libro azul*, p. 125; *Dip. Hist of the Panama Canal*, p. 556.

[32] *Story of Panama*, p. 259. That the company was perfectly aware that Colombia did not share its interpretation of Article I was indicated by the same official in replying to Cromwell's request that a stockholders' meeting be called to approve the proposed sale before the Hepburn bill came to a vote in the Senate. Bô wrote that such a move would be dangerous inasmuch as Colombia, as owner of 50,000 shares, would have to be notified and this might "reawaken her pretension of demanding from us a given sum for the abrogation of articles 21 and 22 . . ." (*ibid.*).

[33] Concha pointed out to his government, perhaps at Cromwell's instance, that even if the New Company's concession was allowed to expire in 1910 the same interests would still control the Panama Railroad, whose charter gave it the right to prevent the construction of any canal along its right of way until 1967 or at least to exact damages for its consent. In that case Colombia would discover the shoe to be on the other foot. For the minister's discussion of his views, see *Libro azul*, pp. 121–124.

United States officially of the conditions his superiors had in mind in authorizing the company to sell its property. Marroquín and his advisers were apparently too much distracted by developments at home to recognize the importance of pressing the matter promptly and publicly. Consequently, it was not until November 11, 1902, that the subject was first introduced into the formal correspondence between the two governments. In his memorandum of that date to the secretary of state Concha declared:

This same article [Article I of the April convention] shall clearly state that the permission accorded by Colombia to the canal and railway companies to transfer their rights to the United States shall be regulated by the previous special arrangement entered into by Colombia with the said companies, and for which they have been notified that they are to appoint an attorney at Bogotá.[34]

By this time the minister's sullen attitude towards the naval intervention at Panama the previous September and his unwillingness to proceed with the negotiations had aroused a feeling of irritation on Hay's part which he made little effort to conceal. This mood doubtless made it easier for Cromwell to convince the secretary that the company was being subjected to a bit of Latin-American sharp practice. However that may be, in his reply on the 18th Hay dismissed the proposed amendment with the comment that "the United States considers this suggestion wholly inadmissible." [35] Cromwell's account of his own role on this occasion is interesting:

It was a vital and fundamental point for the company, and Mr. Cromwell employed all his energy in resisting the acceptance of this amendment. He conferred frequently on this matter with Secretary Hay, and at his request explained to him the full scope of the amendment as well as the relations between the parties. . . . The result of these arguments was that Secretary Hay declared himself in accord

---

[34] *Dip. Hist. of the Panama Canal*, pp. 258–259. This notification had been presented to Cromwell on behalf of the Colombian government on Oct. 29 (*Story of Panama*, pp. 277–278).

[35] *Dip. Hist. of the Panama Canal*, p. 261.

THE COLOMBIAN DOCTOR'S DILEMMA 215

with our views, and in his official reply to Minister Concha he rejected the amendment.[36]

It was this incident that enabled Hay, during an exchange of notes with General Reyes early in 1904, to say that the proposal to charge the company came as an "utter surprise" to the United States Government, that it had not been so much as mentioned in previous discussions, and that after its rejection by the Department of State it was abandoned by Bogotá "and the convention was nearly three months later signed without any modification of the absolute authorization to sell." [37] The secretary's official "surprise" may or may not have been genuine, but it is clear that he was not wholly frank with Reyes in asserting that Colombia altered its intentions in regard to the New Company after receiving his note of November 18. Not only did the Bogotá government insist upon the propriety of its participation in the $40,000,000 with greater consistency and determination than marked other phases of its canal policy during the ensuing year, but Hay's note appears to have awakened Marroquín and Paúl to the real character of the difficulties which faced them as a result of Concha's acceptance of Article I of the April protocol. From December, 1902, on, the Colombian authorities brought increased pressure to bear on the canal company to submit to an assessment. Having been rebuffed somewhat brusquely by the secretary of state, they sought to conclude an agreement through Mancini, the company's Bogotá agent. On December 31 Hart wired a report of these efforts to Washington. Six days later he cabled that the "Minister for Foreign Affairs says his Government is of the opinion that before Colombia can conclude the matter with the United States it is necessary that canal and railroad companies send here representative authorized to cancel existing contracts." [38] Cromwell states that on January 9 Hay told him that he knew "positively" that the delay in the progress

[36] *Story of Panama*, pp. 268–269.
[37] *Dip. Hist. of the Panama Canal*, p. 497.
[38] State Dept., Dispatches from Colombia: Vol. 58, telegram, Dec. 31, 1902; Vol. 59, telegram, Jan. 5, 1903.

216   THE COLOMBIAN DOCTOR'S DILEMMA

of the convention was due to the refusal of the New Company to pay for Colombia's consent to the treaty.[39] A week later the secretary ordered Hart to warn the Colombian government that unless its attitude changed conversations would be closed.[40]

It is plain enough that the reason the treaty was signed "without any modification of the absolute authorization to sell" was simply that the Department of State explicitly forbade such modification under threat of ending the discussions altogether.[41] For our present purpose, however, it is sufficient to note that the prospect of sharing in the sale price of the Panama concessions constituted an important prop in maintaining the negotiations on the Colombian side against domestic opposition from 1901 to 1903 and that Herrán's acceptance of the treaty by no means signified his government's surrender of its claim to such an indemnity.

III

Unquestionably, an earnest desire to avoid losing the economic benefits of having the United States build the canal was a primary factor in determining the Colombian leaders to accept the Hay-Herrán treaty with all its shortcomings. Yet the possibility that the republic might forfeit not only the canal but the Isthmus itself—should the negotiations miscarry—figured perhaps even more decisively in the counsels of the Bogotá administration. In this connection Marroquín later remarked that "the canal question was unfortunately completely linked with the integrity of Colombian territory." [42]

As early as June, 1901, Silva intimated to his superiors that the Panamanians might very well seek annexation to the United States if their vital interests were persistently ignored.[43] In an unofficial letter to the vice-president the following March he enlarged on this subject:

[39] *Story of Panama*, p. 278.
[40] State Dept., Instructions to Colombia, Vol. 19, telegram, Jan. 16, 1903.
[41] See Hay's ultimatum to Herrán on Jan. 22 in *Libro azul*, p. 340.
[42] *Anales diplomáticos y consulares*, IV, 815.   [43] *Libro azul*, p. 56.

... if the men of political influence in this country should become convinced, as is possible and even probable, that the Panama route is that which suits the United States, and if Colombia does not agree in due time to a comparatively advantageous arrangement, it is the logic of events that we shall definitely lose the Isthmus. Nor do I say this lightly: I have serious information which justifies my statement; and the most serious [aspect] of this matter is that the Government of the United States will without much trouble establish a point of aid in the Isthmus, as much because of the actual state of war there, as because the Panamanians of position and financial resources will never willingly submit to the opening of the canal in any other place than at the Isthmus. They understand very well that the adoption of the Nicaragua route will be the moral and material ruin of Panama; and this sacrifice, which will have no compensations, may very well prove superior to the concept of a platonic patriotism.[44]

Both Silva and Francisco Groot regarded a treaty with the North Americans not as a threat to Colombian independence and prestige, but as the best protection the nation could achieve, particularly against European imperialism. The latter wrote Marroquín that he considered the treaty of 1846 largely responsible for the preservation of the department of Panama to the rest of the republic up to that time.[45] Luis M. Isaza, another presidential adviser, took a more fatalistic view. Should the United States select the Panama route, he conjectured, Colombia would discover its own wishes in the matter to be of no moment, since "contemporary history gives evidence that for that nation there are no obstacles in matters of foreign sovereignty nor in principles of International Law when it concerns the expansion of its commerce and power." To him, the canal issue appeared closely associated with the civil war and the question of the maintenance of Colombian sovereignty on the Isthmus. In conclusion, he warned that if the Panamanians, with their slight affection for the rest of the country, became convinced that the canal was not to be opened through their territory it would be very difficult to keep them from separating, "counting, as they will, on assistance from the United States." [46]

[44] *Anales diplomáticos y consulares*, IV, 816.
[45] *Libro azul*, Appendix, p. 18.   [46] *Ibid.*, Appendix, pp. 33-34.

Concha sent home similar admonitions in his dispatch of March 20, 1902:

> ... there prevails in Panama, among the people of position and reputation, the idea that the Government of the United States should be treated with at all events, and at whatever cost in concessions. This predominant manner of thinking on the Isthmus holds much significance, especially if it is considered that the rebels have recovered much strength there in recent days, and that the ancient germ of secession is active once more and can lead to a very difficult state of things. Encouragement of no great amount would be needed for this idea to gather momentum in a short space of time, thus bringing the whole Republic to a terrible complication, whose consequences are incalculable.[47]

Again on April 1 the minister commented anxiously on the dangers of a secession movement, either spontaneous or induced, if the outlook for the treaty became markedly unfavorable. Should Colombia break off the discussions in a belligerent manner, he feared that the United States might follow the course advocated by certain newspapers in the country and abrogate the treaty of 1846. Then, whenever a halt occurred in the railway service, its naval forces could occupy the territory and bring about "damage to Colombian sovereignty of much greater consequence than any limitation to which the Republic might be subjected in the use of a stipulated zone of its territory." [48]

In his dispatch of May 21, 1902, Concha wrote:

> It is my duty to call to your attention that the revolutionaries have been working here persistently to influence the United States towards their cause, and that if the Colombian Government does not proceed now with much tact the sacrifices of two years will be lost in an hour.[49]

Referring to the events of this period in an address to the Colombian congress two years later, Marroquín declared that it was well known that "responsible chiefs of the revolution

[47] *Ibid.*, p. 88.
[48] *Ibid.*, pp. 123–124. During the several weeks that followed, Concha received a series of letters from prominent Panamanians stressing the unanimity of support for the canal among business and commercial people on the Isthmus regardless of the concessions necessary to secure it. Mutis Durán wrote that only the prospect of the canal had sustained business there recently. *Ibid.*, pp. 191–195.
[49] *Anales diplomáticos y consulares*, IV, 824.

promised to treat with the American Government concerning the opening of the Panama Canal, in the event of their triumph, establishing in this manner a dangerous competition for the nation." The chiefs alluded to were obviously Vargas Santos and Foción Soto, who informed American newspapermen in Washington in the early summer of 1902 that "if the final result of the present war favors the Liberal arms, we will, without doubt, take possession [of the concession] in 1904, and we will sell it to the United States." [50]

These communications clearly indicate how closely the Conservative leaders associated the activity of the rebels in Panama with the danger of losing the Isthmus. This does not necessarily mean that they felt that General Herrera was attempting to erect an independent state there, but rather that Liberal successes in that region were attracting attention to the weakness of federal control along the line of the proposed canal and thereby setting the stage for a local separatist movement or possibly for open intervention by the United States. Many Liberals would have welcomed the latter contingency if assured that it would operate favorably to their cause and that Colombian sovereignty over the canal zone would be respected.[51] In any event, they hoped to block Marroquín's chances of concluding a treaty that would

[50] *Ibid.*, IV, 824–825.
[51] According to the testimony of Henry N. Hall before the House Committee on Foreign Affairs, Modesto Garcés, a Colombian lawyer, was in charge of the revolutionist headquarters in New York in the summer of 1902. Part of his duties consisted in attempting to persuade the Department of State to intervene at Panama in favor of the Liberal party. Hall alleged that on July 31, or Aug. 1, 1902, Garces returned to New York from one of his conferences at the State Department in Washington. He informed General Vargas Santos, general-in-chief of the revolutionary forces, who was in the United States just then to purchase arms and seek financial aid, that Acting-Secretary David Jayne Hill had hinted that intervention might be arranged with the independence of Panama in view. Garces thereupon wrote out the rough draft of a memorandum which he said Hill had suggested should be sent to the department. In substance the proposed memorandum asked: "What would be the attitude of the United States in the event that the revolutionary forces should declare the independence of The Cauca and Panama?" General Vargas refused to sign the paper or to become a party to any such proposition. Hall stated that the original memorandum was (in 1912) in the possession of General Celso Rodríguez of Bogotá, formerly one of the chief lieutenants of Vargas Santos. *Story of Panama*, pp. 183–184.

strengthen the Conservatives politically and financially. Although they failed in this purpose, they succeeded in making themselves a source of constant worry to the Bogotá authorities.

This was but one of several ways, however, in which the civil war served to throw the Colombian government on the defensive throughout the course of the canal negotiations and to place it in the difficult position of seeking to avoid a final commitment on a treaty which it ardently desired. Equally serious, in its immediate potentialities, was the threat of invasion from Venezuela. It is very doubtful that the rebellion could have maintained itself as long as it did had it not been for the active assistance which the dictator of Venezuela, General Cipriano Castro, furnished to the Liberals during 1900 and 1901.[52] This support grew out of a bargain which that gentleman made early in 1899, while an exile in Colombia, with the enemies of Sanclemente. It was agreed that Castro was to oust President Andrade of Venezuela with the coöperation of Colombian Liberals and then aid his allies in turn against their own president. The first part of the scheme worked well. Castro invaded his country early in 1899 and took Caracas before the end of the year. In May, 1900, he had himself proclaimed president and summoned a national assembly to frame a new constitution.[53]

Meanwhile, the Liberal revolt had broken out in Colombia. The rebel forces were soon greatly weakened, however, by the sixteen-day battle of Palonegro (May 10–26, 1900), and thereafter the war largely took the form of a series of fierce, spasmodic conflicts, with the principal organized bodies of Liberals concentrated on the Isthmus and along the lower valley of the Magdalena. Late in 1900 Castro seemed on the point of fulfilling his promise to invade Colombia but the expedition failed to materialize.[54] At no time did the dictator formally recognize the belligerency of the revolutionists. He limited himself at first to supplying them with materials of war, permitting them to or-

[52] Rougier, *Les Récentes Guerres civiles*, p. 46.
[53] *Ibid.*, p. 4.   [54] *Ibid.*, p. 47.

ganize their forces on his soil, and offering them a refuge in retreat. Later he allowed them to use his ports for outfitting privateers and the sale of prizes. And finally he went so far as to sanction the exercise of consular authority by commercial representatives of their provisional government.[55]

Marroquín and his ministers watched these developments with growing concern. After a lengthy interchange of notes dealing with specific infractions of neutrality, the Bogotá government summarized its grievances in a memorandum late in January, 1901.[56] Its protest concluded with a sharp demand that Venezuela desist from further instances of unfriendly conduct. No reply came from Caracas. Castro's active aid to the revolutionists declined for the time being, but it would be difficult to say whether this was brought about chiefly by Colombia's note or by the increasingly tense domestic situation at home.[57]

In June, 1901, General Uribe Uribe, the commander of the Liberal forces in the Magdalena Valley, visited Castro in Caracas and thereby started rumors that plans were afoot for a new "Great Colombia" with the Venezuelan adventurer at its head.[58] Marroquín, nevertheless, continued to exert himself to prevent an open break with his eastern neighbor. When, late in July, a corps of Colombian volunteers under a personal enemy and compatriot of Castro's crossed the frontier and invaded Venezuela, Bogotá promptly repudiated the expedition.[59] In response to Secretary Hay's efforts to avert a rupture between the two nations, Silva wrote him on August 28:

The Colombian government has exercised the most scrupulous vigilance to prevent the organization upon its soil of filibustering expeditions against General Castro, though it is notorious that the many expeditions that invaded Colombia from Venezuela, did so with the assistance of General Castro and his official agents. Without this foreign assistance the Colombian rebellion would have long since ended.[60]

---

[55] *Ibid.*, pp. 47–50.
[56] *Ibid.*, p. 51, footnote 2.
[57] *Ibid.*, p. 6.
[58] *Ibid.*, p. 51.
[59] *Ibid.*, p. 53; *Anales diplomáticos y consulares*, II, 972–973.
[60] State Dept., Notes, Colombia, Vol. 10.

Instances of Castro's unfriendliness multiplied as the months passed and at last, in exasperation, the Colombian government severed diplomatic relations on December 16, 1901.

It will be recalled that the isthmian canal negotiations were entering a very critical phase at this time. December 16 was the very day on which the United States Senate gave its approval to the Hay-Pauncefote treaty. Coincidentally, the New Company was on the verge of accepting the Walker Commission's valuation of its property as a figure of sale and the House was preparing to take final action on the Hepburn bill. Silva was writing letters filled with bitter complaints at his neglect. In Bogotá the foreign office was thinking not of the canal but of the imminence of war with Venezuela.

Matters were still further complicated when the Liberals, spurred by several successes early in 1902, began to close in on the capital. For some weeks the city was practically in a state of siege. Hart kept Washington informed of the progress of the fighting and of the activities of the government ministers. His dispatch of February 3 commented on the complete lack of coördination between departments. "Unhappily," he added, "the situation grows worse daily . . . Less attention is being paid to foreign affairs than ever before so far as my experience goes." [61] This attitude toward the nation's external concerns was not entirely an outgrowth of the military crisis. Following Uribe's resignation the previous September the vigor and efficiency of the foreign office had undergone a marked decline. No successor was installed until March 1, 1902. Throughout this long interim such business as could not be postponed was discharged, after a fashion, by the ministers of finance and public education, successively.[62] These circumstances, taken together, throw considerable light on the Colombian government's failure to supervise the discussions with the United States more successfully during the first few months of 1902. By the time Paúl had formulated his plan of procedure

[61] State Dept., Dispatches from Colombia, Vol. 58, No. 559.
[62] For list of foreign ministers and acting ministers, see *Libro azul*, Appendix, p. 159.

and communicated his instructions to Concha, the March and April protocols had been signed and the opportunity for effective negotiation on the fundamental issues had passed.

IV

Another important factor in bringing about the Colombian government's acceptance of the Hay-Herrán treaty was the ominous decline in Marroquín's popularity at home. This is ascribable in good part to his failure to placate the Liberals and reëstablish internal peace. In the weeks immediately following the coup of July 31, 1900, the insurrectionists suspended operations in the hope that the vice-president would grant the concessions previously agreed upon with Dr. Parra.[63] The hope went unfulfilled, however, and fighting recommenced, much to the disappointment of many men of all factions.

For various reasons, some of which were undoubtedly connected with Marroquín's total disregard of the Parra agreement, the personnel of the administration underwent a radical change in character in the first year and a half of Marroquín's term of office. Most of those who had taken the lead in removing Sanclemente from power had resigned their posts on one pretext or another by early 1902, and had been replaced by men of cruder stamp. Aristides Fernández was beyond question the most forceful of these newer advisers. Meticulously honest in the midst of constant opportunities for personal gain, he was nevertheless narrow and unconciliatory in his approach to the problems facing the government. His tactics in dealing with the Liberals became increasingly harsh and sanguinary. Lucas E. Nieto Caballero later recorded the impressions which he, as an ardent young Liberal, formed during these years:

Fernández, a kind of St. Just, without his eloquence, bloodthirsty . . . was personally a suave man. Unctuous manners, excessive exactitude in questions of money, member of a good family, orderly habits. He possessed a good figure. But I detested him. He appeared to me horrible, of iron . . . with all the hideousness of crime. He was

---

[63] *Supra,* pp. 60–61.

no criminal. He was hardly a passionate man. He sought to serve his party up to the point of converting himself into a lightning-rod of all angers, he sought to crush the revolution and he selected a bad way. Had he possessed the qualities of a statesman or more delicate sensibilities, he would have ended rebelliousness by compromise. But he preferred harshness, as did the French of the Terror, as did the Spaniards of the Pacification, and he did not fail to approve the cruel acts of savage subordinates.[64]

In January, 1901, Fernández ordered that all captured rebel chiefs be tried for brigandage and executed upon conviction. Few acts could have been better calculated to infuriate the Liberals and alienate the loyalty of the vice-president's more high-minded followers. The decree was an obvious attempt to circumvent one of the most cherished provisions of the Colombian constitution, that which forbade the imposition of the death penalty for participation in political revolts. Yet protests from all factions proved ineffectual. In July, when news reached the capital that Uribe Uribe was in Caracas, death was prescribed for any citizen entering into an agreement with a foreign power.[65] These orders were carried out in several instances amid a storm of popular disapproval. Miguel Antonio Caro, the archbishop of Bogotá, and nearly all the Nationalist leaders protested to Marroquín about the executions and the mistreatment of prisoners of war.[66] Even Marroquín's own friends remonstrated with him concerning Fernández' conduct. But the vice-president was either unwilling or unable to interfere.[67] In September, General Nel Ospina, one of the ablest of Marroquín's early advisers, was dismissed from the ministry of war and imprisoned. Shortly afterwards Antonio José Uribe gave up the portfolio of foreign relations.

The rising protest soon took the form of a movement for the

[64] *Por qué soy liberal?* pp. 44–45.
[65] Rougier, *Les Récentes Guerres civiles*, pp. 11–14.
[66] Nieto Caballero, *op. cit.*, p. 46.
[67] Rougier, *Les Récentes Guerres civiles*, p. 13, footnote. According to Nieto Caballero (*loc. cit.*), Fernández threatened to shoot three captured Liberal generals belonging to prominent families if certain Conservative officers were not released by the opposition. Public opinion seems to have prevented further action in this case.

reinstatement of Sanclemente. On September 28 a group of leading citizens of Bogotá signed a petition addressed to the executive which cited the recent arbitrary actions of the government, including the suppression of certain newspapers and the incarceration of Nel Ospina.[68] "The true justification of the political move of July 31, 1900," the paper set forth, "would have been the immediate reëstablishment of peace, based solidly on justice, and, consequently, on [public] opinion." The signers declared that, since they had been disappointed not only in this, but in their hope for a disinterested government, they wished assurances from Marroquín that he would place no obstacle in the way of the restoration of the legal president, Sanclemente. Among these petitioners was Luis Martínez Silva, brother of the minister to the United States and one of the chief instigators of the 1900 coup. The vice-president, in his written refusal, commented on the fact that several of the signers had formerly held posts in his government.[69] In the following two months petitions protesting the administration's unnecessarily belligerent policies were presented by prominent citizens of Antioquia and The Cauca.[70]

Not all the pleas for relief were directed to the presidential palace. Eduardo Espinosa, a Bogotá lawyer, sent an appeal to General Reyes, the *Designado,* who was at that time in Mexico City with Silva. In asking him to return to Colombia and restore peace he prophesied that the Liberals would gladly and promptly accept an honorable surrender if offered "with the formal promise of returning to them their guarantees as citizens and of granting them adequate representation in the government." [71]

A Liberal sympathizer, writing in 1902 on conditions in his country, stated that Marroquín seemed unable to realize the significance of the many defections among his former fervent partisans.[72] The vacancies thus created, he added,

were filled by ignorant men of bad precedents, so that men have been seen to attain to the offices of Ministers and Governors who

---

[68] [Eduardo Espinosa], *Colombia,* pp. 1–2.   [69] *Ibid.,* p. 3.
[70] *Ibid.,* pp. 7–9.   [71] *Ibid.,* pp. 23–24.
[72] Morales, "The . . . Situation of Colombia," *North American Review,* CLXXV (1902), 356.

were not capable of filling the post of Chief of Police in the meanest village. . . . A government *de facto* rules the country by the power of its bayonets,—backed by no political party, for the Liberal Party opposes it by force of arms; the Nationalist Conservative Party repudiates it as the offspring of treachery; and the Historical Conservative Party, in a state of dissolution, is only composed of the public officers and the military chiefs for whom warfare is the most profitable of industries.

To add to Marroquín's troubles, the financial situation grew worse as the war dragged on. Nieto Caballero gives a graphic description of the effects of Colombian inflation:

The paper money, an inheritance from Dr. Rafael Núñez, produced sudden ruin and enrichments. The emission had no limits other than the speed of the presses. Every day new paper came forth. Every day the exchange mounted skywards. A government triumph made it descend and permitted some rest for the pressmen. A Liberal triumph made it rise and imposed night work upon them. When fine quality paper was exhausted, use was made of the first that came to hand . . . and the deluge continued. [Exchange] came to be quoted at 25,000%, that is to say, a peso was exchangeable for less than half a centavo. Waste was intensified and gambling spread. It was not bad business to give interest of 10% to 20% monthly, for on the day of payment the bills represented a fifth or tenth part of what they were worth on the day of the loan. . . . The idea of value was absolutely lost and everything became a nauseous speculation.

Fernández could have become a millionaire. He was the master of the country, his very name awakened panic . . . and his constant activity mixed in everything. Nothing easier than to fill a room in his house with paper, than to change it for gold, than to send funds abroad, than to prepare for himself an old age without worries. And he did not take a cent. He was honest. He believed in giving to his party his chief services and he triumphed over all obstacles at the cost of his name. His later life passed obscurely in a little shop . . . where he personally attended his clientele . . . until he died in the greatest poverty.[73]

The only serious efforts made by members of the administration to bring about a harmonious settlement of the issues between the parties were undertaken not in Bogotá, but in Wash-

[73] *Por qué soy liberal?* pp. 47-48.

THE COLOMBIAN DOCTOR'S DILEMMA 227

ington. Both Silva and Concha keenly realized how extensively Colombia's permanent interests at Panama were suffering from the continuation of the war. In February, 1901, Silva and Uribe Uribe, who chanced to be in the United States at the time, were brought together by the Ecuadorean minister for an interview at which possible terms of peace were discussed. The general's proposal was that congress be assembled to reform the constitution and the essential laws. The Liberals were to be guaranteed twenty-five seats in the lower house and nine of the eighteen places in the senate plus control of one-third of the departmental assemblies. Meanwhile public order was to be restored, political prisoners were to be freed, and the press unmuzzled. These overtures were cabled to the Bogotá authorities. The reply was: "Do not proceed with the negotiations." [74]

Uribe Uribe warned Silva that the government's refusal to treat with him freed the Liberals from any responsibility for the prolongation of the fighting. He added that "the war could have ended when Marroquín succeeded to power." In regard to the canal treaty he urged the minister not to be in haste but to see what other nations might be willing to offer. He even suggested that Silva visit the chief European capitals before committing himself to a convention with the United States.[75]

Silva's reply of April 2 is important for the picture it gives of the intraparty divergencies with which Marroquín had to cope. It read in part:

The determining reason for that move [of July, 1900] was to put an immediate end to the war by means of a frank and patriotic understanding with the Liberals who were still in arms, and on this point we were very explicit in the previous conferences which those of us who assumed charge of the movement had with Señor Marroquín. Unfortunately, there interposed a wretched Conservative, or more accurately, Nationalist element which represented all the most odious aspects of the former regime; and, on the other hand, the guerrillas

---

[74] Urueta, *Documentos . . . del General Uribe Uribe*, pp. 168–169.

[75] *Ibid.*, pp. 169, 175–176. It was in this letter, written March 23, 1901, that Uribe Uribe stated his fears that Silva's mission was not one of statesmanship, but a petition for money to be used to wipe out a political party whose members were merely fighting for their rights under the constitution of 1886.

of Cundinamarca [the department which includes Bogotá] did not grasp the extent or the intrinsic meaning of the step taken by us, and believed that it was the moment to enter into an understanding with the Nationalists to take advantage of the situation. If their conduct had been otherwise, if they had had faith in the political and administrative integrity of the new Government, and laid down their arms, the fanatical and violent element of our party would have been left stifled; the republican Conservatives would have dominated the situation, the country would have been spared much bloodshed and misery, and the Liberal Party would have made greater progress toward the recognition of its rights than would have been gained by many battles.[76]

The minister concluded by urging that the Liberals suspend hostilities and trust to the "inevitable logic" of events to place the moderates in power once more.

In March of the following year Concha sounded out Dr. Antonio José Restrepo, a Liberal then residing in New York, with a view to opening parleys with General Vargas Santos which might provide a basis for peace negotiations. The resulting correspondence lasted until August, but accomplished nothing.[77]

Marroquín's only concession to the Liberals prior to the fall of 1902 was an offer of amnesty in June of that year. Full pardon was promised to all insurgents who would lay down their arms before a stated time except those guilty of common law crimes or of conducting intrigues with foreigners. The Liberals, however, spurned any truce which did not include formal guarantees of political rights.[78]

The merits of the administration's handling of the rebellion are not primarily under consideration here. Nevertheless, some of the consequences of the persistent refusal to compromise had a very direct influence upon the outcome of the canal negotiations. As we have seen above, Fernández' methods resulted in a prolongation of the conflict in Colombia, in a dangerous split in the Conservative party, and in the presence on the Isthmus of a well-disciplined army of rebels, ready to profit by any assistance the United States might be willing to extend. The Bogotá

---

[76] *Ibid.*, p. 177.   [77] *Cong. Rec.*, 57th Cong., 2nd Sess., pp. 2260–2261.
[78] Rougier, *Les Récentes Guerres civiles*, pp. 27, footnote 1, 28.

government thus found itself caught as by the action of a vise between the effects of its domestic policies and the constantly growing pressure exerted by the Department of State for a treaty.

V

The specter of North American intervention troubled Marroquín increasingly as the summer of 1902 advanced. The passage of the Spooner bill was considerably more of a victory for the Panama route than for Colombia in the sense that the act called for treaty terms even more advantageous to the United States than those of the April convention. No one was more fully aware than the vice-president of the utter incompatibility between the concessions demanded by Washington and those which the Colombian public was prepared to grant. He entertained no illusions as to the kind of reception his compatriots would accord a canal treaty drafted along the lines urged by Secretary Hay. On the other hand, he was becoming strongly apprehensive of the repercussions within his party and on the Isthmus which might follow a collapse of the parleys. When, about midsummer, he and Paúl came to recognize the critical nature of the dilemma confronting them, further attempts at actual negotiation practically ceased insofar as the Colombian government was concerned. From then until the November revolution of 1903 the administration's tactics seem to have been shaped primarily by its desire to unload upon the national congress full responsibility for choosing between the alternative evils that lay ahead.

An analysis of the records of Colombia's canal diplomacy from January, 1901, to July, 1902, discloses the surprising fact that at no time in those eighteen months were any treaty terms submitted to the United States which had their direct origin in Bogotá. The decisive steps of the negotiation were in every case taken by Silva or Concha on their own initiative, in partial or complete disregard of their instructions and under pressure of events in Washington. The work of formulating the treaty moved so rapidly in the first six months of 1902 that Marroquín and his advisers lost all control over the activities of their ministers.

Troubles at home were so numerous and the postal and cable services so unreliable that Bogotá's effective share in this vital phase of the negotiation was almost negligible.

The successive stages whereby this extraordinary situation developed are pertinent and can be presented in summarized form. Silva's optimistic dispatches of the spring of 1901 led Marroquín to conclude that Colombia was in a favorable bargaining position and that it would be possible to avoid "precipitating" the negotiation until internal peace had been restored.[79] By June, however, the minister's earlier assurance was wavering before his growing realization that the protection of the Clayton-Bulwer treaty was likely to be withdrawn. At a conference with Admiral Walker early in July he accepted without official instructions the principle of United States judicial and police control in the canal zone, in a form which, Marroquín later observed, "was inserted almost textually in the Hay-Herrán treaty." [80] Silva's other great error, in the vice-president's eyes, was the preparation of a treaty project on his own authority in January, 1902. While this paper was never officially presented, it came to the knowledge of Hay and the Walker Commission and "this fact . . . compromised the attitude of the Government, which ought to be prudent and reserved, and in addition made extremely difficult the negotiations which were to follow . . ." [81]

While Silva's advocacy of substantial canal concessions by Colombia and his disregard of instructions in dealing with Walker doubtless caused considerable irritation in Bogotá, there are strong indications that his removal was in good part the result of political animosity. His outspoken criticism of certain policies of the regime he had helped to install created powerful enemies for him within the party. When his close friend, Antonio José Uribe, resigned from the cabinet in September, 1901, Silva's

[79] *Anales diplomáticos y consulares,* IV, 805.
[80] *Ibid.,* IV, 806; *Libro azul,* p. 66. Silva admitted that "the principle of sovereignty will be somewhat affected . . . but it is the inevitable consequence of the circumstances in which Colombia is placed" (*Anales diplomáticos y consulares,* IV, 807).
[81] *Ibid.,* IV, 807.

letter of regret reflected his growing bitterness.[82] He deplored the unwillingness of other high officials to recognize the precarious state of the canal negotiation and spoke of the "insults and diatribes" which had rewarded his efforts in Washington. On other occasions he made no attempt to disguise his hostility to Fernández and his methods.[83] The fact that his brother was among those who had petitioned Marroquín to retire in favor of Sanclemente doubtless strengthened the hands of his foes. The vice-president later stated that Silva was recalled as much because "political differences had arisen between my Government and the minister in Washington concerning the manner of appraising issues connected with the revolution" as because of his "previous personal commitments."[84] Thus it would appear that Silva's abrupt departure from the diplomatic scene can be attributed in part to the same factors of discord within the administration that forced Nel Ospina and Uribe from the cabinet.[85]

Marroquín's own attitude toward the canal negotiations during this period throws much light upon his later difficulties. Although Silva had emphasized the necessity for prompt concessions to the United States if the selection of Nicaragua was to be prevented, Marroquín wrote him on December 6, 1901:

> ... I repeat that I harbor the insuperable resolution not to agree to anything that would diminish our sovereignty; neither North American jurisdiction over a span of our territory nor anything that the Government of the United States would have to refuse to us if the roles were interchanged . . .[86]

---

[82] Uribe, *Colombia y los Estados Unidos*, pp. xxxi–xxxii.
[83] Nieto Caballero, *Por qué soy liberal?* p. 49.
[84] *Anales diplomáticos y consulares*, IV, 809.
[85] Silva was imprisoned by Fernández in August, 1902, with several other citizens for writing a letter to Marroquín protesting the shooting of captured Liberals. State Dept., Dispatches from Colombia, Vol. 58, telegram, Sept. 24, 1902; Nieto Caballero, *Por qué soy liberal?* p. 51.
[86] *Anales diplomáticos y consulares*, IV, 807. This letter was omitted from the correspondence published in the *Libro azul*. In reading it to the Colombian congress in 1904 Marroquín said: "If later I changed my opinion, if I violated my purpose, it was owing to the manner in which the negotiations were planned and carried forward in Washington, . . . doing violence to my disposition and to my most vehement desires." *Ibid.*

Ten days later the Senate in Washington advised ratification of the second Hay-Pauncefote treaty and thereby, contingent upon similar approval by Great Britain, opened the way for the construction of an isthmian canal wholly under the control of the United States. This action, according to Marroquín, "ruptured the dikes placed against so-called American imperialism . . . It changed the face of the question and made the situation for the Government obscure, delicate and complex: action and inaction equally presented great problems and reason for anxiety."[87]

Evidently the risks of inaction were preferred, for Silva's pleading notes of December evoked no responsive sign in Bogotá. It was not until the dispatch of January 6 arrived with the details of the New Company's offer of sale and a final entreaty for specific canal proposals with which to counter the rapid progress of the Hepburn bill that Marroquín made a move.

The tragi-comedy of Colombia's indecisive diplomacy now commenced. Apparently rather dismayed at the magnitude of his responsibility, the vice-president summoned a conference of leading citizens to the San Carlos Palace on February 13 to study Silva's letter of January 8 and advise him on the fundamental points of the negotiation.[88] The conferees entered upon their task in total ignorance of the fact that Silva had completed a treaty draft two weeks before and that only the chance arrival of his orders of recall had prevented him from officially submitting it to Hay. As has been noted above, the majority report of the committee appointed by the junta advised firmly against any canal treaty whatever with the United States. After a lapse of four weeks a summary of this and of the Groot minority report was duly forwarded to Concha together with the bases on which the Colombian government *would* consent to negotiate a convention! As a further complication of the situation, the same communication instructed the minister that nothing was to be done about the canal until an understanding had been reached with the New Company and that his authority was therefore tempo-

---

[87] *Ibid.*, IV, 804–805.   [88] *Libro azul*, pp. 102–103.

THE COLOMBIAN DOCTOR'S DILEMMA 233

rarily limited to serving notice on the company and to "confirming to the United States the manifestation of good-will which animates . . . Colombia . . ."! [89] This confusing collection of material was the final product of two months of deliberation during one of the greatest diplomatic crises of Colombia's history. When Concha received it at long last, on April 26, he had already subscribed to the protocols which afterwards formed the basis of the Hay-Herrán treaty. His proffered resignation was refused by Marroquín and, characteristically enough, a commission of "specialists" was set up about the middle of May to examine the canal problem in the light of the minister's note of April 1.[90] Before the results of this new investigation could be incorporated into a definite policy the Spooner bill had been passed and Hay was suggesting amendments to the April memorandum. The Bogotá administration found itself unable to keep abreast of these developments, much less guide and control them.

Marroquín revealed his mental distress in a letter to General Pompilio Gutiérrez at Panama on July 26, 1902:

Concerning the canal question, I find myself in a horrible perplexity; in order that the North Americans may complete the work by virtue of a convention with the Government of Colombia, it is necessary to make concessions of territory, of sovereignty and of jurisdiction, which the Executive Power has not the power of yielding; and if we do not yield them and the North Americans determine to build the canal, they will open it without stopping at trifles, and then we will lose more sovereignty than we should lose by making the concessions they seek.

History will say of me that I ruined the Isthmus and all Colombia, by not permitting the opening of the Panama Canal, or that I permitted it to be done, scandalously injuring the rights of my country.

I would only be able to free myself of [my] responsibilities if I should succeed in transferring them to the congress and, as for that, God knows when it can be convened. I think that it would be unwise to call for elections until all the municipalities of the Republic are under control of the proper authorities.[91]

---

[89] *Ibid.*, pp. 116–117.
[90] *Anales diplomáticos y consulares*, IV, 820. This committee consisted of Uribe, Groot, and Clímaco Iriarte. All were very critical of the March 31 convention. Their reports are to be found in the *Libro azul*, Appendix, pp. 35–70.
[91] *Anales diplomáticos y consulares*, IV, 841.

Five weeks after this was written two thousand federal troops were captured at Aguadulce on the Isthmus and Herrera's army began to close in on Panama City.[92] This was the most serious setback that had yet befallen the Conservatives in that quarter. Furthermore, the effectiveness of the remaining government forces was seriously impaired by sickness and there seemed no prospect of retaining control of the railroad line. Marroquín, suddenly faced with disaster, determined to act. In defense of his subsequent course he later said:

The negotiations which were afoot, the sorry spectacle which was exhibited to the gaze of the world, the supreme necessity of terminating the war as soon as possible . . . obliged my Government to take an extreme resolution, which was to call upon the United States, through its minister in Bogotá and the legation in Washington, for American forces to reëstablish the freedom of the transit of the Panama railroad. This proceeding was not new, and although extremely distressing, it had not produced up until then results which might arouse the fears of Colombian patriotism.[93]

The first steps in the execution of this plan were designed to win the good-will of the Department of State by removing the chief obstacles from the path of the negotiation. All Hay's terms apart from the financial provisions were to be promptly accepted, subject to the approval of the Colombian congress.[94] Accordingly, on August 9 Marroquín wired Concha that ten millions in cash and an annuity of six hundred thousand after fourteen years were required to make the proposed amendments presentable to the congress.[95] When the minister flashed back word that he would not continue without further instructions, another wire

[92] *Use . . . of a Military Force in . . . Colombia*, p. 282.
[93] *Anales diplomáticos y consulares*, IV, 824.
[94] "I have become convinced," Marroquín wrote to Benjamín Aguilera of Panama on Oct. 24, 1902, "that the only method of contenting the Panamanians and escaping the disasters which await us, is to have the treaty signed in spite of the opposition which is growing" (*ibid.*, IV, 842).
[95] *Libro azul*, p. 235. The suddenness of this decision appears in the contrast between this cable and Paúl's letter of July 31 which was then on its way to Washington. It read in part: "Your determination not to lend yourself to the introduction of modifications in the *Memorandum* which might lessen the sovereignty of Colombia or deprive the interoceanic passage of its neutral character, is in harmony with the resolution of the Government." *Ibid.*, p. 234.

THE COLOMBIAN DOCTOR'S DILEMMA 235

was sent, on August 25: "Say to the American Government that the Colombian Government accepts in principle the recent suggested amendments. . . . Ratifications of congress necessary; the assembling of which awaits only the pacification of Panama." [96] Concha, bewildered at the turn events were taking and wholly in the dark about the reason for these unexpected orders, quietly refrained from delivering the message to Hay. In more extended communications on August 13 and September 9 Paúl stressed the government's desire for haste but offered no hint as to his real motives.[97] The second note conferred special powers upon Concha to sign a treaty *ad referendum* with as little sacrifice of Colombia's sovereignty as would prove compatible with the demands of the United States. Under any circumstances, however, the treaty was to be signed. Paúl's failure to admit his representative to his confidence at this point was a major error, the consequences of which have already been described.[98]

On September 11 the Colombian government officially requested the good offices of the United States toward the restoration of peace, "especially on the Isthmus, where the revolution is strong." [99] The foreign minister stressed the fact that "the continuance of the war will delay submission of the canal matter to the congress." Washington responded by ordering the senior naval officer at Colón to use his influence in arranging a conference between the warring factions.[100] These instructions reached Commander McLean on the 18th, the day after the first detachments had been sent ashore to guard the railroad.

Having offered the United States evidences of his coöperative spirit by yielding on the Hay amendments and by indicating his desire for an early peace, Marroquín was now ready to launch the second part of his plan. Unaware that McLean had already landed his men, he wired Concha on September 20 that General Perdomo would soon reach the Isthmus with a large force and it was time "to demand of the United States the execution of the Convention of 1846 to assure the transit from Panama to Co-

[96] *Ibid.*, p. 253. [97] *Ibid.*, pp. 235–237, 246–249. [98] *Supra*, p. 164 ff.
[99] *Use . . . of a Military Force in . . . Colombia*, p. 284. [100] *Ibid.*

lón."[101] Two days later, apparently in reply to a protest from the Washington legation, he and Paúl cabled: "We do not know the form of the intervention of the Government of the United States of America. We only ask the execution of article thirty-five of the treaty of forty-six, as has already been done in analogous circumstances."[102]

From a military point of view Marroquín's strategy was a complete success. While the North American naval units kept the rebels away from the railroad, Perdomo was able to assemble his troops at Colón unmolested. After October 22 he was permitted to march them along the line of transit and by the end of the month all restrictions on his use of the trains had been removed by Admiral Casey.[103] The insurgents offered no opposition. They understood clearly that the United States had selected the victor in their domestic struggle. To contest that choice would have been futile. Nieto Caballero describes the intervention from the Liberal's angle:

Herrera would have been able to take Panama, that is, the capital, because the department was his, but in endeavoring to realize this a specter appeared. The government had sought American intervention. The same marines which in after years were to offend the dignity of Cuba, of Santo Domingo, of Haiti, of Nicaragua, appeared by the treaty of 1846 . . . to guarantee the free transit of the railroad, threatened by the revolutionary forces. Herrera gave a roar. Later he bowed his head. . . . It was the fatherland that suffered the

---

[101] *Libro azul*, p. 253.

[102] *Ibid.*, p. 254. "If on other occasions," Marroquín declared in 1904, "that means had been justified, on this it was much more so, because the preponderance or the triumph of the revolution in Panama, in addition to placing the government in the gravest danger and postponing the hour of the much-desired peace, engendered threats to the national integrity and lessened the advantages which the republic might obtain in the negotiation of the Panama Canal. . . . The summoning of American forces to the Isthmus in fulfillment of the Treaty of 1846 had already been accomplished during the revolution under circumstances identical with those which confronted me; it had produced the results desired without diminution of sovereignty, and had merited the complete approval of Dr. Concha's predecessor in the Washington legation." *Anales diplomáticos y consulares*, IV, 824–825. The reference to Silva's approval of the intervention of the fall of 1901 is based upon a section of the latter's dispatch of Dec. 6, 1901, which was omitted from the *Libro azul* but which is to be found in *ibid.*, IV, 825.

[103] *Supra*, p. 172.

offense. For the sake of its sovereignty it was necessary to turn his back on victory.[104]

The treaty of Panama, signed on board the *Wisconsin* on November 21, was by no means an unconditional surrender on Herrera's part. Not only was complete amnesty granted to all revolutionists accepting its terms but the government also conceded certain important political guaranties.[105] By article 7 the administration undertook to call special congressional elections and "to employ all its authority to carry them out in a wholly legal manner." The legislature so chosen was to study and act upon three major issues: the Panama Canal negotiations, the reforms suggested to the 1898 congress by Marroquín, and the revision of the monetary system, "permitting an amortization of the paper money by means of the revenues which the Republic will derive from conventions agreed upon concerning the canal." The treaties of Chinácota (of the same date as that of Panama) and Nerlandia (signed on October 24) provided that the Liberal forces of the departments of Santander, Magdalena, and Bolívar should lay down their arms in return for assurances of fair electoral practices in choosing the local and national assemblies.[106] The conclusion of these agreements of October and November, 1902, broke the back of the rebellion, although sporadic disorders continued in various parts of the republic for several months.

With the dangers of internal disruption and external aggression temporarily removed, the Colombian government was at last in a position to devote its energies wholeheartedly to the canal parleys. Unfortunately, there was very little about the convention that remained open to discussion. In the process of securing the good-will and assistance of the Washington authorities Marroquín and his foreign minister had assumed an attitude of tractability regarding Hay's amendments to the April protocol which had been more expedient than sincere. Whether the secre-

[104] *Por qué soy liberal?* p. 54.
[105] Rougier, *Les Récentes Guerres civiles,* p. 31, footnote.
[106] *Ibid.,* pp. 28, 29 footnote.

tary suspected this and anticipated a Colombian attempt to recover lost ground once the pressure on the Isthmus had been relieved, or whether he was motivated only by the need of concluding a canal agreement in time for action by the coming session of the Senate, it is impossible to say with any certainty. In either event, he knew from Concha's note of October 26 that Bogotá had given orders to sign the treaty and he had indicated his unwillingness to humor the minister's obduracy indefinitely. On November 22, the day after the conclusion of the treaty of Panama, he cabled the legation in Bogotá in an effort to bring the negotiation to a head. Hart was instructed first to congratulate the Colombian government on the cessation of the civil war and then to warn it that the time had come for a prompt statement as to whether it wanted the canal or not. The envoy was to point out that all possible concessions in the treaty provisions had been made by the United States and that Nicaragua had offered a "perfectly satisfactory" convention.[107]

Three days later Hart dispatched his reply:

Minister of Foreign Affairs wishes you to be informed that Colombia wants canal and in view of the attitude of Colombian Minister Secretary of Legation has been telegraphed as follows:
First. If Minister refuses to sign treaty Secretary of Legation is to take charge the Legation and to sign.
Second. The Legation is to require in writing your ultimatum declining to make further concessions to Colombia.
Third. The Legation to ask increase in sum to be paid Colombia. Note. This in order to satisfy the views Congress is expected to entertain, and to show that the effort was made.
Fourth. It must be definitely understood that the whole treaty is to be submitted for consideration Congress. . . .[108]

This telegraphic exchange offers a fairly frank picture of the diplomatic situation at the time of Concha's withdrawal. The Colombian government had, in fact, lost its freedom to negotiate on any provision except that dealing with the indemnity. Paúl's dissatisfaction with the pact exudes from every line of his in-

[107] State Dept., Instructions to Colombia, Vol. 19, Nov. 22, 1902.
[108] State Dept., Dispatches from Colombia, Vol. 58, telegram, Hart to Hay, Nov. 25, 1902.

structions to Herrán. It was to be signed because the administration did not care to face the domestic consequences of refusing. The tactics to be employed in presenting it to the electorate were clearly indicated: the edge was to be taken off the national disappointment, if possible, by increasing the pecuniary attractions; a written ultimatum was to be obtained as evidence that the government had done its best, and the responsibility for acceptance, modification, or rejection was to rest with the congress. It was not a statesmanlike program, but it was the best escape Marroquín could devise from the forces closing in upon him. The government's dilemma gives added significance to the efforts Paúl was putting forth at this time to force the New Company to share its $40,000,000. Such an arrangement would have been regarded as a distinct triumph for Colombian diplomacy and would have measurably increased the prospect of ratification.

Herrán's task was to fight a rear-guard skirmish with Hay in the hope that the canal company would succumb or that the United States would consent to further concessions. The instructions which reached him on January 16 ordered him to work for better financial terms, but "if this is not possible and you see that everything may be lost by delay, sign the treaty." [109] The minister did sign on the 22d after receiving the Department of State's ultimatum. Two days later the following dispatch left Bogotá:

> Señor Paúl and I have directed a cable of this same date, in which we said not to sign the treaty relative to the Panama Canal without receiving new instructions.
> Our circumstances have greatly changed; the triumph over the revolution has given the government the power and prestige which might have been lacking before because of the doubt which would have been entertained in the United States and elsewhere as to which political group would finally prove master of the Isthmus. Today the Government of the United States has to recognize that, if some [group] is to be dealt with, it must be mine. Other circumstances make us think that our position is today much better than during the period in which the negotiations began. . . .
> The general opinion in Colombia, or at least that most worthy of

[109] *Libro azul*, p. 335.

being regarded, is that the treaty should not be approved on the conditions proposed by the Government of the United States. Less diminution of our sovereignty is wished and much greater pecuniary advantages are desired than those offered. What I wish now is not to manifest my opinion without consulting that of the Congress, which, fortunately, will meet within two months.[110]

[110] *Anales diplomáticos y consulares,* IV, 840–841.

VII

THE RISE OF PROTEST IN COLOMBIA

W<small>HILE</small> M<small>ARROQUÍN</small>, in isolated Bogotá, was drafting orders for the suspension of the canal negotiations, the North American press was hailing the pact just signed in Washington. Prompt ratification by both parties was generally predicted, although it required little reading between the lines to discern a vague editorial uneasiness regarding Marroquín's dependability. On January 24, the very day on which the vice-president and Paúl cabled Herrán not to sign the treaty, the New York *Times* carried a report from its Washington correspondent that "assurances have been given by the Colombian Government that this Government may rely on the completion of the agreement . . ." Two days later the editor observed pointedly that "having authorized Mr. Herrán to sign the treaty, the Government at Bogotá will naturally be expected to ratify it without delay." [1]

A few dailies which had refused to reconcile themselves to the choice of the Panama route continued to raise voices of protest and warning. The New York *Herald* characterized the convention as a "stupendous blunder" and the Colombian authorities as "not competent to make a binding treaty." After picturing the humiliation of the United States in the event of a rejection, the paper concluded that the "Panama scheme, nurtured in scandal, seems destined to remain tainted until the end." [2]

The Senate's action in approving the treaty on March 17 had been so long expected as to cause little stir among the journalists. The *Review of Reviews* complained that the "details of the arrangement . . . are in some respects so far from being clean-cut and satisfactory that intelligent Americans will prefer not to read the text of the treaty . . ." while the *Nation* was convinced that

[1] N. Y. *Times,* Jan. 26, 1903.   [2] N. Y. *Herald,* Jan. 24, 1903.

"it would be difficult to point out any feature to which reasonable exception could be taken." [3] For the most part the press conceded that the better route had been selected and turned its attention to the views of public men on the prospects of an early exchange of ratifications. Hanna, Lodge, Aldrich, and other Senate leaders were confident that the United States would soon be able to start work on the canal.[4] The Colombian consul-general in New York, de Brigard, was of the opinion that "as political affairs in Colombia stand at present, there is no person or party strong enough to defeat the wishes of the President." He admitted that Senator Vélez might attack the convention for limiting the nation's isthmian sovereignty, but he was careful to add that this would be "for political purposes only, not with the idea that it will have any effect." [5] Edward B. Hill, one of Cromwell's closest legal associates, anticipated no important opposition, although he acknowledged that some objections might be raised around Bogotá, "a State [sic] far removed from the line of the canal." [6] The *Nation* felt that "some little sputtering" might be expected in Colombia, "but it is not to be supposed that the $10,000,000 which we are to pay that country for the privilege of making it the highway of nations will be thrown away for any sentimental considerations by the politicians at Bogotá." [7] The prevalent attitude was well expressed by an editorial comment of the New York *Sun:* "The proposed arrangement is too greatly to the advantage of Colombia to make its rejection conceivable. The Colombian statesmen may be quarrelsome, but they are not fools. President Marroquín, in particular, is far from being a fool." [8]

By the early spring of 1903 the basis of popular misunderstanding of the treaty situation in Colombia had been effectively, if unintentionally, established in the United States. Reliable information seemed to be unobtainable, even through the Colombian legation. Press comment consisted for the most part of hearsay and wishful thinking. The protreaty periodicals, complacent

[3] *Review of Reviews*, XXVII, 388; *The Nation*, LXXVI, 84.
[4] N. Y. *Tribune*, March 18, 1903 [5] *Ibid.*, March 23, 1903.
[6] N. Y. *Times*, March 18, 1903. [7] *The Nation*, LXXVI, 219.
[8] N. Y. *Sun*, March 28, 1903.

THE RISE OF PROTEST IN COLOMBIA 243

over Hay's "generous treatment" of a weak sister republic, regarded the Bogotá government with patronizing indulgence as long as ratification appeared likely, while the opposition minority exhausted its armories of ridicule and abuse. Neither group had any comprehension of the limitations upon Marroquín's power in Colombia nor of the nature of the circumstances under which the treaty was signed. Both depicted the vice-president as an absolute and irresponsible dictator who had entered into the canal pact upon terms quite satisfactory to himself and, presumably, to the little clique of politicians that surrounded him. Such farcical gestures as the convocation of a national congress were conceded in most quarters to be unobjectionable if done in good faith, that is, without imperiling the bargain that had been struck. It was naturally assumed that only such criticism of the treaty would appear as the despot permitted. Since, according to the current belief, power was concentrated in Marroquín's hands, his authorization to sign the convention was generally construed to be the equivalent of a pledge of ratification. Opponents of the treaty accepted without question the vice-president's reputed ability to force through any arrangement he desired, confining themselves rather to pointing out the disadvantages of the route, the insufficiency of the provisions for control, and the possibility that some future regime in Bogotá might denounce the treaty as the act of a usurper. The contingency that the approaching congress might insist upon radical amendments does not seem to have occurred to them as important.[9]

This distorted press version of Marroquín's position left the reading public in the United States wholly unprepared for the developments that followed. Offered in good faith by the majority of publications, it nevertheless precluded any well-informed discussion of the summer's events in Colombia and paved the way for popular approval of the Panama revolution in November.

More striking than the ignorance of the press on Colombian

[9] *Public Opinion*, XXXIV, No. 13, 387; *The Nation*, LXXVI, 84, 219; *Review of Reviews*, XXVII, 271–272, 388–393.

THE RISE OF PROTEST IN COLOMBIA

affairs is the fact that the Department of State was scarcely better informed itself. An adequate knowledge of political conditions in Bogotá would have prevented a series of departmental errors of judgment during the spring and summer of 1903 and might possibly have averted the outright rejection of the treaty. Part of the responsibility for this deficiency is attributable to Minister Charles B. Hart, whose task it was to keep his superiors posted on all aspects of his charge which might directly or indirectly affect the interests of the United States. His dispatches, commendable in their handling of routine matters and the military news of the insurrection, nowhere pointed out in clear-cut fashion the pressures that were relentlessly diminishing the government's freedom of action during the critical months of the canal negotiation. On the other hand, Hart was not sufficiently apprised of the happenings in Washington in the late summer and fall of 1902 to be of full service to the department. Had he seen the diplomatic picture whole he might have been able to enlighten Hay on the strategy behind Marroquín's willingness to accept almost any treaty conditions when the Liberals were knocking at the gates of Panama and Colón. As it was, the secretary of state came to the false conclusion, on receiving Concha's note of October 26, that the vice-president was satisfied with everything except the compensation. Better coördination between Washington and the Bogotá legation in December and January would probably have disclosed the important fact that Marroquín intended to sign the treaty only as a final expedient to prevent a rupture in the negotiations until the Colombian congress could assume charge. If Hay had any inkling of this purpose, his subsequent actions did not disclose it.

Throughout the increasing tension of the spring months, when the seriousness of the Colombian opposition was becoming evident, the Department of State maintained the attitude that the Bogotá administration had eagerly demanded and entered into a treaty with the United States and therefore was obligated to ensure its ratification without change.[10] It was pointed out that

[10] *Dip. Hist. of the Panama Canal*, pp. 385, 392.

THE RISE OF PROTEST IN COLOMBIA 245

Marroquín had given repeated assurances of his readiness to sign if the indemnity provision were increased. That had been done, the pact had been duly signed, and it only remained for the Colombian government to fulfill the rest of the bargain. The implication is clear that the United States proposed to hold the vice-president personally responsible for the legislative fate of the treaty. What Hay and his shrewder assistant, Adee, had apparently overlooked was the significance of Marroquín's reiterated intention to submit the convention to his legislature for final decision. Nothing could have been more emphatic than these persistent declarations. Yet the State Department, dismissing them as unimportant in the winter, denounced Marroquín for acting upon them a few months later. Even the mediocre Hart, given proper coöperation from his superiors, might have thrown timely light on the underlying purpose of these insertions.

Hart took his final departure from Bogotá shortly after the middle of March, 1903. He had been called home the previous spring to answer charges preferred against him by personal creditors in Colombia. Apparently he failed to satisfy the department for, although he was permitted to return to his post in July, he soon sent in his resignation for acceptance at pleasure. The unexpected treaty complications that attended the naval intervention on the Isthmus in the fall and the need for an experienced representative during the protracted negotiations with Herrán probably account for the delayed action in his case. On February 4, however, his resignation was formally accepted and the legation secretary, Arthur M. Beaupré, was appointed to succeed him.[11] The fact that this replacement occurred within a fortnight of the signing of the treaty would seem another indication that the Department of State at that time anticipated no difficulty over Colombia's ratification.

[11] State Dept.: Dispatches from Colombia, Vol. 58, Hart to Hay, Unnumbered, Aug. 27, 1902; Instructions to Colombia, Vol. 19, Hay to Hart, No. 450, Feb. 4, 1903, and Hay to Beaupré, No. 1, Feb. 20, 1903. Hart left Bogotá March 19 and Beaupré was officially received by Marroquín April 13.

II

During the weeks that followed the conclusion of the treaties of Panama and Chinácota in November, 1902, the Bogotá authorities turned to the complex tasks of demobilization and restoration. Late in November all political prisoners were pardoned and exiles permitted to return.[12] The government forces were reduced first to 50,000 and later to 25,000 men.[13] Certain wartime restrictions upon private business were lightened in December and early the next year foreign trade was encouraged by the practical abolition of export duties.[14] By a legislative decree of November 24 elections were ordered for a special session of the national congress. Citizens of all parties were assured in an official circular at the end of the year that they could "freely cast their votes" not in "anxiety and restlessness" but in the "tranquil exercise of the franchise." [15]

On New Year's Day the vice-president published an address to the Colombian people which Washington might well have read to better profit. It said in part:

My Government is faced with this dilemma [in connection with the canal]: We must either allow our sovereign rights to suffer and renounce certain pecuniary advantages to which, as many believe, we have a right, or we must vigorously stand up for our sovereign rights and claim peremptorily the pecuniary indemnity to which we have a right to consider ourselves entitled. In the first case . . . should the canal be opened through Panama, the just wishes of the inhabitants of that department and of all Colombians will be satisfied; but the Government lays itself open to the future charge of not having duly defended our sovereignty and with having sacrificed the interests of the nation. In the second case, should the canal not be opened through Panama, it will be laid to the charge of the Govern-

---

[12] State Dept., Dispatches from Colombia, Vol. 58, Hart to Hay, No. 692, Nov. 27, 1902.

[13] *Ibid.*, Vol. 58, Hart to Hay, No. 696, Dec. 2, 1902; Vol. 59, Hart to Hay, No. 718, Jan. 12, 1903.

[14] *Consular Reports*, LXXI, 465–466, 605, 616.

[15] Legislative Decree No. 1719 of 1902 reported by Hart to Hay, in State Dept., Dispatches from Colombia, Vol. 58, No. 692, Nov. 27, 1902. The election circular appears in *Diario oficial*, 1903, pp. 5–6.

ment that it did not allow Colombia to benefit by this undertaking which is regarded as the foundation of our future greatness. I have already expressed my desire that the interoceanic canal should be opened through our territory. I think that even at the cost of making sacrifices, we should put no obstacle in the way of so great an undertaking, for it means an enormous material improvement for our country, and, should the canal once be opened by the people of the United States, our relations with that people would be drawn closer. The result would be an incalculable gain for our industry, our commerce and our wealth. Happily for me, the immense responsibility of coming to a decision falls to Congress. That is the body which has to give its approbation or disapprobation to the agreement proposed by the Government of the United States.[16]

As a brief statement of the problem this paragraph is admirable. However, the vice-president is—perhaps purposely—vague on one point. While stressing the fact that the national congress must give its "approbation or disapprobation" to the "agreement proposed by the Government of the United States," he does not specifically say that he will commit his administration to its defense by signing it first. This might appear a quibble were it not for the note he dispatched to Washington three weeks later ordering Herrán to withhold his signature until the legislature could take over the negotiations.[17] The question naturally arises whether this device for evading personal responsibility was not already taking form in the executive's mind at the beginning of January. Be that as it may, the New Year's Day address is one more clear indication that Marroquín was deeply dissatisfied with the treaty and that he welcomed the prospect of shifting the burden to other shoulders.

Important cabinet changes in Bogotá followed soon after the signing of the treaty. Paúl resigned the portfolio of foreign affairs on January 24, probably immediately after the arrival of Herrán's cable with the news from Washington. The ministers of public instruction and the treasury successively discharged the duties of the post until Dr. Luis Carlos Rico, former minister to Venezuela and a close friend of Marroquín, took office on

[16] *Diario oficial*, 1903, p. 3. [17] *Supra*, pp. 239–240.

March 11.[18] Meanwhile, hostilities over and the army reduced, Fernández began to improve his political position with an eye on the next presidential election. Early in February he had himself promoted to the ministry of state (*gobierno*), the most important peacetime post in the cabinet. Hart summarized the significance of the general's appointment:

> The incumbent is regarded as the political chief of the cabinet under the President. In the event of the death, resignation or disability of the President, Vice-President and the "Designado" (a kind of second Vice-President), the Minister of Government succeeds at once to the executive power. The titular President is dead; the Vice-President is exercising the executive power; the "Designado," General Rafael Reyes, is out of the country and is not regarded as a potent factor in current politics. In addition to this, General Fernández is now regarded as the most powerful man in the country, and his appointment as Minister of Government is an official recognition of his strength. Moreover, as he is a candidate for the Presidency, the appointment is interpreted as the Government's acceptance of his candidacy. It is believed that the Congress about to be chosen will further strengthen the position of General Fernández by naming him the "Designado." [19]

The congressional elections did not get under way until after the middle of March and then proceeded so slowly that the government delayed its announcement of the day of meeting.[20] Beaupré, newly in charge of the United States legation, showed uneasiness over the trend of treaty discussion in the capital. "Without question," he wrote, "public opinion is strongly against its ratification, but, of course, public opinion in Colombia is not necessarily a potent factor in controlling legislation." Nevertheless, the early returns on the balloting were not encouraging. Although it had been expected that the government would manage the elections sufficiently to ensure that the successful candidates would "be favorable to the administration's view" on the canal question, prominent and able leaders of the Nationalist party,

---

[18] *Libro azul*, Appendix, p. 159; *Diario oficial*, 1903, p. 121.

[19] State Dept., Dispatches from Colombia, Vol. 59, Hart to Hay, No. 723, Feb. 6, 1903.

[20] *Libro azul*, p. 361; *Dip. Hist. of the Panama Canal*, p. 379.

THE RISE OF PROTEST IN COLOMBIA 249

opposed to Marroquín and the Hay-Herrán treaty, were victorious. Ex-President Caro and General Pedro Nel Ospina, for example, were to represent the department of Antioquia in the senate. "It seems altogether probable," Beaupré stated, "that unless the Government is thoroughly in earnest in its desire to have the convention ratified, it will not be done; and there is a possibility that it may not go through in any event." [21]

By the end of March disturbing rumors of Colombian opposition were afloat in the North American press. On the 27th, the New York *World* reported that Silva and Concha "are now in Bogotá laying plans to defeat the treaty" with the latter "personally directing the fight." [22] The opposition was said to be well supplied with funds and relying upon assistance from European sources. Counter-reports quickly put in an appearance from Panama. They were evidently intended to be reassuring, but by their very substance they served to raise doubts where none had been before. The delay in calling the congress was ascribed to the circumstance that the government, "desiring by all means the approval of the treaty, wanted to know the opinion of all the Representatives beforehand and therefore sent special Commissioners through the country." It was added that "lucrative Government positions" had been offered to certain congressmen-elect known to be hostile to the convention for the purpose of preventing their attendance at the capital.[23] To the extent that they re-

---

[21] State Dept., Dispatches from Colombia, Vol. 59, Beaupré to Hay, No. 741, March 30, 1903.

[22] Silva had died on Feb. 10, 1903, in Tunja, Colombia.

[23] N. Y. *Times*, April 5, 1903. There is no corroborating evidence for these reports. They evoked a sharp reply from D. A. González Torres, Colombian consul in Amberes [probably Anvers], Belgium, which was reprinted in *El Correo Nacional* from the *XX Century* of Brussels. The consul protested that it "is absolutely false . . . to say that the Government, with the purpose of assuring votes, has offered lucrative positions to members of Congress recognized as decided adversaries of the Herrán-Hay Treaty. It is equally false that the votes of the Representatives of the Department of The Cauca are already won in favor of the Treaty; very much to the contrary: the majority of these Representatives are absolutely hostile to the mentioned Treaty, and no one has the right to judge them capable of selling their votes. These are unfounded accusations, resulting from the discontent of the United States at seeing that Colombia does not bend to all its pretensions and needs." (Dated April 16, 1903, and reprinted in *El Correo Nacional* of July 3.)

ceived credence these clumsy attempts at electoral manipulation produced an unfavorable newspaper reaction. They did not harmonize well with the journalistic picture of the smoothly functioning political machinery of a dictatorship. By April 16 the New York *Times,* while depreciating stories of European interference, was expressing anxiety over the ultimate fate of the treaty.

The anxiety of the *Times's* editorial writer would have been greatly heightened by a perusal of the report which was then on its way to the Department of State from Colombia. Beaupré's dispatch of April 15 brought tidings of a recent "outburst of controversy, both in the Bogotá press and among the public in this city, with regard to the Panama Canal convention." The minister attributed this unexpected development to a circular issued by Fernández inviting the press of the capital to discuss the treaty. The notice, he explained, "was to the effect that the Government had no preconceived wishes for or against the measure; that it was for Congress to decide, and Congress would be largely guided by public opinion." At the same time what purported to be a translation of the text of the convention was published. According to Beaupré, the strict censorship imposed during the recent civil war had destroyed "anything like public opinion." News of the signing of the treaty had therefore been received with complete apathy except for a feeling of relief at the prospect of acquiring $10,000,000, which was then considered reasonably sufficient to restore the nation's finances. "I am convinced I am right," he added, "in saying that the public had never expected better terms." Since that time a marked change in attitude had occurred, passing from approbation to suspicion and finally to decided opposition. The newspapers of the city

> are full of strongly worded articles denouncing the convention, . . . which they represent as being the attempt of a strong nation to take an unfair advantage of the crisis through which Colombia is passing, and, for a paltry sum, rob her of one of the most valuable sources of wealth which the world contains.

As an example of the absurd arguments advanced in support of these attacks, he cited the contention of one writer that the United States would start the canal with "a clear profit of $190,-000,000." Beaupré concluded his report with a veiled hint that some kind of pressure would improve the treaty's prospects.

> This fact is clear, that if the proposed convention were to be submitted to the free opinion of the people it would not pass. The Congress about to assemble has been elected under the supervision of Government officials, and a system of quite indigenous wirepulling has undoubtedly been used; and yet if Congress, as now constituted, were allowed to give a free vote I feel convinced the convention would not be ratified. . . . As to what will happen, it is impossible to predict; yet this much seems certain to me, if it is the wish of the Government that the convention be ratified it will be done.[24]

This dispatch presents most of the facts and suppositions upon which the Department of State based its subsequent policy towards Colombia. These may be summarized as follows: (1) that the "general public" of Colombia was at first indifferent towards the treaty and the financial terms were all that had been expected; (2) that the government unnecessarily started trouble by lifting the press censorship and inviting free discussion of the convention; (3) that the government, by adopting a neutral attitude on the issue, encouraged attacks upon the treaty; (4) that while the administration "undoubtedly" controlled elections for congress, prominent opponents of the treaty were permitted to win seats; (5) that popular sentiment had been so thoroughly aroused against the treaty that a free poll of either congress or the people would result in a vote of rejection; and (6) that the government still had the power, if it wished to use it, to force the treaty through.

While these conclusions were not entirely in accordance with fact, as will be seen, they constituted reasonable deductions from Beaupré's superficial analysis of the situation. Also, they reflected with substantial accuracy the Colombian government's passive

[24] State Dept., Dispatches from Colombia, Vol. 59, Beaupré to Hay, No. 6, April 15, 1903.

policy towards ratification. Had the department carefully studied the vice-president's New Year's address or had Hart in his many months of contact with high officials in Bogotá correctly fathomed their sincere discontent with the treaty, Beaupré's report would have contained fewer surprises. But Hay and Adee were apparently still working on the premise that Marroquín had been reasonably satisfied with the terms secured by Herrán and that an implied promise of ratification had been given. On the basis of these assumptions the good faith of the Colombian authorities naturally began to come under suspicion. The sudden opposition to a pact negotiated by a freshly victorious dictator could have originated only at the source of power. If, as some observers were hopefully suggesting, the maneuver was no more than a mysterious quirk of Latin-American domestic politics which would somehow straighten itself out before a final vote was taken on the treaty, all might be well. But darker motives, involving possible further pecuniary demands upon the United States, might also have inspired the recent developments. The dispatch of April 15 rudely punctured the department's belief that Colombian ratification could be taken for granted; thereafter it was constantly on the alert for signs of "treachery" in Bogotá. The seeds of the "blackmail" theory had been sown.

III

It may be useful at this point to examine the nature of the newspaper attacks on the treaty to which Beaupré referred. To begin with, the minister was incorrect not only in his statement that the Colombian public was apathetic on the canal question but also in his inference that the censorship had prevented discussion of it previous to the publication of the Fernández circular. All printed matter had been strictly supervised during the revolution, it is true, but for reasons of its own the government had permitted, and even encouraged, free expression of opinion on this topic.[25] In the summer of 1902 some of the correspondence

[25] Francisco Groot in a letter to *El Colombiano* on May 20, 1902, stated that the "free discussion which the Government has permitted even before the re-

between Bogotá and the Colombian legation in Washington was released to the press until Concha advised discontinuance of the practice on the grounds that it might cause a "serious perturbation in the future." [26] On August 5, however, Foreign Minister Paúl announced his desire to give full publicity to the canal question in order that all points of view could be made known.[27] From that time on, pertinent correspondence and documents appeared regularly, though in somewhat jumbled sequence, in *El Colombiano* and *El Correo Nacional* of Bogotá.[28] On September 25, after Concha had been ordered to accept Hay's terms—with a higher indemnity, if possible—and after the assistance of the United States had been invoked to crush the Liberal threat on the Isthmus, Paúl instructed the governors of the provinces to see that the local press discussed the Panama project with complete liberty so that the members of the approaching congress might become familiar with the trend of public opinion.[29] Fernández' circular of March 12, after Paúl had left office, was no more than a restatement of a well-established policy, intended from very early to prepare the way for shifting the treaty responsibility from the administration to congress.

The "sudden outburst of controversy" was not owing to any abrupt awakening of popular interest but to the fact that previously there had been nothing very definite for the publicists to wax controversial over. The first notice of the signing of the convention appeared February 4, but the terms were a matter of speculation until a so-called text was printed on March 12.[30] This, however, did not agree with a version published five days later by *El Correo Nacional*, which had obtained it from *La Estrella*

---

establishment of public order has been completed, seems to indicate that it will not contract any commitment respecting the canal, but that it will leave this solution to Congress."

[26] *Libro azul*, p. 252.   [27] *El Colombiano*, Aug. 5, 1902.

[28] *El Colombiano*, for example, printed the entire text of Senator Morgan's speech of June 12, 1902, attacking the Panama route and immediately under it the manifesto of the Liberal leaders of April, 1900, opposing Sanclemente's extension of the New Company's franchise.

[29] *Diario oficial*, 1903, p. 73.

[30] *El Colombiano*, Feb. 4, 1903; *El Correo Nacional*, March 12, 1903.

de Panamá.[31] The official copy, differing from both the others, was withheld for an unexplained reason until May 13.[32]

Contrary to the impression given by the United States minister, discussions of the canal problem were frequently featured in the daily and periodical press of the capital throughout the fall of 1902. Most of them dealt with the historical background of the project or with its probable status, when completed, in international law. Soon after Concha's dramatic departure from Washington, however, a marked undercurrent of hostility toward the negotiations set in, originating primarily in the growing realization that the United States would insist upon full and permanent jurisdiction over the canal zone and secondarily in recent reports of the highhanded conduct of North American naval officers on the Isthmus.

By January the preservation of Colombian sovereignty had become a favorite journalistic theme. In an editorial entitled "Let Us Be Practical," the conservative *Correo Nacional* lamented that for many years the Colombians had occupied themselves with copious talk and sentiment about the canal, and now

> when in the brief term of one legislature a final decision must be given, the public opinion has still not been enunciated, has not even been formulated, because of all its phases that which has least concerned us has been the practical and concrete, such as must be considered by the congress.

The editor admitted that with the abrogation of the Clayton-Bulwer treaty and the refusal of European governments to intervene no alternative remained to a direct negotiation with the United States. "Today," he wrote, ". . . the Yankee control of the canal is a fact which we must accept as the unavoidable basis of all that is projected in this respect." Since the diplomacy of the United States was based on the Spooner law, which required the acquisition of "dominion" and "jurisdiction" over a strip of territory across the Isthmus, the real question was whether Colombia was ready to cede such a strip. "We believe," he continued,

[31] *El Correo Nacional,* March 17, 1903. The text in *La Estrella* was printed January 27.
[32] *Diario oficial,* 1903, p. 233.

THE RISE OF PROTEST IN COLOMBIA 255

that everything aside from this dilemma does nothing but becloud the negotiation. . . . In fine, let us be practical: fewer advantages if you will, but more solid ones; so that in every negotiation or treaty that is made our rights remain based on realistic grounds and not on air castles of universal justice which disappear on the morrow before the batteries of a squadron.[33]

This appeal was utterly lost on such ebullient spirits as General Julio Fernández M., whose communication appeared in *La Constitución* of Bogotá on January 27:

If we believe—unhappily—that the North Americans alone can construct the greatest work of the Twentieth Century, in which not only Asia, but also Europe holds more interest than the United States, let us not be deceived like children, and let us put our ultimatum in proper and complete form: . . . either a joint company, *or we make it by ourselves alone, before or after, or while the Nicaragua Canal is being made.* Nothing more, nothing less.

A few days later *El Porvenir* sounded a note frequently heard during the next six months:

We imagine that if Dr. Concha's mission was not successful at the Washington chancellery it should be attributed to the fact that our minister did not wish to accede to clauses injurious to the essential interests of Colombia; and that was his duty. The presence of Yankee rule on the Isthmus, call it by its technical name or by those of perpetual domination, possession or undefined control, is incompatible with the sovereignty of the fatherland; it would be equivalent to encasing a powerful state in a weak one, and the most unrealistic understands what our people's fate would be in such an eventuality.

Colombia ought not to meddle in an adventure of this kind. Let us joyfully renounce the honor of a canal across Panama before we accept a treaty with such a large gullet.

Not an atom of our sovereignty nor a stone of our territory.[34]

With the publication of the March 12 version of the treaty the journalistic attacks grew more numerous and, in many instances, more specific. Signs of bitterness increased. The issue seemed to provide a convenient counterirritant for the distemper of the times. It opened a new channel for feelings roiled by years of civil strife. It offered scope for imaginative discourses on the country's

[33] *El Correo Nacional,* Jan. 20, 1903. [34] Reprinted in *ibid.,* Feb. 3, 1903.

future, for appeals to national instead of party loyalty, and for the exaltation of Colombia's honor and territorial unity. For some, the controversy was doubtless an escape from the disappointments of the recent war, for others, an idealistic fight for terms that would hasten the work of reconstruction. One group, though mostly silent during the spring, saw in the treaty an opportunity for political revenge; another, the fearsome shadow of United States control. Nowhere, however, is there the slightest indication that any part of the opposition was officially inspired.

The objections to the treaty most frequently advanced in the press during the spring of 1903 were four: the loss of sovereignty involved, the unconstitutionality of the grant of jurisdiction to a foreign power, the insufficiency of the financial compensation, and the danger of further encroachments by Yankee imperialism. Of these, the sovereignty question was by far the most skilfully presented. Colombia, as a weak nation forced to rely to the full on such protection as international law afforded, had produced a distinguished group of scholars in that field, many of whom were actively engaged in the discussions of these months. Consequently, the Bogotán who kept abreast of the news was likely to be much better informed on such theoretical matters as the "attributes of sovereignty" than his contemporary in New York or Chicago. In a country where man's conquest of nature was still in its early stages and where political systems were often kaleidoscopic, the concept of "sovereignty" was endowed with particularly deep significance. It represented the Colombian people's moral right of dominion over their historic territory, regardless of their ability to maintain constant control. It was the chief symbol of national permanence and unity in a land of disorderly change.

This feeling is clearly reflected in an editorial published by *El Colombiano* on March 24, which reads in part:

> The public knowledge of the treaty signed in Washington last January, between the Colombian Chargé d'Affaires and Secretary of State Hay, not only has not dispersed the instinctive misgivings which that document inspired when partly known, but has completely

THE RISE OF PROTEST IN COLOMBIA 257

justified those misgivings, revealing a clear plan for the actual abrogation of Colombian sovereignty over a considerable part of the Isthmus, if not over all of it.

It means nothing—since the express terms of the Treaty lead to other conclusions—that different articles of the Treaty repeated, with more or less cunning, that Colombian sovereignty would continue in all its strength and vigor, and that the United States would guarantee it in Panama as before. Sovereignty is synonymous with dominion, rule and supreme authority over a stated territory; but from the moment that the laws of a Nation and its courts are limited in power by those of another Nation; from the moment that a Nation ceases to hold authority over the . . . people inhabiting its territory; from the moment it is prevented from levying taxes therein; from the moment that entrance into a given region of the country in pursuit of criminals requires the permission of a foreign power, [from that moment] its authority must be classified as something less than sovereignty; and that portion of its territory must be described by some name other than that of fatherland. . . .

We do not know by what authority the representative of Colombia was able to sign a pact openly contrary, not in one but in many points, to the fundamental law he swore to respect. . . . Neither do we dare, in spite of all, to think that the dismemberment of the fatherland would also find its basis in the all-useful Article 121 of the Constitution, which has already served the preceding administration to ruin the rights of Colombia in the canal. We wish to believe solely that these provisions of the Treaty were not considered with full deliberation and that, drawn up by American officials little versed in our laws, they have been adopted without the discussion they deserve.

The editor pointed out that the convention placed Colombia in the category of a barbaric nation by granting citizens of the United States "extraterritorial" privileges not accorded Colombians. The country's retention of the specific "right" to navigate its own rivers in the region of the canal without charge was cited as a piece of "cruel sarcasm." The outburst ended on the fashionable note of elevation:

Colombia does not record in the pages of its tormented and unfortunate existence an hour more difficult than the present, nor will it have a page more shameful for her, than the acceptance of the pact written in Washington. . . . No, we cannot fear or even suspect, that after so heroic and cruel a struggle—in which more than fifty thousand victims were sacrificed solely in order to demarcate the national frontiers, to repel the intermeddling of foreign powers in our politics, to affirm in an incontestable manner the autonomy of the Republic—[Colombia] would fall beaten and humiliated at the foot of a foreign power; that we might sell for thirty pieces of silver brothers who accompanied us in the national defense, and that this might be the homage we tender the fathers of the great war, and the monument we raise to the fatherland on the first centennial of its independent existence.

The indefatigable *Colombiano* continued its assaults with regularity. It was soon complaining that Article XIII of the treaty referred to controversies in the zone between citizens of the United States and those of "any foreign nation other than the Republic of Colombia" as if Colombia was to be considered an outsider in its own territory! Many difficulties were certain to arise, yet

the most serious of all, in the end, will be that Colombia . . . will lose the attributes of a sovereign nation, will remain subject to a kind of protectorate, prevented from regulating its commerce and external relations. Shall the present generation have the right to sacrifice thus, blindly, the interests of posterity for a few millions which will not begin to solve the financial problem of the present? [35]

From time to time suggestions were advanced designed to preserve Colombia's sovereignty and still permit the building of the canal. A contributor to *El Nuevo Tiempo* proposed the formation of a "perpetual commercial company" by the two governments on the following basis:

The Government of Colombia will contribute as its stake the territory and rights which belong to the present New Company . . . the Panama railroad, the buildings, ports, etc., etc.

The American Government will bring to completion the work of the canal with its own resources.

The management of the company will belong to the American Government, and the method by which the benefits will be dis-

---

[35] *Ibid.*, March 27, 1903. These editorials have been selected as fairly typical presentations of the substance of the sovereignty argument. The various phases of the subject were treated at great length in numerous articles and pamphlets which appeared throughout the spring and early summer.

THE RISE OF PROTEST IN COLOMBIA 259

tributed between the associates will be the subject of a special convention.³⁶

One Carlos Vallarino, who favored the rejection of the Hay-Herrán treaty as "openly damaging to our national sovereignty and to our fiscal interests," brought forward a plan for creating a "Hanseatic country" on the Isthmus guaranteed by a confederation "of the nations of our race." He admitted

that Colombia will cede the most coveted part of its territory; but in return . . . it will assure, with advantages, its own sovereignty, and will obtain, furthermore, greater profit as an important shareholder *in the greatest and most far-reaching affair* that can occur during its lifetime as a nation: the opening of the interoceanic canal. It will also present itself before the world, realizing at the same time the birth of the Latin-American Colossus, and opening [in coöperation with it] the universal highway, as the initiator of perpetual peace and of dignified and just politics throughout that [federated] America, the future of the human species, calling to its full, rich and fecund breasts all the disinherited of Europe to increase its development rapidly for the benefit of all humanity.³⁷

Señor Vallarino did not state who was to dig, and who finance this glorious waterway to the millennium.

F. A. Monsalve D.'s solution likewise had the virtues of breadth and simplicity. Spurning the Hay-Herrán treaty because the moral and material returns were "unworthy" of Colombia, he suggests a scheme which

consists in procuring competent personnel and sufficient capital from all the commercial nations of both worlds, especially from those whose commerce might interest them in the opening of the Canal, for the purpose of organizing a society aimed at the completion and management of the work, a society which ought to be under the direct control of the Colombian Government and with its center of operations in Bogotá.

Moral and material values would then flow to Colombia in abundance. The country would be in communication with the most civilized nations, "implying the development of commerce and industry and ideas, the betterment of the people, the augmenta-

---

³⁶ *El Nuevo Tiempo*, Bogotá, Jan. 20, 1903.   ³⁷ *Ibid.*, April 15, 1903.

tion and repair of river and land highways." The necessity of internal peace would have a stabilizing effect on politics, credit would be strengthened, and immigration would increase.[38]

Closely associated with the discussion of sovereignty was the constitutionality of certain articles of the treaty. The Colombians were not deceived for an instant by the Department of State's phrasing of Articles II and IV.[39] To them a perpetual lease was not intrinsically different from a sale. Accordingly, the legally minded were soon raising the question whether the fundamental law of the land permitted the transfer of territory to another power.

El Colombiano brought the subject to public attention early in March with the query: "Has the Congress which is about to meet sufficient authority to decree the alienation of the tract of land required of us as the essential condition to completing the excavation of the interoceanic canal?" In answer, it pointed out that Article 3 of the constitution fixed the national boundaries and made no provision for altering them except by the regular process of amendment. The basic charter, it continued,

is not amended by means of public treaties, since these are subject to its terms. It follows that nothing can be finally concluded in contravention of its letter and spirit. . . . If then neither the Executive Power nor the Congress, nor both bodies, can alienate, dismember, cede or give away part of the territory, inasmuch as they lack the authority, and also as the soil of the fatherland is inalienable by its very nature, it follows directly that . . . it is necessary either to violate the Law or to agree to change it in advance as Costa Rica and Nicaragua have done.[40]

Clímaco Iriarte, writing to the *Correo Nacional*, emphasized the fact that the treaty was very different in nature from the contract with the New Company. As a "mutilation of the country" it entailed a "real and transcendental" reform of the constitution. He recommended that the congress not consider it, but rather turn its attention to new enabling legislation.[41]

While questions of sovereignty and constitutionality produced

[38] *El Correo Nacional*, April 23, 1903.
[40] March 10, 1903.
[39] Appendix C.
[41] April 25, 1903.

THE RISE OF PROTEST IN COLOMBIA 261

more able and heated discussion in the press than any other aspects of the Hay-Herrán treaty, the financial provisions probably caused the keenest disappointment. Writers who had been prepared to rationalize away a considerable measure of Yankee control, and there were a number of them in 1902, were chagrined and silenced by the slender recompense proposed. Those who objected to any diminution of Colombian authority were correspondingly strengthened in their stand. One of the effective early arguments for an agreement with the United States—i. e., that it offered the most practical prospect of escape from the country's monetary predicament—collapsed completely with the publication of the terms. Nevertheless, the calculation of suitable indemnities continued to be something of a favorite sport with publicists and editors, if only to demonstrate the gross injustice of the pact.

A contributor to *El Correo Nacional* of February 23 sought to find a basis for evaluating the canal zone property in the amount offered by the United States for the Danish West Indies the year before. He argued that, inasmuch as the former had been willing to pay $5,000,000 for the 300 square kilometers of "barren, rocky cliffs" comprising the Danish islands, it would be only right and proper to expect $27,000,000 for the 1,600 square kilometers included in the proposed strip at Panama. Cutting this figure to $20,000,000 to be generous, and capitalizing at three percent, the author arrived at $600,000 as a fair rental. To this he added $275,000 [*sic*] for the railroad annuity, $100,000 yearly for the reversion rights of the Panama Railroad, $40,000 to cover the estimated annual yield from the lighthouses and tonnage dues of Panama and Colón, and $200,000 for the commercial tax collected in those cities. This total, capitalized at three percent, would mean a fixed indemnity of $40,500,000. In contrast he cited Hay's offer of the previous July, the latest figures available to him, which amounted by either alternative to a capitalization of only $10,300,000.[42] Colombia should, in his estimation, insist

[42] This offer, it will be remembered, was the choice between $7,000,000 with a $100,000 annuity and $10,000,000 plus a rental of $10,000. The final treaty terms

upon an annual stipend well in excess of $1,000,000. He regretted the unwillingness of the Yankees to be more generous

> because we desire to see the canal made by the United States and because we believe that the canal's influence will greatly develop our commerce and also will modify our manner of existence, political and social, helping to give us the stability and peace which we need so much. But we cannot sacrifice our rights by not being properly indemnified.[43]

Dr. Samuel Ramírez A. felt there was a serious discrepancy between the respective sums offered the New Company and Colombia, although the former was merely a tenant and the latter owned the land. Not only was Colombia's share inconsistent with its proprietary rights but it did not take into sufficient account the value of the railroad rentals. By the curious process of capitalizing $250,000 at one percent, Ramírez found $25,000,000 to which his country was entitled. Taking the New Company's estimate of $109,000,000 as the "technical value" of its property, he proceeded along this line of reasoning: the company had accepted $40,000,000 for over $100,000,000 worth of property because it was pressed by circumstances; since the Nicaragua route was a delusion, Colombia could safely wait seven years for the existing contract to expire and then charge the United States the interest on the full $100,000,000. He concluded that as "an initial sum $25,000,000 and an annuity of $1,000,000 would not be an excessive price."[44]

On March 28 *El Correo Nacional* carried an article by Dr. Gerardo Pulecio, who, after expressing his opinion that only the United States could complete the canal, disposed of the sovereignty issue with the unorthodox observation that "Colombia does not hold and never has held effective sovereignty in the Isthmus." He then approached the main issue:

> The really grave question in this matter *is the price*. We have about six hundred and fifty millions of pesos in paper money, and this

---

of $10,000,000 cash and $250,000 yearly, if capitalized at three percent, come to $18,000,000.

[43] *El Correo Nacional*, Feb. 23, 1903.   [44] *Ibid.*, March 31, 1903.

dreadful burden devours us and is an inheritance of misery and of shame for our descendants. . . . If the business [of the canal] does not reach a head, or if what is received is very little or not used *scrupulously* . . . we can say that we have reached the finale . . . because we would have to present to the world the not-to-be-imagined spectacle of a country without money, where the inhabitants live hungry in houses of from a million pesos up, of which every beggar is proprietor.

While insisting that he was not among those who believed that the United States should pay the weight in gold of the earth it excavated, Pulecio considered a fair price would be $25,000,000 in cash and $1,000,000 annually, beginning in 1914 whether the work was then completed or not. In addition, he felt that the New Company should pay at least $2,000,000 for the privilege of transferring its concessions.[45] A few days later the same paper printed a communication from General Francisco J. Vergara y Velasco denouncing the "sale" of the zone for $10,000,000 as an act of folly "which the country would never pardon." In his opinion congress should insist not only on a more respectable payment from the United States but also on a contribution from the New Company.[46]

On March 13 the *Correo Nacional* printed a questionnaire covering the chief points involved in the treaty discussion. It was addressed to twenty-eight prominent citizens of various political groups with the request that they submit their opinions for publication. The questions were these:

1. Should Sanclemente's extension to the New Company be ratified by the coming congress?
2. Would it be possible to form a new company to excavate the canal, or is the United States the only possible agent?
3. In case an understanding is reached with the United States, on what bases ought the concession to be given?

---

[45] *Ibid.*, March 28, 1903.
[46] *Ibid.*, April 2, 1903. The general did not favor the ratification of the treaty as signed, but suggested a law of authorization to guide the executive in a new negotiation which would protect the "present and future interests of Colombia without shutting the door to any just and equitable arrangement between the contracting parties." This type of solution was to gain considerable support among the moderates as time went on.

4. Should jurisdiction in the zone of work be granted to the American government?
5. If jurisdiction be granted, can Colombia's sovereignty be saved in the zone?
6. What indemnity ought to be demanded and in what form?
7. On what conditions ought Colombia to permit the New Company to transfer its rights to the American government?

An analysis of the replies indicates clearly that most of the men consulted did not approve of the treaty in its existing form. It was the consensus of opinion that since "sovereignty" implied complete and undivided jurisdiction, a permanent lease to the United States was equivalent to the sale of a portion of the national domain. On the subject of price there was a distinct tendency to favor a lump payment in the neighborhood of $25,000,000 and a rental of about $1,000,000. Most of those who answered agreed that the United States was the sole agent capable of carrying through the work, although some felt that there was good reason for delaying any agreement with that country until the New Company's concessions expired in 1910. It is significant that of those addressed, only one, Cromwell's friend, Enrique Cortés, urged the prompt ratification of the convention as it stood.[47]

So far we have attempted to show how the proposed subversion of national sovereignty, the doubtful constitutionality of a perpetual lease, and the dissatisfaction with the financial terms served as important foci of Colombian opposition to the Hay-Herrán treaty. A fourth powerful factor in shaping public opinion was the ever-present distrust of Yankee imperialism. For a century the United States had been enlarging its territory at the expense of Spanish America. Its absorption of Florida, Texas, New Mexico, and California had been followed more recently by the occupation of Puerto Rico and Cuba. Its annexation of Hawaii and the Philippines in 1898 had greatly increased the military importance of Central American canal sites and, consequently, the uneasiness of the countries possessing them. Great

[47] These replies were printed at intervals from March 28 until the opening of the congress.

THE RISE OF PROTEST IN COLOMBIA 265

Britain, formerly the most serious check upon the aggressiveness of the Colossus of the North, had now abandoned that role insofar as the canal was concerned and thereby cleared the way for the latter's complete domination of the route. Even more disturbing was the recrudescence of the expansionist spirit of the mid-nineteenth century in the writings and speeches of prominent public leaders in the United States. Theodore Roosevelt, for instance, aroused deep resentment among the sensitive Colombians by his patronizing references to the political behavior of Latin-American nations. A characteristic reaction is to be found in an article in *El Porvenir* of Cartagena on June 27, 1902. After citing passages from an address by Roosevelt on the Monroe Doctrine the author remarks:

> The words quoted are a perfect condensation of American thought, with admirable touches of dissimulation. They are a warning to our countries. It is the conviction of his irresistible superiority and vigor that makes the Yankee, from Mr. Roosevelt to the rag-picker, treat the turbulent republics of Latin America with haughtiness and contempt. . . . That is the way all the Yankees are with regard to us. They regard us as conquerable countries, and they treat us with the haughtiness of conquerors. . . . Mr. Roosevelt, arrogating to himself powers derived from nobody knows where, declares that no republic however small, *if it knows how to govern itself,* has anything to fear from the United States, as though the great nation had received from some universal power the mission to put in order those who live in disorder! It is a tutelage which it pretends to exercise by the sole right of its strength. . . . If we live in disorder, we live in our own house, and nobody has the right to meddle in it.[48]

The intervention of the naval forces on the Isthmus in the fall of 1902 furnished numerous incidents of real or fancied slights to Colombian dignity. *El Correo* related with acerbity how Admiral Casey detained the gunboat *Bogotá* until she could prove her right to fly the Colombian flag.[49] Several weeks later, in the course of one of its editorial attacks on the treaty, *El Colombiano* declared:

[48] Quoted from State Dept., Dispatches from Colombia, Vol. 58, Hart to Hay, No. 648, Aug. 18, 1902.
[49] Jan. 12, 1903.

No use to say that the United States reiterates and affirms the guaranty contained in the Treaty of 46-48, because already the Colombians know by sad, humiliating experience what such a guaranty is worth or signifies, and however weak may be their memory, they have not yet forgotten the recollection of the insults and affronts received during the past year from the American Armada.[50]

One of *El Correo's* readers waggishly proposed that the United States annex the Republic of Colombia. Then, as a truly sovereign state in the North American Union, it could contract to let the Washington government construct the canal through its territory. The editor replied in mock exasperation:

Enough. . . . Some clamor up and down against the Yankees, others wish that Colombia were a star in the American banner, it may be there are some to whom it has occurred to seek the *annexation of . . . the United States . . . to Colombia.* What a solution!!! [51]

IV

In the latter part of April, while the denunciation of the treaty in the Bogotá press was at its height, the countrywide balloting for congress was brought to gradual completion. Beaupré reported that the government was evidently "mending fences" in many districts by holding new elections where the first ones had been "illegally conducted." [52] It soon became obvious that the chief opposition to the administration was to come not from the Liberals but from former President Caro's Nationalists, the faction that had been ousted from control by the Marroquín *coup d'état* of July, 1900. Caro had announced at the beginning of the elections in March that in spite of his repugnance for "disputes of all kinds" and his contentment with the "obscurity of his present condition" he considered it imperative to return to public life in view of the critical issues confronting the nation.[53] This step complicated the political situation by reviving many of the old dissensions that had precipitated the civil war. Alignments

---

[50] March 24, 1903.   [51] June 4, 1903.
[52] State Dept., Dispatches from Colombia, Vol. 59, Beaupré to Hay, No. 13, April 27, 1903.
[53] *El Correo Nacional,* March 23, 1903.

quickly appeared for and against the former dictator. Whether the government made serious efforts to defeat him is not clear, but he emerged from the campaign as one of the senators from Antioquia.

On May 7 Marroquín officially summoned congress to meet in special session on the 20th of June. Opposition to the convention showed no signs of abatement during the weeks that followed this decree. Beaupré wrote that feeling was "veering into a current of extreme bitterness against the authors of the pact, especially Mr. Herrán." Mancini confided to the minister that he was "emphatically of the opinion that the Congress will refuse to ratify the convention, and that he has written to his company to that effect." In summarizing the arguments used against the treaty Beaupré noted that in private discussion, "which perhaps more clearly reflects the real situation, . . . the one great determining point . . . is the belief that the price can be greatly augmented." [54]

About the beginning of the month, General Rafael Reyes arrived in the capital after an absence of five years abroad. An imposing figure, a man of wealth and a famous explorer, the general had been the idol of the Colombian people. As the standard-bearer of the Historicals in the preceding presidential campaign, he had unsuccessfully attempted to oust the Nationalist machine. During the recent rebellion he had kept discreetly out of the country. Now, on his return, he let it be known that he would be a candidate in 1904. Beaupré reported that his popularity had not waned materially and that Fernández, the most powerful man in the government during the war, "has seen the light and is for General Reyes, quite content to play an important second part in the programme." Marroquín's relations with Reyes were close and he was said to be favorable to the latter's political aspirations. Beaupré was convinced that the general's desire for the presidency was largely due to the attractive prospects for Colombia's future offered by the Panama Canal and that he was therefore

[54] State Dept., Dispatches from Colombia, Vol. 59, Beaupré to Hay, No. 17, May 4, 1903.

sincerely in favor of ratification.⁵⁵ This belief is supported in part by an account of a newspaper interview granted by Reyes in San José, Costa Rica, on March 22, while he was en route to Bogotá. In this he expressed his opinion that the United States would complete the canal within five years and that the work would prove a great boon to the entire Caribbean region. He was also quoted as stating that he foresaw no danger to the independence of Colombia or the Central American republics because of the adequate guaranties included in the treaty.⁵⁶

On May 6, the day before Marroquín convoked the special session, Beaupré had a conversation with a personage whom he described to Hay as "one of the ablest and most distinguished of Colombians." In the course of the talk the subject of the canal convention "opportunely and confidentially arose." The minister gathered that the tide of public opinion against the treaty was "appalling" to the government.

[There] is, in consequence, a diversity of opinion among its members as to the proper course to pursue. Some are in favor of forcing confirmation through Congress, while others, dreading the effect of such action in the present state of the public mind, counsel moderation and delay and the adoption of measures to change public sentiment into a more favorable channel.

All the enemies of the Government are united in an onslaught upon the canal convention. Many of them are sincere, of course, in their opposition to the proposed treaty as such, but many more, regarding it as an administration measure and at present unpopular, are assailing it with the indirect object of undermining the Government.

My informant is of the opinion that the convention may eventually be confirmed, but only after much discussion and maneuvering in Congress. The probabilities are that when the measure is presented to Congress there will be a lengthy debate and an adverse vote. Then the representatives of the coast departments of the Cauca-Panama, and Bolivar will ask for a reconsideration, and urge a ratification of the convention as the only means of preventing the secession of those

---

⁵⁵ *Ibid.*, Vol. 59, Beaupré to Hay, Unnumbered, May 11, 1903.
⁵⁶ *El Noticiero*, San José, Costa Rica, as reported in *El Correo Nacional*, April 30, 1903.

THE RISE OF PROTEST IN COLOMBIA 269

departments. . . . The debate will be resumed and in the end the friends of the Government and of confirmation will prevail.[57]

Four days later Beaupré wrote a personal message to Hay revealing that his informant had been Reyes and transmitting news of another interview. This time the general declared that he had become convinced by talking with representatives and senators who had already arrived for the session that "Congress is against the Government, and therefore against the confirmation of the convention." He asked the minister to inform his superiors that he did not think ratification possible unless the United States saw fit to pay more money and in a different manner. It was his belief that the majority in the legislature,

> being opposed to the Government, does not wish the entire sum paid at one time, but rather in say five annual installments; that if the United States will pay fifteen million in annual installments of three million, the Convention will be confirmed; otherwise he has grave doubt of the outcome.[58]

Meanwhile a severe cabinet crisis was rocking the administration. Considerations of personal prestige were probably the fundamental issues at stake, although the immediate occasion of the controversy was sufficiently serious to disrupt a far more stable government than that at the San Carlos Palace. The national finances, which had caused so much tribulation during the war, had shown very little permanent improvement since the end of hostilities. Foreign exchange, quoted at about 10,000 percent at the end of January, had dropped to 6,300 percent when the news of the treaty signing reached Bogotá. With this encouragement the government announced on March 1 that the emission of additional paper money had ceased and that the lithographic plates had been stored with a committee representing all parties. In less than a month, however, the situation was again desperate.

---

[57] State Dept., Dispatches from Colombia, Vol. 59, Beaupré to Hay, No. 19, May 7, 1903.

[58] *Ibid.*, Vol. 59, Unnumbered, May 11, 1903. Beaupré suspected that the installment plan was Reyes' own device for postponing most of the payments until he was president.

Credit was exhausted at home and no interest had been paid on the foreign debt since 1899. Claims from the war were reaching "tremendous proportions," according to Beaupré. The temporary hope afforded by the prospect of $10,000,000 in gold from the United States waned rapidly as the protest against the treaty mounted. Further use of the printing press to meet treasury needs would render the outstanding paper completely worthless.[59]

Early in May, Fernández, exasperated by Marroquín's plan to declare the country in a state of peace and thereby automatically destroy his emergency power to emit paper money, determined upon summary action. On the 10th, he and José Joaquín Casas, the minister of public instruction, presented the cabinet with an ultimatum. This document cited the disordered condition of the country and called for the adoption of the following measures: the revocation of the decree summoning the special session of congress; the indefinite postponement of the declaration of internal peace; the transfer of the ministry of hacienda to the control of the ministry of war; the dismissal of all judges refusing to accept the constitutionality of the legislative decrees; severe punishment for those fomenting rebellion; the immediate suspension of all private newspapers; economy in government expenditures; strong measures against usury and speculation in foreign exchange; and the removal of departmental governors not favorable to this program. The insurgent ministers gave notice of their intention to resign if these demands were not promptly and fully accepted.[60]

Probably to Fernández' surprise, these vigorous tactics were met by equally vigorous resistance. The majority of the council of ministers, led by General Alfredo Vásquez Cobo, minister of war, refused to admit the necessity or the wisdom of such repressive measures. The upshot of the bitter debate that followed was

[59] *Ibid.*, Vol. 59, No. 744, April 6, 1903. Beaupré estimated that there was over $1,000,000,000 in irredeemable paper money in circulation. This is about one-third more than most Colombian estimates of the time.

[60] *Ibid.*, Vol. 59, No. 28, May 19, 1903; *Renuncia de dos ministros*, pp. 6, 9–10. The Colombian version makes no mention of the first three demands which Beaupré included in his dispatch and also in a cable of the same date. The weight of indirect evidence seems to favor the American minister's account.

THE RISE OF PROTEST IN COLOMBIA

a decisive defeat for the one-time strong man of Colombia. He and his ally, Joaquín Casas, thereupon formally submitted their resignations to the vice-president. This strategy had been successfully used on previous occasions to force the executive's hand, but this time the tables were turned. Marroquín praised their past services and accepted their withdrawals. To embark upon such a program as they proposed, he told them, would be tantamount to a proclamation of dictatorship and consequently a betrayal of his oath of office. It would provide no remedy for the financial crisis, for

> as frequent revolutions serve to create a very unfavorable impression of our people and of our Government in foreign lands, and deprive us of the credit from them which we require so urgently, should a dictatorship now appear it would . . . make our Government seem less stable and less worthy of doing business with Governments, institutions of credit, and foreign capitalists.[61]

The vice-president followed up his victory on June 1 by issuing a legislative decree declaring the revolution at an end and announcing the restoration of public order.[62]

For some weeks Fernández' intentions caused anxiety in the capital. The general refused an appointment as minister to France in a bitter open letter saying that he considered it his duty to remain in the capital to defend his party and the country. On June 17 *La República* of Bogotá published a communication signed by most of the officers of the governmental forces, Perdomo's name leading, which approved the views of Fernández and criticized the attitude of the rest of the cabinet. The administration immediately summoned the loyal Cauca troops of

---

[61] *Renuncia de dos ministros*, pp. 11–12; State Dept., Dispatches from Colombia, Vol. 59, Beaupré to Hay, No. 28, May 19, 1903. The cabinet crisis started a rumor, which reached the United States by way of Panama, that Marroquín had resigned and that Reyes had replaced him. Loomis, of the State Department, wired Beaupré on May 12 for information. The N. Y. *World* stated on indefinite authority that should Reyes find the treaty opponents too numerous he would not hesitate "to declare the country in a state of war and make the treaty binding by the approval of himself and his Cabinet, which he has authority to do under the Colombian Constitution." (May 13, 1903.)

[62] *Decretos legislativos* (Bogotá, 1903), Decree No. 638 of 1903, p. 520.

General Pinto (who had succeeded Fernández in the ministry of state) and took precautions against a military coup.[63] Marroquín had lost another of his few remaining allies—the army.

[63] State Dept., Dispatches from Colombia, Vol. 59, Beaupré to Hay, No. 54, June 19, 1903.

VIII

PRESSURE DIPLOMACY

Unfortunately for Hay's record as secretary of state, William Nelson Cromwell was considerably more than an interested bystander in the skirmishes that marked the diplomatic correspondence between Washington and Bogotá in the spring and summer of 1903. The story of the Marroquín government's fruitless efforts to charge the New Company for the privilege of selling its property to the United States has already been traced up to the signing of the Hay-Herrán treaty. It will be recalled that Cromwell's strategy was to evade any financial settlement until Colombia's consent to the transfer had been formally incorporated in the convention and then to rely on the pretext that any demand upon the company for money thereafter was in direct violation of that nation's obligations to the United States. The first part of this plan was successfully consummated on January 22, 1903. The second was put into operation soon afterwards when it became evident that the Marroquín administration, though temporarily outmaneuvered, had no intention of abandoning its fight for compensation.

The controversy was reopened on February 3 with the dispatch of identical notes from the ministry of hacienda to the canal and railroad companies informing them that they were expected to appoint representatives in Bogotá empowered to negotiate with the authorities on questions relating to the transfer of their concessions to the United States. Each corporation was assured that Colombia,

> in view of the great interests which the French people have in this colossal enterprise, will not in any way oppose . . . the granting of the permission for the transfer of the concession; but it will demand and require from the concessionary company, if this be done, by way

of return, a sum of money which shall be previously agreed upon, and the cancellation on the part of the company of every undertaking or obligation which the Government of Colombia has contracted by virtue of the concession . . . up to the date on which it passes to the new concern.[1]

Cromwell later declared that Mancini's letters and cables to him repeatedly emphasized Colombia's determination not to ratify the treaty without a previous arrangement with the companies. He added that "other news received through the State Department and its minister in Bogotá, which Secretary Hay communicated to us as soon as received, was equally significant and plain." It was a situation calling for a high degree of audacity and legal adroitness and one for which the attorney was superbly equipped. Upon studying the problem, he concluded that the only way to save his clients from paying a "tribute" of millions of francs

was to convince the American Government that it should refuse to consent to any amendment of Article I or to permit that the treaty should depend in any way on a previous agreement with the canal company, as Colombia was demanding. To this end we had numerous interviews with Secretary Hay, Senators Hanna, Spooner, and Kittredge, Congressman Burton, and on certain occasions, with the President. We pointed out that Colombia had already pledged herself morally to consent, and that her consent should be imposed upon her as being demanded by international good faith, and we thus created a feeling favorable to the support and protection of the company against these demands.[2]

This procedure was sanctioned by the Paris office about the middle of March in a cable stating that "as far as Colombia is concerned, we are entirely in accord with you on all points, and upon the course to pursue we approve your idea to inform the Government of the United States and to act according to its instructions."[3]

On April 7, Cromwell participated in a conference at the State Department with Hay, Admiral Walker, and Attorney-General

---

[1] *Dip. Hist. of the Panama Canal*, pp. 387–388. The notes to the canal and railroad companies were dated, respectively, Dec. 24 and 27, 1902.
[2] *Story of Panama*, pp. 278–279.   [3] *Ibid.*, p. 329.

PRESSURE DIPLOMACY

Knox on plans for the admiral's inspection tour of the Isthmus.[4] That weightier matters were also discussed is evident from the instructions cabled to Beaupré that afternoon:

> Referring to requests of Colombia to canal and railroad companies for appointment of agents to negotiate cancellation of the present concessions, et cetera, if the subject arises inform the Colombian Government that the treaty covers entire matter, and any change would be in violation of Spooner law and not permissible.[5]

Cromwell modestly admitted several years afterwards that "Secretary Hay honored us with his confidence by permitting us to collaborate with him in the writing of these instructions, which conveyed the determinations arrived at." The company congratulated the attorney on his achievement by wire on the 10th.[6]

Beaupré replied to the Hay-Cromwell message on April 24, saying that although the subject had not arisen to his knowledge he deemed it best in two interviews with Foreign Minister Rico to bring the conversation "as cautiously as possible to a point that would enlighten me." He found His Excellency evasive but gathered that negotiations with the companies were being considered by the government, if they had not already been started.[7]

Four days later Hay made one of the gravest missteps of his career. In a lengthy and legal dispatch to Beaupré, which bears no resemblance to his usual style of writing, he committed the United States on the basis of a quibble to the complete support of the New Company's financial interests. It was the master stroke of Cromwell's career as lawyer-diplomat. The principal points raised in the communication may be summarized as follows:

1. Copies of the notices of February 3 from the minister of hacienda to the canal and railroad companies were enclosed. From these notices it was apparent to the Department of State that the Colombian government contemplated a grant by its congress of "a further permission to transfer [the companies'] concessions to the United States besides that contained in the treaty."

[4] N. Y. *World*, April 8, 1903.
[5] State Dept., Instructions to Colombia, Vol. 19, Hay to Beaupré, p. 234.
[6] *Story of Panama*, p. 279.
[7] State Dept., Dispatches from Colombia, Vol. 59, Beaupré to Hay, No. 10.

It was also clear that the companies were expected to enter into preliminary agreements with Colombia for the "canceling of all obligations of Colombia to either of them contracted by Colombia under the concession." Such negotiations by any of the parties involved were declared to be "inconsistent with the agreements already made between this Government and the canal company, with the act of June 28, 1902, under the authority of which the treaty was made, and with the express terms of the treaty itself." By the Spooner Act, it was noted, the president was authorized to purchase the "rights, privileges, franchises, concessions" and other property of the New Company. As it was known to the department that the Salgar-Wyse concession of 1878 forbade the sale of that corporation's property to the United States without Colombia's consent, therefore, "and before entering upon any dealings with the New Panama Canal Company, the present treaty with Colombia was negotiated and signed." Article I expressly provided that Colombia "authorizes the New Panama Canal Company to sell and transfer to the United States its rights, privileges, properties, and concessions." Colombia now indicated a purpose not only to disregard this authorization but also to destroy a great part of the subject matter to which it referred. "This Government," the dispatch added,

cannot approve such a transaction either by Colombia or by the company. If the company were to accede to the demands of Colombia, the President would be unable to consummate the proposed purchase from it, for it would have surrendered to Colombia a material part of the property for which he is authorized to make payment.

2. By such action as seemed contemplated the treaty itself could not be carried out, since the payments to Colombia were intended as compensation not only for the use of the zone and the income renounced, but also for "other rights, privileges, and exemptions granted to the United States." One of the most important of these was the right of acquiring the rights and privileges of the New Company. The action proposed by Colombia "would constitute *pro tanto* an annulment of Article I, would render impossible the execution of the law, and is wholly inadmissible."

PRESSURE DIPLOMACY 277

The plausibility of this ingenious contention advanced in the name of the Department of State does not withstand close analysis. Passing over without further comment the astounding assertion that the United States had no dealings with the New Company before the signing of the treaty, the chief flaw in the argument up to this point is its complete disregard of the wording of Article XXII of the convention. This provides that Colombia

renounces, confirms and grants to the United States, now and hereafter, all the rights and property reserved in the said concessions which otherwise would belong to Colombia at or before the expiration of the terms of ninety-nine years of the concessions granted to or held by the above-mentioned party and companies, and all right, title and interest which it now has or may hereafter have, in and to the lands, canal, works, property and rights held by the said companies under said concessions or otherwise, and acquired or to be acquired by the United States from or through the New Panama Canal Company, including any property and rights which might or may in the future, either by lapse of time, forfeiture or otherwise, revert to the Republic of Colombia under any contracts of concessions, with said Wyse, the Universal Panama Canal Company, the Panama Railroad Company and the New Panama Canal Company.

This clause is phrased so expertly that it covers not only the situation as it existed on January 22, 1903, but also any changes that might occur between that date and the exchange of ratifications.[8] Yet this is quite aside from the fact, well known to the company attorney, that Marroquín's advisers at that time were interested solely in obtaining a money payment, nothing more. Even assuming that some Andean corporation lawyer had cunningly devised this alleged scheme to fleece Uncle Sam, it should be borne in mind that the United States had merely an option on the company's property and rights. Not a dollar had been paid to the

[8] It might be urged in support of the department's point that the Colombian government planned to cancel its obligations to the French companies before it ratified the treaty, so that *on the actual date of its taking effect* Article XXII of the convention would have practically no meaning. This possible interpretation, while of doubtful validity in international law, is, it seems, satisfactorily covered by the inclusion in the article of the words ". . . title and interest which [Colombia] *now has* . . . in and to the lands, canal, works, property and rights held by the said companies under said concessions or otherwise . . . ."

Frenchmen and, naturally, not a dollar would be paid if they meanwhile divested themselves of what they had to sell. Granted the extremely hypothetical case that Colombia, having tricked the New Company out of its "rights, privileges, and exemptions," demanded as its successor in title all or part of the $40,000,000 from the United States, still the latter would find itself put to no extra expense. The only possible losers would be Cromwell's clients. There is not the slightest shred of evidence, however, that the Colombian officials entertained any such aggressive idea. They were fighting a strictly defensive battle for what must be considered very moderate advantages and their wildest flights of fancy never approached the Napoleonic visions which the author of this note found reason to attribute to them.

3. The dispatch continued:

So far as the Panama Railroad Company is concerned, it is enough to point out that Articles XXVIII and XXIX of its contract with Colombia . . . have no bearing upon any transaction now in contemplation. These articles declare that "the present privilege cannot be ceded or transferred to any foreign government," under penalty of forfeiture. No transfer of this privilege by the company is contemplated, nor, indeed, any transfer by the company of anything. The purchase by the United States from the New Panama Canal Company of certain shares of the railroad company is the only operation now proposed, and this does not affect the railroad company itself. To this transfer of shares the railroad company is not a party and in it the company has no part. It neither makes it nor can it prevent it. Plainly, therefore, the provisions of the company's contract with the Colombian Government can have no application to such a transaction.

This was a lesson in legal sophistry that must have caused Rico and his colleagues to rub their eyes in wonder. Speciousness of this order was not only unworthy of the department that sponsored it but a gratuitous gesture of contempt for the Bogotá government. It is hardly conceivable that such an argument would have been presented to the chancellery of Great Britain or any other first-class power.

4. The railroad company having been disposed of, it was admitted that

With regard to the New Panama Canal Company the situation is different in this respect, for that company will make a direct transfer of all its property and concessions to the United States, and such a transfer was originally forbidden by Articles 21 and 22 of the Salgar-Wyse concession of 1878.

But here, in support of its contention that Colombia had no right to enter into any separate agreement with the French concerns, the department pointed out that Colombia had given its consent to the proposed sale "so repeatedly and in so many different ways . . . as to make it impossible for the executive Government of that Republic to retract it." It declared that the treaty had been made in reliance on these assurances and that

> to raise new conditions and impose new terms upon the consent thus freely tendered or to cancel any provisions of the concessions would be a complete departure from [those assurances]. The Government of Colombia initiated the negotiations, and it cannot be conceived that it should now disclaim its own propositions, nor can this Government acquiesce in such a course. . . . These various considerations show that the Republic of Colombia is fully committed to the United States, wholly apart from her express agreement by the treaty, to consent fully and freely to the acquisition of the property of the New Panama Canal Company by the United States without other terms or conditions than those embodied in the treaty. It is not necessary here to consider the questions of good faith toward the canal company which would be raised by new exactions of that company at this time.

5. The memorandum then traced the history of Article I to prove that it was included in "the original proposal of Colombia to the United States" of March, 1902, and that it had undergone no change in the negotiations that followed. The alteration of it suggested by Concha in his note of November 11, 1902, was quoted with the department's reply that it was "inadmissible." The amendment to this article was then

> abandoned by Colombia, and the treaty . . . was signed . . . without any modification of the absolute authorization to the company to sell. . . . It is impossible that this Government should even discuss the matter any further or permit this rejected and abandoned proposition to be put in force in any form.

6. The whole argument was clinched with this remarkable paragraph:

> The consent of Colombia to the sale . . . is a matter of agreement between the two nations. It has not been granted by Colombia to the company alone, but also to the United States. To that agreement neither the canal nor the railroad company is or can be a party; nor can the United States permit its international compacts to be dependent in any degree upon the action of any private corporation. Such a course would be consistent neither with the dignity of either nation nor with their interests. To make the effectiveness of the agreement between Colombia and the United States depend upon the willingness of the canal company to enter into arrangements with Colombia, of a character satisfactory to that country, would not only give that company an influence which it can never be permitted to exercise in the diplomatic affairs and international relations of this country, but would enable it to control the acquisition by the United States of the rights granted by Colombia and the enjoyment by Colombia of the equivalent advantages secured to her by the United States.[9]

For sheer cynicism, this passage would be hard to parallel in the diplomatic archives of the nation. There is no positive proof that Cromwell was the word-for-word author of the dispatch but the sum of evidence indicates that he inspired it and that it closely followed a memorandum prepared by the attorney or one of his associates. His own subsequent description of the circumstances is worth quoting:

> We also wrote, at the request of the Secretary, a detailed note covering the whole history of the negotiations and arguments in support of the attitude thus taken by the United States, which note the Secretary used as a basis for his official instructions to the American minister. . . . We sent a copy of these instructions to the company, which expressed its approval in the following cable:
>
> "We have received Mr. Hay's letter of instructions to the minister of the United States in Bogotá, which satisfies us and for which we thank you."

These instructions were officially communicated to the Colombian Government, and they were bitterly attacked as contrary to the atti-

---

[9] State Dept., Instructions to Colombia, Vol. 19, Hay to Beaupré, No. 6, pp. 236 *et seq.*

PRESSURE DIPLOMACY

tude that Colombia had taken. The President, and Secretary Hay, however, giving the highest proof of their honor, stoutly maintained the attitude which had been thus assumed by common consent.[10]

That the Department of State should allow confidential instructions to be sent to Paris for the approval of the New Company is remarkable in itself. But that the department should concur in this at the very time it was primly advising the Colombians that their plan for a previous agreement with the French company would give that corporation "an influence which it can never be permitted to exercise in the diplomatic affairs" of the United States suggests that Hay was letting the control of matters get out of his hands. It is a situation difficult to reconcile with the undoubted personal integrity and high principles of the secretary of state. Tyler Dennett, his foremost biographer, feels that Hay was not at his best during these months and was slipping into an "indefensible position at Bogotá" by his repeated yielding to Cromwell's pressure.[11] It is regrettable that a sense of duty to his office did not impel Hay to act with greater circumspection in a matter of such importance. As it was, his keen critical faculties seem to have crumbled under the spell of the attorney's persuasive personality.

While this notable communication was on its way to Bogotá, a report emanated from Panama that the New Company had offered the Colombian government $12,000,000 for permission to sell its property to the United States. The State Department promptly denied official knowledge of the reputed offer and observed through a spokesman that it did not "feel called upon to interfere between these parties"! Edward B. Hill of Cromwell's firm declared that Colombia had never demanded such a payment and that the company did not expect to pay any amount to that government.[12] This was a day or so after Cromwell had learned from Mancini's cable of May 7 that Colombia had set the transfer price at 50,000,000 francs and was awaiting information regarding the concessionary's intentions. Former Minister

[10] *Story of Panama*, p. 279. [11] Dennett, *John Hay*, pp. 375–376.
[12] N. Y. *Times*, May 12, 1903.

Hart reached New York on the 30th and visited the attorney to acquaint him with the situation at first hand. He expressed his conviction that the Marroquín administration would make no effort to have the treaty ratified unless a private settlement was first arranged with the canal and railroad enterprises.[13]

Beaupré transmitted a paraphrase of the dispatch of April 28 to Rico on June 10. The latter replied with a counter-memorandum on the 27th in which he stated that the purpose of a separate agreement with the companies was to cancel the legal bonds existing between them and the Colombian government by virtue of their concessions. He pointed out that just as the United States

> must celebrate a contract in order to acquire the rights of the said companies, and that negotiation cannot be included in the treaty which is to be celebrated between the two countries, neither can the resolution of the obligation between Colombia and the two companies be verified in the treaty.

Without a previous understanding Colombia would be relinquishing its rights in regard to those corporations, while leaving its obligations to them still in force. In answer to the Department of State's contention that the Panama Railroad was not transferring its property to a foreign government, Rico called attention to the fact that the necessity of Colombia's consent was recognized in Article I of the treaty. Furthermore,

> each share, by representing a certain proportionate value of the privilege, or, that is, of the railroad itself, and the transfer of that to a foreign government being prohibited, the shares cannot be sold, because with them [the foreign government] would become [a copartner] in the property of the privilege, which is judicially inadmissible. The restrictive conditions of the contracts of 1850 and 1867 do not exclude from the penalty of forfeiture the sale of portions of the privilege. . . . Your excellency knows very well that any interpretation ought to be discarded that makes illusionary that which is stipulated, and in this case the condition in reference would be reached if any proceeding was admitted by which the privilege for the construction and exploitation of the railroad could be transferred to a foreign government.

---

[13] *Story of Panama*, p. 278.

The minister assured Beaupré that he would acquaint the Colombian congress with the interpretation placed upon Article I by the United States.[14]

For present purposes, Cromwell's success in committing the Washington government to the furtherance of his own aims is chiefly significant because the policies and tactics adopted in consequence contributed in very direct fashion to the defeat of the Hay-Herrán treaty at Bogotá. Until the release of the note of April 28 few Colombians seriously doubted that the canal and railroad companies would eventually agree to pay for the permission to transfer their concessions. The realization that the United States was planning to shield the French from an exaction which was accepted throughout Colombia as just and proper did nothing to stimulate enthusiasm for the treaty. The opposition was quick to make capital of the message as an example of what might be expected from a permanent partnership with the Yankees, while the administration, which had counted upon this outside contribution to render the convention more palatable to the public taste, found it difficult to plunge into the ratification fight with much earnestness.

II

By early June the State Department was convinced that Colombian opposition to the treaty was based almost entirely on financial considerations. The peremptory demands upon the New Company had been supplemented by Reyes' broad hint that another $5,000,000 from the United States would do much to ensure the approval of the pact. Talk of the violation of sovereignty was dismissed, at Beaupré's suggestion, as unimportant and largely hypocritical. The reasons for this impression, which Roosevelt later expanded into an elaborate "holdup" myth, seem clear enough. Most of the objections currently raised against the treaty, as has been pointed out, related to its infringement of national sovereignty, its unconstitutionality, its encouragement of impe-

[14] State Dept.: Dispatches from Colombia, Vol. 59, Beaupré to Hay, No. 67, July 1, 1903.

rialism, and its financial inadequacy. All were fully discussed through the columns of the press, but only the last remained within the scope of possible executive action once the treaty was signed. The first three either never had been or else were no longer subject to negotiation. The principle of United States "control" of the zone had been laid down by the Department of State as an indispensable condition of the construction of the Panama Canal and this limitation of sovereignty had been agreed to on several occasions by Colombia's ministers in Washington. Marroquín, in ordering Concha to accept all but the monetary provision of Hay's proposals of July, 1902, had committed himself to the stand that the convention was constitutional and compatible with the nation's safety. On these three fundamental points the administration had taken a position from which it would have been difficult to withdraw on its own initiative. If the legislature chose to adopt another view of them, that was its own affair.

The question of compensation, however, was a different story. It was not a juristic issue, but purely and simply a matter of bargaining. Herrán had assented to the $250,000 annuity only under pressure of an ultimatum and if the United States could be persuaded to make a further financial concession it would naturally improve the chances of ratification. The meagerness of the indemnity was but one of the causes of Colombian discontent with the treaty, yet it was the only one which the vice-president could very well do anything about prior to the meeting of the congress. On the whole it seems closer to the facts to interpret the government's motive in broaching the subject to Beaupré as an attempt to moderate public criticism rather than as a calculated overture for a bribe. As for the campaign to assess the New Company, it long antedated the signing of the treaty, as both Cromwell and Hay knew, and its continuation into the spring of 1903 was the result of the lawyer's Fabian tactics, not of Colombia's sudden greed.

Acting on the assumption that the Marroquín government

was holding out for a double *douceur,* the Department of State cabled another of its unfortunate messages to Bogotá on June 9:

> The Colombian Government apparently does not appreciate the gravity of the situation. The canal negotiations were initiated by Colombia, and were energetically pressed upon this Government for several years. The propositions presented by Colombia, with slight modifications, were finally accepted by us. In virtue of this agreement our Congress reversed its previous judgment and decided upon the Panama route. If Colombia should now reject the treaty or unduly delay its ratification, the friendly understanding between the two countries would be so seriously compromised that action might be taken by the Congress next winter which every friend of Colombia would regret. Confidential. Communicate substance of this verbally to the minister of foreign affairs. If he desires it, give him a copy in form of memorandum.[15]

Cromwell later claimed credit for inspiring this note as well as that of April 28. According to his narrative, Hay accepted his advice as to the proper attitude to take towards the Colombian government and submitted it to Roosevelt, "who, a few days later, sent for Mr. Cromwell, and after due consideration directed that instructions be sent to Colombia . . ." embodying his suggestions.[16]

Beaupré complied with these instructions on the 13th. Rico immediately asked what action the United States Congress contemplated—hostile measures against Colombia or adoption of the Nicaragua route? The envoy answered that he had received no further explanation and could not, therefore, assist the minister in construing the warning. To Rico's observation that, regardless of the executive's actions in the preliminary parleys, a treaty could not be completed without the consent of the national legislature, Beaupré replied that while such a proposition was true in the abstract it was incumbent upon his excellency's gov-

---

[15] *Ibid.:* Instructions to Colombia, Vol. 19, Hay to Beaupré, telegram, pp. 278–279.
[16] *Story of Panama,* p. 280. Some weight is lent to this story by a letter in the Hay Papers, dated June 1, in which the secretary commends Cromwell to the president and suggests that the latter see him (McCaleb, *Roosevelt,* p. 151). From this time on Roosevelt took a more active hand in the Colombian situation.

ernment to acquaint its congress with the circumstances connected with the negotiations and to use all its influence to secure ratification.[17]

A week later the foreign minister submitted a formal counter-memorandum to the American legation. He opened his rebuttal by denying that Colombia was obligated to approve the canal convention merely because it had initiated the negotiations. The ratification of treaties was a legislative prerogative and was specifically recognized as such in Articles XXV and XXVIII of the pact in question. He noted that the debate in the United States Senate was so protracted and vehement that an extra session had been necessary. Yet, he added, "if it had been rejected it would have been without any diminution of any right of Colombia, just as its rejection here will be without any diminution of any right of the United States." In illustration of his point he cited the recent refusal of the United States Senate to approve the first Hay-Pauncefote treaty in its original form, although its own government had proposed the negotiations. With reference to the Department of State's contention that it had accepted Colombia's propositions "with slight modifications" Rico remarked that there was a "very notable difference" between the protocol of March 31, 1902, and the final treaty terms, particularly regarding the establishment of tribunals in the zone and the financial compensation. Likewise, the interpretation placed on Article I by the department had caused the companies to refuse "to enter into arrangements which ought to precede the ratification, . . . a refusal which makes difficult the legislative approval of the pact." The foreign minister professed ignorance of the fact that the United States had "revoked any law in order to make possible the treaty with Colombia." His government, he declared, was under the impression that if the Washington authorities were unable to secure satisfactory terms from Colombia they were, by the explicit provisions of the Spooner law, to construct a canal through Nicaragua. Accordingly, he felt that he had

[17] State Dept., Dispatches from Colombia, Vol. 59, Beaupré to Hay, No. 48, June 13, 1903.

derived the correct conclusion that the only result that can affect adversely the interests of this nation, if their Congress should reject the project of the treaty, is that the Government of the United States will cease negotiations and adopt the Nicaragua route for the construction of the canal.

The undue delay in ratification to which the Department of State referred would occur, in his opinion, only if the executive should disregard the favorable action of his legislature with the evident purpose of causing injury to his own country or to the other nation involved in the pact. Rejection or delay by the congress itself could not be interpreted as cause "for the adoption of measures tending to alter the friendly relations between the two countries." If such were the case the negotiation of a treaty would be the "occasion of a serious danger instead of an element of peace and progress." He concluded with a tribute to the greatness and liberality of the United States and an expression of confidence that, even if his congress should decide that the treaty was not for the best interests of Colombia, the amity between the republics would be in no way disturbed thereby.[18]

It should be added that Hay's statement that the canal negotiations "were energetically pressed upon this Government for several years" was not only inaccurate but a complete reversal of the facts of the case. It was the Department of State, goaded by Cromwell, which did the pressing, while Colombia squirmed and desperately sought pretexts for delay. Nor did the United States Congress reverse its judgment because of the Concha protocol. That proposal would have received scant attention had it not been for the efforts of Senator Hanna and the New Company "lobby." To what extent the threat of June 9 fulfilled its function of cowing the Bogotá legislators will appear below.

III

Throughout the spring months Cromwell kept in close touch with affairs on the Isthmus by means of his contacts with the officials of the Panama Railroad Company. The most important

[18] *Ibid.*, Vol. 59, Beaupré to Hay, No. 55, June 20, 1903.

of these were Colonel J. R. Shaler, the general superintendent, H. G. Prescott, the assistant superintendent, J. R. Beers, the freight agent and captain of the port of La Boca, José Agustín Arango, attorney and land agent, Manuel Amador Guerrero, company surgeon, and Pablo Arosemena, consulting counsel. The attorney kept certain of these men constantly posted on developments in Washington and in Bogotá and received from them in turn prompt information of local events that affected his interests.

The congressional elections in Panama resulted in an overwhelming victory for the Conservative party and particularly for its Nationalist wing. By the Colombian constitution each department of the republic was entitled to send a delegation to the national legislature consisting of three senators chosen by the local assembly and as many representatives selected by property-owners and literate citizens as its total population bore ratio to 50,000. The successful senatorial candidates on the Isthmus were José Agustín Arango, an employee of the railroad company, José Domingo Obaldía, a wealthy rancher of prominent family, and Juan B. Pérez y Soto, a native Panamanian with extensive business connections in Cartagena.[19] Early in the spring Governor Mutis Durán had considered the possibility of nominating Dr. Amador Guerrero for a senate seat but it had been felt that his connections with the railroad were too obvious. Amador's friends had finally consented to the nomination of Obaldía instead.[20] Arango did not make the journey to Bogotá because, he later explained, he foresaw the impossibility of preventing the rejection of the treaty.[21] His place in the senate devolved, consequently, on José María Uricoechea, his first alternate.

Opinion in the department itself was by no means unanimous for the pact. Most of the Liberal leaders seem to have opposed it,

[19] Each senator had a first and second alternate. The six members of the lower house from Panama were: Gerardo Lewis, Oscar Terán, Angel María Herrera, Julio J. Fábrega, Samuel Quintero C., Alejandro V. Orillac (Senado, *Anales,* and Cám. de Rep., *Anales,* June 20, 1903).

[20] Terán, *Del tratado Herrán–Hay al tratado Hay–Bunau-Varilla,* I, 420 footnote.

[21] Arango, *Datos para la historia,* p. 11.

though this may have been partly due to fear that the administration would use the payments from the United States to strengthen its political power. Petitions for and against ratification were everywhere in circulation and thousands of signatures were collected, many of them over and over again.

Outstanding among the isthmian opponents of the treaty was Pérez y Soto, senator-elect from Panama and inhabitant of Cartagena in Bolívar. Effusively patriotic in the fashion of his countrymen, the ardor of his sentiments moved him to declare in a letter to *El Correo Nacional:*

> I shall prepare myself, then, for the hour of the Congress . . . hoping to harmonize the progress and prosperity of my native Department with the security and glory of the Republic, without losing sight for an instant of the principal, the essential [consideration] for nations as for individuals, Honor.[22]

The security and glory of the Republic appear, however, to have been rather closely identified in his own mind with the interests of Cartagena, an historic Atlantic port which would gain little and might lose much from the improvement of transit facilities to the west coast of the continent.[23] For this reason and, it may be, for others of a loftier kind, the senator quickly brought his talent for vituperative writing into play against the Yankees and all whom he consided guilty of truckling to them. The following excerpt from another part of the letter quoted above illustrates his method of attack:

> The Herrán treaty will be rejected, and rejected by a unanimous vote in both chambers. That is what I hope, since there will not be a single representative of the nation who will believe the voice of people who have sold themselves; who have had the brazenness to recommend the shameful compact. The insult, however, which Herrán has cast upon the Colombian name will never be wiped out.
> The gallows would be small punishment for a criminal of this class.

---

[22] May 11, 1903.
[23] Opinion in Cartagena was not entirely unfavorable to the treaty. A long memorial to the national congress, urging ratification, contained the names of a number of well-known men who had previously signed an adverse petition (*La Estrella de Panamá*, July 1, 1903).

Cromwell realized the necessity for prompt measures to counteract the effects of such an untimely outburst from an official spokesman for Panama. He used his contacts with "influential people" on the Isthmus to inspire articles and petitions in favor of ratification. Ricardo Arias, a well-to-do landowner and a Liberal, made his first appearance in the role of publicist on June 1 in an "Open Letter" to his countrymen. He declared that the proposed treaty

> is not dishonorable to the nation. . . . For the Isthmus of Panama it is a question of life or death. . . . The gravest responsibility will rest on whomsoever, letting slip this opportunity, the last offered us, may sink this land into eternal ruin.[24]

Juan Antonio Henríquez, special counsel for the railroad in Colón, contributed two articles to *La Estrella de Panamá*. In one of them, entitled "The Sovereignty of Colombia: Where Lie the Dangers of Losing It?" he argued that the real threat to the nation's sovereignty over the Isthmus was not in the acceptance of the canal convention but in its rejection. An unfavorable vote, he warned, would result in peril to the country's integrity and humiliation to its dignity.[25]

The most notable effort in this series came from the pen of Pablo Arosemena, also a legal adviser of the railroad company.[26] He examined at length Articles III and VIII of the treaty with regard to their bearing upon Colombia's sovereignty in the light of international law and concluded that they unquestionably constituted a limitation of national control. Nevertheless, he felt that good reasons existed for accepting such conditions.

> [The pact] is not a vulgar contract for the sale or lease of Colombian territory; it is an international Convention of great scope, of inap-

---

[24] Terán, *op. cit.*, I, 376–377.   [25] June 17, 1903.

[26] Dr. Arosemena was one of the most distinguished Liberals in Colombia. Born in Panama City in 1836, he had received his doctorate of law from the National University in Bogotá at the age of seventeen. His political career commenced two years later with his election to the departmental assembly of Panama. For the next thirty years he held important legislative and executive offices almost continually either on the Isthmus or in Bogotá. He also headed several important diplomatic missions. He was not a member of the revolutionary

preciable transcendency, celebrated for purposes of universal interest.

The Republic does not sell or lease territory to fill its coffers, and to care for the opportune payment of its national expenses. It cedes a section of land, accepting a limitation of political dominion over it, for the excavation of a maritime canal between the two great oceans; a colossal, magnificent work, which has been a dream for centuries, whose execution claims the legitimate interest of mankind and imposes the implacable law of progress. To sell or lease territory to pay the public service—most reprehensible; to cede a territorial zone for a work destined for the innocent use of all nations—justifiable. The proper estimation of the Herrán-Hay Treaty requires the use of an extensive and noble criterion. . . .

I hold this view. The sovereignty of Colombia in the belt of land in which the excavation of an interoceanic canal is possible is not absolute. I do not believe the Republic can obstruct the execution of this work through its territory except for reasons of extreme weight. . . . I maintain that there is no absolute sovereignty on the planet. . . . The world is the property of mankind—it does not belong exclusively to a certain nation or race. Humanity possesses, then, the right to the innocent use of our territory.

Arosemena did not consider the concessions demanded of Colombia to be unduly great. In return the nation received very positive advantages, one of the most important being a guaranty of protection from the imperialistic designs of the European powers, particularly Germany and Great Britain. In view of the frequent disorders along the line of the railroad in the past he thought it natural that the United States should insist on keeping the regulation and defense of the canal in its own hands.[27]

La Estrella de Panamá, which published Arosemena's essay, was the principal organ of the protreaty forces. It was owned and edited by José Gabriel Duque, a native of Cuba and a naturalized citizen of the United States, whose son was in business in the Colombian capital with the son of former Minister Hart. Duque also controlled the Panama Lottery and was considered one of the

---

junta of 1903 and did not approve of the secession movement. Once Panama's independence had been proclaimed, however, he contributed freely of his ability and experience towards the solution of the political problems facing the young nation. He died at Panama City in 1920.

[27] *La Estrella de Panamá*, June 17, 1903.

most influential men on the Isthmus. He knew Cromwell casually from a meeting several years before.[28]

Early in June the municipal council of Panama adopted a resolution asking the national congress to approve the convention and requesting other towns in the department to take similar action. While not necessarily the determining factor in its activities, it is worth noting that the council's thirteen members included a son and a son-in-law of Arango and that its president, Demetrio H. Brid, was an employee of *La Estrella*.[29]

Among the petitions directed to Marroquín during these weeks was one from "Colombians born and resident on the Isthmus, without distinction as to political party." It assured the vice-president that

> we consider the approval of the Herrán-Hay Treaty of vital importance, as affecting our interests and hopes of the present and future. To reject the Treaty, which would work for the adoption of the Nicaragua route, would be equivalent to decreeing the ruin of the Isthmus, causing evil without repair and without measure, and would give rise to unpatriotic sentiments. We beg you to communicate this to Congress. The mail will bring the originals.

The signers included Eusebio A. Morales, a prominent Liberal, José Agustín Arango, Nicanor A. de Obarrio, Federico Boyd, Manuel Amador Guerrero, the company surgeon, Demetrio H. Brid, Samuel Lewis, Arango's son-in-law, Ricardo Arias, and more than a score of other well-known citizens. All of those just mentioned were to play important parts in the establishment of the Republic of Panama the following November.[30]

The opposition faction was meanwhile actively engaged in the propagation of its own views, particularly through the agency of the native-owned press. *El Cronista, El Mercurio, El Duende, El Lápiz* and *El Istmeño* of Panama and *La Verdad* and *El Estímulo* of Colón carried articles condemning the convention.[31] Dr. Carlos

---

[28] *Story of Panama*, pp. 359–360; Terán, *op. cit.*, I, 377.

[29] Terán, *op. cit.*, I, 378–379.

[30] *Anales diplomáticos y consulares*, IV, 842–843. This petition was dated June 19.

[31] Terán, *op. cit.*, I, 418, footnote 2. Terán maintains that the majority of the

A. Mendoza, a Liberal leader, undertook a refutation of Ricardo Arias' "Open Letter," while Dr. Belisario Porras, who had distinguished himself with the Liberal army during the recent struggle, published a denunciation of Marroquín's attempt to "sell" the Isthmus to a foreign government.[32] Some municipalities in which Liberal influence was strong voted down the invitation of the Panama City council to endorse its petition to the national congress.

IV

Faced with the almost certain prospect of defeat in Bogotá, Cromwell had recourse to a final stratagem before the meeting of the legislature. His plan evidently met with the approval of the New Company officials for they wired him from Paris on June 13:

Your cables and letters received. Are completely in accord with you on the program and are happy commencement execution. We hope for favorable results. We thank you for all your efforts.[33]

This dispatch found the attorney already in action. He spent half an hour at the White House with Roosevelt on the morning of the 13th and continued his conference at three o'clock that afternoon. On leaving he refused to be interviewed but sent his press agent, Roger L. Farnham, over to Charles S. Albert of the New York *World* with a suggestion for a story on the Panama affair. Farnham stipulated that he was not to be quoted and that his name was not to be mentioned.[34] The following morning the *World* "scooped" its rival papers with an official prediction of a revolution on the Isthmus in the event that Colombia turned down the treaty. The article read in part:

Panamanians was opposed to the canal treaty because of its diminution of Colombia's sovereignty.

[32] Castillero R., "La causa immediata de la emancipación de Panamá," *Boletín de la Academia Panameña de la Historia*, I, No. 3, 342, footnote; Terán, *op. cit.*, I, 418, footnote 2. It is interesting to note that Mendoza, so highly critical of the Hay-Herrán treaty in June, accepted, as minister of justice of the Republic of Panama, the less advantageous Hay–Bunau-Varilla treaty in November. There are other indications that much of the Liberal opposition on the Isthmus was largely political in character.

[33] *Story of Panama*, p. 280.   [34] *Ibid.*, p. 344; *N. Y. Tribune*, June 14, 1903.

President Roosevelt is determined to have the Panama canal route. He has no intention of beginning negotiations for the Nicaragua route.

The view of the President is known to be that as the United States has spent millions of dollars in ascertaining which route is most feasible; as three different Ministers from Colombia have declared their Government willing to grant every concession for the construction of a canal, and as two treaties have been signed granting rights of way across the Isthmus of Panama, it would be unfair to the United States if the best route be not obtained.

Advices received here daily indicate great opposition to the canal treaty at Bogotá. Its defeat seems probable for two reasons:

1. The greed of the Colombian Government, which insists on a largely increased payment for the property and concession.

2. The fact that certain factions have worked themselves into a frenzy over the alleged relinquishment of sovereignty to lands necessary for building the canal.

Information also has reached this city that the State of Panama . . . stands ready to secede from Colombia and enter into a canal treaty with the United States.

. . . It is known that the following suggestion has been communicated to representatives of the Administration:

The State of Panama will secede if the Colombian Congress fails to ratify the canal treaty. . . . This plan is said to be easy of execution, as not more than 100 Colombian soldiers are stationed in the State of Panama.

The citizens of Panama propose, after seceding, to make a treaty with the United States, giving this Government the equivalent of absolute sovereignty over the Canal Zone. . . . There will be no increase in price or yearly rental. . . .

President Roosevelt is said to strongly favor this plan, if the treaty is rejected. The treaty of 1846, by which the United States guarantees the sovereignty of Colombia over the Isthmus of Panama, is now construed as applicable only to foreign interference, and not to the uprisings of her own people. The formal abrogation of the treaty of 1846 is, however, under consideration.

It is known that the Cabinet favors the President's idea of recognizing the Republic of Panama, if necessary to secure the canal territory. The President has been in consultation both personally and by wire with leading Senators, and has received unanimous encouragement. . . .

It is intended to wait a reasonable time for action by the Colombian Congress, which convenes June 20, and then, if nothing is done, to make the above plan operative.

William Nelson Cromwell . . . had a long conference with the President today. Mr. Cromwell's advices are that much opposition to the treaty has developed, but he still expects ratification.[35]

On the 19th the New Company cabled Cromwell: "We have received your dispatch of the 15th. We hope step taken will produce decisive results." [36]

By coincidence or prearrangement, Bunau-Varilla, who was then in Paris, sent a wire to Marroquín on the 13th urging ratification of the treaty as the only way to avert the loss of Panama. This message was in the engineer's typical style, setting forth the "fundamental principle" that only the United States could build a canal and that the failure of the convention would result either in a shift to Nicaragua or in the "construction of Panama Canal after secession and declaration of independence of the Isthmus of Panama under protection of the United States as has happened with Cuba." He appealed to the "high patriotic policy" of the vice-president to save his country from the "two precipices . . . whither would lead the advice of blinded people or of evildoers who would wish to reject Treaty—or to modify it, which would amount to the same thing." [37] Bunau-Varilla makes no reference in his writings to any reconciliation with the New Company or of any plea for aid on Cromwell's part. Instead, he ascribes his impulse to send the cablegram to an interview with "a distinguished personage," recently arrived from Bogotá with vague news of a "conspiracy" that was baffling the efforts of the aged executive. Whether or not this is the entire explanation is a matter for conjecture.

Having set fires in the enemy's rear with the aid of his White House conferences, Cromwell returned to the task of prodding the Department of State. On June 14, the day the *World* article appeared, he wrote to Hay:

[35] N. Y. *World*, June 14, 1903.   [36] *Story of Panama*, p. 281.
[37] Bunau-Varilla, *Panama: The Creation, Destruction, and Resurrection*, pp. 267–268.

The truth of the matter is, Mr. Secretary, that the Marroquín Government is unpopular and thoroughly distrusted; the elements lately in rebellion, restored to liberty and given a voice in Congress, are naturally hostile to the Government. *The Marroquín Government has become subdued, non-aggressive and apprehensive of dethronement.* Marroquín, too, notes the rise of his rival Reyes, and is afraid to take a position which may not be sustained by Congress. Therefore, unless the Marroquín Government is forced to it, they will only submit the Treaty as the best the United States offers, but without endorsement or recommendation, as they intended to do when the Treaty was made.

The money element also plays a great part and the scheme of a large faction is to repudiate the last Canal extension; wait until next year and forfeit the concession; then sell to the United States direct and get the whole $40,000,000 (this being boldly and frequently stated in the public prints), or else force the United States and the Canal Company to make up a purse of $20,000,000.

I think Marroquín must be *forced* to take a definite stand of *recommendation* in support of the Treaty which he proposed to the United States and induced it to sign and ratify. If he *does that* then all the resources of Government will be employed to carry the Treaty, for it will then become an administrative measure and he must stand or fall by the result and he will probably then put it through.

Further, the idea that by the repudiation of the Canal Extension for which they received five million francs, they can make the United States a party to an unholy bargain of sale based on such an iniquity, should be promptly extinguished, so that this influence against ratification will be dissipated.[38]

This letter, so replete with quotable arguments and phrases, is typical of the artful methods by which the secretary was prevailed upon to imperil the ratification of the treaty through the extension of official protection to the private interests of a French corporation. Cromwell's description of the Colombian administration's attitude was substantially correct, but the reasons he advanced for its lack of vigor were operative only to a secondary degree. The unwillingness of the vice-president to press the convention grew out of the circumstances of its negotiation, not out of the political situation in May and June. The tactics suggested by the attorney were subsequently adopted by the Department of

[38] Dennis, *Adventures in American Diplomacy*, pp. 338–339, footnote.

State and constituted the basis of its policy towards Colombia for the next two months.

Beaupré meanwhile was reporting a slight improvement in the general outlook. Influential leaders who had opposed the treaty shortly before were now said to be working for it, although "the great majority of people still continue to believe . . . that the convention will not be ratified." [39] As the *sabana* trains brought parties of legislators and their families into Bogotá in increasing numbers the social life of the capital quickened. An air of expectancy seemed to hang over the city with the approach of the day set for the opening session. It was an event of more than ordinary significance, for it symbolized the conclusion of four years of chaos and suffering and a return to the ways of orderly government. The press took occasion to plead for the submergence of old feuds and dissensions in a common effort to meet the issues of the hour with calmness and tranquillity. It was an idea that received wide acclaim and, custom-like, soon proved more honored in the breach than the observance.

[39] State Dept., Dispatches from Colombia, Vol. 59, Beaupré to Hay, No. 45, June 10, 1903.

IX

THE DEFEAT OF THE TREATY

At one o'clock in the afternoon of June 20 the Colombian congress convened for a session which was to mark an epoch in the nation's history. Foreign diplomats and such citizens as were fortunate enough to gain entrance crowded the galleries to watch the spectacle of the opening ceremonies. Although more than forty days had elapsed since the official announcement of the assembly date, a liberal sprinkling of vacant seats was noticeable in both halls as the gavels fell. Beaupré, attentively following the proceedings, observed with satisfaction that the administration had a "full and ample majority" in each chamber and concluded that "such legislation as the Government may seriously desire will be enacted."[1] Nevertheless, the senate's first important action was hardly encouraging, for it chose General Joaquín F. Vélez, an outspoken opponent of the treaty, as its presiding officer for the first thirty-day term. José Medina Calderón was elected president of the lower house.[2]

Marroquín's address of welcome was long but rather vague in its recommendations to the legislature. It congratulated the nation upon its return to representative government, emphasized the difficulties of reconstruction, suggested the use of foreign capital for the betterment of river and rail communications, deplored the straitened financial condition of the country, and

---

[1] State Dept., Dispatches from Colombia, Vol. 59, Beaupré to Hay, No. 57, June 20, 1903.

[2] Senado, *Anales*, and Cám. de Rep., *Anales*, June 20, 1903. Vélez was a member of a distinguished and influential family of the department of Bolívar and was known to have presidential ambitions. According to a news report reaching the United States through Colón, the general met with an "enthusiastic reception" on his arrival in Bogotá for the session. Nationalists and Historicals alike participated. It was reported that Reyes was among the first to greet him and that Marroquín sent a state carriage to the train (N. Y. *Times*, June 26, 1903).

THE DEFEAT OF THE TREATY

quoted *in extenso* from the New Year's Day address. The position taken at that time on the Panama Canal question was reaffirmed and made more explicit. The intervening months had neither diminished the vice-president's desire for a canal nor increased his enthusiasm for the Hay-Herrán treaty. He now disclaimed any intention of using his influence for or against ratification.

Since I have thrown upon you all the responsibility that the decision of this negotiation brings, it is not my purpose to allow my opinion to weigh in the matter. Whenever I have transmitted instructions to our representatives in Washington, I have directed them to express formally my resolution to submit the study and decision of this most serious affair . . . to the supreme Congress.

While refusing to take the initiative himself, the executive clearly intimated to the legislature that he thought amendments could be obtained.

Fortunately for transacting business with the American Government in connection with the canal, the present time is more propitious than that in which, being inundated by difficulties and dangers, we were unable to work on behalf of our interest with serenity and liberty. On the other hand, after many years, during which that matter had been dealt with in a vague manner and without any precise conditions, today it is presented to us in such a light that the discussion thereof cannot but lead to practical and positive results.[3]

The anti-administration faction wasted no time in polite preludes to action. On Monday, the 22d, its leaders in the house opened hostilities by calling for the publication of all important documents relating to the treaty. The government objected that it was not yet prepared to submit the pact to congress and was sustained by a vote of 38 to 5.[4] Meanwhile, the vice-president and his advisers, in spite of their professions of neutrality, were occupied in sounding out opinion in the upper branch and bringing pressure to bear on wavering legislators. Beaupré cabled on the 26th that the administration would not present the treaty until it was

[3] *Libro azul,* Appendix, pp. 83–85; State Dept., Dispatches from Colombia, Vol. 59, Beaupré to Hay, No. 72, July 6, 1903.
[4] State Dept., Dispatches from Colombia, Vol. 59, Beaupré to Hay, telegram, June 23, 1903.

confident of success. According to his information, the house was favorable, but an "unfriendly influence makes the majority in the Senate uncertain." [5]

By the end of the first week Rico had made no move to bring in the convention. The cabinet was apparently anxious to defer the beginning of debate until certain of its supporters, particularly Obaldía of Panama, could reach the capital. The foreign minister did ask for a secret session of the senate on the 30th, but evidently for the principal purpose of acquainting it with Hay's warning note of June 9.[6] Beaupré learned several days later through private sources that the dispatch had caused a sensation when read and that it was "construed by many as a threat of direct retaliation against Colombia in case the treaty is not ratified."

Rico's object in communicating this note may have been revealed on the day following the meeting when Marroquín summoned a number of influential senators to the San Carlos Palace to impress upon them the need for favorable action on the treaty. His efforts resulted in a heated argument and a discouraging demonstration of opposition within the group. Beaupré, convinced that this obstructionist sentiment would disappear if confronted by firmness on the part of Marroquín or the United States, erroneously interpreted the excited reaction to the Hay note as a "favorable" sign. He felt the same way about the effect of a statement attributed to Obaldía on his arrival at Bogotá that Panama would revolt if the treaty were not ratified.[7]

For nearly a fortnight the senate waited upon the administration's pleasure, busied with such questions as whether the congress was legal or illegal, ordinary or extraordinary. Not until July 2 did the foreign minister finally submit his government's "project for a convention" with the United States.[8] It then developed that the document bore the signatures of Secretary Hay and Minister Herrán but not those of Marroquín and Rico. This

[5] *Ibid.*, telegram, June 26, 1903.   [6] Senado, *Anales*, June 30, 1903.
[7] State Dept., Dispatches from Colombia, Vol. 59, Beaupré to Hay, No. 68, July 2, 1903; telegram, July 5, 1903.
[8] Senado, *Anales*, July 2, 1903.

THE DEFEAT OF THE TREATY   301

discovery precipitated a bitter wrangle that occupied every meeting devoted to the treaty until July 14. Throughout these two weeks not a single significant reference was made to the provisions of the treaty itself. It soon became apparent that the instigators of the dispute were less concerned with the shortcomings of the pact than with those of the vice-president. The kernel of the matter was that the omission of the latter's endorsement threatened the success of a preconcerted plan to link the chief executive as closely as possible with the unpopular convention and then crush both together under the guise of championing the national honor and integrity. Outwitted in this first skirmish, the discomfited senatorial cabal turned to the precedents in an effort to prove that Marroquín had violated the rules of procedure, meanwhile subjecting the head of the government and his advisers to a thorough castigation for their alleged insincerity and lack of good faith. The rest of the upper house, probably taken by surprise, found itself helpless for a time to deflect the current of debate into less vindictive channels.[9]

The attack on the administration was brilliantly directed by Núñez' disciple and political heir, Miguel Antonio Caro. Medium in stature, with high forehead and Roman profile distinguishing the massive head that surmounted his broad shoulders, Caro was an impressive figure in debate. Few of his countrymen could rival his eloquence or match his satirical thrusts. Kindly and gracious in private life, his self-assurance on public questions frequently took the form of overweening arrogance in the heat of forensic combat.[10] No administration could have had a more

[9] *Ibid.*, "Relación de debates," pp. 17-162.
[10] López de Mesa, *Introducción a la historia de la cultura en Colombia*, pp. 77-79; Ospina, *Diccionario biográfico*, I, 477-478. Caro (1843-1909), a native of Bogotá, achieved early distinction in the fields of philology, history, and constitutional law. A close student of the classics throughout his life, he translated Vergil into Spanish and collaborated with the famous grammarian, Rufino Cuervo, in writing a Latin grammar. His poetry attracted considerable attention in the Spanish-speaking world. He was one of the founders of the *Academia Colombiana*. His strong devotion to the Roman Catholic Church naturally brought him into conflict with the Liberal party, although he does not seem to have favored clericalism in its extreme forms. Reference has been made in chap. ii to his association with Núñez and his dominating position in Colombian politics

dangerous and implacable foe. His enmity toward Marroquín dated back to 1898 when the latter, placed in the vice-presidency through his efforts, scrapped his policies and spurned his counsel during the several months' interval before the more tractable Sanclemente took office.[11] The break was made irreparable by the coup of July 31, 1900, which imprisoned the puppet president and ended the period of Nationalist domination. Since then Caro had been nursing his anger in retirement and watchfully biding his time. The special session now provided him with a unique opportunity to humiliate his enemy before the nation and the world. Congress would be the setting for his retribution, the canal treaty his timely instrument.

Caro's allies were drawn from two main sources. Owing to the impartiality, or perhaps more properly, the political blundering of some of the governors during the elections, a number of the former dictator's strong adherents were returned to the senate by the departmental assemblies. These quickly formed themselves into a *bloc* under their leader, dedicated to a campaign of reprisal against the administration. They soon received active reinforcement from several followers of Fernández, who had been counted upon at the time of their election to support the government's policies, but who were now alienated by the general's ousting from the cabinet.[12] Certain other senators, known to be adverse to the treaty, held aloof from this obviously partisan assault upon the administration. Notable among them were Vélez, soon to be named opposition candidate for the presidency, and Pérez y Soto. Neither of these men took any part in the debate over the signature.

---

in the middle nineties. Endowed though he was with unusual powers of intellect and eloquence, the quality of his statesmanship frequently suffered from the limitations of his temperament. His passionate hatreds sometimes distorted his judgment and deflected his talents into the pursuit of personal grudges. His conduct in the 1903 session was a conspicuous example of this failing.

[11] *Supra*, p. 54.

[12] State Dept., Dispatches from Colombia, Vol. 59, Beaupré to Hay, No. 133, Sept. 11, 1903; *El Colombiano*, July 11, 1903. Senator Zárate was a near relative of Fernández while Uribe Buenaventura was a close friend. It was reported that Fernández himself disapproved of the fight made over the signature (*El Colombiano, loc. cit.*).

THE DEFEAT OF THE TREATY

Marroquín's failure to sign the pact was soon shown to be a violation of custom but not of law. Nevertheless, it was a sufficient opening for his opponents. Senators Indalecio Saavedra, Marcelino Arango, and Joaquín M. Uribe B. immediately proposed the following resolution:

> The Senate will abstain from considering the Herrán–Hay Treaty as long as it is not approved by the Government; and it bases this determination on these motives:
> (1) It has always been customary for the Government to approve conventions and treaties before submitting them to Congress.
> (2) Such a usage is practically essential, as treaties are acts of the Government and not of subordinate agents, a character which comes to them by ratification of the former.
> (3) The Government with whom this treaty is contracted might doubt the good faith of Colombia, for having neglected to authorize at one place and one date, what it had authorized, through instructions, at another date and place.[13]

Of the three sponsors of this resolution only Marcelino Arango spoke in its support. He insisted that the question he had raised concerned not parties alone but the entire nation. The executive approval of treaties had become such a traditional practice in his opinion that the few exceptions that might be cited did not invalidate the rule.

> The Congress does not possess authority to approve treaty projects, but treaties. This document, notwithstanding its high origin and transcendency, has been brought to the Senate with as little consideration as if it were being brought to a confectioner's. If our minister departed from his powers and instructions, the vice-president ought to have remarked on it . . . and then we would not have to occupy ourselves with this question; but if the minister confined himself to the instructions which were communicated to him, we cannot adduce that the vice-president did not wish it to be signed. . . .
> There should have been presented here a legitimate and authentic offspring of the constitutional authority of the vice-president of the Republic, and what has been presented is a foundling, so that we might adopt it and burden ourselves with the shame of its sins if it turns out to be a criminal.

[13] Senado, *Anales,* July 2, 1903.

For all his high indignation Arango was careful to preserve his bridges intact behind him. He explained that his protest at the chief executive's behavior was not to be taken as an indication of his stand on the treaty. When the time came he would vote as he thought proper regardless of the consequences to himself.[14] The senator returned to the attack on July 6, climaxing his speech with a warning that Marroquín's failure to sustain his own handiwork might possibly lead to the seizure of the canal zone by the United States.[15]

Caro was soon in the thick of the fight, blasting the vice-president with a titanic vigor that dwarfed the efforts of his fellow senator. It was not his intention, he had assured his colleagues shortly after his installation, to promote discussions or even participate in them "unless in some exceptional case." Yet he had made it clear in the same speech that he would consider anything that might embarrass Marroquín an "exceptional case." [16] He now proposed an "invulnerable" substitute for the resolution of Saavedra, Arango, and Uribe B. and took an active share in the debates that followed. Like Arango he termed the treaty a "fatherless child" which the administration did not dare to recognize. He dwelt upon its unconstitutionality, arguing that the eight months allowed for the exchange of ratifications was insufficient for the reform of the fundamental charter.[17]

The government was by no means left friendless under fire. Roused by the virulence of the Antiochian's attack, senators and cabinet ministers sprang to the defense. Angulo, irritated by the fruitless delay, inquired whether any legal barrier prevented the senate from examining treaties which did not bear the executive signature or whether the vice-president's possible delinquency necessitated a similar fault in congress.[18] Luis V. González ob-

[14] *Ibid.*, "Relación de debates," pp. 25–27.
[15] *Ibid.*, pp. 50–52.   [16] *Ibid.*, pp. 45–46.
[17] The government excluded most of Caro's speeches from the printed report of the senatorial debates. The main points of his attacks can be pieced together, however, by a study of the detailed replies made by Rico, Angulo, González, Mesa, and Antonio José Uribe. The statements made above are based upon Senado, *Anales*, "Relación de Debates," pp. 59, 61, 107–108, 115–117, 143–144.
[18] *Ibid.*, p. 57 (July 8).

served that the United States would certainly accept ratification without the vice-president's signature and that he doubted it would be reconciled to its defeat, if that should occur, by the fact that Marroquín had signed the rejected document under pressure.[19] Rico, who had been invited to be present at the senate meetings and who found himself a particular object of Caro's denunciations, defended himself and his chief with spirit and ability. He asserted that the government had done its best under very difficult circumstances, that it had ordered Herrán to sign rather than sacrifice the entire negotiations, and that its approval of the minister's work was implied by its act of submitting the convention to the legislature.[20]

The most effective defense of the administration was made on July 10, by Antonio José Uribe, who had been appointed to the cabinet as minister of public instruction that he might bring his learning and prestige to bear in the debates. This distinguished jurist's address stood out as an all-too-rare instance of informed discourse and unimpassioned argument. Step by step he reviewed the efforts of the government to achieve a diplomatic agreement with the United States, and, having sought to justify the constitutionality of those efforts, he tactfully took the senate to task for its partisan squabbling:

Now [the government] has sent [the treaty] to the Legislative Chambers, respecting completely their full freedom of action to study and resolve the question. It falls to the Colombian Congress thus to say the last word in this grave matter . . . inasmuch as it has been discussed in the principal chancelleries of Europe and in some of those of America; the diplomacy and press of the world have analyzed the treaty: all these studies are known to us; the world has no further word to add to the question; it pertains to the Colombian Congress to pronounce this final word. That is why this debate is, or ought to be, so solemn; the governments and the principal organs of the word press are following it with great interest, and they know by cable from hour to hour the course of the discussion which has been initiated.

Unfortunately, the debate, which has been in progress several days,

---

[19] *Ibid.*, pp. 107–108, 115 (July 8).
[20] *Ibid.*, pp. 58–59 (July 8), 126 (July 9).

has revolved on questions of mere form; and time, so precious in these moments, is wasted in angry and sterile discussions. Let us raise the line of sight and penetrate to the substance of the matter which should be examined.

The current impasse he attributed to a confusion between public treaties and simple administrative or civil contracts, such as were covered by the commercial, political, and municipal codes. From this misunderstanding had arisen an attempt to apply domestic codes to what was "perhaps the most weighty and transcendental question in world politics and international commerce." Correctly construed, the minister pointed out, treaties were contracts between sovereign governments and therefore enforceable not by national laws but by the law of nations. Accordingly,

the Herrán–Hay Treaty is a complete diplomatic document, for the perfection of which there is lacking only the approval of the Legislative Body of Colombia and the exchange of ratifications between the two governments: it is a most important international question; not a matter of a mere municipal or political code.

Uribe protested that he could not see the advantage to be derived from a debate over the detail in question. The United States did not ask for the vice-president's signature and it was of no use to Colombia. If the treaty was ratified, it was thereby a perfect compact; if it was not, the executive's name would possess no significance anyway. He warned his hearers against creating the impression that Colombia was capable of jeopardizing the permanent interests of two peoples because of a bureaucratic technicality, thereby proclaiming itself before the world a nation governed by pettifoggers rather than statesmen.[21]

The barb in Uribe's last remark brought cries of disapproval, but the speech seems to have had its effect in putting an end to the long dispute. The Colombian legislators were extremely conscious of the world's attention, now fixed upon them as never before. Also, quite apart from their personal feelings about the treaty, the senators were fast losing interest in baiting Marroquín

[21] *Ibid.*, pp. 138–149.

THE DEFEAT OF THE TREATY

for his refusal to sign. The vituperation of Caro and his friends had somewhat overshot the mark. Ospina probably voiced the sentiment of a number of his fellows when he administered a dignified rebuke to Arango for seeking to classify the membership into two parties, which he referred to as the "presidential" and "ours." His own vote, Ospina insisted, would be cast on the merits of the treaty, not on the instructions of a factional leader.[22]

On July 10 Caro's substitute resolution was defeated by a vote of 14 to 11. Pérez y Soto and Vélez supported the government on this question, as did Ospina, whom Fernández had imprisoned. The original Saavedra-Arango-Uribe B. proposal was referred to the committee on foreign relations and quickly buried.[23] Four days later the upper house turned its attention for the first time to the convention itself. A committee consisting of Pérez y Soto, chairman, Obaldía, Ospina, Gerlein, De Narváez (later replaced by Uribe B.), Uricoechea, Campo, and Rivas Groot was appointed to make a study of the document and return a report with a project of law within eight days.[24] This period was twice subsequently extended owing to the illness of Pérez y Soto.

II

While the senatorial debate over the vice-president's signature was still at its height the administration evidently came to the conclusion that this otherwise unwelcome outburst might provide an opportune means of liberalizing the financial terms of the treaty. If it could be used to convince the United States that Marroquín was confronted with a vigorous opposition and that the coöperation of the two governments was necessary to secure ratification, important concessions might be forthcoming from Washington. On July 9 Reyes informed Beaupré that in his opin-

[22] *Ibid.*, p. 150.
[23] Voting negatively on the Caro substitute were Angulo, Campo, González Luis, González Valencia, Gerlein, Jiménez López, Lorenzo Marroquín, Mésa, Obaldía, Ospina, Pérez y Soto, Rivas Groot, Tobar, and Vélez. The affirmative votes were cast by Arango, Caro, Gómez Restrepo, De Narváez, Márquez, Pacheco, Quintero Calderón, Uribe B., Uricoechea, Saavedra, and Zárate.
[24] Senado, *Anales*, July 14, 1903.

308 THE DEFEAT OF THE TREATY

ion the convention could not be passed without two amendments, one requiring a payment of $10,000,000 from the New Company and the other increasing the indemnity provision in Article XXV to $15,000,000. The general added that immediate approval of the treaty would be assured by these alterations. He requested the minister to get a confidential expression of his government's views on the subject.[25]

The cabled report of this interview reached the State Department on the 12th. Hay's reply was prompt and uncompromising.

Neither of the proposed amendments mentioned in your telegram received to-day would stand any chance of acceptance by the Senate of the United States, while any amendment whatever or unnecessary delay in the ratification of the treaty would greatly imperil its consummation.[26]

Roosevelt, on learning the substance of this exchange, wrote from Oyster Bay on the 14th:

Make it as strong as you can to Beaupré. Those contemptible little creatures in Bogotá ought to understand how much they are jeopardizing things and imperilling their own future.[27]

As nearly as can be determined from the fragmentary evidence available, the administration's strategy before congress opened was based on the assumption that the membership of the upper house would include a noisy opposition minority. The vice-president and his advisers probably anticipated that the majority of senators would favor the treaty with moderate amendments. It is significant that fully six weeks before the legislature assembled Reyes predicted "a lengthy debate and an adverse vote" followed by a change in sentiment and eventual approval.[28] Although he naturally said nothing about it to Beaupré, he probably hoped

[25] State Dept: Dispatches from Colombia, Vol. 59, Beaupré to Hay, telegram, July 9, 1903.

[26] *Ibid.*: Instructions to Colombia, Vol. 19, Hay to Beaupré, telegram, pp. 254-255, July 13, 1903. Beaupré's message was received on the 12th, but Hay's reply in answer to "your telegram received to-day," was not sent until the next day.

[27] Pringle, *Roosevelt*, p. 311. This note was in reply to Hay's letter of July 13 (Roosevelt Papers, Hay to Roosevelt).

[28] State Dept.: Dispatches from Colombia, Vol. 59, Beaupré to Hay, No. 19, May 7, 1903; Vol. 60, same to same, No. 133, Sept. 11, 1903.

THE DEFEAT OF THE TREATY 309

that Washington would be sufficiently impressed by the opposition to accept a number of modifications advantageous to Colombia. However that may have been, it is certain that by early July the administration was meeting with more resistance than it had counted upon, and worst of all, a resistance centered on itself rather than on the treaty. Under these circumstances Reyes was now advising Marroquín not to press the convention but to rely upon, and work for, a gradual shift of opinion both in congress and the press.[29] His interview with Beaupré on July 9 was in harmony with this policy. Nothing would have produced a more favorable reaction in certain quarters than the news that the United States was willing to permit an increase of $15,000,000 in the total compensation.

Beaupré suspected that the government might have tactical reasons for its apparent indifference to the fate of the convention, but his uneasiness over the final result was growing steadily more pronounced. "If one could know," he wrote in his dispatch of July 11,

just what would be the attitude of the Government later on, it would be easy enough to predict the outcome, for I still adhere to my oft-repeated opinion that if the Government shall seriously desire it the treaty will be ratified. Its present attitude of washing its hands of the whole matter will not do, for while the House is favorable, there is a declared majority in the Senate against ratification, and only the influence of the Government can win it over.

I am inclined to believe, from information obtained at different times, some of which I have reported to the department, that the Government intends to use its influence later on, and at what it shall deem the proper time, in favor of the treaty. If so, the treaty will be ratified; if not, then it will be defeated.[30]

The minister summarized this note in a wire sent off the same day and added:

The danger is delay, which the opposition fights for. I think strong intimation from you through the Colombian minister or this legation that unnecessary delay should be avoided would be effective.

---
[29] *Ibid.*, Vol. 60, same to same, No. 154, Sept. 25, 1903.
[30] *Ibid.*, Vol. 59, same to same, No. 78.

Otherwise debate may continue until September, necessitating instructions communicated by telegraph for exchange of ratifications.[31]

By the 15th, with the government triumphant in the signature fight and the treaty in the hands of the special senate committee, the prevailing opinion in official circles seemed to be that the pact would be ratified, but with amendments. Beaupré himself believed that it could be ratified unaltered were it not for the widespread impression that additional concessions were obtainable. He again asked Hay for a firm declaration of the State Department's position in the matter of amendments and suggested that he be given "secret instructions as a guide in case of emergency."[32]

Further telegraphic communication was cut off at this critical juncture owing to a disagreement between the Colombian government and the Central and South American Telegraph Company over the renewal of the latter's charter. Although the existing contract had more than a year to run, the company closed its Buenaventura office, through which diplomatic messages were sent, on July 15 as a means of "persuading" the government to accept certain terms it wished to include in the new agreement. Beaupré, finding the situation "embarrassing and unpleasant," complained to Rico and was assured that the government would seek a temporary adjustment. Herrán, meanwhile, filed a vigorous protest with the company's New York office demanding compliance with the unexpired contract. A copy of this note was sent to Hay with the comment that the "closing of the Buenaventura office absolutely deprives Colombia of direct telegraphic communication with the United States and Europe."[33]

The senate, awaiting the report of its special committee, elected officers on the 18th for the second thirty-day term. Beaupré was encouraged by the fact that both Quintero Calderón, the new president, and Pedro Nel Ospina, first vice-president, were generally considered to be favorable to the treaty. The minister still

[31] *Ibid.*, Vol. 59, same to same.
[32] *Ibid.*, Vol. 59, same to same, telegram, July 15, 1903.
[33] *Ibid.*, Vol. 59, same to same, No. 82, July 21, 1903; No. 88, July 29; State Dept., Notes, Colombia, Vol. 10, Herrán to Hay, July 16 and enclosure.

THE DEFEAT OF THE TREATY

felt, however, that "there may be enough members of the Senate to carry certain amendments." He was under the impression that Marroquín, at least, realized the impossibility of securing the consent of the United States to any changes in the convention, but he repeated his request to the department for a definite statement of policy in order "to bolster up and strengthen this understanding." [34]

This dispatch had no more than started northward when an inquiry from Rico reached the legation which made it clear that the question of amendments was still very much in the thoughts of the administration. The foreign minister asked to be informed whether the statement in Beaupré's note of April 24 that "any change would be in violation of the Spooner law and therefore not permissible" referred only to Colombia's desire to charge the New Company for the privilege of transferring its rights or to alterations in the text of the treaty as well. Beaupré replied the next day that the Spooner law had been fully complied with insofar as the Panama route was concerned when the Hay-Herrán treaty was signed and that it could "only again become a subject for discussion, and then in reference to the Nicaragua route, in the event of the rejection of the treaty by Colombia." He admitted that this was his personal opinion, which he was unable to confirm by cable, but he had no grounds for belief that his government would "consider or discuss again any modifications whatever to the treaty as it stands." He reasoned that if the Department of State viewed a change in the status of the companies' concessions as a violation of the Spooner Act, then, "with much more reason, it would seem that the treaty itself, as the official interpretation of the law, can not be modified at all without violating that law." [35]

This evidence of the administration's continued interest in amendments heightened Beaupré's apprehensions. He looked upon it as a possible prelude to open cabinet support of the move-

[34] State Dept., Dispatches from Colombia, Vol. 59, Beaupré to Hay, No. 83, July 21, 1903.
[35] *Ibid.*, No. 85, July 22, 1903.

ment for revision. Furthermore, it strengthened the suspicion that his earlier warnings were not regarded as particularly authoritative in government circles. While interruption of the cable service continued, however, he found himself obliged to proceed as best he could without diplomatic guidance from Washington.

III

Among the legation's tasks during the course of the session was the investigation of reports that foreign influences were at work to defeat the treaty. Persistent rumors to this effect had been reaching the Department of State for several months. The German government, in particular, was suspected by the administration of nurturing expansionist schemes in the region of the projected canal. Secretary of War Root regarded the Germans as a "predatory nation" and later admitted that the Platt Amendment had been drafted with an eye to possible trouble from their quarter.[36] Henry White wrote Hay from London in April that he had "little doubt" that the Wilhelmstrasse was responsible for blocking the sale of the Danish West Indies to the United States.[37] Washington naval strategists were watching the Kaiser's vigorous naval and colonial policies with undisguised apprehension. The comparatively recent scholarly investigations of Vagts, Perkins, Tansill, and others have clearly demonstrated the lack of any solid basis for these fears insofar as the Caribbean was concerned. In 1903, however, the Berlin state archives were still closed to outsiders. No one at the North American capital at that time could do more than guess at the actual objectives behind Germany's periodic outbursts of aggressiveness.

As early as January 12, ten days before the signing of the treaty, Hay instructed Ambassador Tower in Berlin to discover "discreetly and informally" whether any foundation existed for a press notice from London stating that the New Company had received a German offer of $40,000,000 for its rights upon the expiration of the United States' option and that the German gov-

[36] Jessup, *Elihu Root*, I, 314.   [37] Nevins, *Henry White*, p. 206.

THE DEFEAT OF THE TREATY

ernment was willing to purchase Colombia's shares in the enterprise at par in liquidation of all claims of its citizens against that country.[37] Tower found no evidence of such a scheme, but the newspapers seized upon the London dispatch and kept the story in circulation for several weeks. *El Porvenir* of Bogotá exclaimed that the German offer, if true, "will completely change the face of things and will give incalculable amplitude to the negotiations." [39] The New York *World* attributed German activity at the Colombian capital to suspicion that the United States and Great Britain had reached an understanding over the management of the canal that would eventually prove inimical to the interests of their commercial rivals, particularly in South America. The same paper reported that representatives of French stockholders in the New Company who considered the sale price too low were "co-operating against the treaty." [40] Herrán, meanwhile, was warning his superiors that the transcontinental railroads had aided Morgan in his fight against the ratification in the United States Senate and "they will send to Bogotá a commission well equipped to foment and strengthen the opposition which is organizing in our Congress against the treaty." [41]

As disconcerting accounts of the Colombian reaction to the convention began to pour in on Washington during May the Department of State grew watchful for signs of European or North American intrigue. On June 2 Hay was writing to Beaupré:

From your long residence [in Colombia] you ought to be in a position to be in close touch with every phase of the situation and to know and understand the intricacies of Colombian politics as they may bear upon the very important question at issue. The department desires all of the pertinent, accurate information that it can obtain, and wants it promptly. . . . It is also expected that you will know what hostile influences, if any, are at work against the ratification of the

---

[38] State Dept., Instructions to Germany, Vol. 21, Hay to Tower, telegram.
[39] Feb. 26, 1903.   [40] March 27, 1903.
[41] *Libro azul*, p. 360. There is not the slightest evidence that any such commission was sent to Bogotá. Possibly Cromwell and Herrán had discovered that they, as well as Morgan, could capitalize on the "bogey" value of the transcontinental railroads.

treaty, and whether or not there is opposition to it from European sources. The situation is seemingly a grave one, but the department has confidence that you will rise to the full measure of its requirements.[42]

The minister replied on July 21:

At times I have thought, from the . . . conversation of certain opponents, that foreign hostile influences were at work, but I have never been able to be certain of this. If there be opposition from this source, it is of too secret a nature to be discovered, and can not, therefore, be particularly effective. On the whole, I am inclined to believe that no direct hostile influence is being used here, but that, if any exists, it comes through Colombian legations or consulates in Europe.

Through private sources Beaupré learned that Uricoechea, a member of the special senate committee on the treaty, had called upon Baron Grünau, the German chargé d'affaires, to inquire what the attitude of the Berlin government would be in case trouble arose over the canal question and whether it would be willing to undertake or aid the construction of the waterway in the event that the Hay-Herrán pact was rejected. Grünau replied that he had no instructions on the subject but that, in view of his government's desire to remain on friendly terms with the United States, it was his opinion that no steps would be taken in connection with the construction of the canal or any controversy growing out of the negotiations. About the same time a member of the house of representatives approached the British minister on a similar errand. He was informed that Great Britain regarded the Hay-Pauncefote treaty as a sufficient guaranty for the commerce of the world and was, therefore, willing to permit the United States a free hand in any further developments concerning the canal.[43]

IV

The senate committee appointed to study the treaty completed its labors on July 31 and four days later submitted its report, ac-

[42] State Dept.: Instructions to Colombia, Vol. 19, Hay to Beaupré, No. 15.
[43] *Ibid.*, Dispatches from Colombia, Vol. 59, Beaupré to Hay, No. 83.

THE DEFEAT OF THE TREATY

companied by a "project of law for the approval with amendments of the treaty between the Republic of Colombia and the United States of America for the construction of an interoceanic canal between the Atlantic and Pacific Oceans." It confined its analysis to questions of law with the suggestion that other possible changes be postponed until after the main issues had been discussed in the first debate. Nine amendments were incorporated in the report:

First. References to the Spooner law in the preamble of the treaty were to be suppressed as inappropriate in a pact between sovereign nations and a possible source of later disagreement.

Second. Article I was to stipulate explicitly that the canal and railroad companies must reach an understanding with Colombia before its consent to the transfer of the concessions would become effective. Also, provision was to be made in the same article that all land grants possessed by the companies on the Isthmus were to revert to Colombia upon ratification of the treaty "to the end that the cities of Panama and Colón may remain effectively excluded from the zone . . ."

Third. Articles II and III were to be modified in such a way as to make clear that the rights granted to the United States in the zone and its adjacent territories were those of tenancy and not of ownership. The boundary of the concession was to be determined with the greatest precision. In addition, the guaranty of Colombian sovereignty embodied in the treaty of 1846–48 was not to be modified in any respect, but was to continue to apply to the entire department of Panama, including the zone.

Fourth. The right conceded to the United States to use the rivers and lakes needed to supply the canal was not to be considered exclusive beyond the point required for such purpose.

Fifth. The "uncertainty" in Article VIII concerning the right of Colombia to collect duties in the cities of Panama and Colón was to be clarified.

Sixth. Article XIII, relating to the establishment of the United States tribunals and the application of United States laws in the zone was to be suppressed as contrary to Article 10 of the Colombian constitution. The police and sanitary regulations to be enforced in the leased area were to be made the subject of a special agreement between the two governments.

Seventh. The evaluation of damages resulting from the expropriation of private property by the United States was to be determined by a joint commission, the awards to be based upon value at the time of seizure rather than before the commencement of construction as provided in Article XIV.

Eighth. An article was to be included providing for the forfeiture of all rights and properties to Colombia should the canal not be completed within the time agreed upon.

Ninth. Specific mention was to be made of the tribunal which was to decide differences of interpretation.

These proposals represented the views of the majority of the committee, consisting of Nel Ospina, Obaldía, Uricoechea, Campo, Gerlein, Rivas Groot, and González Valencia. Uribe B. appended a separate opinion which attempted to show that the treaty violated seven articles of the constitution. He rejected his colleagues' proposed changes as inadequate and denounced the entire agreement as "inconvenient, illegal, and detrimental to the national dignity." The most detailed analysis of all was submitted by the chairman, Pérez y Soto. He raised lengthy objections to practically every article. The effectiveness of his arguments was considerably weakened, however, by repeated indications of his profound aversion to everything Yankee. He expressed doubt that the United States wanted any isthmian canal whatever and hinted broadly that its practical motive in negotiating the treaty was to forestall the possibility of construction by a rival nation. He supported this ingenious thesis by pointing to the undeveloped state of the North American merchant marine as compared with those of other commercial powers. His own attitude, he was careful to state, was favorable to the idea of a canal. No one, it appeared, desired more earnestly than he to assist in furthering the progress of mankind. Yet the senator from Panama considered it his duty to remind the congress of the many substantial reasons why his constituents would not profit from an interoceanic canal.[44]

The presentation of this committee's report marked the real crisis in the Colombian senate's consideration of the treaty. The amendments suggested by the majority were, on the whole, reasonable and statesmanlike. Any mention of change in the amount of the annuity or the cash indemnity to be paid by the United States was carefully avoided. The requirement of a previous understanding with the canal and railroad companies had been regarded as fundamental by the Colombian government since the beginning of the negotiations. Its revival at this time was certainly in line with the private wishes of the administration and was probably an indispensable condition of ratification by the senate. On one point only did the report recommend an alteration which would seriously affect the privileges of the United States as set forth in the convention. The suppression of the article providing for the extension of United States courts and laws to the canal zone in cases concerning its citizens would undoubtedly have given rise to a host of difficulties between the two governments and eventually necessitated some such arrangement as that already proposed in Article XIII. In view of the virulence of the newspaper attacks on this article, however, the committee was obliged to make some show of opposition. The report was essentially a compromise designed to muster the strength of the senate "moderates" behind a practical set of proposals. In this it was successful, if we may credit Beaupré's "positive information" that twenty of the twenty-seven votes in the upper house had been secured in its support before it was formally submitted on August 4.

Rico undoubtedly awaited the reaction of the United States minister with some anxiety. He was not kept long in suspense. Cut off from cable communication with Washington, Beaupré determined upon a "course of energetic action" which he later

[44] *Libro azul,* Appendix, pp. 86 *et seq.* As has been mentioned above, Pérez y Soto was an Isthmian by birth, but his residence and business interests were now located in the city of Cartagena, a mainland port which had no reason to expect any considerable direct benefits from the canal.

admitted "might . . . seem undiplomatic unless viewed in the light of the exigency and the circumstances." Early in the morning of the 5th he called upon the foreign minister and handed him a note containing a "further interpretation" of his instructions. After calling attention to the reasons for its author's inability to consult his government, the dispatch came to the point without further ceremony.

It would appear to me that the committee has either been insufficiently acquainted with the contents of my notes of April 24 and June 10, 1903, or that they have failed to attach to these direct communications the importance they demand as definite expressions of opinion and intention on the part of my Government.

From them it is clear that the committee's proposed modification of article 1 is alone tantamount to an absolute rejection of the treaty. I feel it my duty to reiterate the opinion I have before expressed to your excellency that my Government will not consider or discuss such an amendment at all.

Furthermore, it continued, the suppression of Article XIII would "not be acceptable in any case." The other suggested alterations, while not so serious in principle, were, in the envoy's opinion, of too slight a value to Colombia to warrant the risk of having them discussed further by the United States Senate, even assuming that they were submitted to that body, which was "more than doubtful." The interpretation of individual articles could be better handled through "separate emphatic assurances" by the Department of State or by specific legislation when the time arrived for dealing with them.

If the present modifications of the committee constitute really the final decision that is likely to be arrived at by the Congress of Colombia, the matter should be voted without any delay, and so give at least a slight opportunity to my Government to consider the matter before the expiration of the time for exchange of ratifications as provided in the treaty. . . .

I take this opportunity to respectfully reiterate what I have before expressed to your excellency, that if Colombia really desires to maintain the present friendly relations existing between the two countries, and at the same time secure to herself the extraordinary advantages that the construction of the canal in her territory will undoubtedly produce, . . . the pending treaty should be ratified exactly in its present form, without any modifications whatever. I say this from a deep conviction that my Government will not in any case accept amendments.[45]

During the afternoon of the same day the cable service was partially restored and Beaupré received a departmental message dated July 31, the first orders regarding the canal he had had from Washington since the 13th of that month. Its contents were precisely what he had been requesting.

Instructions heretofore sent to you show the great danger of amending the treaty. This Government has no right or competence to covenant with Colombia to impose new financial obligation upon canal company and the President would not submit to our Senate any amendment in that sense, but would treat it as voiding the negotiation and bringing about a failure to conclude a satisfactory treaty with Colombia. No additional payment by the United States can hope for approval by the United States Senate, while any amendment whatever requiring reconsideration by that body would most certainly imperil its consummation. You are at liberty to make discreet unofficial use of your instructions in the proper quarters. The Colombian Government and Congress should realize the grave risk of ruining the negotiation by improvident amendment.[46]

Beaupré lost no time in rushing another communication to Rico. "I have," he informed the minister, "received such definite instructions from my Government as enable me not only fully to confirm, but materially amplify the terms of all my previous notes . . . ." He thereupon paraphrased Hay's telegram and "implored" the Colombian government "to urge upon Congress the necessity of ratifying the treaty in its present form." Apparently in the belief that the situation called for something even stronger, Beaupré reintroduced the theme of the message of June 9:

I may say that the antecedent circumstances of the whole negotiation of the canal treaty . . . are of such a nature as to fully warrant the United States in considering any modifications whatever of the

---

[45] State Dept.: Dispatches from Colombia, Vol. 60, Beaupré to Hay, No. 98, enclosure, Aug. 7, 1903; same to same, No. 105, Aug. 15, 1903.
[46] *Ibid.*: Instructions to Colombia, Vol. 19, Hay to Beaupré, telegram.

terms of the treaty as practically a breach of faith on the part of the Government of Colombia, such as may involve the very greatest complications in the friendly relations which have hitherto existed between the two countries.

In conclusion he expressed regret at the senate committee's insistence on the "practical reenactment of the treaty of 1846–1848," an attitude seeming to imply "almost a doubt as to the good faith of the intention of the United States in its compliance therewith." That agreement, he asserted confidently, unless denounced in accordance with its own provisions, would never be "disregarded in the slightest degree by the Government of the United States." [47]

Both of these notes were read in a secret session of the senate a day or two later and created an uproar. Indignation was by no means confined to the opponents of the administration. Historicals and Nationalists alike were cut to the quick by the envoy's imperious tone and his implied contempt for the prerogatives of the congress. Their pride was hurt and their sense of decorum outraged. Conscious of the relative weakness of their country, the legislators were particularly sensitive about any matter touching its independence of action. The American minister could hardly have chosen a more certain method of infuriating these men than to threaten them with Yankee coercion. This was a fact which Hay clearly did not appreciate, although a more efficiently organized department would have been in a position to enlighten him on the point. For Beaupré's clumsy and amateurish tactics there is no excuse. He was, of course, under the necessity of following his instructions from Washington, but he was at all times permitted a wide discretion as to the manner of handling the business of his mission. It must be remembered also that from the early weeks of his incumbency he had been a consistent advocate of pressure diplomacy and that Hay's peremptory cable of July 31 was thoroughly in line with his own requests for "firm representations."

The Beaupré notes completely disrupted the plans of the sen-

[47] *Ibid.:* Dispatches from Colombia, Vol. 60, Beaupré to Hay, No. 98, enclosure, Aug. 7, 1903.

ate moderates. The attitude of the United States made it clear that any attempt to use the special committee's report as the basis for further negotiations was futile. The administration, moreover, had been placed in a position where any move it might make in favor of unconditional ratification would be publicized by its enemies as evidence of truckling to the foreigner. Caro, sensing that the humiliation of the vice-president was at hand, secured passage of a resolution admitting the public to the debates upon the committee report.[48]

Meanwhile, a group of the executive's advisers, including Lorenzo Marroquín, Reyes, various senators, and a number of prominent citizens, had set to work devising ways and means of averting the political dangers of the situation. It was generally conceded that as matters stood the treaty was doomed in the senate. It was necessary, therefore, for the government to steer a course that would dissociate it as completely as possible from the ostensible causes of the rejection. By August 10 a plan had been perfected which would, if successful, save the administration's face without sacrificing the canal. In accordance with this strategy the committee report would be brought up for first debate on the 12th, the correspondence with the United States legation would be introduced in such a manner as to emphasize Rico's defense of the rights and dignity of the Colombian congress, and finally, when the vote was taken, no effort would be made to prevent an overwhelming defeat of the convention. The suddenness of this decisive action would, it was hoped, arouse the coastal departments to vehement protest, send foreign exchange up enormously and so generally disturb the country that a sharp reaction in public sentiment would set in, enabling the government to "yield" to domestic pressure for a reconsideration of the treaty or at least to push through a law empowering the vice-president to complete the negotiations without further recourse to the legislature.[49]

[48] Senado, *Anales*, p. 90 (Aug. 6).
[49] State Dept., Dispatches from Colombia, Vol. 60, Beaupré to Hay, No. 105, Aug. 15, 1903; same to same, No. 133, Sept. 11, 1903; same to same, No. 154, Sept. 25, 1903.

Possibly with the purpose of drawing Beaupré out still further, Rico addressed a note to him on the 8th to inquire whether there were any other circumstances in the course of the treaty negotiation beyond those cited in Beaupré's notes which had led him to state that any modification of the terms signed by Herrán would be "practically a breach of faith on the part of the Government of Colombia, such as may involve the very greatest complications in the friendly relations which have hitherto existed between the two countries." Beaupré replied promptly that the circumstances referred to had been fully covered in his note of June 10. Unfortunately, he did not stop there. Instead, he played squarely into the foreign minister's hands with "a few more words" on the "extraordinary efforts made by my Government to keep faith with Colombia after an agreement had been reached between the executive Governments of the two nations." The fight for ratification in the United States was, he remarked,

> a momentous struggle, and the final and close victory was secured in the end only by the most stupendous efforts on the part of the administration, imbued as they were with the idea that such a compact, made after mature and careful consideration . . . must be ratified as it stood.

In view of this experience, the envoy added, it was his government's view that no Colombian amendment could be safely submitted to the Senate in Washington. He felt that the strength of the Nicaragua faction and the anti-canal interests was not sufficiently appreciated in Bogotá. The note concluded with a half apology for the tone of his communications on the 5th. The latter "may have expressed an almost exaggerated desire to impress upon your excellency the dangers of delay or modification . . . ," but the foreign minister was assured that the writer had the "deepest personal concern" for the honor and glory of Colombia and that he would always work for the "ultimate good" not only of the country which he represented but of that in which he had "the privilege and pleasure of residing." [50]

Rico dispatched an answer on the 11th. After summarizing the

[50] *Ibid.*, Vol. 60, Beaupré to Hay, No. 101, enclosure, Aug. 10, 1903.

apposite passages in the preceding correspondence he declared that in his government's opinion the position adopted by the United States—that any modification of the treaty as signed constituted a violation of the pact—was "not compatible with diplomatic usages nor with the express stipulation of article 28 of the same convention." In succinct and able fashion he reviewed the procedure prescribed by the Colombian constitution for the negotiation and ratification of treaties and noted its fundamental resemblance to that followed in the United States. He called attention to Beaupré's own statement that various amendments had been proposed by senators in Washington. He assumed that since the propriety of their action had not been questioned there was no reason to "consider that the Government of the United States was bound to approve the treaty without modifications, as has been claimed in regard to the Government of Colombia." Before ending on his customary note of ceremonial politeness, Rico hinted at the use he was about to make of this latest exchange of views.

I might observe that the general opinion which has been developing itself in favor of the Panama route might induce the Senate in Washington to accept some or all of the modifications which may be adopted by the Colombian Congress; but as the Government of your excellency does not think possible the presentation of modifications to the pact, I will call the attention of the Congress of Colombia to this grave circumstance.[51]

V

The historic treaty debate of August 12 opened at half-past one in the afternoon in the crowded chamber of the upper house. Before the opposition could catch the significance of his move, Senator Marroquín obtained consent to have the discussion preceded by the reading of the correspondence between Beaupré and the minister for foreign affairs. Caro then announced his intention of introducing a law providing, first, for the rejection of the Hay-Herrán treaty and, secondly, for a communication

[51] *Ibid.*, Vol. 60, Beaupré to Hay, No. 107, enclosure, Aug. 17, 1903.

to the United States Government to the effect that the adverse decision of the Colombian congress carried no implication of hostility nor any antagonism to its construction of the Panama Canal.[52]

As the reading of the Rico-Beaupré notes proceeded the galleries gave free expression to their feelings. The American envoy's dispatches were greeted with loud murmurs of disapproval, while Rico's responses, read principally by himself, evoked prolonged applause. Caro quickly perceived that the administration was turning the open session, for which he was responsible, to its own advantage. He secured the floor as soon as possible and launched into one of the most vigorous philippics of his career. The treaty itself was hardly mentioned. Instead, he denounced the government for its conduct of the negotiations and accused it of courting the crowd's acclaim as champion of the rights of the congress in order to evade responsibility for its diplomatic blundering. This was an opportunity the veteran *politico* had long awaited. Throwing every ounce of energy into the effort, he turned his full powers of verbal castigation upon his foes. The spectators were held spellbound by the force of his eloquent fury. One observer recorded that he "reached his peak as a parliamentary orator." Another compared him to a "caged lion" as he paced back and forth before his desk. Impressive as his speech undoubtedly was from the standpoint of delivery, its statesmanlike contribution to the debate was slight. The personal animus

[52] According to the rules of the Colombian senate the procedure for dealing with treaties was as follows: The treaty, on submission, was turned over to a committee which prepared a favorable project of law and recommended changes if it saw fit. To be approved, the project of law must pass three debates. In the first, the treaty was read in its entirety and the question of its convenience or inconvenience for the public interest was discussed. This debate closed with the question: "Does the senate wish that a second debate be held on this project?" If the treaty was not rejected at this point, a second debate was held in which the pact was discussed article by article. Amendments could be proposed at this time by any member of the senate. If the vote at the conclusion of this session was favorable, another committee incorporated the changes adopted and a final debate occurred which terminated with the question: "Does the senate desire that this project be a law of the republic?" The method used in the lower house was substantially the same.

THE DEFEAT OF THE TREATY

which inspired his remarks robbed them of any important constructive value.[53]

In marked contrast to Caro, Rico delivered a calm and carefully reasoned address. While he refrained from making any direct recommendation regarding the treaty, he emphasized the fact that Colombia faced the choice of accepting the convention without alterations or of abandoning its hopes of a canal. He sought to show, by reviewing the history of the isthmian project from the Spanish period to 1903, that the United States remained the sole agency able and willing to undertake the gigantic task of uniting the oceans. Yet the Washington government had been most explicit in insisting that it would not assume the cost and the responsibility without control over the zone. Inasmuch as the alternatives were clearly defined, the foreign minister requested the legislators to limit their debate to the points at issue and thus avoid irrelevant considerations of domestic politics. He soon ignored his own suggestion, however, by commending the administration for permitting free discussion of the canal question during the recent civil disturbances instead of completing the ratification by dictatorial means. The latter remark brought interruptions from the floor and evidences of vociferous disapproval from the spectators.[54]

General Nel Ospina criticized Rico, rather unjustly in view of the facts, for having given the United States the opportunity to refuse to accept amendments by his poor judgment in putting the question to Beaupré. In his opinion the convention violated existing laws which would have to be repealed before he could conscientiously vote in the affirmative. He suggested that when once obstacles had been eliminated, a new agreement could be for-

---

[53] *Ibid.*, same to same, No. 105, Aug. 15, 1903; Castillero R., "La Causa Inmediata de la Emancipación de Panamá," *Boletín de la Academia Panameña de la Historia*, I, 349; López de Mesa, *Introducción a la historia de la cultura en Colombia*, p. 80.

[54] Senado, *Canal de Panamá*, pp. 3 *et seq*. The "Relación de debates," ordinarily published with the *Anales del Senado* omits all discussions of the treaty from July 31 to September 10. Rico's address was published in *Diario oficial* for September 17. *El Correo Nacional* summarized the speeches in its issue of August 14.

mulated with the United States which would prove honorable for both countries.⁵⁵ There was a specious quality to the general's arguments that suggests he was coöperating with the administration's plan to throw the treaty down hard enough to get it ratified on the rebound.

Besides those mentioned above, the only speakers during the afternoon were Arango and Rodríguez. Apparently, the result of the debate was perfectly clear to the principal senators in advance. It is significant that neither Pérez y Soto nor Vélez, the leaders of the antitreaty faction, as distinguished from Caro's anti-administration *bloc,* felt it necessary to join the attack. Obaldía, the most ardent advocate of the canal in the upper house, sat in silence through most of the session and then left.

At half-past six a vote was taken on the question of giving further consideration to the treaty as reported with amendments by the special committee. Of the twenty-seven members of the senate, twenty-four recorded themselves in the negative. Ospina and Uricoechea abstained and Obaldía was absent.⁵⁶

VI

Beaupré immediately wired the result of the senate's action to his department with the comment that the rejection was not to be taken as final. Shortly after nine o'clock that evening Reyes called to inform the envoy that the vote

was in accordance with plans perfected by the Government and influential Senators and citizens in the belief that the treaty could not

---

⁵⁵ State Dept., Dispatches from Colombia, Vol. 60, Beaupré to Hay, No. 105, Aug. 15, 1903.

⁵⁶ Senado, *Anales,* p. 123. Obaldía was taken severely to task by the opposition press for his departure from the hall before the balloting began. He was accused of attempting to escape the consequences of standing alone in opposition to his colleagues' patriotic action. The senator replied in a letter to *El Correo Nacional,* dated August 16, that he was ill on the day of the debate and left late in the afternoon for his home, thinking that the discussion would continue into the following session. He asserted that he was still, as in the past, wholeheartedly in favor of the canal. "The honest landlords," he wrote, "the citizens who have founded honest hearths and raised moral families, those who have contributed with deeds to the advancement of the Isthmus . . . these are, with rare exceptions, ardent partisans of the Canal and I will always be with them." *El Nuevo Tiempo,* Aug. 14, 1903; *El Correo Nacional,* Oct. 26, 1903.

THE DEFEAT OF THE TREATY

now be passed without amendments, but that within a very short time such a reaction [in] public sentiment can be created as will enable the President to present the treaty again to the Senate and secure its passage without amendments.

The general asked two weeks' grace in which to put the scheme into operation. He doubted that the constitution could be amended in time but considered a change unnecessary.[57]

The day after the rejection the senate adopted a resolution expressing its desire to maintain "the most cordial relations" with the United States and its firm belief that a canal at Panama was of "the greatest importance for the commerce and progress of the world as well as for the development and prosperity of the American nations." In harmony with this sentiment it empowered its presiding officer to appoint a committee of three to work out the bases for a new canal convention which would be compatible with the laws and interests of the Colombian people.[58]

For a few days the news of the defeat of the treaty seemed about to produce the reaction anticipated by Reyes. Beaupré reported on the 15th that "there has been an almost hysterical condition of alarm and uncertainty in Bogotá as to the future action of the United States." A rumor was widely circulated that North American troops had already landed on the Isthmus. As it became generally known, however, that the senate had appointed a committee to consider means of renewing the negotiations, popular anxiety was allayed and the country seemed to settle into a state of indifference. The newspapers gave more attention to the election of the new Pope than to the canal while congress devoted its chief energies to the political preliminaries of the presidential and congressional elections scheduled for December.[59]

The new senate committee on the canal, consisting of Nel Ospina, Rodríguez, and Campo, submitted a project of law on September 2. By its provisions the rejection of the treaty on

[57] State Dept., Dispatches from Colombia, Vol. 60, Beaupré to Hay, telegram, 9 P.M., Aug. 12, 1903 (received Aug. 23); same to same, telegram, 10 P.M., Aug. 12, 1903 (received Aug. 19).
[58] Senado, *Anales*, p. 125.
[59] State Dept., Dispatches from Colombia, Vol. 60, Beaupré to Hay, No. 105, Aug. 15, 1903; same to same, No. 110, Aug. 18, 1903; same to same, No. 154, Sept. 25, 1903.

August 12 was approved and the vice-president empowered to negotiate another convention for the opening of the waterway under certain conditions which were set forth in detail. The Panama Railroad was granted permission to transfer its concession to a corporation or government provided the purchaser undertook to continue the $250,000 annual rental and to surrender the property to Colombia in 1967, or alternatively, in that year, to buy it at a price set by agreement or arbitration. The canal company, likewise, could sell its rights and holdings to a foreign government in return for a payment of $10,000,000 to Colombia. The chief executive was authorized, in such event, to conclude a treaty with the government concerned for the construction and operation of a canal through a zone ten miles in width, excluding the cities of Panama and Colón. This privilege would take the form of a lease for one hundred years, renewable at the option of the lessee for similar periods. The compensation would consist of a minimum of $20,000,000 in gold on the exchange of ratifications and a rental of $150,000 until 1967 and $400,000 thereafter until the expiration of the first hundred-year term. The annuity would then be increased on each renewal by 25 percent above the base for the preceding period. The treaty would have to include an explicit recognition of the neutrality of the canal and a guaranty of Colombian sovereignty over the zone and the department of Panama. Civil, criminal, and admiralty jurisdiction in cases involving foreigners, or Colombians and foreigners, would be vested in tribunals consisting of justices named in equal number by the two governments. Colombia would retain the duty of maintaining order, security, and public sanitation, but it might at its discretion call upon the concessioner to provide these services at the latter's expense. Differences of interpretation of the treaty would be settled by appeal to a nation friendly to both parties.[60]

Deliberation upon this project of law was postponed repeatedly for various reasons, the most important being the political storm which had just broken in connection with the coming elections.

[60] Senado, *Anales*, p. 161; *Libro azul*, Appendix, pp. 142 *et seq.*

On August 30 Marroquín, acting apparently on the advice of Reyes, had replaced the governors of the departments of Bolívar, Magdalena, and Panama with substitutes pledged to support the treaty and the Reyes campaign for the presidency. The opponents of the administration were infuriated by this bald admission of intent to "supervise" the poll. Most exasperating of all was the fact that Obaldía, whom many suspected of secessionist sympathies, had been appointed to the post on the Isthmus. Beaupré cabled an account of the stir to Washington on the day of the announcement. A few hours later he had further news to report.

Confidential. General Reyes requests me to inform you that the Presidential candidature has been offered him by Marroquín and the Governors of all the departments. He has privately answered that he will accept. Without certain knowledge that the treaty will be approved by this Congress or the next (for without the ratification of the treaty, and the assured friendship of the United States, he did not desire to become President) he wishes to know whether sufficient time would be granted by the Government of the United States to allow the Congress of July twenty, next year, which he is certain he will have control over, to reconsider the treaty in case it will not be possible to force it through the present Congress. If you think it necessary that this Congress take action he wishes to know if you can accept any modification, and how long you will wait for the ratification of the treaty.[61]

The denunciation of the government in the Colombian congress and press continued without abatement throughout the remainder of the session. Late in September Beaupré forwarded more details of the political situation. Several of the presidential candidates, he noted, were members of the legislature and "fearing public sentiment, have allowed this to interfere with their better judgment concerning the Panama Canal and other important matters." He considered Reyes the only important nominee. He was the official government candidate and "all the usual combinations are being made with the view to his election." Quite apart from this fact, the general possessed considerable

---

[61] State Dept., Dispatches from Colombia, Vol. 60, Beaupré to Hay, telegram, 8 A.M., Aug. 30, 1903; same to same, telegram, same date. Both messages were received by the department on September 12.

strength of his own. Both parties esteemed him and he was acceptable to the mass of the electorate. The envoy emphasized, however, that "public opinion" was not a particularly influential factor since the departmental governors "have the election machinery so completely in their hands that, if there be unanimity among them, they are virtual dictators of the course of events." [62]

Inasmuch as Marroquín had done nothing unconstitutional in removing the governors, the anti-administration forces concentrated their fire upon the most vulnerable of his appointees. Obaldía was widely reported to have declared that Panama would set up an independent state if the canal treaty were rejected, and that it would be justified in so doing. Although it was not generally known at this time, he had frankly told the vice-president in accepting the governorship that he would feel it his duty to go with the people of the Isthmus should they decide to secede.[63]

On September 10 Pérez y Soto introduced this resolution in the senate:

The Senate of the Republic cannot see with indifference the appointment which has been made for the post of governor of the department of Panama which it regards as a menace to the safety of the Republic.[64]

The debate lasted two hours and consisted principally of a series of vituperative attacks upon the government. At the end of that time the resolution was amended to omit specific reference to Panama and in this form it passed unanimously. Such action amounted to a vote of censure of the chief executive and his advisers. Whatever influence those men had formerly wielded in the upper house had now completely disappeared. The once-loyal Nel Ospina was roundly applauded for a passionate speech in which he warned the vice-president that a new revolution was imminent if he persisted in his present course. The only senator who tried to defend the administration was Lorenzo Marroquín.

[62] *Ibid.*, same to same, No. 153, Sept. 24, 1903. General Joaquín F. Vélez had been selected as the opposition candidate. Reyes was not formally nominated by the Conservative party until November 5.
[63] *Ibid.*, same to same, telegram, Aug. 31, 1903 (received Sept. 5).
[64] Senado, *Anales*, p. 172.

THE DEFEAT OF THE TREATY

His remarks were accompanied throughout by jeers and hisses from all parts of the hall. Beaupré, whose observations had about convinced him that nothing more of importance would be done regarding the treaty, reported to Washington that "it really begins to appear that the majority of the senate care little about the canal, except in so far as that subject administers to their own political ends." [65]

The Ospina-Rodríguez-Campo project of law was brought up for its first debate on September 14, during a lull in the partisan war. The senators discussed it in a desultory way, passed it without dissent and, in accordance with procedure, turned it over to another committee for study and possible alteration in preparation for the second debate.[66]

The work of this new group was delayed by the illness of Quintero Calderón, the chairman, and by the many complex aspects of one of the amendments under consideration. For some time sentiment had been increasing in favor of a law declaring invalid the extension of the New Company's franchise granted by Sanclemente in 1900. Certain influential newspapers had been urging congress to refuse its approval to this "emergency" decree and thus place Colombia in a position to collect an additional $40,000,000 from the United States when the French concession expired in 1904. Yet there were good reasons why the committee hesitated to recommend such action. In the first place, Caro had been an intimate friend of Sanclemente and would not look kindly upon any proposition which implied that the former president had overstepped his powers. Secondly, Mancini had discovered what was in the wind and was busy explaining to the senate leaders that even if Colombia canceled the extension, the New Company would still own the railroad and could, in the exercise of one of the privileges of its charter, prevent the cutting of any canal across its line without compensation for its loss. He admitted that his clients could not permanently block a water-

---
[65] State Dept., Dispatches from Colombia, Vol. 60, Beaupré to Hay, No. 133, Sept. 11, 1903.
[66] Senado, *Anales*, p. 185.

way, but their rights prevented Colombia from granting clear title to the route to any other concessioner. Finally, should congress decide to annul the 1900 decree, it would be necessary to make provision in the budget for the return of the $1,000,000 in gold which the New Company had paid.[67]

Largely because of the difficulty of reaching a decision regarding the Sanclemente extension, the report of the Calderón committee did not reach the senate until October 14.[68] It unreservedly attacked every aspect of the project under examination. The article approving the rejection of the treaty on August 12 was termed superfluous and likely to set a dangerous precedent for the future. The innovation of listing conditions binding upon the executive in negotiating future canal agreements was criticized as an unconstitutional infringement of presidential powers. The committee held that any pact, even though drawn in conformity with these stipulations, would require ratification by the succeeding congress. Its treatment of the New Company extension was a masterpiece of evasion. The report set forth the arguments on both sides, stressed the fact that the question constituted an important "duty of Congress . . . that cannot be shirked" and then deftly slipped out of the line of fire with the observation that "we respect, in advance, the decision of Congress in so delicate a matter." [69]

The second debate on the Ospina-Rodríguez-Campo project of law occurred on October 27. Caro opened his address with an endorsement of the Calderón committee's strictures, but soon turned, as if by uncontrollable habit, to his favorite sport of baiting the administration. He centered his attention upon two of its errors which he felt might well lead to unhappy consequences. The first was the government's insincere maneuver in having the correspondence with Beaupré read in the session of August 12. This, he declared, had the effect of making the senate's rejection

[67] State Dept., Dispatches from Colombia, Vol. 60, Beaupré to Hay, No. 176, Oct. 10, 1903.
[68] The time limit specified for the exchange of ratifications of the Hay-Herrán treaty expired on September 22.
[69] Senado, *Anales*, p. 314; *Libro azul*, Appendix, pp. 149 *et seq.*

THE DEFEAT OF THE TREATY

of the treaty appear as a protest against the attitude of the United States and a reflection upon the conduct of President Roosevelt and his secretary of state, when, in reality, its unfavorable decision was based on the realization that the terms of the pact were unconstitutional and harmful to the interests of the republic. The second error which the senator discussed was the appointment of Obaldía to the governorship of Panama, a step which, he said, left no doubt in his mind of the vice-president's willingness to endanger the integrity of the nation for the advancement of his party's political fortunes.

The most significant speech of the debate was delivered by Arango. He denounced the project of law as a clumsy attempt to befog the issue. The proposal amounted, in substance, to no more than a series of amendments to the Hay-Herrán treaty. A franker procedure, in his opinion, would be to attach them to the treaty, in spite of Beaupré's warnings, and send them back to Washington for further action. Arango's suggestion had the merit of offering a concrete method of disposing of the issue for the current congress and there is evidence that it was advanced at this juncture by general agreement among the senators.[70]

For some time it had been clear to the American minister that both the administration and the congress were playing a waiting game to see what move the United States would make concerning the canal. Many legislators had left for their homes and the rest were accomplishing nothing of importance by remaining. Attacks on the government continued and the treaty was mentioned, when at all, chiefly in that connection. On October 30 the senate voted unanimously to suspend consideration of amendments to the convention indefinitely. As a result, the canal question remained exactly where it had been on August 12.[71]

The congress assembled for its final meeting on the 31st. The upper house rose at 11 o'clock in the morning and did not trouble to return to listen to Marroquín's formal message in the after-

[70] State Dept., Dispatches from Colombia, Vol. 60, Beaupré to Hay, No. 199, Nov. 2, 1903.
[71] Senado, *Anales*, p. 430.

noon. The representatives sat until two-thirty when the session was adjourned *sine die*.⁷²

The vice-president had the last word. On November 1 he issued a long manifesto to the nation which was published in the press and posted in the streets. It reviewed the efforts of the administration to deal with the many complicated problems which troubled the country as a consequence of the war and severely criticized the senate for wasting its time in political attacks upon the executive. The lower house was praised for its more coöperative attitude and its businesslike attention to the public interests. In respect to the canal, the message stated that the government had decided to resume the negotiations with the United States in the hope that a new agreement could be reached which would meet with the approval of the next congress. The Colombian chargé d'affaires, it added, had been instructed to convey this information to the Department of State in Washington.⁷³

Five days later word arrived that the department of Panama had declared its independence.

⁷² State Dept., Dispatches from Colombia, Vol. 60, Beaupré to Hay, telegram, Oct. 23, 1903; same to same, No. 199, Nov. 2, 1903.
⁷³ *Ibid.*, same to same, No. 207, Nov. 4, 1903.

X

REVOLUTION IN PANAMA

NEWS OF THE REJECTION of the Hay-Herrán treaty reached Washington on August 15. Hay was then vacationing in Newbury, New Hampshire, the president was at Oyster Bay, and Cromwell was at the capital, consulting with the acting secretary of state and helping Herrán compose cables to Bogotá. While the unanimity of the Colombian senate's action doubtless came as a surprise, it appears that those close to the situation had already abandoned any serious expectation that the convention would be ratified in the form demanded by the United States. Roosevelt, among his books and bronzes at Sagamore Hill, had been revolving possible courses of action in his mind for several days. Hay had been watching his chief somewhat anxiously from a distance, and waiting. Cromwell, in his inimitable fashion, had been playing with the idea of a "spontaneous" revolution in Panama.

The attorney for the New Company had become convinced early in June that Article I of the treaty stood very little chance of acceptance by the congress about to meet in Bogotá.[1] We have already seen the manner in which he used his "contacts" on the Isthmus to inspire articles and petitions favorable to ratification and to work upon the Colombian government's fears of an uprising. Inasmuch as these maneuvers had not produced the desired results, he had turned his attention to the possibility of encouraging the efforts of a small but energetic separatist *junta* in Panama City.[2]

There is unquestionably considerable truth in the contention of apologists for the revolution of 1903 that the majority of

[1] *Story of Panama*, pp. 282–283 (Cromwell Brief).
[2] *Ibid.*, pp. 348 *et seq.* (Hall testimony).

Panamanians had never felt any strong attachment for the rest of Colombia.[3] The Isthmus was at this period an undeveloped area, rich in soil and minerals but lacking in the capital essential for exploiting its resources. Geographically, it was completely severed from the mountain departments where lived the bulk of the population and the majority of the ruling class of the republic. Its internal communications depended to a large extent upon the services of the Panama Railroad. There were trails, but no roads between the villages; and no bridges except the railroad trestles crossed the 475 rivers and streams of the department. Despite a coast line extending for 1,300 miles along two oceans, there was no native maritime commerce of importance. The 300,000 inhabitants lived principally by agriculture, tilling the earth in a manner similar to that used by the aborigines of 1500.[4] In the preceding seventy-five years occasional attempts had been made to set up an independent state. These had invariably failed, but the region had at times enjoyed relative autonomy. Under the "Regeneration," however, existing political privileges had been suppressed in favor of a centralized control from Bogotá, which paid only incidental attention to the interests of the locality. The edge of Panamanian discontent had been somewhat dulled during the last years of the nineteenth century by the prospect of a canal under United States supervision which would place the department on one of the great commercial arteries of the world, to the benefit of the world in general and of Panama in particular. This may explain the lack of any serious effort on the part of the Isthmians to establish their independence during the civil war of 1899–1902. Likewise, it may explain why Cromwell felt so confident that the embers of separatism could be readily fanned into blaze should the treaty fail of ratification.

The story of the conspiracy on the Isthmus has been told by

[3] See the monographs by Nicanor A. de Obarrio, Ricardo J. Alfaro, Ismael Ortega B., José Augustín Arango, and Ramón M. Valdés in Instituto Nacional de Panamá, *Documentos historicos*, and Academia Panameña, *Publicaciones*, Vols. I–II.

[4] International Union of American Republics, *Monthly Bulletin*, XVI, 328; Morales, "The Republic of Panama," *North American Review*, CLXXVII, 916.

many persons and in many conflicting ways. There is, however, general agreement that the plot centered about *El Maestro* José Agustín Arango and that he was discussing the subject with his family at the end of May. The original *junta* consisted of himself, his three sons, his three sons-in-law, and Carlos Constantino Arosemena. In his own account of the affair he states that "after mature meditation" and with the consent of his fellow conspirators, he approached Captain Beers, "a respectable man, of sound and clear judgment, of absolute integrity and honor," and disclosed his hope of bringing about a separation in the event— which he considered likely—that the treaty were rejected. Such action, he told the captain, would leave Panama in a position to negotiate directly with the United States. Beers reacted cordially to the scheme and it was soon agreed that he should go north to interview

persons of high position and influence who could give assurances that the American Government would not lend any assistance to Colombia in reincorporating the Isthmus into that republic; and that, on the contrary, [the conspirators] would be able to count on the decided protection of the United States, in the sense of recognizing [their] independence once that government had been convinced that it was a unanimous movement of the isthmian people.[5]

Although no direct evidence on the point has come to light, it is probable that Henry N. Hall of the New York *World* was correct in his opinion, offered before the House Committee on Foreign Affairs in 1912, that Beers did not leave his post as freight agent for the railroad and journey up to New York on his own initiative, even though his trip involved the interests of the company. It seems more likely that he reported his conversations with Arango to his superiors in the United States and that his departure was in conformity with instructions from them.[6]

While Beers was visiting the United States Arango was cautiously sounding out other influential citizens.[7] One of the first to

---

[5] Arango, *Datos para la historia,* pp. 11 *et seq.*

[6] *Story of Panama,* p. 348 (Hall testimony).

[7] Arango, as mentioned above, had been elected to the national senate. According to Henry N. Hall, *El Maestro* received a message requesting him to go to

be admitted to the plot was the physician of the Panama Railroad, Manuel Amador Guerrero. Born in the department of Bolívar in 1833, Amador had studied medicine and surgery in Cartagena and then settled on the Isthmus to practice. His likable personality had won him acceptance in the exclusive social circles of Panama City and he eventually became connected with a prominent local family through his marriage to the brilliant María de la Ossa. Politically, he had long been affiliated with the Conservative party. Amador had a quick mind, resolution, and a tendency to push himself into positions of responsibility and honor. He offered the presidency of the proposed republic to Arango in such a way that the latter, in declining it, felt obliged to offer it to him. He accepted. He then asked to be named to the commission which would go to the United States to conclude arrangements for the revolt should Beers return with an encouraging report.

By the early part of July the *junta* had been reorganized. It now consisted of Amador, Arosemena, and Arango, with the last named using his relatives as a kind of private family council. Others, added to the inner circle as their views were found acceptable, included Nicanor A. de Obarrio, Ricardo Arias, Federico Boyd, Tomás Arias, and Manuel Espinosa B. Boyd's home in Panama became a frequent meeting place of the group.[8] Matters were progressing so satisfactorily toward the end of the month that Pedro and Ramón Arias gave a luncheon for about twenty-six "key" persons at their house in the savannahs. Among the guests were Hezekiah A. Gudger, United States consul-general in Panama, J. Gabriel Duque, the proprietor of

---

Kingston, Jamaica, on his way to Bogotá and there confer with Cromwell or his representative. Apparently this engagement was canceled at the last minute and Arango decided not to attend the congress. *Ibid.*

[8] Arango, *Datos para la historia*, p. 17. During the late summer and fall other men were admitted to the plot. These included Carlos A. Mendoza, Juan Antonio Henríquez, and Eusebio A. Morales, who were placed in charge of preparing a declaration of independence and all other documents necessary to regularize the proceeding. Ramón Valdés López was commissioned by the *junta* to go into the interior to await word of the outbreak and stir up sentiment for independence in the provinces.

the Panama *Star and Herald,* Herbert G. Prescott, assistant superintendent of the railroad in charge of transportation, Major William Murray Black, U.S.A., Corps of Engineers, representing the Walker Commission on the Isthmus, two of his assistants, and General Ruben Varón of the Colombian "navy." Plans for a revolution were freely discussed and several speeches were made advocating an independent republic under the protection of the United States.[9]

Beers returned to Panama City on August 4 with a code book provided by Cromwell and the news that the attorney could be depended upon to "go the limit" in supporting any separatist project. Two days later Arango held a luncheon at his country home; the freight agent, who was the guest of honor, and Assistant Superintendent Prescott were the only United States citizens present. Beers is supposed to have made a private report to the members of the *junta* and, later, a general speech to the guests.[10] The prospects of tangible assistance from the north appeared so encouraging, as a result of the Beers mission, that the conspirators determined to proceed with their plans. When about a week later news of the fate of the canal treaty reached the Isthmus, the revolutionary movement was in full swing.

II

On August 12, the day the treaty was rejected in Bogotá, the Department of State in Washington received Beaupré's delayed cable of the 5th listing the recommendations of the majority of the Pérez y Soto committee to the Colombian senate. Herrán was reported to have been "astounded and disappointed," while a "high official" of the department was quoted as remarking that alterations in the treaty meant "certain death to that measure." [11] Several correspondents informed their papers that the proposed modifications called for an increased payment by the United States—a misapprehension which circulated widely without denial from Washington.[12]

[9] *Story of Panama,* p. 349 (Hall testimony).   [10] *Ibid.,* pp. 349–350.
[11] N. Y. *Herald,* Aug. 14, 1903.   [12] *Story of Panama,* p. 353.

On learning the gist of the Beaupré message Roosevelt immediately sent for Senator Cullom, chairman of the Committee on Foreign Relations. The two men discussed the Panama situation and the Cuban reciprocity treaty at Oyster Bay on the 14th. Interviewed shortly after his departure, the senator remarked that the administration was not yet ready to abandon the Panama route. When questioned as to how the canal could be built, if Colombia insisted on terms the United States was unwilling to grant, he answered blandly that "we might make another treaty, not with Colombia, but with Panama." The reporters, sensing a "story," inquired whether the United States would promote a revolution on the Isthmus. Cullom replied:

No; I suppose not. But this country wants to build that canal and build it now. It needs it for its own defense, and it is needed by the whole world. The treaty is blocked by a country that has been treated well by us, and there are very weighty considerations which make us feel that at all hazards this great work should be undertaken at the earliest possible minute.[13]

Under these circumstances, the news of the actual defeat of the convention came almost as an anticlimax. Hay wrote to the president from Newbury on the 16th:

Mr. Loomis wires me that the Bogotá Congress has rejected the Canal Treaty. I would come at once to Oyster Bay to get your orders, but I am sure there is nothing to be done, for the moment. You will, before our Congress meets, make up your mind which of the two courses you will take, the simple and easy Nicaragua solution, or the far more difficult and multifurcate scheme of building the Panama Canal *malgré* Bogotá.

Before you resolve on either solution you will probably want to talk with some of the leading Panama senators, Hanna, Spooner, Aldrich, etc. If you could get a word with Root before he sails it would be valuable. I have written to Adee to get up the treaty of 1846 in all its bearings to have the case ready for me when I go to Washington the last of next week. It may be advisable to take a lesson from

---

[13] N. Y. *Herald*, Aug. 15, 1903. On the same day Cromwell called at the Department of State twice to see Acting Secretary Loomis and Third Assistant Secretary Adee. From there he went to the Colombian legation and helped Herrán prepare cables to Rico reiterating that the United States would not modify its insistence upon ratification without amendments. *Ibid.*

their fears about that treaty. Corea, who has plenipotentiary powers from Nicaragua, is in Europe—so that nothing will be lost by waiting a few weeks. If you finally conclude to close with Nicaragua, it will be quick work to get a treaty ready. But I presume you may think best to do nothing definite until our Congress meets, and then lay the matter before them, for some modification of the Spooner act.[14]

This tactful application of the brakes to his chief's impetuosity shows Hay at his best. The advice was good, but probably not needed in this instance. Roosevelt's attention had been caught by certain ideas advanced in a memorandum by John Bassett Moore which Assistant Secretary of State Loomis had forwarded on the previous day.[15] This document contributed so importantly to the president's subsequent interpretation of United States rights under the convention of 1846-1848 that its most notable points are summarized below.

The treaty with Colombia, Moore explained, had assumed an unnecessarily elaborate form owing to the fact that it was modeled upon drafts prepared with reference to the Nicaragua route, regarding which previous stipulations were insufficient. In the event that Colombia rejected the treaty it would be im-

[14] Dennis, *Adventures in American Diplomacy*, pp. 342-343.
[15] The full text of the memorandum, taken from the Roosevelt Papers, appears in Appendix D. Loomis' letter to the president on the subject reads: "When I was at Oyster Bay some time ago, I had the honor of speaking to you for a moment with reference to the views of Professor John Bassett Moore concerning the diplomatic and international aspects of our relations to the Panama Canal Treaty and problem. It will be admitted, I think, that Professor Moore is one of the most profound and accurate students of international law in the United States, and that he has had a great deal of extremely valuable experience in the practical application of the principles of both public and private international law. I asked Professor Moore to put his views into writing in order that you might look over them if you so desire, and I herewith enclose a copy for your perusal. I think you will find some strong and well supported suggestions in this memorandum, which, in the event of the failure of the treaty at Bogotá, which now seems possible, may be of the very greatest importance." Quoted from Dennis, *op. cit.*, Loomis to Roosevelt, Aug. 15, 1903. In the course of a correspondence several months later Moore informed the president that this document embraced the substance of a conversation which he had with Loomis sometime around the 7th or 8th of August, that it was written and sent to the assistant secretary of state on August 14 in accordance with a request from that official which reached him on the 13th or 14th. (*Ibid.*, Moore to Roosevelt, Jan. 7, 1904.)

portant to consider the state of the canal question. The supposition that the United States might then abandon the Panama route and conclude agreements with Nicaragua and Costa Rica was one that might "serve the present purposes of diplomacy but certainly not those of permanent policy." If the Panama route was adjudged the best and most practicable, it was the one the nation should have. The United States, in building the canal, was contributing not only to its own well-being, but to that of the world.

To the question, "May Colombia be permitted to stand in the way?" the memorandum offered a general and a specific answer. The former was to be found in a note from Secretary Cass to Lamar, minister to Central America, dated July 25, 1858.

> The progress of events has rendered the interoceanic routes across the narrow portions of Central America vastly important to the commercial world, and especially to the United States, whose possessions, extending along the Atlantic and Pacific coast[s] demand the speediest and easiest modes of communication. While the just rights of sovereignty of the States occupying this region should always be respected, we shall expect that these rights will be exercised in a spirit befitting the occasion and the wants and circumstances that have arisen. Sovereignty has its duties as well as its rights, and none of these local Governments . . . would be permitted in a spirit of Eastern isolation to close these gates of intercourse on the great highways of the world, and justify the act by the pretension that these avenues of trade and travel belong to them, and that they choose to shut them . . .

The specific answer was contained in the provisions of Article XXXV of the treaty of 1846 with New Granada. In return for a guaranty "that the right of way or transit across the Isthmus of Panama upon any modes of communication that now exist, or may be hereafter constructed, shall be free and open to the Government and citizens of the United States" the latter nation guaranteed the perfect neutrality of the Isthmus, "with the view that the free transit from one to the other sea may not be interrupted nor embarrassed in any future time while this treaty exists . . ." The object of assuming this "offensive and defensive alliance" [Moore's phrase] was primarily to secure a canal, as Polk's message of transmittal to the Senate clearly showed.

"Since the day the treaty was ratified," the memorandum continued, "the United States has faithfully performed its guarantee." Not only had it saved Colombia from foreign attacks on the Isthmus, but it had on numerous occasions protected the route from domestic disturbances.

In reality, Colombia has again and again claimed that it was our *duty* to protect the route against domestic interruption or attack, thus construing the treaty more broadly than we have done and less favorably to her own sovereignty. Our claim has been that we had under the treaty a *right* to intervene for the purpose of keeping open the transit, while Colombia has asserted that we were *bound* to intervene also for the purpose of supporting the authority of her titular governments. Her claim has in reality approached the point of making us responsible sovereign on the Isthmus.

Seward had, in Moore's opinion, "exactly expressed" the position of the United States:

The United States have taken, and will take, no interest in any question of internal revolution in the State of Panama . . . but will maintain a perfect neutrality in regard to such domestic controversies. The United States will nevertheless hold themselves ready to protect the transit trade across the Isthmus against invasion by either the domestic or foreign disturbers of the peace of the State of Panama.

Having set forth the diplomatic precedents which formed the basis of his argument, Moore proceeded to some striking conclusions.

In view of the fact that the United States has for more than fifty years secured to Colombia her sovereignty over the Isthmus, for the mutually avowed purpose of maintaining a free and open transit, the United States is in a position to demand that it shall be allowed to construct the great means of transit which the treaty was chiefly designed to assure. *In reality, the Panama canal, so far as built, has actually been constructed under the protection of this very guarantee.* The persons that undertook it failed to finish it. The United States would be justified in asserting and maintaining a right to finish it. . . .

The Government and citizens of the United States indeed have never as yet enjoyed the full benefit, nor even the chief benefit, that the treaty was intended and expected to secure. That benefit would be realized only when the ships of the United States and of its citizens should be able to pass from ocean to ocean by way of the Isthmus.

Colombia, on the other hand, has from the beginning enjoyed the full benefit that was to accrue to her, namely, the guarantee of her sovereignty. She is therefore not in a position to obstruct the building of the canal. . . .

Colombia's consent to the transfer of the rights of property (as distinguished from distinctively concessionary rights) of the Panama Canal Company, and an unqualified license to construct and operate, or perhaps merely to operate, a canal, are all the United States needs; and these the United States has a perfect right to require. Elaborate stipulations as to the future are at least superfluous. The United States in constructing the canal would own it; and, after constructing it, would have the right to operate it. The ownership and control would be in their nature perpetual.

Some years must elapse before the canal can be completed; and it is not to be supposed that the United States would be unable meanwhile to arrange all expedient details. Once on the ground and duly installed, this Government would find no difficulty in meeting questions as they arose. It has done so under the treaty of 1846. Colombia's guarantee of a free and open transit has not secured it to us. We have usually found, when the emergency arose, that we were dependent upon our own resources for the enjoyment of the privileges which the treaty was designed to secure to us.

The ominous tone of these final paragraphs is perhaps more obvious than the limited scope of the matter to which they refer. It should be noted that Moore confines his discussion to an interpretation of mutual obligations existing *within the framework of the treaty*. He expresses his opinion that the pact of 1846–1848 gave the United States extensive rights relating to the canal, among which was the right to "require" from Colombia a license to operate a waterway. He does not say that the United States consequently had the right to seize the zone or take any other forcible measures if Colombia failed to comply with its "agreement." He says nothing about methods of obtaining redress in the event of noncompliance. In fact, the context indicates that he did not believe such a contingency had at the time arisen. The memorandum was drafted on the assumption that the Hay-Herrán treaty would be rejected and that it would therefore be proper to remind Colombia of its "implicit" obligation to continue the parleys until an agreement should finally be reached. In writing the document, Moore says, the thought occurred to him "that it might strengthen the United States in further negotiations with Colombia, and that further discussions might take place at Bogotá either through our minister there or through a special representative." [16] It is not impossible that Moore, who had handled Latin-American questions during his previous service in the State Department, hoped that it might be his good fortune to be selected as the special representative. In any case, it is certain that in August, 1903, his attention was focused upon diplomatic, not military, solutions to the canal problem. This does not mean, of course, that Roosevelt necessarily construed the memorandum in a similar manner.

On the 19th, the president dispatched the memorandum to his secretary of state with a note.

Loomis sent me the enclosed paper from John Bassett Moore. It seems to me important.

On your way back cannot you stop here, and we will go over the canal situation? The one thing evident is to do nothing at present. If under the treaty of 1846 we have a color of right to start in and build the canal, my off-hand judgment would favor such proceeding. It seems that the great bulk of the best engineers are agreed that that route is the best; and I do not think that the Bogotá lot of jack rabbits should be allowed permanently to bar one of the future highways of civilization. Of course under the terms of the Act we could now go ahead with Nicaragua and perhaps would technically be required to do so. But what we do now will be of consequence, not merely decades, but centuries hence, and we must be sure that we are taking the right step before we act.[17]

---

[16] Moore to the author, Oct, 20, 1939.

[17] Roosevelt Papers, Roosevelt to Hay, Aug. 19, 1903. An even greater care to avoid anything approaching precipitate action is noticeable in Adee's letters. On the 18th he wrote Hay with reference to suggestions that the United States might assist Panama in separating from Colombia: "Such a scheme could, of course, have no countenance from us—our policy before the world should stand, like Mrs. Caesar, above suspicion. Neither could we undertake to recognize and protect Panama as an independent state, like a second Texas. Such a state would have a

Reassured by this indication that matters would be allowed to drift along quietly for a while, Hay wired Beaupré on the 24th that the president would make no engagement as to his next step regarding the canal, but that it was improbable that any definite action would be taken within two weeks.[18] Four days later he visited Oyster Bay. The New York *Herald's* correspondent at the summer capital telegraphed his paper that the chief executive and his cabinet head "take little interest in the despatches from Minister Beaupre . . . which purport to detail efforts being made by the Colombians to 'save the treaty' by amending it." Three choices, according to this report, faced the administration. The first was to ignore Bogotá, proceed to construct the canal under the treaty of 1846, fight if objection was raised and create an independent State of Panama. Such a course would "give the United States what would be expected to be a short and inexpensive war, but would insure a permanent settlement of the question of the sovereignty of a canal zone across the Isthmus of Panama." The second possibility was to turn to Nicaragua, and the third was to mark time "until something transpires to make Colombia see light, and then negotiate for another treaty." [19]

The day following his conference with Roosevelt Hay wired Beaupré again:

The President is bound by the Isthmian Canal Statute, commonly called the Spooner law. By its provisions he is given a reasonable time to arrange a satisfactory treaty with Colombia. When, in his judgment, the reasonable time has expired and he has not been able

---

hard time of it between Colombia on one side and Costa Rica on the other." Thayer, *John Hay*, II, 313–314. On the 19th Adee was more specific in his remarks to the secretary of state: "At first blush I would be inclined to do nothing [with regard to the treaty rejection] that would smack of resentment. I would prefer to stand pat on the Spooner law, by which the authority of the President is measured. . . . He is no longer competent to negotiate on different bases and certainly cannot acquiesce in any new proposals whether in the form of Colombian amendments to the present treaty or as propositions put forward by way of inviting fresh negotiation—which may depart from the purview of the Spooner law." Dennis, *Adventures in American Diplomacy*, p. 344.

[18] State Dept., Instructions to Colombia, Vol. 19, p. 262.
[19] N. Y. *Herald*, Aug. 29, 1903.

REVOLUTION IN PANAMA

to make a satisfactory arrangement as to the Panama route, he will then proceed to carry into effect the alternative of the statute. Meantime the President will enter into no engagement restraining his freedom of action under the statute.[20]

III

While the discussions at Sagamore Hill were in progress, Amador was on the Atlantic, northward bound, for the ostensible purpose of visiting his "sick" son in Massachusetts. He was making the journey alone, as his fellow commissioner, Ricardo Arias, was obliged at the last minute to remain in Panama. The physician's chief resources were his wits, a letter from Arango to Cromwell, and a cable code for communication with the *junta*.[21] His duties were to confirm the promises of assistance from Cromwell which Beers had brought and to obtain, if possible, direct assurance from the secretary of state or the president that the provisional government would receive armed support and prompt recognition from the United States. He was also to procure the money and munitions required for the uprising. Upon landing at New York September 1, he took up his quarters at the Hotel Endicott in that city.

Among Amador's fellow travelers had been J. Gabriel Duque, editor of the Panama *Star and Herald,* who was making one of his periodic business trips to the United States. On dropping in at the exporting house of Andreas & Company soon after his arrival, Duque encountered Roger L. Farnham, Cromwell's utility man and press agent, and was informed that Cromwell wished to see him on matters of business. Together they went down to the attorney's offices in Wall Street. During the course of the interview that followed Cromwell is supposed to have offered Duque the presidency of the Republic of Panama if he would bring about a revolution. According to Henry N. Hall, the lawyer

---

[20] State Dept., Instructions to Colombia, Vol. 19, p. 264. This dispatch strongly reflects Adee's view of the situation.

[21] *Story of Panama,* pp. 357–359. In the code "X" stood for Hay, "W" for Cromwell, and "Ministro" for Herrán. Complete statements appropriate to situations which might arise were represented by numbers. The code is printed in *ibid.,* pp. 358–359.

stated that he was willing to supply security for a loan of $100,000 for immediate expenses. Before they parted Cromwell called the Department of State on the long-distance telephone and arranged for Duque to see Hay the next morning—September 3. Duque returned to Andreas & Company before packing and this time met an old acquaintance, Charles Burdett Hart. The former minister readily agreed to accompany his isthmian friend to Washington and introduce him to the secretary of state personally.[22]

Hay apparently made no promises of direct assistance at this meeting with Duque on September 3, but he emphasized that the United States would build the Panama Canal and did not propose to let Colombia stand in its way. He is said to have added that if revolutionists seized the cities of Panama and Colón, the United States would see to it that the free and uninterrupted transit on the railroad was not disturbed by the troops of either side.[23]

Duque's procedure, on leaving the State Department, shows that Cromwell had badly mistaken his man. The editor promptly called at the Colombian legation and warned Herrán that if the treaty were not ratified the Isthmus would declare its independence. The minister lost no time in spreading the alarm. He advised the consul-general in New York that conspirators were using the office of Andreas & Company as headquarters for their activities. "The canal and Panama Railroad companies," he added, "are deeply implicated in this matter." On the 4th he wired his government:

Revolutionary agents of Panama here. Yesterday the editor of the Estrella de Panamá had a long conference with the Secretary of State. If treaty is not approved by September 22 it is probable that there will be a revolution with American support.[24]

---

[22] *Ibid.*, pp. 359–360. The sons of Duque and Hart were business partners in Bogotá. Hart was, incidentally, very friendly with Cromwell.

[23] *Ibid.*, p. 360.

[24] *Libro azul*, p. 363. Duque's behavior is somewhat difficult to account for. After warning Herrán of what was afoot he returned to the Isthmus and commenced a series of weekly letters to Hay, running from Sept. 21 to Nov. 16, describing conditions in Panama. On Sept. 21 he wrote that the feeling for independence was

Suspecting that Amador was compromised in the plot, Herrán hired detectives to trace his movements. He also sent word to Cromwell and the company in Paris that Colombia would hold them responsible for any secessionist attempt on the Isthmus.[25]

In a note to Rico on the 11th the minister accurately predicted the situation which was to occur eight weeks later.

As long as our Government maintains its authority in the cities of Panama and Colón, the American intervention will contribute powerfully to impeding the realization of the plans of the revolutionaries; but in the event that a conspiracy succeeds in gaining possession of the city of Panama, the recovery of that place will prove very difficult, since our forces would probably not be able to make use of the railroad, nor would we be permitted to undertake operations in the terminal cities which might suspend or disturb the traffic.

The warning I gave relative to the probable future attitude of the President is founded on threatening statements which he has uttered in private conversations, and which by indirect means have come to my knowledge.

Special reference is made to the promptness with which the independence of our Department of Panama will be recognized.

President Roosevelt is a decided partisan of the Panama route, and hopes to begin excavation of the canal during his administration.

Your excellency knows the vehement character of the President, and you are aware of the persistence and decision with which he pursues anything to which he may be committed. These considerations have led me to give credit and importance to the threatening expressions attributed to him.[26]

Meanwhile Amador had been introduced to Cromwell by the vice-president of the Panama Railroad. He was greatly pleased by the lawyer's enthusiasm for his undertaking and his profuse offers of assistance. His hopes were rudely shattered a few days later, however, when, on arriving at the Sullivan & Cromwell

---

intense but that leaders and funds were lacking. The Colombian soldiers, he said, were starving and their pay was twelve or thirteen weeks in arrears. "Now you will readily see," he concluded, "how easy it is to buy these men over as necessity knows no law." Dennis, *Adventures in American Diplomacy*, pp. 322, 339. It will appear below that Duque had converted his volunteer fire brigade in Panama City into a revolutionary organization.

[25] *Story of Panama*, p. 361 (Hall testimony).
[26] *Libro azul*, pp. 363–364.

offices to keep an appointment made at the first meeting, he was refused admittance by the reception clerks in a manner that grew firmer as his protests increased. This sudden rebuff was, of course, the result of Cromwell's panic on receiving Herrán's sharp note of warning. So fearful did the attorney become that Colombia might seize upon his activities as an excuse to cancel the canal concessions that he wired Colonel Shaler, the superintendent of the railroad, to exercise the greatest care to observe all obligations of the 1867 contract and to avoid participation in "any movements or hostilities whatever."

Knowing no reason for the complete alteration in Cromwell's attitude, the perplexed and angry Amador wired his friends the single word "Disappointed" and, having no other apparent recourse, prepared to sail for home. Information soon reached him, however, that if he remained quietly in New York help would come from another quarter. About a fortnight later Bunau-Varilla arrived from Paris.[27]

IV

Whatever criticism may be leveled at Roosevelt for his later actions on the Isthmus, it cannot be fairly said that he chose his course without reflection. There is no indication that he came to any final decision in September. John Bassett Moore's suggestion that the 1846–1848 treaty gave the United States a right to "require" Colombian coöperation in its canal plans continued to interest him and he invited Moore to spend the night at Sagamore Hill to discuss "some matters of foreign policy."[28] Hay was still advising caution in a tone of studied deference:

There is a question whether we ought—
1. To save time and to dissipate any uncertainty about our position—say to Colombia that we will not for a moment consider the proposition they are now discussing; or
2. Say nothing and let them go on making fools of themselves until you are ready to act on some other basis. It is now perfectly clear that in the present state of Colombian politics we can not now, nor

---
[27] *Story of Panama*, p. 362.
[28] Roosevelt Papers, Roosevelt to Moore, Sept. 5, 1903.

for some time to come, make a satisfactory treaty with Colombia.

It is altogether likely that there will be an insurrection on the Isthmus against that government of folly and graft that now rules at Bogotá.

It is for you to decide whether you will (1) await the result of that movement, or (2) take a hand in rescuing the Isthmus from anarchy, or (3) treat with Nicaragua.

Something we shall be forced to do in the case of a serious insurrectionary movement in Panama, to keep the transit clear. Our intervention should not be at haphazard, nor, this time, should it be to the profit, as heretofore, of Bogotá. I venture to suggest you let your mind play a little about the subject for two or three weeks, before finally deciding. For my part, I think nothing can be lost, and something may be gained, by awaiting developments for a while.[29]

Roosevelt replied from Oyster Bay on the 15th:

I entirely approve of your idea. Let us do nothing in the Colombia matter at present. I shall be back in Washington by the 28th instant and you a week or two afterwards. Then we will go over the matter very carefully and decide what to do. At present I feel that there are two alternatives. (1) To take up Nicaragua; (2) in some shape or way to interfere when it becomes necessary so as to secure the Panama route without further dealing with the foolish and homicidal corruptionists in Bogotá. I am not inclined to have any further dealings whatever with those Bogotá people.[30]

From London Lodge was voicing a hope that the administration would not turn to Nicaragua. His advice was to gain time by having a bill introduced at the approaching session of Congress modifying the mandatory clause of the Spooner Act. "I am in strong hopes," he added, "that either under the treaty of '46 or by the secession of the Province of Panama we can get control of what is undoubtedly the best route." [31]

As the weeks slipped by and the chief executive showed no signs of forcing a solution that would save the New Company's interests, Cromwell's anxiety mounted. Unwilling to risk further dealings with the isthmian *junta* and uncertain as to the result of

[29] Dennett, *John Hay*, p. 377, Hay to Roosevelt, Sept. 13, 1903.
[30] Roosevelt Papers, Roosevelt to Hay, Sept. 15, 1903.
[31] Lodge, *Selections from the Correspondence of Theodore Roosevelt and Henry Cabot Lodge*, II, 54, Sept. 5, 1903.

the movement in Bogotá to invalidate the 1900 extension, the usually resourceful attorney found himself practically helpless. His complaints evidently reached the ears of the secretary of state, for the latter wrote Adee on the 21st:

[Cromwell] must not whimper over the ruin of the treaty through the greed of the Colombians and the disinclination of the Canal Company to satisfy it. If they were willing to be bled, why not say so at the time? It is a thing we could not share in, nor even decently know.[32]

The president seems to have reached his decision early in October. He would wait for Congress to assemble, lay the case before it, and request authority to dig the canal despite Colombia. He wrote out a message in rough draft, skilfully centering his argument around the "hold-up" theme:

The Isthmian Canal bill was, of course, passed upon the assumption that whatever route was used, the benefit to the particular section of the Isthmus through which it passed would be so great that the country controlling this part would be eager to facilitate the building of the canal. It is out of the question to submit to extortion on the part of a beneficiary of the scheme.

Having given Morality his customary embrace, Roosevelt was prepared to suggest that the United States purchase all the rights of the French company and start construction without further diplomatic fencing with Bogotá. He was careful to state, however, that should this course meet with congressional disapproval he was ready to proceed at once with the Nicaraguan alternative.[33]

Mark Hanna had no part in the formulation of this audacious scheme, but Roosevelt was shrewd enough not to ignore the old senator altogether. On October 5 the president wrote home:

You may have noticed that I have not said a word about the canal. I shall have to allude to it in my message, but I shall go over this part of my message with you before putting it in its final form. I am not as sure as you are that the only virtue we need exercise is patience. I think it well worth considering whether we had not better warn those cat-rabbits that great though our patience has been, it can be

---

[32] Thayer, *John Hay*, II, 312.
[33] Roosevelt, *Autobiography*. The text of this draft appears on pp. 572 *et seq.*

exhausted. This does not mean that we must necessarily go to Nicaragua. I feel that we are certainly justified in morals, and therefore justified in law, under the treaty of 1846, in interfering summarily and saying that the canal is to be built and that they must not stop it.[34]

Cromwell learned of the projected message at a White House conference on October 7 and immediately plunged into a study of the legal technicalities involved. On the 15th he sailed for France to acquaint his clients with the recent developments in Washington and Panama. His law partners, Curtis and Hill, had been thoughtfully placed at the president's call in case questions concerning the New Company should arise during his absence.[35] On the 31st the attorney wired from Paris that he was authorized

in the name of the president of the canal company, with the unanimous approval of the board of directors at its meeting today, and with that of the liquidator of the old company, to give you . . . the assurance of their loyal support . . . and to express to you their entire confidence in the success of your masterful policy.[36]

The day following Cromwell's departure Roosevelt personally interviewed Captain Chauncey B. Humphrey and Lieutenant Grayson M. P. Murphy, both of the regular army, who had just returned from a four-months' military intelligence tour of the northern portions of Venezuela and Colombia. As an "unpremeditated incident" of their return journey they had compiled a remarkably detailed set of statistics which would be of use in any campaign on the Isthmus.[37] The president was deeply impressed by what these officers had to say regarding secret military preparations in Panama. Reports had already reached him from a variety of sources that a revolution was imminent, but here was evidence of a kind which might fairly be relied upon. The picture of affairs on the Isthmus which Humphrey and Murphy presented on October 16 was later to figure prominently in Roosevelt's speeches and writings as proof that the outbreak of November 3 was not instigated by him. In December, 1903, Lieutenant-General Young submitted to Secretary of War Root

[34] Roosevelt Papers. [35] *Ibid.*, Cromwell to Roosevelt, Oct. 14, 1903.
[36] *Story of Panama*, p. 282. [37] *Ibid.*, pp. 367–368 (Hall testimony).

an official summary of the Humphrey-Murphy observations.

Complying with your request of this date, I have the honor to state that Captain C. B. Humphrey, 27th Infantry, and Lieutenant Grayson M. P. Murphy, 17th Infantry, reported to the Chief of Staff on the 14th day of October at the Office of the Chief of Staff in the City of Washington; that on the 12th of September they embarked at La Guira, Venezuela, for Colón, thence proceeded across the Isthmus by the Panama Railroad and return, and thence by steamer to the City of New York; that while on the Isthmus they became satisfied beyond question that, owing largely to the dissatisfaction because of the failure of Colombia to ratify the Hay-Herran treaty, a revolutionary party was in course of organization having for its object the separation of the State of Panama from Colombia, the leader being Dr. Richard Arango, a former governor of Panama; that when they were on the Isthmus arms and ammunition were being smuggled into the city of Colón in piano boxes, merchandise crates, etc., the small arms received being principally the Gras French rifle, the Remington and the Mauser; that nearly every citizen of Panama had some sort of rifle or gun in his possession with ammunition therefor; that in the city of Panama there had been organized under the supervision of Mr. Carlos Duque . . . a fire brigade which was really intended for a revolutionary military organization; that there were representatives of the revolutionary organization at all important points on the Isthmus; that in Panama, Colón, and other principal places of the Isthmus police forces had been organized which were in reality revolutionary forces; that the people on the Isthmus seemed to be unanimous in their sentiment against the Bogota government, and their disgust over the failure of that government to ratify the treaty providing for the construction of the canal, and that a revolution might be expected immediately upon the adjournment of the Colombian Congress without ratification of the treaty.[38]

V

At this point it is necessary to take another glance at the activities of the conspirators. The arrival of Bunau-Varilla in New York on September 22 was the turning point in their fortunes. The engineer had spent the summer in Paris, watching develop-

[38] Root Papers, Young to Root, Dec. 24, 1903 (War Dept. File). "Richard" Arango and "Carlos" Duque obviously refer to José Augustín Arango and J. Gabriel Duque.

ments in Colombia and sending lengthy cables to Marroquín and Nel Ospina. The defeat of the treaty convinced him that the same dark forces that had been responsible for the de Lesseps failure were again in the ascendancy. On September 2 he published an article through the columns of his brother's paper, *Le Matin,* in order "to raise the veil concealing the unknown" regarding the situation which would exist on September 23, the day after the expiration of the period for the exchange of ratifications. By examining the logical components of the problem he deduced that three courses were open to Roosevelt, none of them involving the use of the Nicaragua route. The president could conduct further negotiations with Bogotá, wait for a revolution in Panama, or "demand from the Republic of Colombia itself, on the strength of explicit stipulation, what it refuses to concede amicably." After summarizing Article XXXV of the 1846–1848 treaty he concluded:

> The "right of way" is, in the legal parlance of the American Union, the right of passing in its fullest sense, that is, not only the right of material transport, but also the right to carry out all the works necessary to transport under any system of transit or transport.
> The "right of way" is in reality the right to establish the works necessary for the passage of trains if a railway be contemplated, or for the passage of a boat if a canal be under consideration.
> If we are correctly informed it is to this third method—to this legal coercion exercised in virtue of a treaty—that President Roosevelt would be minded to resort in order to obtain from the Republic of Colombia the indispensable control over the territory required for the operation of the Canal.[39]

This shrewd prediction was made about a month before Roosevelt formulated his draft message to Congress, but more than a fortnight after he had received John Bassett Moore's memorandum. Moore stated in a letter of the following January

> I never saw Bunau-Varilla nor had any communication with him, directly or indirectly, till early in October last, when one day I met

---

[39] Bunau-Varilla, *Panama: The Creation, Destruction, and Resurrection,* pp. 286–288.

him and was introduced to him. He mentioned the canal question, but, as I was at the moment on my way to keep an engagement, our conversation was brief. On the same or the following day, namely, October 3rd, he sent me a copy of *Le Matin* of September 2, 1903, containing his article. I have not since looked at it; but I remember in a general way its drift, though not just how far it went. He told me that the position which he had taken was arrived at by what he called the purely logical examination of the various elements of the question, which had been the object of his life's study. I have seen him only once since, on the evening of the 10th of November. . . . I may add that my two brief conversations with Bunau-Varilla sufficed to give me the impression that he is one of the cleverest men I have met.[40]

Whether the Frenchman came to the United States for reasons of his own, as he asserts in his book, or in response to a call from Cromwell, is an open question. There is no direct evidence that he was summoned, and plenty that he disliked the canal company's counsel, but it is certain that Amador learned of the engineer's presence immediately and had an interview with him on September 23. Bunau-Varilla listened to a recital of the doctor's grievances, told him it was "unpardonable folly" to have believed Cromwell's "empty talk" and promised to see what he could do. After a futile trip to Washington in the first few days of October, he succeeded, through his friendship with Loomis, in meeting the president briefly on the 9th. He came away without any word of open encouragement but with the conviction that Roosevelt was greatly interested in the possibilities of a revolution. On the 16th he had an interview with Hay, again with the help of Loomis. According to his own account, he told the secretary, in reply to a query as to what he thought would happen on the Isthmus, that the "whole thing" would end in a revolution and that "you must take your measures, if you do not want to be taken yourself by surprise." Hay is recorded as having answered that he would not be caught napping, for "orders have been given to naval forces on the Pacific to sail towards the Isthmus." [41]

[40] Roosevelt Papers, Moore to Roosevelt, Jan. 7, 1904.
[41] Bunau-Varilla, *op. cit.*, pp. 289–293, 304 *et seq.*

Bunau-Varilla hurried back to New York and apprised Amador that the *junta* would be protected by United States forces forty-eight hours after the proclamation of the new republic. He promised to provide $100,000 to defray the immediate expenses of the movement.[42] Apart from his genuine desire to see the canal constructed at Panama, the Frenchman seemed to delight in the minutiae of creating a new state. He had prepared, and now turned over to Amador, a program of military operations, a cable code, a declaration of independence, the basis for a constitution, and a flag designed by his wife. Once the break with Colombia had been made, he explained, the "delicate period, that of the complete recognition of the new Republic" would begin. The fight would be in Washington, and he was ready to bear the responsibility of it. He stated candidly that nobody was better fitted to carry it through than himself. It would therefore be necessary, he added, to entrust him with the diplomatic representation of Panama in Washington. Amador at first objected that his countrymen would wish to grant that honor to one of their own number, but finally consented to urge the appointment. On the 20th he departed for Colón on the *Yucatan*.[43]

The Bunau-Varilla version of Hay's remark concerning the movement of warships towards the Isthmus is substantiated by an order issued by the Navy Department to the commanding officer of the Pacific squadron on October 15, the day preceding the conference. Admiral Glass at San Francisco was instructed to proceed "about 22nd instant on exercise cruise to Acapulco." Four days later, Secretary Moody directed Glass to

[42] With regard to Henry N. Hall's statement that this $100,000 was placed to Bunau-Varilla's credit in New York by order of the New Company, the Frenchman's papers in the Library of Congress include very substantial evidence that the money was raised by his own efforts. On Oct. 22 Bunau-Varilla cabled the Balser banking house in Brussels and the Agence Champs Elysées of the Crédit Lyonnais requesting each of them to advance him 250,000 francs, to be guaranteed by his securities in their care. He asked that the money be deposited at his call with Agence B of the Crédit Lyonnais. On the 26th he wired Agence B to transfer 500,000 francs to his account with Heidelbach, Ickelheimer & Co. in New York. The cabled replies to these requests are in the Bunau-Varilla Papers. Hall's testimony can be found in *Story of Panama*, pp. 372, 384.
[43] Bunau-Varilla, *op. cit.*, pp. 320 *et seq.*

send the *Boston* with all possible dispatch to San Juan del Sur, Nicaragua. She must arrive by November 1, with coal sufficient for returning to Acapulco. Secret and confidential. Her ostensible destination Acapulco only.

At the same time the *Dixie*, at the Brooklyn Navy Yard, was warned to be ready for sea by the 23d, and the *Atlanta* was ordered to Guantanamo.[44]

In Bogotá, meanwhile, the air was filled with rumors of secessionist intrigues at Panama. On the 20th, the day that Amador sailed from New York, Beaupré wrote the department:

I have the honor to inform you that it would be of great utility and satisfaction to me to be kept posted as to the course of events on the Isthmus, and, if not inconsistent with the rules, I would be glad to have it arranged so that our consular officers at Panama and Colón could send me copies of their dispatches to the department on the political situation, and that the consul-general could telegraph me whenever anything of unusual importance occurs.[45]

In his dispatch of the 21st the minister referred to "the alarm existing as to the possible action of the Government of the United States should the feeling of disaffection undoubtedly existing in the Department of Panama find expression in overt acts." [46]

Amador's ship docked at Colón on the morning of the 27th. Prescott went aboard to see whether the doctor had any documents that he could take for safer keeping. The conspirators remained quietly in Panama City. That evening they assembled at Boyd's house to learn the result of their colleague's mission. Their disappointment grew as the report progressed. They had apparently expected some kind of secret treaty of alliance with the United States instead of vague assurances from an unofficial third party. When Amador announced that the plan called for the independence of a strip of only fifty miles on either side of the canal, Boyd and Ricardo Arias indignantly pointed out that such action would leave the landed members of the group at the

---

[44] *Story of Panama*, pp. 367, 369 (Hall testimony).
[45] State Dept., Dispatches from Colombia, Vol. 60, No. 185.
[46] *Ibid.*, same to same, No. 186.

mercy of the Colombians. It was thereupon decided to extend the revolution to the entire department.[47]

VI

It is clear that by the end of October Roosevelt and Hay were well aware that an isthmian uprising was about to occur. They did not initiate the movement, but they welcomed it, and they fully realized that the conspirators were counting on the North American fleet to prevent interference from Colombia.[48] A revolution was the easiest path to the president's goal, far more certain of success, if properly handled, than any expropriatory scheme that might be submitted to Congress. Once convinced of the justice of his aims, Roosevelt was not inclined to stickle over what appeared to him small points of procedure. Having decided upon his final course in Panama, he was determined not to sacrifice his opportunity through halfway measures.

A detailed account of the actual outbreak lies outside the scope of this work.[49] Yet in view of the prominent part played by the treaty of 1846–1848 throughout the entire course of the canal

[47] *Story of Panama*, pp. 377–378 (Hall testimony).

[48] During the subsequent fight over the ratification of the Bunau-Varilla treaty Roosevelt wrote John Bigelow: "The opposition, apparently under the guidance of Mr. MacVeagh, who is the confidential adviser of General Reyes in this matter, are, I am told, intending to insist that Bunau-Varilla knew or had assurance from either Hay or myself as to what our own action would be, and advised the revolutionists in accordance therewith. Of course I have no idea what Bunau-Varilla advised the revolutionists, or what he said in any telegrams to them as to either Hay or myself; but I do know, of course, that he had no assurance in any way, either from Hay or myself, or from any one authorized to speak for us. He is a very able fellow, and it was his business to find out what he thought our Government would do. I have no doubt that he was able to make a very accurate guess, and to advise his people accordingly. In fact, he would have been a very dull man had he been unable to make such a guess." Roosevelt Papers, Jan. 6, 1904.

[49] The N. Y. *World*, in preparing its defense in the case of U. S. *v.* The Press Publishing Co., before the federal circuit court of the Southern District of New York, gathered the largest single collection of source material existing on this subject. Most of it is based upon sworn statements of participants and witnesses. A summary of it was presented before the House Committee on Foreign Affairs in 1912 by Henry N. Hall, representing Don Seitz, then editor of the *World*. See *Story of Panama*, pp. 374 *et seq.* Other important material can be found in Arango's *Datos para la historia* and in the *Dip. Hist. of the Panama Canal*, pp. 345 *et seq.*

negotiations with Colombia, it is perhaps not irrelevant to touch briefly upon the administration's application of Article XXXV during the period in which the Republic of Panama was born.

As we have seen, the *junta's* plans were based wholly upon the expectation that United States warships would make an opportune appearance and maintain free and uninterrupted transit—that is, for everyone except Colombian troops. The kind of revolution Arango and his friends contemplated did not involve a Panamanian triumph on the field of battle. In this they were unquestionably wise, for the Colombian army, though numbering in the neighborhood of only 10,000 men, was composed of well-equipped veterans of the civil war. The revolutionary forces, on the other hand, consisted of 287 members of J. Gabriel Duque's Panama fire brigade, reinforced by the police corps of the city and the purchased services of General Huertas' regulars of the Colombia Battalion. General Ruben Varón had agreed to support the movement with the gunboat *Padilla* for $35,000 in silver as soon as Amador and Arango could satisfy him that the United States Government would furnish protection from any Colombian attack. Huertas' adherence to the plot was on the same conditional basis.[50]

It was this fundamental necessity of persuading their "allies" of the reality of North American aid that determined Arango and his friends to postpone their attempt until five o'clock in the morning of November 4, a day later than originally scheduled. The plan was to employ the firemen, consisting of the young aristocrats of the city, to arrest Governor Obaldía (for appearances' sake) and such officials and influential citizens as were thought to be out of sympathy with secession. The populace was then to be aroused and led to the Cathedral Plaza where the declaration of independence would be read and the provisional government announced.[51]

In spite of these precautions, however, the entire project nearly miscarried. On October 25 Obaldía had sent about a hundred soldiers under Captain Tascon, whom Huertas could

[50] *Story of Panama*, p. 382 (Hall testimony).   [51] *Ibid.*, pp. 382, 385.

not win over, into the interior to repel an imaginary invasion from Nicaragua. He telegraphed the "news" to Bogotá with the reassurance that order prevailed and that the leaders of the Liberal party were coöperating with him. The Colombian cabinet acted with unaccustomed celerity. General Alfredo Vásquez Cobo, the minister of war, instructed General Tobar at Cartagena to reinforce the garrison in Panama at once. Obaldía was directed to refuel the gunboats *Padilla* and *Bogotá* and dispatch them immediately to the Pacific port of Buenaventura to pick up a battalion stationed there.[52]

The governor, somewhat taken by surprise, showed these orders to Amador. The physician was too deeply involved to withdraw at this stage of the preparations. He therefore cabled Bunau-Varilla on October 29 that more than two hundred Colombian troops were expected to reach Colón within five days and warships must be sent. The Frenchman rushed to Washington and told his friend Loomis that a situation was developing on the Isthmus which would undoubtedly lead to fighting along the railroad. The assistant secretary would not commit himself, but his attitude prompted Bunau-Varilla to assume that suitable action would be taken. On his way back to New York on the 30th Bunau-Varilla stopped off at Baltimore and dispatched the following wire to the Panama office of the commercial firm of Piza, Nephews & Company: "All right will reach two days and half. This cablegram for Amador."[53]

At this moment the *Nashville* was already on its way to Colón and there was no means of communication with her commander until she arrived. On November 2 the acting secretary of the Navy wired to the consul there:

Nashville, *care American consul, Colon:*
Maintain free and uninterrupted transit. If interruption threat-

---

[52] Cám de Rep., *Investigación sobre la rebelión del Istmo de Panamá*, pp. 44–46.
[53] Bunau-Varilla, *Panama: The Creation, Destruction, and Resurrection*, pp. 327–331. Amador's message read in code: "Tower, New York. Fate news bad powerful tiger urge vapor Colon. Smith." Bunau-Varilla's reply read: "Pizaldo, Panama. Allright will reach ton and half obscure jones." The original cable from Amador and a draft of the answer to him are in the Bunau-Varilla Papers.

ened by armed force, occupy the line of railroad. Prevent landing of any armed force with hostile intent, either Government or insurgent, either at Colon, Porto Bello, or other point. Send copy of instructions to the senior officer present at Panama upon arrival of *Boston*. Have sent copy of instructions and have telegraphed *Dixie* to proceed with all possible dispatch from Kingston to Colon. Government force reported approaching the Isthmus in vessels. Prevent their landing if in your judgment this would precipitate a conflict. Acknowledgment is required.[54]

Admiral Glass, waiting with the *Marblehead* and the *Concord* at Acapulco, Mexico, was ordered to proceed to Panama immediately. His instructions regarding the transit were identical with those sent to the *Nashville*. In addition, he was to prevent the

> landing of any armed force, either Government or insurgent, with hostile intent at any point within 50 miles of Panama. If doubtful as to the intention of any armed force, occupy Ancon Hill strongly with artillery.[55]

The *Nashville* reached Colón early in the evening of November 2, but owing to a misunderstanding, the instructions did not come into the possession of the consulate until two days later. About midnight Tobar and his Tiradores Battalion arrived on the steamer *Cartagena*. They disembarked after daylight only to find that Superintendent Shaler had no means of transporting them across the Isthmus. Warned of their approach, the official had taken care to send most of the rolling stock to other points on the line.[56]

The uneasiness of the conspirators in Panama was so pronounced at this time that Amador, on learning from Assistant Superintendent Prescott of the arrival of the soldiers, did not dare inform the others. His wife is credited with having suggested the stratagem of bringing the officers over separately and placing them under arrest while the troops were being detained at Colón on any pretext that Shaler could devise. The details were worked out by the company officials over the telephone. After some persuasion the superintendent lured Tobar, Amaya,

[54] *Dip. Hist. of the Panama Canal*, p. 362. [55] *Ibid.*, pp. 362–363.
[56] *Story of Panama*, pp. 386–388 (Hall testimony).

and their aides aboard a special train on the understanding that the men, under Colonel Torres, would follow in a few hours. The generals were received with great cordiality and pomp upon their arrival at the departmental capital about half-past eleven. As the afternoon wore on, however, their suspicions were aroused by the rapidly spreading rumors of an uprising and by the failure of their troops to put in an appearance. Tobar inspected the defenses and prepared to take over command of the garrison.[57]

With the tension increasing hourly, the *junta* hastily revised its plans. At Huertas' suggestion it was agreed that the Colombian commanders were to be arrested at a parade and band concert at eight o'clock that evening. About four o'clock Vice-Consul-General Felix Ehrman received a telegram from Loomis which was to figure prominently in later attacks upon the administration's conduct: "Uprising on the Isthmus reported. Keep department promptly and fully informed." He cabled back at once: "No uprising yet. Reported will be in the night. Situation is critical."[58] It should be pointed out that Loomis' wire is not in itself, as has been so frequently charged, conclusive proof of the department's previous knowledge of the day and hour set for the revolt. It was clearly prompted by a telegram which had arrived at 2:35 P. M. from Consul Malmros at Colón advising that an outbreak was "imminent."[59]

Shortly after five the now thoroughly suspicious Tobar announced that he and his staff would spend the night in the barracks instead of at the house assigned to them by the local authorities. Huertas decided that it would be dangerous to delay action any longer. Accordingly, at the first opportunity he encircled the officers with a patrol and placed them under arrest.

Word of Tobar's capture reached Amador while he was conferring with Prescott at the latter's house. He immediately gave orders that Obaldía be taken into formal custody and then sought out Ehrman to inform him that Panama had severed its

[57] *Ibid.*, pp. 388 *et seq.*
[58] State Dept.: Instructions to Consuls, Vol. 189, Nov. 3, 1903; Consular Letters, Panama, Vol. 25, Nov. 3, 1903.
[59] *Ibid.*: Consular Letters, Aspinwall (Colón), Vol. 19, Nov. 3, 1903.

political bonds with Colombia. The consul-general wired Hay a few minutes later:

Uprising occurred to-night, 6; no bloodshed. Army and navy officials taken prisoners. Government will be organized to-night, consisting three consuls, also cabinet. Soldiers changed. Supposed same movement will be effected in Colon. Order prevails so far. Situation serious. Four hundred soldiers landed to-day, Barranquilla.[60]

Within the next hour Arango, Boyd, and Tomás Arias constituted themselves a provisional governing committee and repaired to the Cathedral Plaza where they were enthusiastically greeted by the crowd. Soon afterwards the gunboat *Bogotá*, whose commanding officer was among those arrested with Tobar, threw five or six shells into the city, killing a Chinese and mortally wounding an ass in the slaughterhouse. It then withdrew to the shelter of an island in the bay.

While the bombardment was still going on, the municipal council met under the presidency of Demetrio Brid, the editor of the English section of the Panama *Star and Herald*. In the presence of the most prominent conspirators it recognized the *de facto* government and set two o'clock the following afternoon for the formal proclamation of the new republic.[61]

The successful consummation of this almost bloodless coup is chiefly attributable to the fact that the Tiradores Battalion was detained in Colón throughout the day. Torres exerted himself to the utmost to arrange for the transportation of his men. When three visits to Shaler failed to bring results, he even appealed to Consul Malmros for aid. The railroad officials taxed their ingenuity for new excuses to put him off. First they maintained that an order from the governor was required, then that the money had to be paid in advance. Shortly after the departure of the generals for Panama, Commander Hubbard of the *Nashville* received his orders of the 2d, which had been delivered by error to one of the launches. He thereupon cabled the Navy Department:

[60] *Ibid.:* Consular Letters, Panama, Vol. 25, Nov. 3, 1903 (received 9:50 P.M.); *Story of Panama,* pp. 393-395 (Hall testimony).
[61] *Story of Panama,* pp. 395 *et seq.* (Hall testimony).

REVOLUTION IN PANAMA 365

Receipt of your telegram of November 2 is acknowledged. Prior to receipt this morning about 400 men were landed here by the Government of Colombia from Cartagena. No revolution has been declared on the Isthmus and no disturbances. Railway company have declined to transport these troops except by request of the governor of Panama. Request has not been made. It is possible that movement may be made to-night at Panama to declare independence, in which event I will . . . [message mutilated here] here. Situation is most critical if revolutionary leaders act.[62]

By some chance Malmros was not told of the delivery of these instructions, nor did the Department of State learn, at least until the following day, of Hubbard's acknowledgment. At four o'clock Loomis asked the consul whether the Colombian forces had landed. Half an hour later he inquired whether the instructions to Hubbard had been received. In response, Malmros confirmed the debarkation and denied the receipt of the instructions. At 8:45 P. M., twenty-five minutes after this reply reached Washington and a full hour before learning of the actual outbreak in Panama from Ehrman, Loomis telegraphed: "The troops which landed from the *Cartagena* should not proceed to Panama." At 10:30 P. M. Hay added:

If dispatch to *Nashville* has not been delivered inform her captain immediately that she must prevent Government troops departing for Panama or taking any action which would lead to bloodshed, and must use every endeavor to preserve order on the Isthmus.

So eager was the department to get these orders to Hubbard that a final cable was sent at 11:18 P. M. to Ehrman in Panama enclosing the message and instructing him to use a special train, if necessary, to deliver it.[63] The consul-general, aroused from sleep, had the railroad officials telephone it across the Isthmus shortly before their agents cut the wires.

Having heard through Shaler in the meantime of the arrest of the generals, Hubbard wrote out the following order to the superintendent about ten o'clock in the evening:

[62] *Dip. Hist. of the Panama Canal*, p. 365; *Story of Panama*, pp. 440–441.
[63] State Dept.: Instructions to Consuls, Vol. 189, Nov. 3, 1903; Consular Letters, Aspinwall (Colón), Vol. 19, Nov. 3, 1903.

Sir: The condition of affairs at Panama being such that any movement of troops in the neighborhood must inevitably produce a conflict and interrupt the transit of the Isthmus which the United States Government is pledged to maintain uninterrupted, I am obliged to prohibit the carrying of troops of either party or in either direction by your railroad, and hereby notify you that I do so prohibit it.[64]

Early in the morning of the 4th Shaler and the local revolutionary committee received copies of this communication. Torres, unaware of the developments in Panama, tried again to procure trains for his men. Porfirio Meléndez, the representative of the *junta* in Colón, finally took the colonel to the Astor House for a drink and broke the news about the uprising and the arrest of Tobar. He pointed out that the United States was behind the independence movement and that more vessels were expected hourly. He advised the officer to come to an "arrangement" and take his men back to Cartagena. Torres returned to the wharf in a rage. His fury increased when he was handed a note from Hubbard setting forth the existing dangers to the freedom of traffic and concluding: "I have therefore the honor to notify you that I have directed the superintendent of the Panama Railroad at Colon that he must not transport on his line troops of either party." [65]

In an effort to force the release of his superiors Torres sent an emissary to Malmros at half-past twelve to warn him that he was determined to burn the town and kill every American in it if his demands were not complied with by two o'clock.[66] Hubbard promptly placed the women and children aboard ships in the port, collected the men in a stone shed belonging to the railroad company, and landed a detachment of sailors with an extra supply of rifles. The Colombians surrounded the structure and for a while fighting seemed inevitable. The *Nashville* cleared its decks and moved in close to shore with its guns trained on the wharf and the *Cartagena*. The latter immediately got up steam

---

[64] *Story of Panama*, p. 440 (Hall testimony).
[65] *Ibid.*, pp. 441–442 (Hall testimony).
[66] State Dept., Consular Letters, Aspinwall (Colón), Vol. 19, Malmros to Hay, Nov. 5, 1903.

and left the harbor, thereby thwarting a carefully prepared plan of the revolutionary committee to seize her. About half-past three Torres apparently thought better of his conduct and opened negotiations with Hubbard. It was agreed that while he awaited orders from the incarcerated Tobar the sailors would be reëmbarked and the troops withdrawn to Monkey Hill, outside the town.

On the morning of the 5th the Tiradores reappeared in Colón and Hubbard repeated his defensive measures of the previous day. Since the generals in Panama refused to take advantage of their captors' generous permission to cross to the Atlantic side on parole or to issue orders to their subordinate from prison, Torres began to show interest in Meléndez' suggestion that he take passage with his men on the Royal Mail steamer *Orinoco*. A basis of understanding was finally reached and he sailed shortly after sunset with his battalion, $8,000 in gold, and two cases of champagne. The U.S.S. *Dixie* steamed into the harbor just as the *Orinoco* was preparing to get under way.[67]

With the departure of the Colombian forces from Colón on the 5th the revolution was for the time being an accomplished fact in the sense that no armed opposition remained on the Isthmus. The question as to whether the new republic would survive for longer than the time necessary for Bogotá to land an army of pacification depended entirely upon the attitude the United States chose to assume. Early recognition and direct protection were the indispensable conditions of continued Panamanian independence.

Convinced by Hubbard's actions in Colón that the Roosevelt administration would fend off any immediate attempt on Colombia's part to recover the lost territory, the provisional government set about its task of securing prompt recognition and a treaty guaranty of its sovereignty over the Isthmus. On the 4th it cabled Secretary Hay that "in consequence of a popular and spontaneous movement" the Republic of Panama had been established and that Arango, Boyd, and Arias constituted the

[67] *Story of Panama*, pp. 442-444, 454-458 (Hall testimony).

executive board. A few hours later the municipal council of Panama wired Roosevelt that it had joined the secession movement and that it hoped for his recognition.[68]

As long as Colón remained in the possession of the Colombian government the Department of State made no open move. When Ehrman, on the 5th, reported the receipt of an official circular letter announcing the creation of the new government, Loomis replied: "Acknowledge the receipt of circular letter and await instructions before taking any further action in this line." Two hours later he asked both Ehrman and Malmros to keep the department informed as to the situation. At seven that evening the latter wired that all the Colombian soldiers at Colón were embarking for Cartagena and that a vessel, supposed to be the *Dixie,* was in sight.[69] This was unquestionably the news that Washington had been waiting for. An independent republic which controlled only one end of the canal route would have been of no use to the administration. With the revolutionists controlling Panama, the Colombians Colón, and Uncle Sam sitting on the railroad between them preventing a victory for either side, the whole situation would have become farcical. Had the imprisoned Tobar been less concerned with his own injured dignity, he might have realized that as long as Torres remained quietly in Colón the trumps were in his government's hand. Bogotá's claims to *de facto* sovereignty over the Isthmus would have been as good as the *junta's* and its *de jure* rights superior. It would then have been up to the United States, since it was interested in a canal and not an impasse, to propose an acceptable solution. Tobar's opportunity to tie matters up in this fashion had presented itself that afternoon. The insurgents, feeling confident of North American support, had unwittingly furnished an excellent opening. Every arrangement had been made to bring the general to the Atlantic side for a conference with his subordinate, but, since no troops were allowed on the trains, he had

[68] *Dip. Hist. of the Panama Canal,* pp. 353–354.
[69] State Dept.: Instructions to Consuls, Vol. 189, Loomis to Ehrman, telegrams, Nov. 5, 1903; same to Malmros, same date; *ibid.*: Consular Letters, Aspinwall (Colón), Vol. 19, Malmros to Hay, Nov. 5, 1903.

been asked to give his promise not to escape. The general had haughtily—and foolishly—refused these terms and had thereupon been escorted back to confinement. Torres, abandoned by his commander and impressed by Meléndez' stories about what the Yankees intended to do, had then decided to accept his bribe and withdraw from the scene. It was this action which cleared the principal obstacles from the path of the recognition of Panama.

At ten o'clock the following morning—November 6—the declaration of independence was read and the republic proclaimed at the prefecture in Colón, before a gathering of townspeople, foreign consuls, and officers from the warships in the harbor. As a gesture of gratitude for the services of the United States, the revolutionary committee requested Major William Murray Black, U.S.A., to raise the Panamanian flag. The officer complied, with a fine disregard for the fact that he was wearing the uniform of a nation which had not yet recognized the new republic.[70]

Major Black's action was just barely premature. Two telegrams addressed to Hay, sent from the Isthmus during the morning, definitely settled the question of recognition. The first, received at 10:40 A. M., read as follows:

Colon and all the towns of the Isthmus have adhered to the declaration of independence proclaimed in this city. The authority of the Republic of Panama is obeyed throughout its territory.

Arango.
Arias.
Boyd.[71]

The second, from Ehrman, reached the North American capital just before noon:

The situation is peaceful. Isthmian movement has obtained so far success. Colon and interior provinces have enthusiastically joined independence. . . . Bunau Varilla has been appointed officially confidential agent of the Republic of Panama at Washington.[72]

---

[70] *Story of Panama*, p. 458 (Hall testimony).
[71] *Dip. Hist. of the Panama Canal*, p. 354.
[72] State Dept.: Consular Letters, Panama, Vol. 25, Nov. 6, 1903.

At 12:51 Hay communicated the administration's decision to the consul-general:

The people of Panama have, by an apparently unanimous movement, dissolved their political connection with the Republic of Colombia and resumed thei. independence. When you are satisfied that a de facto government, republican in form, and without substantial opposition from its own people, has been established in the State of Panama, you will enter into relations with it as the responsible government of the territory and look to it for all due action to protect the persons and property of citizens of the United States and to keep open the isthmian transit in accordance with the obligations of existing treaties governing the relation of the United States to that territory.

Communicate above to Malmros, who will be governed by these instructions in entering into relations with the local authorities.[73]

---

[73] *Ibid.:* Instructions to Consuls, Vol. 189, Hay to Ehrman, telegram, Nov. 6, 1903.

XI

THE TRIUMPH OF PANAMA

THE FATEFUL CABLE of November 6 conclusively ended whatever slight chance may have remained of reopening the Hay-Herrán negotiations. With the recognition of the *de facto* government of Panama the diplomatic and political history of the canal enters upon another phase, which it is not our present purpose to examine in detail. Some of the immediate consequences of the creation of the new republic are so pertinent to our theme, however, that they merit a brief consideration.

The first reliable reports that an outbreak had occurred on the Isthmus reached the Colombian government the very day that Hay entered into relations with the infant state. Popular excitement mounted as the news became generally known. Crowds paraded the streets shouting "Down with Marroquín!" while a mass meeting before the palace called for his resignation. Troops were summoned to disperse the gatherings and martial law was proclaimed in the city. Strong guards were placed about the United States legation.[1]

At six o'clock on the evening of the 6th Beaupré cabled his report of an interview with Reyes which indicates the complete desperation of the Bogotá authorities.

Knowing that the revolution has already commenced in Panama, General Reyes says that if the Government of the United States will land troops to preserve Colombian sovereignty, and the transit, if requested by the Colombian chargé d'affaires, this Government will declare martial law, and by virtue of vested constitutional authority, when public order is disturbed, will approve by decree the ratification of the canal treaty as signed; or, if the Government of the United States prefers, will call extra session of Congress with new and friendly members next May to approve the treaty. General Reyes has

---

[1] State Dept., Dispatches from Colombia, Vol. 60, Beaupré to Hay, telegram, Nov. 9, 1903.

the perfect confidence of Vice President, he says, and if it becomes necessary will go to the Isthmus or send representatives there to adjust matters along above lines to the satisfaction of the people there. If he goes he would like to act in harmony with commander of United States forces. This is the personal opinion of Reyes, and he will advise this Government to act accordingly. There is a great reaction of public opinion in favor of the treaty, and it is considered certain that the treaty was not legally rejected by Congress. Tomorrow martial law will be declared; 1,000 troops will be sent from the Pacific side; about the same number from the Atlantic side. Please answer by telegraph.[2]

When once the first shock had passed, hostility to Marroquín faded before a growing determination to preserve the integrity of the fatherland. With few exceptions the newspapers of the capital suspended their partisan feuds and devoted their editorials to discussions of the national emergency. Seldom had the country experienced so strong a sense of solidarity. Powerful political leaders, regardless of differences on domestic issues, pledged their support to the executive. From all the continental departments offers of military service and money poured in. Pérez y Soto organized a volunteer legion, while even Caro abstained from his customary attacks on the vice-president.

Owing to the lack of precise knowledge as to the situation in Panama, the cabinet advised the creation of a special commission with wide military and diplomatic powers to proceed to the Isthmus for the purpose of making whatever settlement seemed most advantageous to the nation's interests, short of recognizing the independence of the seceded region. Reyes was named chief of this delegation, with Pedro Nel Ospina and Lucas Caballero as associates.[3] Before taking his departure on the 10th, Reyes requested the United States Government, through Beaupré, not to recognize the revolutionists, but to preserve the freedom of the transit and to await his arrival at Colón before taking any definite action.[4]

[2] *Ibid.*, Beaupré to Hay, Nov. 6, 1903 (received Nov. 8, 11:05 P. M.).
[3] *Libro azul*, pp. 372–373.
[4] State Dept.: Dispatches from Colombia, Vol. 60, Beaupré to Hay, telegram, Nov. 7, 1903.

The announcement from Washington which Marroquín and his advisers had been dreading reached Bogotá on the 11th. It read:

> The people of Panama, having, by an apparently unanimous movement, dissolved their political connection with the Republic of Colombia and resumed their independence, and having adopted a government of their own, republican in form, with which the Government of the United States of America has entered into relations, the President of the United States, in accordance with the ties of friendship which have so long and happily existed between the respective nations, most earnestly commends to the Governments of Colombia and Panama the peaceable and equitable settlement of all questions at issue between them. He holds that he is bound, not merely by treaty obligations, but by the interests of civilization, to see that the peaceable traffic of the world across the Isthmus of Panama shall not longer be disturbed by a constant succession of unnecessary and wasteful civil wars.[5]

Upon communicating this dispatch to the vice-president and his cabinet at the San Carlos Palace, Beaupré was asked whether it was to be understood that no Colombian troops would be permitted to land on the Isthmus. He declared that he was not in a position to amplify the message. Rico delivered a long and formal protest the following day, denouncing the action of the United States as a violation of its obligations under the treaty of 1846–48 and threatening to sever diplomatic relations unless his government was permitted to suppress the revolt without interference. A national council of eminent citizens, summoned to advise the administration in the emergency, proved so belligerent in its attitude that a recommendation for war against the United States was defeated only by a narrow margin and after a bitter debate.[6]

Reyes accomplished nothing constructive by his visit to the

---

[5] *Ibid.:* Instructions to Colombia, Vol. 19, Hay to Beaupré, telegram, Nov. 6, 1903, p. 279.
[6] *Ibid.:* Dispatches from Colombia, Vol. 60, Beaupré to Hay, telegram, Nov. 12, 1903; same to same, telegram, Nov. 14, 1903; same to same, telegram, Nov. 17, 1903; Uribe, *Colombia y los Estados Unidos,* pp. xxxiii–xxxiv; *Libro azul,* pp. 592 et seq.

Isthmus beyond ascertaining that his country would have to fight the United States as well as Panama if it sought forcibly to reëstablish its authority there. He and his colleagues were informed by Admiral Coghlan, commanding the North American naval forces in the area, that orders had been issued to prevent the landing of any Colombian soldiers or officials within the borders of the new republic.[7] The commissioners were allowed to enter Colón harbor but not to leave their steamer. A conference with a Panamanian delegation headed by Tomás Arias, which came aboard on the 20th, convinced them of the futility of seeking reunion by direct negotiation. In accordance with supplementary instructions, therefore, they continued directly on to Washington, where they arrived on November 28.[8]

While the Reyes mission was at Colón, a new canal treaty was being put into final shape in Washington. It will be recalled that Bunau-Varilla had insisted upon appointment as Panama's diplomatic representative in return for his assistance to the revolution. This had been a difficult concession for Amador to grant as it deprived him of a distinction on which his own heart had been set. After the proclamation of the republic deliberate efforts seem to have been made to confine the Frenchman's duties to an empty formality. He was commissioned as diplomatic agent, not minister plenipotentiary, and the provisional government announced that Amador and Boyd were starting for the United States to supervise the actual negotiations. They carried a letter of instructions to their "colleague" in Washington which stated:

[7] *Libro azul*, pp. 563 *et seq*. In answer to Rico's query of the 7th on this point, the department had wired on the 11th: "It is not thought desirable to permit landing of Colombian troops on Isthmus, as such a course would precipitate civil war and disturb for an indefinite period the free transit which we are pledged to protect." State Dept.: Dispatches from Colombia, Vol. 60, Beaupré to Hay, telegram, Nov. 7, 1903; Instructions to Colombia, Vol. 19, Hay to Beaupré, telegram, Nov. 11, 1903. In view of its recognition of Panama's independence five days previously, the department was guilty of an amusing inconsistency in expressing fear that the landing of Colombian troops on the Isthmus would precipitate a "civil war."

[8] *Libro azul*, pp. 365–366.

TRIUMPH OF PANAMA 375

You will have to adjust a Treaty for the Canal construction by the United States. But all the clauses of this Treaty will be discussed previously with the delegates of the Junta, MM. Amador and Boyd. And you will proceed in everything strictly in accord with them . . .[9]

Bunau-Varilla was not the man to be shoved aside in this fashion. Sensing Amador's motive in coming north, he brought pressure on Arango, while the delegation was at sea, to cable him plenipotentiary powers. This was accompanied by a suave intimation that he would otherwise block the opening of credits for which he had arranged. Upon receiving word of Arango's capitulation to his demand for full authority, Bunau-Varilla hurried to Washington to start work. Roosevelt received him on the 13th and five days later the new treaty was signed. The intensity of effort which characterized this feat is vividly recorded in a letter Hay wrote his daughter on the 19th:

As for your poor old dad, they are working him nights and Sundays. I have never, I think, been so constantly and actively employed as during the last fortnight. Yesterday morning the negotiations with Panama were far from complete. But by putting on all steam, getting Root and Knox and Shaw together at lunch, I went over my project line by line, and fought out every section of it; adopted a few good suggestions: hurried back to the Department, set everybody at work drawing up final drafts—sent for Varilla, went over the whole treaty with him, explained all the changes, got his consent, and at seven o'clock signed the momentous document in the little blue drawing-room, out of Abraham Lincoln's inkstand, and with [Clarence's] pen. Varilla had no seal, so he used one of mine.[10]

Bunau-Varilla's part in the formulation of the treaty was considerably more important than Hay's letter suggests. The new Panamanian minister not only worked out suggestions for improving the draft which the secretary of state sent him on the 15th but prepared an entirely new treaty project of his own. Both documents were dispatched to Hay's office on the morning of the 17th. In an accompanying note Bunau-Varilla explained that he was willing to accept whichever proposal the secretary preferred.

[9] Bunau-Varilla, *Panama: The Creation, Destruction, and Resurrection*, p. 360.
[10] Thayer, *John Hay*, II, 318.

The old form has the advantage of rendering easier the comparison between the Treaty with Colombia and the Treaty with Panama, and to show the progress made from one to the other. But it has the great disadvantage of bearing the trace of the long diplomatic fight with M. Concha, who never wished to accede to anything in one article without withdrawing it in the other.

The new form has the advantage of conferring upon the United States in broad and general terms the rights she is entitled to have; rendering it thus unnecessary to enumerate in an infinity of *cas particuliers,* what right [*sic*] Colombia was generous enough to grant.[11]

The minister had acted none too soon. Hardly had the new convention been delivered to the State Department when a telegram reached him from J. J. Lindo, of the commercial firm of Piza, Nephews & Company, announcing that Amador and Boyd had disembarked at New York and would probably continue on to the capital the next day.[12] The Frenchman, torn by anxiety, awaited a summons from the secretary of state. It did not come until late in the evening, and then only in response to a respectful but urgent request for an interview. In the course of the conference Hay disclosed that there was powerful senatorial support for a plan to divide the $10,000,000 cash indemnity between Panama and Colombia. Bunau-Varilla, who knew very well the kind of reception any such scheme would meet with on the Isthmus, argued strongly against it. On the following morning he sent Hay a letter summarizing his views on the subject. He pointed out that a payment to Colombia would be interpreted by the world in general as an admission that the United States had acted in bad faith and by Latin-American nations in particular as an "insulting offer of a little money compensation for a patriotic wrong."[13] This plea was

---

[11] Bunau-Varilla Papers: Hay to Bunau-Varilla, Nov. 15, 1903; Bunau-Varilla to Hay, Nov. 17, 1903. Frank D. Pavey, a New York lawyer and friend of the French engineer, went down to Washington to assist in the work of phrasing and polishing the new convention. Hay later expressed to Bunau-Varilla his irritation over Pavey's indiscreet remarks to reporters about his share in the authorship. *Ibid.,* Hay to Bunau-Varilla, Nov. 23, 1903.

[12] *Ibid.,* Lindo to Bunau-Varilla, Nov. 17, 1903.

[13] Bunau-Varilla, *Panama: The Creation, Destruction, and Resurrection,* pp. 372–375.

evidently effective, for the proposal was dropped. The convention was signed early in the evening of the 18th. With the exception of a few alterations, the text was that submitted by the Panamanian minister.

The Hay–Bunau-Varilla treaty empowered the United States to construct a canal through a zone ten miles in width (as compared with ten kilometers in the Hay-Herrán pact), extending across the Isthmus, but excluding the cities of Panama and Colón. Article III, incorporating the most significant changes, provided:

The Republic of Panama grants to the United States all the rights, power and authority within the zone mentioned and described in Article II of this agreement and within the limits of all auxiliary lands and waters mentioned and described in said Article II which the United States would possess and exercise if it were the sovereign of the territory within which such lands and waters are located to the entire exclusion of the exercise by the Republic of Panama of any such sovereign rights, power or authority.

By other articles Panama granted permission to the canal and railroad companies to transfer their concessions and property to the United States and agreed that the latter nation should have at all times the right to employ its armed forces in the defense of the canal and its auxiliary works. The small islands in the Bay of Panama named Perico, Naos, Culebra, and Flamenco, which the Hay-Herrán treaty had specifically placed outside the zone, were now granted to the United States in perpetuity. In return for these privileges the convention stipulated that the United States "guarantees and will maintain the independence of the Republic of Panama." The pecuniary compensation was identical with that in the Colombian convention. Since North American authority was to be absolute in the zone, no provision was made for the establishment of joint tribunals.[14]

Bunau-Varilla's plan to complete the negotiations before the appearance of Amador and Boyd succeeded principally because the delegates, unaware of any necessity for speed, tarried in New

[14] Malloy, *Treaties,* II, 1349 *et seq.*

York for a day to await Cromwell's return from Paris. After an interview with the attorney they entrained for Washington late in the afternoon of the 18th. Bunau-Varilla greeted them at the station in the evening with the tidings that the treaty had been signed a few hours before. Amador, taken utterly by surprise, "nearly swooned on the platform." [15]

Fearing that the chagrin of the two Panamanians would possibly lead them to interject difficulties in the path of ratification, and fully appreciating the value of placing an accepted treaty before Congress when it gathered on December 7, the minister plenipotentiary again resorted to the cables. He succeeded, after a period of anxious delay, in wringing a pledge from Arango that the agreement would be ratified without change immediately upon its arrival at the Isthmus. The provisional government kept the pledge and formally approved the convention on December 2.[16]

Despite the success of these maneuvers, the treaty was by no means past the rocks. The Reyes mission, now at the capital, retained the services of Wayne MacVeagh, a skilful lawyer well versed in the techniques of "pressure" politics. MacVeagh lost no time in organizing an intensive campaign designed to force the rejection of the convention.

In his annual message to Congress on December 7 Roosevelt devoted several pages to a description of the negotiations with Colombia which preceded the decisive action of August 12. He examined the interpretations placed upon the treaty of 1846–1848 by successive secretaries of state and listed the disturbances which had occurred on the Isthmus during the preceding half-century. He felt that his "recital of facts" established beyond question:

[15] Bunau-Varilla, *Panama: The Creation, Destruction, and Resurrection*, pp. 377–378. In his book the Frenchman makes a great show of hurt pride that Amador should have visited Cromwell rather than himself first. If it was a snub, it would seem that the delay involved made it a fortunate one from the minister's point of view.

[16] Bunau-Varilla Papers: Bunau-Varilla to Amador–Boyd, telegram, Nov. 25, 1903; Bunau-Varilla to de la Espriella, telegram, Nov. 25, 1903; Bunau-Varilla to Hay, telegram, Nov. 25, 1903; Bunau-Varilla to Paris *Matin*, telegram, Dec. 2, 1903.

First, that the United States has for over half a century patiently and in good faith carried out its obligations under the treaty of 1846; second, that when for the first time it became possible for Colombia to do anything in requital of the services thus repeatedly rendered to it for fifty-seven years by the United States, the Colombian Government peremptorily and offensively refused thus to do its part, even though to do so would have been to its advantage and immeasurably to the advantage of the State of Panama, at that time under its jurisdiction; third, that throughout this period revolutions, riots, and factional disturbances of every kind have occurred one after the other in almost uninterrupted succession, some of them lasting for months and even for years, while the central government was unable to put them down or to make peace with the rebels; fourth, that these disturbances instead of showing any sign of abating have tended to grow more numerous and more serious in the immediate past; fifth, that the control of Colombia over the Isthmus of Panama could not be maintained without the armed intervention and assistance of the United States. In other words, the Government of Colombia, though wholly unable to maintain order on the Isthmus, has nevertheless declined to ratify a treaty the conclusion of which opened the only chance to secure its own stability and to guarantee permanent peace on, and the construction of a canal across, the Isthmus.

Under such circumstances, the president continued, "the Government of the United States would have been guilty of folly and weakness, amounting in their sum to a crime against the Nation," had it acted otherwise than it did when the revolution occurred. It could not permit so great an enterprise to be obstructed by the "sinister and evil political peculiarities" of a nation which asserted "an unreal supremacy" over the territory. The possession of such a region carried with it obligations to mankind which, in spite of every warning from the United States, were flouted for small and selfish ends. The new republic had immediately offered to negotiate a treaty which was now submitted to the Senate.

By it our interests are better safeguarded than in the treaty with Colombia which was ratified by the Senate at its last session. It is better in its terms than the treaties offered to us by the Republics of Nicaragua and Costa Rica. . . . All that remains is for the American Congress to do its part, and forthwith this Republic will enter upon the execution of a project colossal in its size and of well-nigh incalculable possibilities for the good of this country and the nations of mankind.[17]

This statement, as Roosevelt quickly discovered, was not sufficiently explicit to meet the questions which were being raised in Congress and the press. The critics wanted to know how much the president knew about the Panama revolution in advance and to what extent he had been its instigator. Blanket denials proved useless. The issue had its political aspect in Washington as in Bogotá. Some Democratic senators were eager to contribute anything within their power to the embarrassment of the man who was generally conceded to be the Republican standard-bearer in the presidential race of 1904. Others, like Morgan, remained sincerely wedded to the Nicaragua route. In both parties were legislators who regarded the administration's decisive share in the isthmian coup as a reflection upon the nation's good name and a source of future ill-will in Latin America. The leading journals split sharply in their reactions. If the New York *Sun* stood fast by the executive, the New York *Post* deserted him to join the *World* in its severe condemnation of his conduct. Albert Shaw, of the *Review of Reviews,* who had raised a minor storm early in November by recommending a revolt to the Panamanians, and Joseph Bucklin Bishop, of the New York *Commercial Advertiser,* viewed the secession movement as a just requital for the "bad faith" shown by the Colombian "dictator."

Placed squarely on the defensive for the first time in office, Roosevelt determined to justify his course in detail. With the assistance of John Bassett Moore a lengthy special message was prepared for submission to both houses of Congress on January 4, 1904.[18] The Moore interpretation of the rights of the

[17] *Cong. Rec.,* 58th Cong., 2nd Sess., pp. 8-11.
[18] "I hope you liked 'our' message in its final form," Roosevelt wrote to Moore on January 6. "I say 'our' message advisedly, for I feel that you had about as much to do with it as I had. You may have noticed that I accepted all your suggestions excepting the cf. with San Domingo. . . . In addition to the invaluable help you rendered, I also received excellent suggestions from Root,

United States under the treaty of 1846–1848 formed the basis of the president's argument. Working from that assumption he sought to meet and demolish the principal objections of his critics. By the time the Hay-Herrán treaty was sent to Colombia for ratification, he contended, three things had already been settled. First, the canal was to be built. The time for delay was past. The United States had assumed in connection with the canal "certain responsibilities not only to its own people, but to the civilized world . . ." Secondly, it had been clearly demonstrated that it was the nation's purpose to deal not merely justly, but in a spirit of liberality with the Colombians.

The Hay-Herran treaty, if it erred at all, erred in the direction of an overgenerosity towards the Colombian Government. In our anxiety to be fair we had gone to the very verge in yielding to a weak nation's demands what that nation was helplessly unable to enforce from us against our will. The only criticisms made upon the Administration for the terms of the Hay-Herran treaty were for having granted too much to Colombia, not for failure to grant enough.

He emphasized that during the protracted negotiations Colombia gave no intimation that there were constitutional barriers to United States control over the zone. The refusal of the Bogotá congress to grant such control was "necessarily a refusal to make any practicable treaty at all." This attitude in turn, he added, "squarely raised the question whether Colombia was entitled to bar the transit of the world's traffic across the Isthmus." The third matter which had been settled by the summer of 1903 was the location of the canal. The Spooner Act provided for a treaty covering the Panama route, with the alternative of Nicaragua should such a treaty not be made within a reasonable time.

The treaty has been made; for it needs no argument to show that the intent of Congress was to insure a canal across Panama, and that whether the Republic granting the title was called New Granada, Colombia, or Panama mattered not one whit. As events turned out, the question of "reasonable time" did not enter into the matter at all.

---

as well as Hay, Loomis, Moody and Lodge. The final result I think was pretty satisfactory." Roosevelt Papers.

Although, as the months went by, it became increasingly improbable that the Colombian Congress would ratify the treaty . . . yet all chance for such action on their part did not vanish until the Congress closed at the end of October; and within three days thereafter the revolution in Panama had broken out. . . . The condition under which alone we could have gone to Nicaragua thereby became impossible of fulfillment. If the pending treaty with Panama should not be ratified by the Senate this would not alter the fact that we could not go to Nicaragua. The Congress has decided the route, and there is no alternative under existing legislation.

Roosevelt then sketched the evidence which had indicated to him that an uprising on the Isthmus was likely as soon as the Colombian congress adjourned. While admitting that the administration "had special means of knowledge," he insisted that the same conclusions could have been reached by anyone who had followed the newspapers closely. That he had in any way encouraged the conspirators, or even conversed with them, he emphatically denied. His orders to the naval vessels to take stations within striking distance of Panama were, he explained, in conformity with the practice of the government in 1901 and 1902 and necessary precautions under the treaty of 1846–1848. The report of Commander Hubbard

shows that, instead of there having been too much provision by the American Government for the maintenance of order and the protection of life and property on the Isthmus, the orders for the movement of the American warships had been too long delayed; so long, in fact, that there were but forty-two marines and sailors available to land and protect the lives of American women and children. It was only the coolness and gallantry with which this little band of men wearing the American uniform faced ten times their number of armed foes, bent on carrying out the atrocious threat of the Colombian commander, that prevented a murderous catastrophe.[19]

That this desperate situation, which appealed to Roosevelt's love of the martially heroic, would not have arisen had the forty-two sailors and marines not appeared on the scene, does not seem to have occurred to the president. He praised Hubbard

[19] *Cong. Rec.*, 58th Cong., 2nd Sess., pp. 418 *et seq.*

for preventing the shedding of Colombian or Panamanian blood, though in fulfillment of what treaty obligation this was done, he did not make clear.

General Reyes, meanwhile, was conducting an able correspondence with the Department of State, not so much in the hope that the administration would see and admit the error of its ways as to furnish the opponents of the pending treaty with arguments in debate and also to record the nature of Colombia's grievances for use in future claims for reparation. These notes sought to establish that the United States had been guilty of violating its obligation to maintain Colombian sovereignty over the Isthmus, had interfered with the movements of troops sent to suppress disorder, had forbidden any attempt by the Bogotá authorities to reëstablish their control in the seceded region, and had recognized the Republic of Panama with unprecedented and improper haste. Hay countered with the arguments used by Roosevelt in his messages on the subject.[20] The earlier exchanges in this series were sent to Congress on January 18 and were quoted extensively in the fight over ratification.[21]

There was danger for a time that some of the administration senators would introduce amendments to the treaty. This would, of course, provide Panama with an excellent excuse to propose changes of its own. To head off this possibility, Hay wrote Spooner on January 20, 1904:

As it stands now as soon as the Senate votes we shall have a treaty in the main very satisfactory, vastly advantageous to the United States, and we must confess, with what face we can muster, not so advantageous to Panama. If we amend the treaty and send it back there some time next month, the period of enthusiastic unanimity, which, as I said to Cullom, comes only once in the life of a revolution, will have passed away, and they will have entered on the new field of politics and dispute. You and I know too well how many points there are in this treaty to which a Panaman patriot could object. If it is again submitted to their consideration they will attempt to amend

---

[20] At least one of these replies, that dated Jan. 5, was based on a draft prepared by John Bassett Moore. Roosevelt Papers, Roosevelt to Moore, Jan. 6, 1904.
[21] *Dip. Hist. of the Panama Canal*, pp. 480 et seq.

it in many places, no man can say with what result, then they will feel that we had passed definitely upon the main subject; that the treaty was safe; that their independence was achieved, and that now it was time for them to look out for a better bargain than they were able to make at first.[22]

The Senate debate on the Hay–Bunau-Varilla treaty was one of the most bitter in the stormy congressional history of the Roosevelt administrations. Morgan, in the last supreme effort of his long fight for Nicaragua, again headed the assault. He not only attacked the convention at length in executive sessions but constantly injected references to the president's conduct into the discussion of other measures. Hanna, the hero of the debate on the Spooner bill, took no part. His exertions on behalf of his friend, Myron Herrick, in the Ohio gubernatorial elections the previous November, had undermined his strength. He fell ill soon afterwards and died on February 16, 1904, just as the final debate on the canal pact commenced. Spooner, Lodge, and Cullom carried the brunt of the fight for the administration. Party discipline, strengthened by the approach of the presidential campaign, was enforced to bring the wavering senators into line. On February 23 the upper house advised ratification of the Hay–Bunau-Varilla treaty by a vote of 66 to 14.[23]

II

With the formal proclamation of the treaty on February 26 the fight for Panama passed into history. Slightly more than five years had elapsed since the New Company fired the opening gun in the momentous battle of the routes. During that half-decade the Panama forces had accomplished a remarkable feat against tremendous odds. By bold and well-directed attacks

---

[22] Dennis, *Adventures in American Diplomacy*, p. 341. Sixteen days before, as we have seen, Roosevelt informed Congress that "the only criticisms made upon the Administration for the terms of the Hay-Herran treaty were for having granted too much to Colombia, not for failure to grant enough." Evidently the administration, in its efforts to forestall similar criticism of the new treaty, was conscious of having leaned very far in the other direction.

[23] N. Y. *Times*, Feb. 24, 1904.

they had routed the entrenched defenders of the Nicaragua line to capture, in June, 1902, the coveted prize of congressional favor. By a series of adroit, and sometimes devious, maneuvers they had subsequently preserved their advantage in the face of Colombia's defection and Morgan's spirited counterthrusts. Many factors contributed to the final victory, but the triumph of the Panama route was basically due to the energy and resourcefulness of a few indomitable personalities.

Cromwell's activities have been traced in considerable detail and need not be recapitulated here. His role throughout was strictly that of the attorney operating in the interest of his clients. The French stockholders were thrice-blessed in their choice of counsel, though they seem to have been rather slow in recognizing that fact. Had the cause of Panama been placed in any less extraordinary hands, events would probably have moved along a very different course. It is doubtful, in the first place, whether the Walker Commission would have been created. The disagreement between the Senate and House committees in 1899 over the form of government participation in the construction of a Nicaragua canal would have been ironed out on some other basis. Bunau-Varilla, whose later contribution was undeniably important, did not open his personal campaign in the United States until nearly two years after Congress provided for the impartial investigation of all isthmian routes. In the second place, it is extremely unlikely that a satisfactory Colombian convention could have been prepared in time for the Senate's consideration in June, 1902, without the prodigious aggressiveness of a Cromwell. If the slow-paced Bogotá government had actually controlled the negotiations carried on in Washington in its name, it would almost certainly have lost the canal then and there.

Once the Spooner Act had been passed, Cromwell's determination to avoid any payment by the New Company to Colombia developed into one of the major obstacles to the consummation of a treaty. The Colombian leaders were clearly disappointed over the low compensation offered by the United States, but they were shocked and angered by the Department of State's belligerent defense of Cromwell's clients. They could see no reason why the Washington administration should spread the mantle of official protection over the prospective profits of a group of French investors and bluntly challenge Colombia's right to make a separate agreement with its own concessioners. Others, too, have found those actions difficult to justify. The argument, offered over Hay's signature, that the United States could never permit its diplomatic arrangements to depend upon the action of a private company, would have a more convincing ring were it not so obvious that the United States was, at that very time, permitting the agent of a private company to jeopardize one of the most momentous diplomatic arrangements in the country's history. The accomplishment of the administration's purpose to build the canal at Panama called for the elimination of every possible barrier to Colombian acceptance of the treaty. Yet Cromwell received official coöperation in raising just such a barrier—to the detriment of the nation's interests and the advantage of his own. Had the department kept hands off the dispute between Bogotá and the New Company, the directors in Paris would undoubtedly have submitted to some kind of assessment rather than lose the entire $40,000,000. Such a victory for Marroquín in the spring or summer of 1903 would certainly have improved the chances for ratification. The treaty might have been rejected despite this help, but at least Hay would have been clear of any responsibility for the outcome.

Only once prior to the summer of 1903 did Roosevelt directly enter the fight for Panama. That was in January, 1902, when he ordered the Isthmian Canal Commission to reconsider its verdict for Nicaragua in the light of the New Company's sudden offer to sell its property at the commission's valuation. It will be recalled that it was the supplementary Walker report that prepared the way for Spooner's amendment to the Hepburn bill. The president appears to have allowed Hay a relatively free hand in the conduct of the subsequent negotiations with Concha and Herrán, although he kept himself constantly posted.

The situation began to change, however, about the middle of July, 1903, as it became evident that the treaty was encountering formidable opposition in the Colombian congress. Roosevelt's notes in the weeks that followed show that the direction of affairs was gradually shifting to Oyster Bay. By the time news of the rejection arrived, Hay had withdrawn into a merely advisory position. The secretary of state was ill and probably not displeased at having the responsibility of decision placed on sturdier shoulders. The president acted as his own foreign minister, insofar as Panama was concerned, until after the November revolution.

Roosevelt never comprehended the Colombian situation nor the nature of the difficulties confronting Marroquín. He based his actions upon a distorted version of the facts, to which he clung doggedly for the rest of his life. The account in the *Autobiography* is typical and succinct:

President Marroquin, through his Minister, had agreed to the Hay-Herran Treaty of January, 1903. He had the absolute power of an unconstitutional dictator to keep his promise or break it. He determined to break it. To furnish himself an excuse for breaking it he devised the plan of summoning a Congress especially called to reject the canal treaty. This the Congress—a Congress of puppets—did, without a dissenting vote; and the puppets adjourned without legislating on any other subject.[24]

Except for the first sentence, every statement in this passage is inaccurate. Roosevelt was not deliberately misrepresenting the facts; he undoubtedly believed what he wrote. But he was content to form judgments of far-reaching importance on the basis of inadequate data. He jumped to conclusions that satisfied him because they harmonized with his preconceptions. There is no indication that he ever made any serious effort to grasp the Colombian point of view.

Roosevelt correctly estimated the strategic value of the canal and the effect its construction would have upon the country's commerce and international prestige. Moreover, he was among

[24] *Autobiography*, pp. 561–562.

the first of the nation's leaders to recognize the advantages of a route which had been traditionally scorned in the United States. Yet he did not bring this same clear vision into his dealings with Colombia. He was thwarted and angry, and he chose to interpret the inconvenient behavior of the Bogotá government in the light of his personal resentment. As on other occasions, he sought to reduce a complicated situation to simple terms by introducing moral considerations which were either overdrawn or wholly fanciful. He preferred to rationalize his desire for prompt action on the treaty rather than soberly to investigate the facts. This was certainly not a conscious process with him, but it was one that gave his conduct the appearance of insincerity. In the case of Marroquín, Roosevelt's imagination transmuted a distracted but well-meaning old man into a powerful and unscrupulous dictator who, with his bandit followers, was attempting to exact tribute from the United States on a flimsy "constitutional" pretext. By contrast, the president pictured himself the champion of Right and the spokesman of progress and "universal utility."

There is reason to believe that the United States might have obtained the Panama route on its own terms without an isthmian revolution. A satisfactory arrangement was probably chiefly a matter of time and patience. It should be remembered that while the Colombians had long counted on a canal, until about 1901 they had generally assumed that it would be built and managed by private enterprise. A divided sovereignty over the line of transit had not been contemplated—even in the treaties of 1869 and 1870. When negotiations were opened in Washington in response to Cromwell's hurry call, therefore, questions of military and civil control arose which had no counterpart in the provisions of the Wyse concession. Consequently, there was much discussion among Colombian publicists and government officials as to the proper limits to be set upon North American rights in the proposed zone. The more ardent advocates of a convention argued that slight sacrifices of jurisdiction would be more than compensated for by the substantial material benefits such a partnership would bring. To an impoverished and war-torn republic the prospect of a large cash indemnity was particularly alluring. It could be used to rebuild the country, to improve transportation, and to stabilize the currency. Many Colombians, accordingly, anticipated an agreement embodying liberal financial payments and minor concessions of authority. The Hay-Herrán treaty proved disappointing in both respects. The unfavorable reaction to these terms was magnified by an element of personal animosity to Marroquín and the failure of the government to obtain anything from the New Company. The convention went down to defeat under a combination of these pressures.

Yet the plight of the treaty was not as hopeless as outward appearances would indicate. Most of the leaders of the Colombian senate did, evidently, want the United States to construct the Panama Canal. Their actions and comments after August 12 point directly to this conclusion. Furthermore, the approaching retirement of Marroquín from office promised a clearing of the political atmosphere. Reyes stood an excellent chance of election to the presidency. He was the administration's choice, he had the backing of the departmental governors, and he was popular throughout the nation. The general possessed a more powerful personality and a far keener political touch than the aged vice-president. He favored close coöperation with Washington and was eager to garner the credit for concluding the canal negotiation. It is obviously out of the question to say with assurance that he would have succeeded in pushing even a modified Hay-Herrán treaty through the Bogotá congress of 1904, but his activities both preceding and following the Panama revolution revealed a talent for opportunism which might well have turned the scale.

A statesmanlike procedure for the Department of State in the autumn of 1903 would have provided for a close analysis of the causes of the treaty rejection and a careful appraisal of the factors which presaged a shift in Colombian attitude. Indeed, a thorough study of the situation would have disclosed much relevant information, for Beaupré's reports on events in

Bogotá were frequently lacking in penetration and unfriendly in tone. No attempt at such an investigation was made, partly because the department was content in this instance to accept the dispatches of a casually-trained diplomat at face value, but principally because Roosevelt had brought the isthmian affair under his personal direction. The chief executive was wholly unwilling to submit to the further delays which a diplomatic solution would have entailed.

More congenial to the president's mood were the enterprising tactics of Bunau-Varilla. The Frenchman had made some highly effective contributions to the fight for Panama previous to the defeat of the convention, although the campaign in the United States had been largely under the control of others. His great opportunity came late in September, when Cromwell was about to leave for Paris in desperation and the White House was considering a dramatic appeal to Congress. By a combination of tact and initiative, the engineer gained the confidence of Amador and the attentive ear of the administration. He convinced Roosevelt and Hay that a revolution was imminent, and satisfied the Panamanian agent that the United States would intervene as soon as an outbreak had occurred. His clever liaison work established a tacit understanding between the two parties which enabled them to coördinate their plans and movements. The shrewdness and audacity of Bunau-Varilla were primary factors in the creation of the Republic of Panama.

The man whose advice would have been most helpful to Roosevelt in the fall of 1903 was unfortunately absent in England attending the sessions of the Alaskan Boundary Commission. Elihu Root afterward defended the course taken at Panama, but he was in no way responsible for it. He was apparently not even consulted in the matter. Had he been in Washington in the critical weeks of decision, his influence would undoubtedly have been cast on the side of restraint. The secretary of war stood closer to Roosevelt, at this time, than any other man in public life. He admired the president, but was not overawed by him. His sagacity and mental poise, unapproached in White House councils, prevented him from being carried away on the swift tides of his chief's enthusiasms and angers. Roosevelt once remarked that Root was the most valuable of his cabinet officers because he was "the only one who will fight with me." [25] Their differences, in these years, were more frequently over tactics than aims. Root would probably have agreed with the president on the desirability of securing control of the Panama canal site, but his orderly and constructive mind would have sought a formula for accomplishing this end without riding roughshod over the sovereign rights and the pride of the Colombian people.

One is tempted to speculate as to the probable course of events had Root became secretary of state early enough to have supervised the entire canal negotiation with Bogotá. His later record in the State Department suggests that he would have leaned less heavily upon outsiders and more upon his own investigations for information and guidance. As a former corporation lawyer he would at least have been able to draw a clear distinction between the interests of the United States and those of private parties. His subsequent skilful handling of Latin-American affairs indicates, furthermore, that the treaty would have been presented to and urged upon the Colombian government with notable tact and understanding. These same qualities would probably have been invoked—and perhaps successfully—to keep Roosevelt patient and comparatively serene during the trying period that would inevitably have preceded the exchange of ratifications.

By the time Root actually did take over the direction of the nation's foreign affairs, in July, 1905, the damage had been done. It became his task, consequently, to inaugurate the delicate process of repairing fractured friendships and restoring Latin-American confidence in the good faith and pacific intentions of the United States. The secretary labored earnestly, but unsuccessfully, to induce the Colombian government to accept the situation created by the revolution of November, 1903.[26] In an effort

[25] Pringle, *Roosevelt*, p. 255.
[26] After protracted negotiations, the Root–Cortés, Root–Arosemena, and Cortés–Arosemena conventions were signed at Washington on Jan. 9, 1909, by the plenipotentiaries of the United States, Colombia, and Panama. By the terms of these

to stimulate trade and neutralize the wider repercussions of the Panama affair, he undertook his arduous journey of 1906, which carried him to half a dozen countries on both coasts of the southern continent. Outwardly, the trip was a great success. Yet the cheering crowds and the champagne toasts were more truly demonstrations of Latin-American hospitality and esteem for Root than indications that old fears and suspicions had been permanently laid aside. Recollections of Yankee warships at the Isthmus were still too fresh to permit a sudden shift in attitude. Nevertheless, by the time Root left the State Department, in January, 1909, the foundations of a better understanding had been laid for later statesmanship to build upon.

Meanwhile, construction of the canal went swiftly forward, despite a faltering start. Under the direction of Colonel William C. Gorgas the zone of operations was transformed into one of the healthiest areas of the globe. The triumphs of the engineers were no less epoch-making. Unprecedented obstacles were surmounted with a competence that gradually silenced the clamor of the critics. Year by year the low hills of the continental divide crumbled under the sustained assault of Goethals' men. The dam at Gatun was raised, the intricate mechanism of the locks was set in place, and the once unruly waters of the Chagres harnessed to the service of the world's commerce. In August, 1914, the first merchant vessel passed through the completed canal. Saavedra Ceron's vision of four hundred years earlier had become an accomplished fact.

Unfortunately, the great achievement that united East and West had raised a barrier between the North and South which

---

agreements Colombia recognized the independence of Panama; the common boundary of the two republics was delimited; and Panama agreed to turn over to Colombia the first ten annual $250,000 payments from the United States in full satisfaction of Panama's share of the Colombian national debt. The United States agreed to start the canal zone rental as of 1908 instead of 1913 and granted the Colombian government certain privileges in the use of the canal and the Panama Railroad. None of the conventions was to go into effect until all were ratified. The project fell through, after Panama and the United States had taken favorable action, owing to Colombia's refusal to ratify either of the agreements entered into by Cortés. See *Dip. Hist. of the Panama Canal*, pp. 314 *et seq.*

Goethals' drills and dredges could not penetrate. Techniques of a different sort were needed to overcome resentment and distrust. The Wilson administration made an admirable start towards the adjustment of Colombia's grievances soon after it took office in 1913. By the terms of the Thompson–Urrutia pact, signed at Bogotá in April, 1914, the United States Government expressed "sincere regret that anything should have occurred to interrupt or to mar the relations of cordial friendship that had so long subsisted between the two nations." [27] Colombia agreed to recognize the Republic of Panama in return for an indemnity of $25,000,000 and certain privileges in the use of the canal. Roosevelt, who had boasted three years before that he "took" Panama, was infuriated by what he regarded as an official admission of wrongdoing on his part. His vehement assaults on the "blackmail treaty" were undoubtedly among the reasons for the Senate's long delay in acting on the agreement.

By the time Harding entered the White House, the situation had changed in several important respects. The British were working their way uncomfortably close to the Canal Zone in their search for oil. The postwar scramble for South American markets had placed a heightened value upon "goodwill." The rapprochement with Colombia was made easier by the fact that the voice of Theodore Roosevelt was now stilled. In April, 1921, the Senate in Washington ratified an amended form of the Thompson–Urrutia convention which retained the indemnity but omitted the apology. Colombia accepted the compromise the following year.[28] Insofar as the two governments were concerned, the Panama affair was closed. Events in the years immediately following were to show, however, that a single injustice righted could not, of itself, produce a new diplomatic order in the Western Hemisphere. Not until the decade of the thirties did the constructive statesmanship of Henry L. Stimson and Franklin D. Roosevelt provide reasonable grounds for hope that the "Colossus of the North" had been finally vanquished by the "Good Neighbor."

[27] *Foreign Relations*, 1914, p. 163.   [28] Malloy, *Treaties*, III, 2538–2541.

APPENDICES

APPENDIX A

The Hay-Concha Memorandum of April 18, 1902

Memorandum of points to be embodied in a convention between the Republic of Colombia and the United States of America for the construction of an interoceanic canal by the Panama route and the management of the railroad over said Isthmus, in furtherance of article 35 of the treaty of 1846–1848 existing between said nations.

Article I

The Government of Colombia authorizes the New Panama Canal Company to sell and transfer to the United States its rights, privileges, properties, and concessions, as well as the Panama Railroad and all the shares or part of the shares of that company, with the exception of the public lands situated outside of the zone hereinafter specified, now corresponding to the concessions to both said enterprises, which public lands shall revert to the Republic of Colombia.

But it is understood that Colombia reserves all its rights to the special shares in the capital of the New Panama Canal Company to which reference is made in Article IV of the contract of December 10, 1890, which shares shall be paid their full nominal value at least.

The railroad company (and the United States as owner of the enterprise) shall be free from the obligations imposed by the railroad concession, excepting as to the payment at maturity by the railroad company of the outstanding bonds issued by said railroad company.

Article II

The United States shall have the exclusive right to excavate, construct, maintain, operate, control, and protect a maritime canal from the Atlantic to the Pacific Ocean, to and across the territory of Colombia, such canal to be of sufficient depth and capacity for vessels of the largest tonnage and greatest draft now engaged in commerce, and also the same rights for the construction, maintenance, operation, control, and protection of railway, telegraph and telephone lines, canals, dikes, dams, reservoirs, and such other auxiliary works as may be necessary and convenient for the construction, maintenance, protection, and operation of the canal.

Article III

To enable the United States to exercise the rights and privileges granted by the foregoing articles, the Republic of Colombia grants to that Government the use of a zone of territory along the route of the canal to be opened 5 kilometers in width on either side thereof measured from its center line, excluding the cities of Panama and Colon. So far as necessary for the construction, maintenance, and operation of the canal, the United States shall have the use and occupation of the group of small islands in the Bay of Panama, named Perico, Naos, and Flamenco, together with 10 fathoms of water in the Bay of Limon in extension of the canal; but the same shall not be construed as being within the zone herein defined nor governed by the special provisions applicable to the zone. This concession shall be for the term of one hundred years, renewable at the option of the United States for periods of similar duration and subject to the payment of the amount hereinafter expressed.

This grant shall in no manner invalidate the titles of rights of private landholders in the said zone of territory, nor shall it interfere with the rights of way over the public roads of the department.

All the stipulations contained in article 35 of the treaty of 1846-48 between the contracting parties shall continue and apply in full force to the cities of Panama and Colon and to the accessory community lands within the said zone, and the territory thereon shall be neutral territory, and the United States shall continue to guarantee the neutrality thereof and the sovereignty of Colombia thereover in conformity with the above-mentioned article 35 of said treaty.

In furtherance of this provision there shall be created a joint commission by the Governments of Colombia and the United States that shall establish and enforce sanitary and police regulations.

Article IV

The rights and privileges granted to the United States by the terms of this convention shall not affect the sovereignty of the Republic of Colombia over the territory within whose boundaries such rights and privileges are to be exercised.

The United States freely acknowledges and recognizes this sovereignty and disavows any intention to impair it in any way whatever or to increase its territory at the expense of Colombia or of any of the sister Republics in Central or South America, but, on the contrary, it desires to strengthen the power of the republics on this continent and to promote, develop, and maintain their prosperity and independence.

Article V

The Republic of Colombia authorizes the United States to construct and maintain at each entrance and terminus of the proposed canal a port for vessels using the same, with suitable light-houses and other aids to navigation, and the United States is authorized to use and occupy, within the limits of the zone fixed by this convention, such parts of the coast line and of the lands and islands adjacent thereto as are necessary for this purpose, including the construction and maintenance of breakwaters, dikes, jetties, embankments, coaling stations, docks, and other appropriate works. And the United States undertakes the construction and maintenance of such works and will bear all the expense thereof. The ports when established shall be declared free, and their demarcations shall be clearly and definitely defined.

To give effect to this article the United States will give special attention and care to the maintenance of works for drainage, sanitary, and healthful purposes along the line of the canal and its dependencies, in order to prevent the invasion of epidemics, or of securing their prompt suppression should they appear. With this end in view the United States will organize hospitals along the line of the canal, and will suitably supply the towns of Panama and Colon with the necessary aqueducts and drainage works, in order to prevent their becoming centers of infection on account of their proximity to the canal.

The Government of Colombia will secure the possession of the land that may be required in the towns of Panama and Colon to effect the improvements above referred to, and the Government of the United States shall be authorized to impose and collect equitable water rates, previously agreed upon with the Government of Colombia, during fifty years for the service rendered; but on the expiration of said term the use of the water shall be free for the inhabitants of Panama and Colon, except to the extent that may be necessary for the maintenance of said aqueducts.

Article VI

The Republic of Colombia agrees that it will not cede or lease to any foreign government any of its islands or harbors within or adjacent to the Bay of Panama; nor on the Atlantic coast of Colombia, between the Atrato River and the western boundary of the department of Panama, for the purpose of establishing fortifications, naval or coaling stations, military posts, docks, or other works that might interfere with the construction, maintenance, operation, protection, safety, and free use of the canal and auxiliary works. In order to enable Colombia to comply with this stipulation, the Government of the United States agrees to give Colombia the material support that may be required in order to prevent the occupation of said islands and ports, guaranteeing there the sovereignty, independence, and integrity of Colombia.

Article VII

The Republic of Colombia includes in the foregoing grant the right, without obstacle, cost, or impediment, to the free navigation and use of the waters of the Chagres River and other streams, lakes, and lagoons, and of all waterways, natural and artificial, within the jurisdiction and under the dominion of the Republic of Colombia in the department of Panama that may be necessary or desirable for the construction, maintenance, and operation of the canal and its auxiliary works, including the right to raise and lower the levels of the waters and to deflect them, and to rectify and navigate any and all streams, lakes, and lagoons. All damages caused to private landowners by inundation, or by the deviation of water course, or in other ways, arising out of the construction or operation of the canal, shall in each case be appraised and settled by a joint commission appointed by the Governments of Colombia and the United States, but the cost of the indemnities so agreed upon shall be borne solely by the United States.

Article VIII

The Government of Colombia declares free for all time the ports at either entrance of the canal and the waters thereof in such manner that there shall not be collected by the Government of Colombia custom-house tolls, tonnage, anchorage, light-house, wharf, pilot, or quarantine dues, nor any other charges or taxes of any kind shall be levied or imposed by the Government of Colombia upon any vessel using or passing through the canal or belonging to or employed by the United States, directly or indirectly, in connection with the construction, maintenance, and operation of the main work or its auxiliaries or upon the cargo, officers, crew, or passengers of any such vessel; it being the intent of this convention that all vessels and their cargoes, crews, and passengers shall be permitted to use and pass through the canal and the ports leading thereto, subject to no other demands or impositions than such tolls and charges as may be imposed by the United States for the use of the canal and other works. It being understood that such tolls and charges shall be equal for vessels of all nations.

The ports leading to the canal also shall be free to the commerce of the world, and no duties or taxes shall be imposed, except upon merchandise destined to be introduced for the consumption of the rest of the Republic of Colombia, or the Department of Panama, and upon vessels touching at the ports of Colon and Panama and which do not cross the canal. Though the said ports shall be free and open to all, the Government of Colombia may establish in them such customhouses, and guards as Colombia may deem necessary to collect duties on importations destined to other portions of Colombia and to prevent contraband trade. The United States shall have the right to make use of the ports at the two extremities of the canal as places of anchorage, in order to make repairs for loading, unloading, depositing, or transshipping cargoes either in transit or destined for the service of the canal.

Article IX

There shall not be imposed any taxes, national, municipal, departmental, or of any other class, upon the canal, the vessels that may use it, tugs and other vessels employed in the service of the canal, the railways and auxiliary works, storehouses, workshops, offices, quarters for laborers, factories of all kinds, warehouses, wharves, machinery and other works, property, and effects appertaining to the canal or railroad or that may be necessary for the service of the canal or railroad and their dependencies, whether situated within the cities of Panama and Colon or any other place authorized by the provisions of this convention.

Nor shall there be imposed contributions or charges of a personal character of whatever species upon officers, employees, laborers, and other individuals in the service of the canal and its dependencies.

Article X

It is agreed that telegraph and telephone lines, when established for canal purposes, may also, under suitable regulations, be used for public and private business in connection with the systems of Colombia and the other American Republics and with the lines of cable companies authorized to enter the ports and territory of these Republics; but the official dispatches of the Government of Colombia and the authorities of the Department of Panama shall not pay for such service higher tolls than those required from the officials in the service of the United States.

Article XI

The Government of Colombia shall permit the immigration and free access to the lands and workshops of the canal enterprises of all employees and workmen of whatever nationality under contract to work upon the said canal and its dependencies, with their respective families, and all such persons shall be free and exempt from the military service of the Republic of Colombia.

Article XII

The United States may import at any time into the said zone, free of customs duties, imposts, taxes, or other charges, and without any restriction, any and all vessels, dredges, engines, cars, machinery, tools, explosives, materials, supplies, and other articles necessary and convenient in the construction, maintenance, and operation of the canal and auxiliary works; also all provisions, medicines, clothing, supplies, and other things necessary and convenient for the officers, employees, workmen, and laborers in the service and employ of the United States within the said zone and for their families. If any such articles are disposed of for use without the zone and within the territory of the Republic, they shall be subject to the same import or other duties as like articles under the laws of Colombia or the ordinances of the Department of Panama.

Article XIII

The United States shall have authority within the said zone to protect and make secure the canal, as well as railways and other auxiliary works, and to preserve order and discipline among the laborers and other persons who may congregate in that region in consequence of the proposed work.

The Governments of Colombia and the United States shall agree upon the regulations necessary for said purpose, as well as to the capture and delivery of criminals to the respective authorities. Special regulations also shall be agreed upon, in the manner aforesaid, for the establishment of laws and jurisdiction to decide controversies that may arise respecting contracts relative to the construction and management of the canal and its dependencies, as well as to the trial and punishment of crimes that may be committed within the said zone of the canal.

Article XIV

The works of the canal, the railways, and their auxiliaries shall be declared of public utility, and in consequence all areas of land

and water necessary for the construction, maintenance, and operation of the canal and the other specified works may be expropriated in conformity with the laws of Colombia, except that the indemnity shall be conclusively determined, without appeal, by a joint commission appointed by the Governments of Colombia and the United States.

The indemnities awarded by the commission for such expropriation shall be borne by the United States, but the appraisal of said lands and the assessment of damages shall be based upon their value before the commencement of the work upon the canal.

Article XV

The Republic of Colombia grants to the United States the use of all the ports of the Republic open to commerce as places of refuge for any vessels employed in the canal enterprise, and for all vessels in distress having the right to pass through the canal and wishing to anchor in said ports. Such vessels shall be exempt from anchorage and tonnage dues on the part of Colombia.

Article XVI

The canal, when constructed, and the entrances thereto shall be neutral in perpetuity, and shall be opened upon equal terms to the vessels of all nations at uniform tonnage and other rates that may be imposed in virtue of the stipulations of this convention, and in conformity with the stipulations of the treaty entered into by the Governments of the United States and Great Britain on November 18, 1901, and known as the Hay-Pauncefote treaty.

Article XVII

The Government of Colombia shall have the right to transport over the canal its vessels, troops, and munitions of war at all times without paying charges of any kind. This exemption is to be extended to the auxiliary railway for the transportation of persons in the service of the Republic of Colombia or of the Department of Panama, or of the police force charged with the preservation of public order, as well as to their baggage, munitions of war, and supplies.

Article XVIII

The United States shall have full power and authority to establish and enforce regulations for the use of the canal, railways, and the entering ports and auxiliary works, and to fix rates of tolls and charges thereof, subject to the limitations stated in Article XVI.

Article XIX

The rights and privileges granted to the United States by this convention shall not affect the sovereignty of the Republic of Colombia over the real estate that may be acquired by the United States by reason of the transfer of the rights of the New Panama Canal Company and the Panama Railroad Company lying outside of the said canal zone.

Article XX

If, by virtue of any existing treaty between the Republic of Colombia and any third power, there may be privileges or concessions relative to an interoceanic means of communication which especially favors such third power, and which in any of its terms may be incompatible with the terms of the present convention, the Republic of Colombia agrees to cancel or modify such treaty in due form, for which purpose it shall give to the said third power the requisite notification within the term of four months from the date of the present convention, and in case the existing treaty contains no clause permitting their involuntary annulment, the Republic of Colombia agrees to procure its modification or annulment in such form that there shall not exist any conflicts with the stipulations of the present convention.

Article XXI

The rights and privileges granted by the Republic of Colombia to the United States in the preceding articles are understood to be free of all anterior concessions or privileges to other governments, corporations, syndicates, or individuals, and consequently, if there should arise any claims on account of the present concessions and privileges, the claimants shall resort to the Government of Colombia and not to the United States for any indemnity or compromise which may be required.

Article XXII

The Government of Colombia renounces the participation to which it might be entitled in the future earnings of the canal under Article XV of the contract with the "Universal Panama Canal Company," and it likewise renounces now and hereafter all the rights reserved in the said concession which shall belong to Colombia at the expiration of the term of ninety-nine years of the concession granted to the above-mentioned company.

APPENDIX A

Article XXIII

If it should become necessary at any time to employ armed forces for the safety or protection of the canal, or of the ships that make use of the same, or the railways and other works, the Republic of Colombia agrees to provide the forces necessary for such purpose, according to the circumstances of the case, but if the Government of Colombia can not effectively comply with this obligation, then, with the consent of or at the request of Colombia, or of her minister at Washington, or of the local authorities, civil or military, the United States shall employ such force as may be necessary for that sole purpose; and as soon as the necessity shall have ceased will withdraw the forces so employed. Under exceptional circumstances, however, on account of unforeseen or imminent danger to said canal, railways, and other works, or to the lives and property of the persons employed upon the canal, railways, and other works, the Government of the United States is authorized to act in the interest of their protection, without the necessity of obtaining the consent beforehand of the Government of Colombia; and it shall give immediate advice of the measures adopted for the purpose stated; and as soon as sufficient Colombian forces shall arrive to attend to the indicated purpose, those of the United States shall retire.

Article XXIV

The Government of the United States agrees to complete the construction of the preliminary works necessary, together with all the auxiliary works, in the shortest time possible; and within two years from the date of the exchange of ratification of this convention the main works of this canal proper shall be commenced, and it shall be opened to the traffic between the two oceans within twelve years after such period of two years. In case, however, that any difficulties or obstacles should arise in the construction of the canal which are at present impossible to foresee, in consideration of the good faith with which the Government of the United States shall have proceeded, and the large amount of money expended so far on the works and the nature of the difficulties which may have arisen, the Government of Colombia will prolong the terms stipulated in this article up to twelve years more for the completion of the work of the canal.

Article XXV

As the price or compensation for the right to use the zone granted in this convention by Colombia to the United States for the construction of a canal, together with the proprietary right over the Panama Railroad, and for the annuity of $250,000 gold, which Colombia ceases to receive from the said railroad, as well as in compensation for other rights, privileges, and exemptions granted to the United States, and in consideration of the increase in the administrative expenses of the department of Panama consequent upon the construction of the said canal, the Government of the United States binds itself to pay Colombia the amount of $7,000,000 in American gold on the exchange of the ratification of this convention after its approval by the legislative bodies of both countries, and fourteen years after the date aforesaid a fair and reasonable annuity, that shall be agreed upon by the contracting Governments three years before the expiration of the above-mentioned term of fourteen years.

In fixing this fair and reasonable annuity there shall be taken into consideration the present price of the usufruct of the railway as well as the compensation that is to be stipulated for the use of the zone and for the additional administrative expenses that the construction of the canal will impose upon Colombia; and also the advanced payment of $7,000,000 and the comparative cost and conditions upon which the United States reasonably could have expected to acquire concessions satisfactory to it in respect of any other canal route.

Three years before the expiration of each term of one hundred years the annuity for the following term shall be fixed in a similar manner.

But in the event that the parties are unable to come to an understanding within the periods above referred to as to such fair and reasonable annuity, then before the second year prior to the termination of the periods above referred to, the contracting parties shall proceed to constitute a high commission, to be composed of five members, of whom two shall be appointed by Colombia, two by the United States, and the fifth (who shall be the president of such high commission) shall be the president, for the time being, of the International Peace Tribunal of The Hague; and the determination reached by said commission, by a majority vote, concerning such fair and reasonable annuity that is to be paid to Colombia by the United States in conformity with this article, shall be binding upon the contracting parties.

But no delay nor difference of opinion in fixing such amount shall affect nor interrupt the full operation and effect of this convention in all other respects.

Article XXVI

If after the lapse of five years from the date of this convention the necessary works for the opening of the canal should not have been commenced by the United States, or if after the expiration of the twelve years stipulated for the completion of the work, and the extension of twelve years referred to in Article XXIV, the canal should not be opened to commerce, all the concessions granted by this convention shall be forfeited and all the works, principal and accessory, machinery and properties of the canal, shall become the property of the Republic of Colombia, and the same Republic shall recover its actual rights over the Panama Railway, without any obligation to return any of the sums that it may have received in conformity with this convention.

Article XXVII

This convention, when signed by the contracting parties, shall be submitted for legislative approval, and shall be exchanged within a term of eight months from this date.

APPENDIX B

The Spooner Act *

An Act To provide for the construction of a canal connecting the waters of the Atlantic and Pacific oceans.

Be it enacted by the Senate and House of Representatives of the United States of America in Congress assembled, That the President of the United States is hereby authorized to acquire, for and on behalf of the United States, at a cost not exceeding forty millions of dollars, the rights, privileges, franchises, concessions, grants of land, right of way, unfinished work, plants, and other property, real, personal, and mixed, of every name and nature, owned by the New Panama Canal Company, of France, on the Isthmus of Panama, and all its maps, plans, drawings, records on the Isthmus of Panama and in Paris, including all the capital stock, not less, however, than sixty-eight thousand eight hundred and sixty-three shares of the Panama Railroad Company, owned by or held for the use of said canal company, provided a satisfactory title to all of said property can be obtained.

SEC. 2. That the President is hereby authorized to acquire from the Republic of Colombia, for and on behalf of the United States, upon such terms as he may deem reasonable, perpetual control of a strip of land, the territory of the Republic of Colombia, not less than six miles in width, extending from the Caribbean Sea to the Pacific Ocean, and the right to use and dispose of the waters thereon, and to excavate, construct, and to perpetually maintain, operate, and protect thereon a canal, of such depth and capacity as will afford convenient passage of ships of the greatest tonnage and draft now in use, from the Caribbean Sea to the Pacific Ocean, which control shall include the right to perpetually maintain and operate the Panama Railroad, if the ownership thereof, or a controlling interest therein, shall have been acquired by the United States, and also jurisdiction over said strip and the ports at the ends thereof to make such police and sanitary rules and regulations as shall be necessary to preserve order and preserve the public health thereon, and to establish such judicial tribunals as may be agreed upon thereon as may be necessary to enforce such rules and regulations.

* *United States Statutes at Large,* Vol. XXXII, Pt. I, Chap. 1302.

APPENDIX B 409

The President may acquire such additional territory and rights from Colombia as in his judgment will facilitate the general purpose hereof.

SEC. 3. That when the President shall have arranged to secure a satisfactory title to the property of the New Panama Canal Company, as provided in section one hereof, and shall have obtained by treaty control of the necessary territory from the Republic of Colombia, as provided in section two hereof, he is authorized to pay for the property of the New Panama Canal Company forty millions of dollars and to the Republic of Colombia such sum as shall have been agreed upon, and a sum sufficient for both said purposes is hereby appropriated, out of any money in the Treasury not otherwise appropriated, to be paid on warrant or warrants drawn by the President.

The President shall then through the Isthmian Canal Commission hereinafter authorized cause to be excavated, constructed, and completed, utilizing to that end as far as practicable the work heretofore done by the New Panama Canal Company, of France, and its predecessor company, a ship canal from the Caribbean Sea to the Pacific Ocean. Such canal shall be of sufficient capacity and depth as shall afford convenient passage for vessels of the largest tonnage and greatest draft now in use, and such as may be reasonably anticipated, and shall be supplied with all necessary locks and other appliances to meet the necessities of vessels passing through the same from ocean to ocean; and he shall also cause to be constructed such safe and commodious harbors at the termini of said canal, and make such provisions for defense as may be necessary for the safety and protection of said canal and harbors. That the President is authorized for the purposes aforesaid to employ such persons as he may deem necessary, and to fix their compensation.

SEC. 4. That should the President be unable to obtain for the United States a satisfactory title to the property of the New Panama Canal Company and the control of the necessary territory of the Republic of Colombia and the rights mentioned in sections one and two of this Act, within a reasonable time and upon reasonable terms, then the President, having first obtained for the United States perpetual control by treaty of the necessary territory from Costa Rica and Nicaragua, upon terms which he may consider reasonable, for the construction, perpetual maintenance, operation, and protection of a canal connecting the Caribbean Sea with the Pacific Ocean by what is commonly known as the Nicaragua route, shall through the said Isthmian Canal Commission cause to be excavated and constructed a ship canal and waterway from a point on the shore of the

Caribbean Sea near Greytown, by way of Lake Nicaragua, to a point near Brito on the Pacific Ocean. Said canal shall be of sufficient capacity and depth to afford convenient passage for vessels of the largest tonnage and greatest draft now in use, and such as may be reasonably anticipated, and shall be supplied with all necessary locks and other appliances to meet the necessities of vessels passing through the same from ocean to ocean; and he shall also construct such safe and commodious harbors at the termini of said canal as shall be necessary for the safe and convenient use thereof, and shall make such provisions for defense as may be necessary for the safety and protection of said harbors and canal; and such sum or sums of money as may be agreed upon by such treaty as compensation to be paid to Nicaragua and Costa Rica for the concessions and rights hereunder provided to be acquired by the United States, are hereby appropriated, out of any money in the Treasury not otherwise appropriated, to be paid on warrant or warrants drawn by the President.

The President shall cause the said Isthmian Canal Commission to make such surveys as may be necessary for said canal and harbors to be made, and in making such surveys and in the construction of said canal may employ such persons as he may deem necessary, and may fix their compensation.

In the excavation and construction of said canal the San Juan River and Lake Nicaragua, or such parts of each as may be made available, shall be used.

SEC. 5. That the sum of ten million dollars is hereby appropriated, out of any money in the Treasury not otherwise appropriated, toward the project herein contemplated by either route so selected.

And the President is hereby authorized to cause to be entered into such contract or contracts as may be deemed necessary for the proper excavation, construction, completion, and defense of said canal, harbors, and defenses, by the route finally determined upon under the provisions of this Act. Appropriations therefor shall from time to time be hereafter made, not to exceed in the aggregate the additional sum of one hundred and thirty-five millions of dollars should the Panama route be adopted, or one hundred and eighty millions of dollars should the Nicaragua route be adopted.

SEC. 6. That in any agreement with the Republic of Colombia, or with the States of Nicaragua and Costa Rica, the President is authorized to guarantee to said Republic or to said States the use of said canal and harbors, upon such terms as may be agreed upon, for all vessels owned by said States or by citizens thereof.

SEC. 7. That to enable the President to construct the canal and works appurtenant thereto as provided in this Act, there is hereby

APPENDIX B 411

created the Isthmian Canal Commission, the same to be composed of seven members, who shall be nominated and appointed by the President, by and with the advice and consent of the Senate, and who shall serve until the completion of said canal unless sooner removed by the President, and one of whom shall be named as the chairman of said Commission. Of the seven members of said Commission at least four of them shall be persons learned and skilled in the science of engineering, and of the four at least one shall be an officer of the United States Army, and at least one other shall be an officer of the United States Navy, the said officers respectively being either upon the active or retired list of the Army or of the Navy. Said commissioners shall each receive such compensation as the President shall prescribe until the same shall have been otherwise fixed by the Congress. In addition to the members of said Isthmian Canal Commission, the President is hereby authorized through said Commission to employ in said service any of the engineers of the United States Army at his discretion, and likewise to employ any engineers in civil life, at his discretion, and any other persons necessary for the proper and expeditious prosecution of said work. The compensation of all such engineers and other persons employed under this Act shall be fixed by said Commission, subject to the approval of the President. The official salary of any officer appointed or employed under this Act shall be deducted from the amount of salary or compensation provided by or which shall be fixed under the terms of this Act. Said Commission shall in all matters be subject to the direction and control of the President, and shall make to the President annually and at such other periods as may be required, either by law or by the order of the President, full and complete reports of all their actings and doings and of all moneys received and expended in the construction of said work and in the performance of their duties in connection therewith, which said reports shall be by the President transmitted to Congress. And the said Commission shall furthermore give to Congress, or either House of Congress, such information as may at any time be required either by Act of Congress or by the order of either House of Congress. The President shall cause to be provided and assigned for the use of the Commission such offices as may, with the suitable equipment of the same, be necessary and proper, in his discretion, for the proper discharge of the duties thereof.

Sec. 8. That the Secretary of the Treasury is hereby authorized to borrow on the credit of the United States from time to time, as the proceeds may be required to defray expenditures authorized by this Act (such proceeds when received to be used only for the purpose of meeting such expenditures), the sum of one hundred and thirty million dollars, or so much thereof as may be necessary, and to prepare and issue therefor coupon or registered bonds of the United States in such form as he may prescribe, and in denominations of twenty dollars or some multiple of that sum, redeemable in gold coin at the pleasure of the United States after ten years from the date of their issue, and payable thirty years from such date, and bearing interest payable quarterly in gold coin at the rate of two per centum per annum; and the bonds herein authorized shall be exempt from all taxes or duties of the United States, as well as from taxation in any form by or under State, municipal, or local authority: *Provided,* That said bonds may be disposed of by the Secretary of the Treasury at not less than par, under such regulations as he may prescribe, giving to all citizens of the United States an equal opportunity to subscribe therefor, but no commissions shall be allowed or paid thereon; and a sum not exceeding one-tenth of one per centum of the amount of the bonds herein authorized is hereby appropriated, out of any money in the Treasury not otherwise appropriated, to pay the expense of preparing, advertising, and issuing the same.

Approved, June 28, 1902.

APPENDIX C

The Hay-Herrán Treaty

The United States of America and the Republic of Colombia, being desirous to assure the construction of a ship canal to connect the Atlantic and Pacific Oceans and the Congress of the United States of America having passed an Act approved June 28, 1902, in furtherance of that object, a copy of which is hereunto annexed, the high contracting parties have resolved, for that purpose, to conclude a Convention and have accordingly appointed as their plenipotentiaries,

The President of the United States of America, John Hay, Secretary of State, and

The President of the Republic of Colombia, Thomas Herran, Chargé d'Affaires, thereunto specially empowered by said government,

who, after communicating to each other their respective full powers, found in good and due form, have agreed upon and concluded the following Articles:

Article I

The Government of Colombia authorizes the New Panama Canal Company to sell and transfer to the United States its rights, privileges, properties, and concessions, as well as the Panama Railroad and all the shares or part of the shares of that company; but the public lands situated outside of the zone hereinafter specified, now corresponding to the concessions of both said enterprises shall revert to the Republic of Colombia, except any property now owned by or in the possession of the said companies within Panama or Colon, or the ports and terminals thereof.

But it is understood that Colombia reserves all its rights to the special shares in the capital of the New Panama Canal Company to which reference is made in Article IV of the contract of December 10, 1890, which shares shall be paid their full nominal value at least; but as such right of Colombia exists solely in its character of stockholder in said Company, no obligation under this provision is imposed upon or assumed by the United States.

The Railroad Company (and the United States as owner of the enterprise) shall be free from the obligations imposed by the railroad concession, excepting as to the payment at maturity by the Railroad Company of the outstanding bonds issued by said Railroad Company.

Article II

The United States shall have the exclusive right for the term of one hundred years, renewable at the sole and absolute option of the United States, for periods of similar duration so long as the United States may desire, to excavate, construct, maintain, operate, control, and protect the Maritime Canal with or without locks from the Atlantic to the Pacific Ocean, to and across the territory of Colombia, such canal to be of sufficient depth and capacity for vessels of the largest tonnage and greatest draft now engaged in commerce, and such as may be reasonably anticipated, and also the same rights for the construction, maintenance, operation, control, and protection of the Panama Railroad and of railway, telegraph and telephone lines, canals, dikes, dams and reservoirs, and such other auxiliary works as may be necessary and convenient for the construction, maintenance, protection and operation of the canal and railroads.

Article III

To enable the United States to exercise the rights and privileges granted by this Treaty the Republic of Colombia grants to that Government the use and control for the term of one hundred years, renewable at the sole and absolute option of the United States, for periods of similar duration so long as the United States may desire, of a zone of territory along the route of the canal to be constructed five kilometers in width on either side thereof measured from its center line including therein the necessary auxiliary canals not exceeding in any case fifteen miles from the main canal and other works, together with ten fathoms of water in the Bay of Limon in extension of the canal, and at least three marine miles from mean low water mark from each terminus of the canal into the Caribbean Sea and the Pacific Ocean respectively. So far as necessary for the construction, maintenance and operation of the canal, the United States shall have the use and occupation of the group of small islands in the Bay of Panama named Perico, Naos, Culebra and Flamenco, but the same shall not be construed as being within the zone herein defined or governed by the special provisions applicable to the same.

This grant shall in no manner invalidate the titles or rights of private land holders in the said zone of territory, nor shall it interfere with the rights of way over the public roads of the Department; provided, however, that nothing herein contained shall operate to diminish, impair or restrict the rights elsewhere herein granted to the United States.

This grant shall not include the cities of Panama and Colon, except so far as lands and other property therein are now owned by or in possession of the said Canal Company or the said Railroad Company; but all the stipulations contained in Article 35 of the Treaty of 1846–48 between the contracting parties shall continue and apply in full force to the cities of Panama and Colon and to the accessory community lands and other property within the said zone, and the territory thereon shall be neutral territory, and the United States shall continue to guarantee the neutrality thereof and the sovereignty of Colombia thereover, in conformity with the above mentioned Article 35 of said Treaty.

In furtherance of this last provision there shall be created a Joint Commission by the Governments of Colombia and the United States that shall establish and enforce sanitary and police regulations.

Article IV

The rights and privileges granted to the United States by the terms of this convention shall not affect the sovereignty of the Republic of Colombia over the territory within whose boundaries such rights and privileges are to be exercised.

The United States freely acknowledges and recognizes this sovereignty and disavows any intention to impair it in any way whatever or to increase its territory at the expense of Colombia or of any of the sister republics in Central or South America, but on the contrary, it desires to strengthen the power of the republics on this continent, and to promote, develop and maintain their prosperity and independence.

Article V

The Republic of Colombia authorizes the United States to construct and maintain at each entrance and terminus of the proposed canal a port for vessels using the same, with suitable light houses and other aids to navigation, and the United States is authorized to use and occupy within the limits of the zone fixed by this convention, such parts of the coast line and of the lands and islands adjacent thereto as are necessary for this purpose, including the construction and maintenance of breakwaters, dikes, jetties, embankments, coaling stations, docks and other appropriate works, and the United States undertakes the construction and maintenance of such works and will bear all the expense thereof. The ports when established are declared free, and their demarcations shall be clearly and definitely defined.

To give effect to this Article, the United States will give special attention and care to the maintenance of works for drainage, sanitary and healthful purposes along the line of the canal, and its dependencies, in order to prevent the invasion of epidemics or of securing their prompt suppression should they appear. With this end in view the United States will organize hospitals along the line of the canal, and will suitably supply or cause to be supplied the towns of Panama and Colon with the necessary aqueducts and drainage works, in order to prevent their becoming centers of infection on account of their proximity to the canal.

The Government of Colombia will secure for the United States or its nominees the lands and rights that may be required in the towns of Panama and Colon to effect the improvements above referred to, and the Government of the United States or its nominees shall be authorized to impose and collect equitable water rates, during fifty years for the service rendered; but on the expiration of said term the use of the water shall be free for the inhabitants of Panama and Colon, except to the extent that may be necessary for the operation and maintenance of said water system, including reservoirs, aqueducts, hydrants, supply service, drainage and other works.

Article VI

The Republic of Colombia agrees that it will not cede or lease to any foreign Government any of its islands or harbors within or adjacent to the Bay of Panama, nor on the Atlantic Coast of Colombia, between the Atrato River and the western boundary of the Department of Panama, for the purpose of establishing fortifications, naval or coaling stations, military posts, docks or other works that might interfere with the construction, maintenance, operation, protection, safety, and free use of the canal and auxiliary works. In order to enable Colombia to comply with this stipulation, the Government of the United States agrees to give Colombia the material support that may be required in order to prevent the occupation of said islands and ports, guaranteeing there the sovereignty, independence and integrity of Colombia.

Article VII

The Republic of Colombia includes in the foregoing grant the right without obstacle, cost, or impediment, to such control, consumption and general utilization in any manner found necessary by the United States to the exercise by it of the grants to, and rights conferred upon it by this Treaty, the waters of the Chagres River and other streams, lakes and lagoons, of all non-navigable waters, natural and artificial, and also to navigate all rivers, streams, lakes and other navigable water-ways, within the jurisdiction and under the domain of the Republic of Colombia, in the Department of Panama, within or without said zone, as may be necessary or desirable for the construction, maintenance and operation of the canal and its auxiliary canals and other works, and without tolls or charges of any kind; and to raise and lower the levels of the waters, and to deflect them, and to impound any such waters, and to overflow any lands necessary for the due exercise of such grants and rights to the United States; and to rectify, construct and improve the navigation of any such rivers, streams, lakes and lagoons at the sole cost of the United States; but any such water-ways so made by the United States may be used by citizens of Colombia free of tolls or other charges. And the United States shall have the right to use without cost, any water, stone, clay, earth or other minerals belonging to Colombia on the public domain that may be needed by it.

All damages caused to private land owners by inundation or by the deviation of water courses, or in other ways, arising out of the construction or operation of the canal, shall in each case be appraised and settled by a joint commission appointed by the Governments of the United States and Colombia, but the cost of the indemnities so agreed upon shall be borne solely by the United States.

Article VIII

The Government of Colombia declares free for all time the ports at either entrance of the Canal, including Panama and Colon and the waters thereof in such manner that there shall not be collected by the Government of Colombia custom house tolls, tonnage, anchorage, light-house, wharf, pilot, or quarantine dues, nor any other charges or taxes of any kind shall be levied or imposed by the Government of Colombia upon any vessel using or passing through the Canal or belonging to or employed by the United States, directly or indirectly, in connection with the construction, maintenance and operation of the main work or its auxiliaries, or upon the cargo, officers, crew, or passengers of any such vessels; it being the intent of this convention that all vessels and their cargoes, crews, and passengers shall be permitted to use and pass through the Canal and the ports leading thereto, subject to no other demands or impositions than such tolls and charges as may be imposed by the United

States for the use of the Canal and other works. It being understood that such tolls and charges shall be governed by the provisions of Article XVI.

The ports leading to the Canal, including Panama and Colon, also shall be free to the commerce of the world, and no duties or taxes shall be imposed, except upon merchandise destined to be introduced for the consumption of the rest of the Republic of Colombia, or the Department of Panama, and upon vessels touching at the ports of Colon and Panama and which do not cross the Canal.

Though the said ports shall be free and open to all, the Government of Colombia may establish in them such custom houses and guards as Colombia may deem necessary to collect duties on importations destined to other portions of Colombia and to prevent contraband trade. The United States shall have the right to make use of the ports at the two extremities of the Canal including Panama and Colon as places of anchorage, in order to make repairs for loading, unloading, depositing, or transshipping cargoes either in transit or destined for the service of the Canal and other works.

Any concessions or privileges granted by Colombia for the operation of light houses at Colon and Panama shall be subject to expropriation, indemnification and payment in the same manner as is provided by Article XIV in respect to the property therein mentioned; but Colombia shall make no additional grant of any such privilege nor change the status of any existing concession.

Article IX

There shall not be imposed any taxes, national, municipal, departmental, or of any other class, upon the canal, the vessels that may use it, tugs and other vessels employed in the service of the canal, the railways and auxiliary works, store houses, work shops, offices, quarters for laborers, factories of all kinds, warehouses, wharves, machinery and other works, property, and effects appertaining to the canal or railroad or that may be necessary for the service of the canal or railroad and their dependencies, whether situated within the cities of Panama and Colon, or any other place authorized by the provisions of this convention.

Nor shall there be imposed contributions or charges of a personal character of whatever species upon officers, employees, laborers, and other individuals in the service of the canal and its dependencies.

Article X

It is agreed that telegraph and telephone lines, when established for canal purposes, may also, under suitable regulations, be used for public and private business in connection with the systems of Colombia and the other American Republics and with the lines of cable companies authorized to enter the ports and territories of these Republics; but the official dispatches of the Government of Colombia and the authorities of the Department of Panama shall not pay for such service higher tolls than those required from the officials in the service of the United States.

Article XI

The Government of Colombia shall permit the immigration and free access to the lands and workshops of the canal and its dependencies of all employees and workmen of whatever nationality under contract to work upon or seeking employment or in any wise connected with the said canal and its dependencies, with their respective families, and all such persons shall be free and exempt from the military service of the Republic of Colombia.

Article XII

The United States may import at any time into the said zone, free of customs duties, imposts, taxes, or other charges, and without any restriction, any and all vessels, dredges, engines, cars, machinery, tools, explosives, materials, supplies, and other articles necessary and convenient in the construction, maintenance and operation of the canal and auxiliary works, also all provisions, medicines, clothing, supplies and other things necessary and convenient for the officers, employees, workmen and laborers in the service and employ of the United States and for their families. If any such articles are disposed of for use without the zone excepting Panama and Colon and within the territory of the Republic, they shall be subject to the same import or other duties as like articles under the laws of Colombia or the ordinances of the Department of Panama.

Article XIII

The United States shall have authority to protect and make secure the canal, as well as railways and other auxiliary works and dependencies, and to preserve order and discipline among the laborers and other persons who may congregate in that region, and to make and enforce such police and sanitary regulations as it may deem necessary to preserve order and public health thereon, and to protect navigation and commerce through and over said canal, railways and other works and dependencies from interruption or damage.

I. The Republic of Colombia may establish judicial tribunals within said zone, for the determination, according to its laws and judicial procedure, of certain controversies hereinafter mentioned.

Such judicial tribunal or tribunals so established by the Republic of Colombia shall have exclusive jurisdiction in said zone of all controversies between citizens of the Republic of Colombia, or between citizens of the Republic of Colombia and citizens of any foreign nation other than the United States.

II. Subject to the general sovereignty of Colombia over said zone, the United States may establish judicial tribunals thereon, which shall have jurisdiction of certain controversies hereinafter mentioned to be determined according to the laws and judicial procedure of the United States.

Such judicial tribunal or tribunals so established by the United States shall have exclusive jurisdiction in said zone of all controversies between citizens of the United States, and between citizens of the United States and citizens of any foreign nation other than the Republic of Colombia; and of all controversies in any wise growing out of or relating to the construction, maintenance or operation of the canal, railway and other properties and works.

III. The United States and Colombia engage jointly to establish and maintain upon said zone, judicial tribunals having civil, criminal and admiralty jurisdiction, and to be composed of jurists appointed by the Governments of the United States and Colombia in a manner hereafter to be agreed upon between said Governments, and which tribunals shall have jurisdiction of certain controversies hereinafter mentioned, and of all crimes, felonies and misdemeanors committed within said zone, and of all cases arising in admiralty, according to such laws and procedure as shall be hereafter agreed upon and declared by the two governments.

Such joint judicial tribunal shall have exclusive jurisdiction in said zone of all controversies between citizens of the United States and citizens of Colombia, and between citizens of nations other than Colombia or the United States; and also of all crimes, felonies and misdemeanors committed within said zone, and of all questions of admiralty arising therein.

IV. The two Governments hereafter, and from time to time as occasion arises, shall agree upon and establish the laws and procedures which shall govern such joint judicial tribunal and which shall be applicable to the persons and cases over which such tribunal shall have jurisdiction, and also shall likewise create the requisite officers and employees of such court and establish their powers and duties; and further shall make adequate provision by like agreement for the pursuit, capture, imprisonment, detention and delivery within said zone of persons charged with the commitment of crimes, felonies or misdemeanors without said zone; and for the pursuit, capture, imprisonment, detention and delivery without said zone of persons charged with the commitment of crimes, felonies and misdemeanors within said zone.

Article XIV

The works of the canal, the railways and their auxiliaries are declared of public utility, and in consequence all areas of land and water necessary for the construction, maintenance, and operation of the canal and other specified works may be expropriated in conformity with the laws of Colombia, except that the indemnity shall be conclusively determined without appeal, by a joint commission appointed by the Governments of Colombia and the United States.

The indemnities awarded by the Commission for such expropriation shall be borne by the United States, but the appraisal of said lands and the assessment of damages shall be based upon their value before the commencement of the work upon the canal.

Article XV

The Republic of Colombia grants to the United States the use of all the ports of the Republic open to commerce as places of refuge for any vessels employed in the canal enterprise, and for all vessels in distress having the right to pass through the canal and wishing to anchor in said ports. Such vessels shall be exempt from anchorage and tonnage dues on the part of Colombia.

Article XVI

The canal, when constructed, and the entrance thereto shall be neutral in perpetuity, and shall be opened upon the terms provided for by Section I of Article three of, and in conformity with all the stipulations of, the treaty entered into by the Governments of the United States and Great Britain on November 18, 1901.

Article XVII

The Government of Colombia shall have the right to transport over the canal its vessels, troops, and munitions of war at all times without paying charges of any kind. This exemption is to be extended to the auxiliary railway for the transportation of persons in the service of the Republic of Colombia or of the Department of Panama, or of the police force charged with the preservation of public order outside of said zone, as well as to their baggage, munitions of war and supplies.

Article XVIII

The United States shall have full power and authority to establish and enforce regulations for the use of the canal, railways, and the entering ports and auxiliary works, and to fix rates of tolls and charges thereof, subject to the limitations stated in Article XVI.

Article XIX

The rights and privileges granted to the United States by this convention shall not affect the sovereignty of the Republic of Colombia over the real estate that may be acquired by the United States by reason of the transfer of the rights of the New Panama Canal Company and the Panama Railroad Company lying outside of the said canal zone.

Article XX

If by virtue of any existing treaty between the Republic of Colombia and any third power, there may be any privilege or concession relative to an interoceanic means of communication which especially favors such third power, and which in any of its terms may be incompatible with the terms of the present convention, the Republic of Colombia agrees to cancel or modify such treaty in due form, for which purpose it shall give to the said third power the requisite notification within the term of four months from the date of the present convention, and in case the existing treaty contains no clause permitting its modification or annulment, the Republic of Colombia agrees to procure its modification or annulment in such form that there shall not exist any conflict with the stipulations of the present convention.

Article XXI

The rights and privileges granted by the Republic of Colombia to the United States in the preceding Articles are understood to be free of all anterior concessions or privileges to other Governments, corporations, syndicates or individuals, and consequently, if there should arise any claims on account of the present concessions and privileges or otherwise, the claimants shall resort to the Government of Colombia and not to the United States for any indemnity or compromise which may be required.

Article XXII

The Republic of Colombia renounces and grants to the United States the participation to which it might be entitled in the future earnings of the canal under Article XV of the concessionary contract with Lucien N. B. Wyse now owned by the New Panama Canal Company and any and all other rights or claims of a pecuniary nature arising under or relating to said concession, or arising under or relating to the concessions to the Panama Railroad Company or any extension or modification thereof; and it likewise renounces, confirms and grants to the United States, now and hereafter, all the rights and property reserved in the said concessions which otherwise would belong to Colombia at or before the expiration of the terms of ninety-nine years of the concessions granted to or held by the above mentioned party and companies, and all right, title and interest which it now has or may hereafter have, in and to the lands, canal, works, property and rights held by the said companies under said concessions or otherwise, and acquired or to be acquired by the United States from or through the New Panama Canal Company, including any property and rights which might or may in the future either by lapse of time, forfeiture or otherwise, revert to the Republic of Colombia under any contracts of concessions, with said Wyse, the Universal Panama Canal Company, the Panama Railroad Company and the New Panama Canal Company.

The aforesaid rights and property shall be and are free and released from any present or reversionary interest in or claims of Colombia and the title of the United States thereto upon consummation of the contemplated purchase by the United States from the New Panama Canal Company, shall be absolute, so far as concerns the Republic of Colombia, excepting always the rights of Colombia specifically secured under this treaty.

Article XXIII

If it should become necessary at any time to employ armed forces for the safety or protection of the canal, or of the ships that make use of the same, or the railways and other works, the Republic of Colombia agrees to provide the forces necessary for such purpose, according to the circumstances of the case, but if the Government of Colombia cannot effectively comply with this obligation, then, with the consent of or at the request of Colombia, or of her Minister at Washington, or of the local authorities, civil or military, the United States shall employ such force as may be necessary for that sole purpose; and as soon as the necessity shall have ceased will withdraw the forces so employed. Under exceptional circumstances, however, on account of unforeseen or imminent danger to said canal, railways and other works, or to the lives and property of the persons employed upon the canal, railways, and other works, the

Government of the United States is authorized to act in the interest of their protection, without the necessity of obtaining the consent beforehand of the Government of Colombia; and it shall give immediate advice of the measures adopted for the purpose stated; and as soon as sufficient Colombian forces shall arrive to attend to the indicated purpose, those of the United States shall retire.

Article XXIV

The Government of the United States agrees to complete the construction of the preliminary works necessary, together with all the auxiliary works, in the shortest time possible; and within two years from the date of the exchange of ratification of this convention the main works of the canal proper shall be commenced, and it shall be opened to the traffic between the two oceans within twelve years after such period of two years. In case, however, that any difficulties or obstacles should arise in the construction of the canal which are at present impossible to foresee, in consideration of the good faith with which the Government of the United States shall have proceeded, and the large amount of money expended so far on the works and the nature of the difficulties which may have arisen, the Government of Colombia will prolong the terms stipulated in this Article up to twelve years more for the completion of the work of the canal.

But in case the United States should, at any time, determine to make such canal practically a sea level canal, then such period shall be extended for ten years further.

Article XXV

As the price or compensation for the right to use the zone granted in this convention by Colombia to the United States for the construction of a canal, together with the proprietary right over the Panama Railroad, and for the annuity of two hundred and fifty thousand dollars gold, which Colombia ceases to receive from the said railroad, as well as in compensation for other rights, privileges and exemptions granted to the United States, and in consideration of the increase in the administrative expenses of the Department of Panama consequent upon the construction of the said canal, the Government of the United States binds itself to pay Colombia the sum of ten million dollars in gold coin of the United States on the exchange of the ratification of this convention after its approval according to the laws of the respective countries, and also an annual payment during the life of this convention of two hundred and fifty thousand dollars in like gold coin, beginning nine years after the date aforesaid.

The provisions of this Article shall be in addition to all other benefits assured to Colombia under this convention.

But no delay nor difference of opinion under this Article shall affect nor interrupt the full operation and effect of this convention in all other respects.

Article XXVI

No change either in the Government or in the laws and treaties of Colombia, shall, without the consent of the United States, affect any right of the United States under the present convention, or under any treaty stipulation between the two countries (that now exist or may hereafter exist) touching the subject matter of this convention.

If Colombia shall hereafter enter as a constituent into any other Government or into any union or confederation of States so as to merge her sovereignty or independence in such Government, union, or confederation, the rights of the United States under this convention shall not be in any respect lessened or impaired.

Article XXVII

The joint commission referred to in Articles III, VII and XIV shall be established as follows:

The President of the United States shall nominate two persons and the President of Colombia shall nominate two persons and they shall proceed to a decision; but in case of disagreement of the Commission (by reason of their being equally divided in conclusion) an umpire shall be appointed by the two Governments, who shall render the decision. In the event of death, absence or incapacity of any Commissioner or umpire, or of his omitting, declining or ceasing to act, his place shall be filled by the appointment of another person in the manner above indicated. All decisions by a majority of the Commission or by the umpire shall be final.

Article XXVIII

This convention when signed by the contracting parties, shall be ratified according to the laws of the respective countries and shall be exchanged at Washington within a term of eight months from this date, or earlier if possible.

In faith whereof, the respective plenipotentiaries have signed the present convention in duplicate and have hereunto affixed their respective seals.

Done at the City of Washington, the 22d day of January in the year of our Lord nineteen hundred and three.

(Signed) JOHN HAY.   [SEAL.]
(Signed) TOMÁS HERRÁN. [SEAL.]

APPENDIX D

The John Bassett Moore Memorandum of August, 1903

Considerations on the present situation with respect to the canal treaty with Colombia.

1. When, some years ago, negotiations were begun with the local sovereigns, to enable the United States to construct an interoceanic canal, the Nicaragua route was the only one in contemplation. The negotiations were therefore carried on with Nicaragua and Costa Rica, and, in defect of sufficient stipulations on the subject with the former power and of any whatever with the latter, the treaty-drafts not unnaturally assumed an elaborate form. When at length the Panama route was examined and found to be preferable, and Colombia became the local sovereign in the negotiations, the previous drafts not unnaturally continued to be made use of. Moreover, the act of June 28, 1902, was framed with reference to a treaty on such lines.

2. There has resulted an elaborate treaty with Colombia, to the ratification of which the Congress of that country objects. Should the Colombian Congress reject the treaty, it is important to consider what would be the state of the canal question in that event.

3. That the United States would then abandon the Panama route and close with Nicaragua and Costa Rica is a supposition that may serve the present purposes of diplomacy but certainly not those of permanent policy. If the Panama route is, as we are advised, the best and the most practicable route, both for construction and for operation, it is the one that we should have.

4. The United States, in undertaking to build the canal, does a work not only for itself but for the world. The experience of a hundred years has demonstrated that private enterprise without the responsible guarantee of a great government cannot assure a canal; this has been most signally demonstrated at Panama. The United States now holds out to the world for the first time a certain prospect of a canal. May Colombia be permitted to stand in the way?

5. Let us answer this question, first, on general grounds. The spirit of the answer may be found in the following words of an American statesman:

"The progress of events has rendered the interoceanic routes across the narrow portions of central America vastly important to the commercial world, and especially to the United States, whose possessions, extending along the Atlantic and Pacific coast, demand the speediest and the easiest modes of communication. While the just rights of sovereignty of the States occupying this region should always be respected, we shall expect that these rights will be exercised in a spirit befitting the occasion and the wants and circumstances that have arisen. Sovereignty has its duties as well as its rights, and none of these local Governments, even if administered with more regard to the just demands of other nations than they have been, would be permitted in a spirit of Eastern isolation to close these gates of intercourse on the great highways of the world, and justify the act by the pretension that these avenues of trade and travel belong to them, and that they choose to shut them, or, what is almost equivalent, to encumber them with such unjust regulations as would prevent their general use." (Mr. Cass, Sec. of State, to Mr. Lamar, minister to Cent. Am., July 25, 1858, Cor. in relation to the Proposed Interoceanic Canal [1885], 281.)

6. We will now answer the question on particular grounds, affecting the national rights of the United States in the matter.

In 1846 the United States entered into a treaty with New Granada (Colombia).

By Art. XXXV. of that treaty, New Granada guarantees "that the right of way or transit across the Isthmus of Panama upon any modes of communication that now exist, or that may be hereafter constructed, shall be free and open *to the Government* and citizens of the United States."

The United States, on the other hand, as "an especial compensation" for these advantages, guarantees, "positively and efficaciously, to New Granada, by the present stipulation, the perfect neutrality of the before-mentioned Isthmus, with the view that the free transit from one to the other sea may not be interrupted or embarrassed in any future time while this treaty exists; and in consequence, the United States guarantee, in the same manner, the rights of sovereignty and property which New Granada has and possesses over the said territory."

7. That these engagements created on the part of the United States an offensive and defensive alliance with Colombia and constituted a sort of supportant partnership in sovereignty with that country, and that the object in assuming this burden was to secure primarily a canal, are facts shown by President Polk's message transmitting the treaty to the Senate. In this message, President Polk said:

"The importance of the concession to the commercial and political

APPENDIX D 429

interests of the United States cannot be overrated. The route by the Isthmus of Panama is the shortest between the two oceans; and, from the information herewith communicated, it would seem to be the most practicable for a railroad or canal.

"The vast advantages to our commerce which would result from such a communication, not only with the west coast of America, but with Asia and the islands of the Pacific, are too obvious to require any detail. Such a passage would save us from a long and dangerous navigation of more than nine thousand miles around the Horn, and render our communication with our own possessions on the northwest coast of America comparatively easy and speedy. . . .

"The treaty does not propose to guaranty a territory to a foreign nation in which the United States will have no common interest with that nation. On the contrary, we are more deeply and directly interested in the subject of the guarantee than New Granada herself, or any other country."

These reasons, which continue to be valid today, are not rendered less important by our recent acquisition of Hawaii and the Philippines.

8. Since the day the treaty was ratified, the United States has faithfully performed its guarantee.

As early as 1853, Mr. Everett intimated to the Peruvian minister that the United States would maintain the neutrality of the Isthmus in the event of war between that country and Colombia. (Mr. Everett, Sec. of State, to Mr. Osma, Peruvian min., Feb. 22, 1853, MS. Inst. Peru, I. 79.)

In 1864 the Colombian Government expressed its expectation that, in the event of war between Peru and Spain, the United States would carry into effect the guarantee of neutrality. (Mr. Seward, Sec. of State, to the Attorney General, Aug. 16, 1864, 65 MS. Dom. Let. 523.)

Mr. Fish stated in 1871 that the Department of State had "reason to believe" that an attack upon Colombian sovereignty on the Isthmus had "upon several occasions been . . . averted by warning from this Government." (For. Rel. 1871, 247, 248.)

In 1886, when Colombia was threatened by Italy with hostilities in the Cerruti case, Mr. Bayard expressed "the serious concern the United States could not but feel were a European power to resort to force against a sister Republic of this hemisphere *as to the sovereign and uninterrupted use of a part of whose territory we are guarantors,* under the solemn faith of a treaty." (Mr. Bayard, Sec. of State, to Mr. McLane, min. to France, telegram, Jan. 29, 1886, MS. Inst. France, XXI. 278.)

Not only then, but at a later time, it is altogether probable that the interposition of the United States, under the treaty of 1846, saved Colombia from hostile measures in the case of Cerruti.

9. While the United States has thus saved Colombia from foreign attacks on the Isthmus, it has on numerous occasions protected the route from domestic disturbance. It is unnecessary here to specify the instances, since some of them are very recent.

It is furthermore to be observed that the United States, in so protecting the route, has usually acted with the express approval of the Colombian Government, whose invocations of the treaty of 1846 have often preceded our interposition. In reality, Colombia has again and again claimed that it was our *duty* to protect the route against domestic interruption or attack, thus construing the treaty more broadly than we have done and less favorably to her own sovereignty. Our claim has been that we had under the treaty a *right* to intervene for the purpose of keeping open the transit, while Colombia has asserted that we were *bound* to intervene also for the purpose of supporting the authority of her titular governments. Her claim has in reality approached the point of making us responsible sovereign on the Isthmus.

The position of the United States was exactly expressed by Mr. Seward as follows:

"The United States have taken, and will take, no interest in any question of internal revolution in the State of Panama, or any other State of Panama [*sic*], or any other State of the United States of Colombia, but will maintain a perfect neutrality in regard to such domestic controversies. The United States will nevertheless hold themselves ready to protect the transit trade across the Isthmus against invasion by either the domestic or foreign disturbers of the peace of the State of Panama."

10. Art. XXXV. of the treaty of 1846 guarantees, as has been seen, a free and open transit not only for the citizens but also for the "Government" of the United States. This means for the use of the Government itself, for persons in its military and civil service and for its property. As early as July 1852 the United States sent several hundred troops across the Isthmus, without asking leave of the Colombian Government. The same privilege has since been exercised, as occasion required; and it has been extended to the transit of fugitives from justice in custody of American officials. By a protocol signed at Bogota, February 22, 1879, and afterwards approved by the Colombian Senate, it was expressly acknowledged that this right of transit for troops and extradited fugitives belonged to the United States—"a right," it was declared, "which is established in compensation for the guaranty of the sovereignty and property of the Isthmus,

APPENDIX D 431

to which the same government is bound." (Moore on Extradition, I. 714–718.)

11. In view of the fact that the United States has for more than fifty years secured to Colombia her sovereignty over the Isthmus, for the mutually avowed purpose of maintaining a free and open transit, the United States is in a position to demand that it shall be allowed to construct the great means of transit which the treaty was chiefly designed to assure. *In reality, the Panama canal, so far as built, has actually been constructed under the protection of this very guarantee.* The persons that undertook it failed to finish it. The United States would be justified in asserting and maintaining a right to finish it.

Let us suppose that insurgents should tear up a section of the Panama railway; or even that the Colombian Government itself should do so. Can it be said that the United States might rightfully have prevented the road from being destroyed, but is forbidden to rebuild it? Certainly not.

True it is, that the Panama canal has not been finished, and therefore has never reached the condition of one of the "modes of communication," of which the United States was to have the free and open use. But it may be observed that the treaty expressly refers to modes of communication "that now exist, or that may be hereafter constructed." It looked to the future as well as the present, and above all to the construction of a canal.

The Government and citizens of the United States indeed have never as yet enjoyed the full benefit, nor even the chief benefit, that the treaty was intended and expected to secure. That benefit would be realized only when the ships of the United States and of its citizens should be able to pass from ocean to ocean by way of the Isthmus.

Colombia, on the other hand, has from the beginning enjoyed the full benefit that was to accrue to her, namely, the guarantee of her sovereignty. She is therefore not in a position to obstruct the building of the canal.

If it be suggested that the treaty did not refer to the possible construction of the canal by the United States, the answer may readily be made that the Government of the United States would not in 1846 have proposed such a thing, not because the proposal would have been considered derogatory to Colombia's sovereignty, but because it is not probable that a dozen men could then have been found in Congress who would have sanctioned the opinion that the Government of the United States could *constitutionally* build a canal in foreign territory or incorporate a company to do so. In fact Mr. Clayton in defending in the Senate, in 1853, the joint guarantee by the Clayton-Bulwer treaty of the investments of private capital, challenged any one of his opponents to say that the United States could, within its constitutional powers, itself build the canal, and none of them responded.

In the evolution of opinion, our views on constitutional questions have undergone a change.

12. Colombia's consent to the transfer of the rights of property (as distinguished from distinctively concessionary rights) of the Panama Canal Company, and an unqualified license to construct and operate, or perhaps merely to operate, a canal, are all the United States needs; and these the United States has a right to require. Elaborate stipulations as to the future are at least superfluous. The United States in constructing the canal would own it; and, after constructing it, would have the right to operate it. The ownership and control would be in their nature perpetual.

It may be said that the treaty of 1846 is not in terms perpetual. But the rights of property, when once acquired, and the license to dig, when once secured, would not be dependent on the treaty.

Some years must elapse before the canal can be completed; and it is not to be supposed that the United States would be unable meanwhile to arrange all expedient details. Once on the ground and duly installed, this Government would find no difficulty in meeting questions as they arose. It has done so under the treaty of 1846. Colombia's guarantee of a free and open transit has not secured it to us. We have usually found, when the emergency arose, that we were dependent upon our own resources for the enjoyment of the privileges which the treaty was designed to secure to us.

The position of the United States is altogether different from that of private capitalists, who, unless expressly exempted, are altogether subject to the local jurisdiction, and who, before invoking their governments' protection, may be required to tread the paths of ordinary litigation and establish their rights before the tribunals of the governments against which they assert them. Under such conditions, the private capitalist must have everything beforehand nominated in the bond. The United States is not subject to such disabilities, and can take care of the future.

(*Signed*) J. B. M.

BIBLIOGRAPHY

BIBLIOGRAPHY

Manuscripts

U. S. DEPARTMENT OF STATE

Consular Letters, Aspinwall (Colón), Vol. 19.
Consular Letters, Panama, Vol. 25.
Dispatches from Central America, Vols. 69–71.
Dispatches from Colombia, Vols. 58–60.
Dispatches from Panama, Vol. 1.
Instructions to Colombia, Vol. 19.
Instructions to Consuls, Vol. 189.
Instructions to Germany, Vol. 21.
Instructions to Nicaragua, Vol. 22.
Instructions to Panama, Vol. 1.
Notes to Department, Colombia, Vol. 10.
Notes to Department, Panama, Vol. 1.
Notes to Colombian Legation, Vol. 7.
Notes to Nicaraguan Legation, Vol. 2.
Notes to Panamanian Legation, Vol. 1.
Register of Miscellaneous Letters to Department, Vols. 8–10.

LIBRARY OF CONGRESS

Bunau-Varilla Papers. Papers of Philippe Bunau-Varilla.
Haupt Papers. Papers of Lewis M. Haupt.
Morgan Papers. Papers of John T. Morgan.
Roosevelt Papers. Papers of Theodore Roosevelt.
Root Papers. Papers of Elihu Root.
Spooner Papers. Papers of John C. Spooner.

Government Publications

REPÚBLICA DE COLOMBIA

Anales diplomáticos y consulares de Colombia, ed. by Antonio José Uribe. 6 vols. Bogotá, 1900–1920.
Cámara de Representantes. Anales. Bogotá, 1903.
——— Investigación sobre la rebelión del Istmo de Panamá. Bogotá, 1913.
Comisión investigadora de la separación de Panamá. Panamá: comienza la reparación. Bogotá, 1911.

Decretos legislativos. Bogotá, 1903.
Diario oficial. Bogotá, 1903.
Libro azul, documentos diplomáticos sobre el canal y la rebelión del Istmo de Panamá. Bogotá, 1904.
Ministerio de Relaciones Exteriores. Canal de Panamá: Documentos relativos a las negociaciones para la apertura de esta vía interoceánica. Bogotá, 1903.
——— Memoria del Ministro de Relaciones Exteriores al Congreso. Bogotá, 1904.
Protesta de Colombia contra el tratado entre Panamá y los Estados Unidos. Bogotá, 1904.
Renuncia de dos Ministros y contestación del Vicepresidente de la República. Bogotá, 1903.
Senado. Anales. Bogotá, 1903, 1904.
——— Canal de Panamá. Documentos relacionados con este asunto. Bogotá, 1903.

UNITED STATES OF AMERICA

(Figures in parentheses represent serial numbers.)
Congressional Record, 54th Cong., 2nd Sess., to 58th Cong., 2nd Sess.
Consular Reports, Department of State, Vol. 71.
Correspondence in Relation to the Proposed Interoceanic Canal between the Atlantic and Pacific Oceans. Washington, D. C., 1885.
Davis, Rear-Admiral Charles Henry, U.S.N. Report on Interoceanic Canals and Railroads between the Atlantic and Pacific Oceans. Washington, D. C., 1867.
Diplomatic History of the Panama Canal. Senate Documents, 63rd Cong., 2nd Sess., No. 474 (6582). Washington, D. C., 1914.
Foreign Relations. Papers Relating to the Foreign Relations of the United States. (Published also as House Document No. 1 of the various regular sessions of Congress.) 1873, 1876, 1879, 1880, 1881, 1886, 1888, 1900, 1914. Washington, D. C.
Hale, Captain H. C., U.S.A. Notes on Panama. Washington, D. C., 1903.
House Documents.
  54th Cong., 1st Sess., No. 279 (3456).
  57th Cong., 1st Sess., No. 611 (4377).
House Executive Documents.
  31st Cong., 1st Sess., No. 75 (579).
House Reports.
  55th Cong., 3rd Sess., No. 2104 (3841).

BIBLIOGRAPHY

56th Cong., 1st Sess., No. 351 (4022).
57th Cong., 1st Sess., No. 15 (4399).
Malloy, William M., comp. Treaties, Conventions, International Acts, Protocols and Agreements between the United States of America and Other Powers, 1776–1909. 2 vols. Washington, D. C., 1910.
Moore, John Bassett. A Digest of International Law. 8 vols. Washington, D. C., 1906.
—— The Interoceanic Canal and the Hay-Pauncefote Treaty. Washington, D. C., 1900.
Official Opinions of the Attorneys-General of the United States, ed. by John L. Lott and James A. Finch. Vol. XXIV (1902). Washington, D. C., 1903.
Richardson, James D., comp. A Compilation of the Messages and Papers of the Presidents, 1789–1908. 11 vols. New York, 1909.
Senate Documents.
    56th Cong., 1st Sess., No. 50 (3848); 1st Sess., No. 160 (3852); 1st Sess., No. 161 (3853); 1st Sess., No. 237 (3853); 1st Sess., No. 268 (3868); 2nd Sess., No. 5 (4029); 2nd Sess., No. 41 (4033).
    57th Cong., 1st Sess., No. 54 (4225); 1st Sess., No. 123 (4230); 1st Sess., No. 253 (4238); 1st Sess., No. 357 (4245); 2nd Sess., No. 34 (4417); 2nd Sess., No. 95 (4422).
    58th Cong., 2nd Sess., No. 51 (4587); 2nd Sess., No. 102 (4588); 2nd Sess., No. 133 (4589).
    59th Cong., 1st Sess., No. 285 (4914); 1st Sess., No. 457 (4915); 2nd Sess., No. 401 (5097–5100).
Senate Executive Documents.
    46th Cong., 1st Sess., No. 15 (1869); 2nd Sess., No. 112 (1885).
Senate Journal.
    23rd Cong., 2nd Sess. (265).
Senate Reports.
    55th Cong., 3rd Sess., No. 1417 (3739); 3rd Sess., No. 1418 (3739).
    56th Cong., 1st Sess., No. 1337 (3894); 2nd Sess., No. 2402 (4067).
    57th Cong., 1st Sess., No. 1 (4256); 1st Sess., No. 783 (4260).
The Statutes at Large of the United States of America. Vols. 30, 32. Washington, D. C.
The Story of Panama: Hearings on the Rainey Resolution before the Committee on Foreign Affairs of the House of Representatives. Washington, 1913.
Use by the United States of a Military Force in the Internal Affairs of Colombia. Senate Documents, 58th Cong., 2nd Sess., No. 143 (4589). Washington, D. C., 1904.
Walker Commission Report (Report of the Isthmian Canal Com-

mission, 1899–1901). Senate Documents, 58th Cong., 2nd Sess., No. 222 (4609). Washington, D. C., 1904.

Newspapers

El Colombiano (Bogotá), 1902–1904.
Commercial Advertiser (New York), 1902–1903.
La Constitución (Bogotá), 1903.
El Correo Nacional (Bogotá), 1903–1904.
El Eco Nacional (Bogotá), 1903.
La Estrella de Panamá (Panama), 1902–1903.
Herald (New York), 1902–1904.
Inquirer (Philadelphia), 1903.
Le Matin (Paris), 1903.
El Nuevo Tiempo (Bogotá), 1903.
El Porvenir (Bogotá), 1903.
Post (Washington), 1903.
El Relator (Bogotá), 1903.
Sun (New York), 1900–1904.
Times (New York), 1896, 1900–1904.
Tribune (New York), 1898, 1902–1904.
World (New York), 1898, 1900, 1902–1904, 1908.

Other Published Works

Abbot, Brigadier-General Henry L., U.S.A. "The Present Status of the Panama Canal," in *Engineering News and American Railway Journal* (New York), XL (1898), 210–213.
——— Problems of the Panama Canal. New York, 1907.
Academia Panameña de la Historia. *Publicaciones*. Vols. I–II (Panama, 1933–1934).
Alba C., Manuel María. "Cronología de los gobernantes de Panamá, 1510–1932," in *Boletín de la Academia Panameña de la Historia* (Panama), III, No. 8 (1935), 3–182.
Aldana, Abelardo. The Panama Canal Question: a Plea for Colombia. New York, 1904.
Alexander, Thomas S. "Colombia: The Government, the Country, and the People," in *The World's Work* (New York), VII (1904), 4336–4343.
——— "The Truth about Colombia," in *The Outlook* (New York), LXXV (1903), 993–996.
The American Monthly Review of Reviews. Vols. XXVI–XXVII (1902–1903). New York.
Anonymous. I Took the Isthmus: ex-President Roosevelt's Confession, Colombia's Protest and Editorial Comment of American

BIBLIOGRAPHY

Newspapers on "How the United States Acquired the Right to Build the Panama Canal." New York, 1911.

Arango, José Agustín. Datos para la historia de la independencia del istmo. Panama, 1922.

Arboleda, Gustavo. Historia contemporánea de Colombia desde la disolución de la antigua república de ese nombre hasta la época presente. Vols. I–VI, Bogotá, 1918–1932.

Arias, Harmodio. The Panama Canal: a Study in International Law and Diplomacy. London, 1911.

Arosemena, Pablo. Escritos. 2 vols. Panama, 1930.

——— "La secesión de Panamá y sus causas," in Documentos históricos sobre la independencia del Istmo de Panamá. Instituto Nacional de Panamá, Panama, 1930, pp. 241–262.

Beaupré, Arthur M. "Conditions in Colombia," in *The Independent* (New York), LVI (1904), 121–123.

Beer, Thomas. Hanna. New York, 1929.

Bemis, Samuel Flagg, ed. The American Secretaries of State and Their Diplomacy. 10 vols. New York, 1927–1929.

Bennett, Ira E. History of the Panama Canal: Its Construction and Builders. Washington, D. C., 1915.

Biard, Pierre. Le Canal interocéanique et son régime juridique. Paris, 1902.

Bigelow, John. The Panama Canal. New York, 1886.

Bishop, Joseph Bucklin. The Panama Gateway. New York, 1915.

——— Theodore Roosevelt and His Time Shown in His Own Letters. 2 vols. New York, 1920.

Bonilla Lara, Alvaro. Los Estados Unidos y los canales interoceánicos de América. Panama, 1929.

Bullard, Arthur. Panama: the Canal, the Country, the People. New York, 1914.

Bunau-Varilla, Philippe. De Panama á Verdun: Mes combats pour la France. Paris, 1937.

——— Nicaragua or Panama. New York, 1901.

——— Panama: the Creation, Destruction, and Resurrection. New York, 1920.

——— Panama: Le Passé, le présent, l'avenir. Paris, 1892.

Burr, William H. "The Panama Route for a Ship Canal," in *Popular Science Monthly* (New York), LXI (1902), 252–268, 304–316.

——— "The Republic of Panama," in *Annual Report,* 1903, of the Smithsonian Institution (Washington, D. C., 1904).

Bustamente, Antoine S. de. "Le Canal de Panama et le droit international," in *Revue de droit international et de législation comparée* (Brussels), XXVII (1895), 112–142, 223–253.

Calderón, Carlos, R. Samper, and Marceliano Vargas. La Question de Panama. Paris, 1903.
Camacho Roldán, Salvador. Memorias. Bogotá, 1923.
Cárdenas y Echarte, Raúl de. La política de los Estados Unidos en el continente americano. Habana, 1921.
Casas, Joaquín José. Semblanza de Don José Marroquín. Bogotá, 1927.
Castillero R., Ernesto J. "La causa inmediata de la emancipación de Panamá," in *Boletín de la Academia Panameña de la Historia* (Panama), I, No. 3 (1933), 253–433.
——— "El Doctor Manuel Amador Guerrero (semblanza del prócer)" in *Publicaciones de la Academia Panameña de la Historia* (Panama), II (1933), 121–128.
——— "El profeta de Panamá y su gran traición," in *Boletín de la Academia Panameña de la Historia* (Panama), IV, No. 10 (1936), pp. 1–60.
Chamberlain, Leander T. "A Chapter of National Dishonor," in *The North American Review* (New York), CXCV (1912), 145–174.
Chapman, Charles E. A History of Spain. New York, 1925.
Cowles, Anna Roosevelt, ed. Letters from Theodore Roosevelt to Anna Roosevelt Cowles, 1870–1918. New York, 1924.
Croly, Herbert. Marcus Alonzo Hanna, His Life and Work. New York, 1912.
Curtis, W. J. The History of the Purchase by the United States of the Panama Canal, the Manner of Payment and the Distribution of the Proceeds of Sale. Birmingham, Ala. [?], 1909.
Davis, Rear-Admiral Charles Henry, U.S.N. Report on Interoceanic Canals and Railroads between the Atlantic and Pacific Oceans. Government Printing Office, Washington, D. C., 1867.
Dennett, Tyler. John Hay. New York, 1933.
Dennis, Alfred L. P. Adventures in American Diplomacy, 1896–1906. New York, 1928.
Eder, Phanor James. Colombia. London, 1913.
Enock, C. Reginald. The Panama Canal: Its Past, Present, and Future. London and Glasgow, 1914.
Escobar, Francisco. "President Roosevelt's Message and the Isthmian Canal," in *The North American Review* (New York), CLXXVIII (1904), 122–132.
Esguerra, Nicolás. El canal de Panamá y la verdadera historia de la prórroga. Bogotá, 1903.
[Espinosa, Eduardo]. Colombia: la legitimidad y el gobierno de facto. New York, 1902.
Espinosa, Eduardo, ed. Manifiestos y protestas del presidente de

Colombia, Sr. Sanclemente, y otros documentos relativos al crimen de alta traición consumado en Bogotá et 31 de julio de 1900. New York, 1901.
Foulke, William Dudley. A Hoosier Autobiography. New York, 1922.
Fox, George L. President Roosevelt's Coup d'Etat: the Panama Affair in a Nutshell. New Haven, Conn., 1904.
Freehoff, Joseph C. America and the Canal Title. New York, 1916.
González Valencia, José María. Separation of Panama from Colombia: Extracts of Letters Addressed by José M. González Valencia, Former Minister of Foreign Affairs of Colombia, to a Friend of Colombia in the United States. Washington, D. C., 1916.
——— Separation of Panama from Colombia: Refutation of the Misstatements and Erroneous Conception of Mr. Roosevelt in His Article Entitled "The Panama Blackmail Treaty." Washington, D. C., 1916.
Graell, C. Arrocha. Historia de la independencia de Panamá: sus antecedentes y sus causas, 1821–1903. Panama, 1933.
Hale, Captain H. C., U.S.A. Notes on Panama. Government Printing Office, Washington, D. C., 1903.
Harrisse, Henry. The Discovery of North America. London, 1892.
Haupt, Lewis M. "Why Is an Isthmian Canal Not Built?" in *The North American Review* (New York), CLXXV (1902), 128–135.
Heilprin, Angelo. A Defense of the Panama Route. Philadelphia, 1902.
Henao, Jesús María, and Gerardo Arrubla. History of Colombia. Translated and edited by J. Fred Rippy. Chapel Hill, N. C., 1938.
Hill, Howard C. Roosevelt and the Caribbean. Chicago, 1927.
Hispano, Cornelio [Ismael López]. Cesarismo teocrático. San José de Costa Rica, 1922.
Historicus. "The Fifty Miles Order," in *The North American Review* (New York), CLXXVIII (1904), 235–245.
Holt, W. Stull. Treaties Defeated by the Senate: a Study of the Struggle between President and Senate over the Conduct of Foreign Affairs. Baltimore, 1933.
Huberich, Charles H. The Trans-Isthmian Canal: a Study in American Diplomatic History (1825–1904). Austin, Texas, 1904.
Humbert, Jules. Histoire de la Colombie et du Vénézuéla des origines jusqu'à nos jours. Paris, 1921.
Instituto Nacional de Panamá. Documentos historicos sobre la independencia de Panamá. Panama, 1930.
International Union of American Republics. *Monthly Bulletin*, 1902–1904.

Jessup, Philip C. Elihu Root. 2 vols. New York, 1938.
Johnson, Willis Fletcher. Four Centuries of the Panama Canal. New York, 1906.
Keasbey, Lindley Miller. Early Diplomatic History of the Nicaragua Canal. Newark, N. J., 1890.
────── The Nicaragua Canal and the Monroe Doctrine. New York, 1896.
Latané, John Holladay. A History of American Foreign Policy. New York, 1927.
────── "The Treaty Relations of the United States and Colombia," in the *Annals* of the American Academy of Political and Social Science (Philadelphia), XXII (1903), 115–126.
Leigh, John George. "The Republic of Colombia and the Panama Canal," in *The Engineering Magazine* (New York), XXVI (1903), 1–19.
Lévine, V. Colombia. New York, 1914.
Lindsay, Forbes (C. H. A. Forbes-Lindsay). Panama and the Canal Title. Boston, 1912.
Lodge, Henry Cabot, ed. Selections from the Correspondence of Theodore Roosevelt and Henry Cabot Lodge, 1884–1918. 2 vols. New York, 1925.
Loewel, Pierre. Le Canal de Panama. Paris, 1913.
López, Jacinto. "El gobierno de Colombia y la compañía del canal de Panamá," in *La Reforma Social* (Habana), III (1915), 455–469.
────── "Situación política, económica y social de Colombia en el período de las negociaciones con los Estados Unidos para la celebración del tratado del canal de Panamá," in *Cuba Contemporánea* (Habana), VIII (1915), 224–239.
López de Mesa, Luis. Introducción a la historia de la cultura en Colombia. Bogotá, 1930.
McCaleb, Walter F. Theodore Roosevelt. New York, 1931.
Mahan, A. T. "The Isthmus and Sea Power," in *The Atlantic Monthly* (Boston), LXII (1893), 459–472.
Malloy, William M., comp. Treaties, Conventions, International Acts, Protocols and Agreements between the United States of America and Other Powers, 1776–1909. 2 vols. Government Printing Office, Washington, D. C., 1910.
Martínez Delgado, Luis. A propósito del Dr. Carlos Martínez Silva, capítulos de historia política de Colombia. Bogotá, 1926.
Martínez Delgado, Luis, and Gustavo Otero Muñoz, eds. Obras completas del doctor Carlos Martínez Silva. 9 vols. Bogotá, 1934–1938.

Mendoza, Diego. El canal interoceánico y los tratados. Bogotá, 1903.
Merriman, Roger Bigelow. The Rise of the Spanish Empire in the Old World and the New. 4 vols. New York, 1918–1934.
Miller, Hugh Gordon. The Isthmian Highway. New York, 1929.
Mills, J. Saxon. The Panama Canal. London, 1913.
Moore, John Bassett. A Digest of International Law. 8 vols. Government Printing Office, Washington, D. C., 1906.
——— The Interoceanic Canal and the Hay-Pauncefote Treaty. Government Printing Office, Washington, D. C., 1900.
——— The Principles of American Diplomacy. New York, 1918.
Morales, Eusebio A. "The Political and Economical Situation of Colombia," in *The North American Review* (New York), CLXXV (1902), 347–360.
——— "The Republic of Panama," in *The North American Review* (New York), CLXXVII (1903), 914–918.
Mowat, R. B. The Life of Lord Pauncefote. London, 1929.
The Nation. Vol. LXXVI (1903). New York.
[Nel Ospina, Pedro]. The Panama Canal Question: a Plea for Colombia. New York, 1904.
Nevins, Allan. Grover Cleveland: a Study in Courage. New York, 1933.
——— Henry White: Thirty Years of American Diplomacy. New York, 1930.
———, ed. Polk: the Diary of a President, 1845–1849. New York, 1929.
Nieto, Máximo A. Recuerdos de la regeneración. Bogotá, 1924.
Nieto Caballero, L. E. El dolor de Colombia. Bogotá, 1922.
——— Por qué soy liberal? Bogotá, 1931.
Núñez, Rafael. La reforma política en Colombia. Bogotá, 1886.
Obarrio, Nicanor A. de. "Reminiscencias históricas," in *Publicaciones de la Academia Panameña de la Historia* (Panama), II (1933), 41–45.
Official Correspondence and Other Documents Respecting the Panama Canal Question. London, 1904.
Offutt, Milton. The Protection of Citizens Abroad by the Armed Forces of the United States. Baltimore, 1928.
Olarte Camacho, Vicente. Tratado de 6 de abril 1914. Bogotá, 1914.
Ortega B., Ismael. La jornada del día 3 de noviembre de 1903 y sus antecedentes. Panama, 1931.
Ospina, Joaquín. Diccionario biográfico y bibliográfico de Colombia. 2 vols. Bogotá, 1927–1937.

Otero, Luis Alfredo. Panamá. Bogotá, 1926.
Otis, Fessenden Nott. Illustrated History of the Panama Railroad. New York, 1861.
Parks, E. Taylor. Colombia and the United States, 1765–1934. Durham, N. C., 1935.
Pensa, Henri. La République et le canal de Panama. Paris, 1906.
Pérez, Raúl. "The Treacherous Treaty: a Colombian Plea," in *The North American Review* (New York), CLXXVII (1903), 934–946.
Pérez, y Soto, Juan B. Inri (sobre el canal de Panamá). Habana, 1905.
Perkins, Dexter. The Monroe Doctrine, 1823–1826. Cambridge, Mass., 1927.
——— The Monroe Doctrine, 1867–1907. Baltimore, 1937.
Petre, F. Loraine. The Republic of Colombia. London, 1906.
Political Handbook of the World, 1937. New York, 1937.
Pratt, Julius W. "American Business and the Spanish-American War," in *Hispanic American Historical Review* (Durham, N. C.), XIV (1934), 163–201.
——— Expansionists of 1898: the Acquisition of Hawaii and the Spanish Islands. Baltimore, 1936.
Pringle, Henry F. Theodore Roosevelt: a Biography. New York, 1931.
Public Opinion. Vols. XXVIII–XXXIV (1900–1903). New York.
Rebolledo, Alvaro. Reseña historico-política de la comunicación interoceánica: La separación de Panamá y los arreglos entre los Estados Unidos y Colombia. San Francisco, 1930.
Reeves, Jesse S. American Diplomacy under Tyler and Polk. Baltimore, 1907.
Renaut, F. P. Le Canal océanique de Panama et les voies ferrées transcontinentales américaines. Paris, 1915.
Restrepo, Antonio José. Canal de Panamá: La verdad sobre la prórroga; replica al Ex-Ministro de Hacienda, Señor Carlos Calderón. Lausanne, 1903.
——— Al pueblo colombiano, replica a la legación en Washington: Labor por la paz: cuestión canal y cuestión constitucional; peligros imaginarios; la paz; intervención personal. Madrid, 1902.
Reyes, Rafael. "Colombia and the United States," in *The Independent* (New York), IV (1903), 2899–2900.
——— Misión diplomática y militar, 1903–1904. Bogotá, 1904.
——— Por Colombia, por Ibero América. London, 1912.
——— The Two Americas. New York, 1914.
Richardson, James D., comp. A Compilation of the Messages and Papers of the Presidents, 1789–1908. 11 vols. New York, 1909.

Rippy, J. Fred. The Capitalists and Colombia. New York, 1931.
—— Latin America in World Politics. New York, 1931.
—— Rivalry of the United States and Great Britain over Latin America (1808–1830). Baltimore, 1929.
Rivas, Raimundo. Relaciones internacionales entre Colombia y los Estados Unidos, 1810–1850. Bogotá, 1915.
Robertson, William Spence. History of the Latin-American Nations. New York, 1926.
Roosevelt, Theodore. An Autobiography. New York, 1913.
—— "How the United States Acquired the Right to Dig the Panama Canal," in *The Outlook* (New York), XCIX (1911), 314–318.
—— "The Panama Blackmail Treaty," in *Metropolitan* (New York), XLI (1915), 8–10, 69–72.
Root, Elihu. The Ethics of the Panama Question (address before the Union League Club of Chicago, Feb. 22, 1904). Chicago, 1904.
Rougier, Antoine. Les Récentes Guerres civiles de la Colombie et du Vénézuéla. Paris, 1904.
Rousseau, H. H. The Isthmian Canal. Washington, D. C., 1910.
Samper Brush, José María, and Luis Samper Sordo, eds. Escritos político-económicos de Miguel Samper. 4 vols. Bogotá, 1925–1927.
Scruggs, William L. The Colombian and Venezuelan Republics. Boston, 1900.
Sears, Louis Martin. A History of American Foreign Relations. New York, 1927.
Secerra, Ricardo. Opiniones de un patriota. Barranquilla, 1904.
Smith, Darrell H. The Panama Canal. Baltimore, 1927.
Sondregger, C. L'Achèvement du canal de Panama. Paris, 1902.
Stephens, H. Morse, and Herbert E. Bolton, eds. The Pacific Ocean in History. New York, 1917.
Sullivan & Cromwell. A Compilation of Executive Documents and Diplomatic Correspondence Relative to a Trans-Isthmian Canal in Central America; with Specific Reference to the Treaty of 1846 between the United States and New Granada (United States of Colombia) and the "Clayton-Bulwer" Treaty of 1850 between the United States and Great Britain. New York, 1905.
Taussig, Rudolph J. "The American Inter-Oceanic Canal: an Historical Sketch of the Canal Idea," in Stephens and Bolton, eds., The Pacific Ocean in History (New York, 1917), pp. 114–136.
Tavernier, E. Etude du canal interocéanique de l'Amérique centrale au point de vue diplomatique, juridique et économique. Paris, 1908.

Taylor, Hannis. Why the Impending Treaty with Colombia Should Be Ratified. Washington, D. C., 1914.
Terán, Oscar. Del tratado Herrán–Hay al tratado Hay–Bunau-Varilla. 2 vols. Panama, 1934–1935.
Thayer, William Roscoe. "John Hay and the Panama Republic from the Unpublished Letters of John Hay," in *Harper's Magazine* (New York), CXXXI (1915), 165–175.
―――― Life and Letters of John Hay. 2 vols. Boston, 1915.
Thomson, Norman. Colombia and the United States. London, 1914 [?].
Tomes, Robert. Panama in 1855: an Account of the Panama Rail-Road, of the Cities of Panama and Aspinwall, with Sketches of Life and Character on the Isthmus. New York, 1855.
Travis, Ira Dudley. British Rule in Central America, or, A Sketch of Mosquito History. Ann Arbor, Mich., 1895.
―――― History of the Clayton-Bulwer Treaty. Ann Arbor, Mich., 1900.
Uribe, Antonio José. Colombia y los Estados Unidos de América: El canal interoceánico; la separación de Panamá; política internacional económica; la cooperación. Bogotá, 1931.
―――― Cuestiones internacionales, económicas, políticas y sociales. Bogotá, 1925.
―――― El gobierno del excmo. Sr. Marroquín ante la República y ante la constitución. Bogotá, 1901.
Uribe Uribe, Rafael. La separación de Panamá. Bogotá, 1906.
Urrutia, Francisco José. A Commentary on the Declaration of the Rights of Nations Adopted by the American Law Institute of International Law. Washington, D. C., 1916.
Urueta, Carlos Adolfo, ed. Documentos militares y políticos relativos a las campañas del General Uribe Uribe. Bogotá, 1904.
Valdés, Ramón M. La independencia del Istmo de Panamá, sus antecedentes, sus causas y justificación. Panama, 1903.
Vásquez Cobo, Alfredo. Pro patria: cuestiones internationales con los Estados Unidos y Panamá. Panama, 1910.
Vega, José de la. La federación en Colombia (1810–1912). Madrid, 1916 [?].
Vélez R., Pedro. Asuntos de Panamá. Bogotá, 1909.
Viallate, Achille. Essais d'histoire diplomatique américaine: le développement territorial des Etats-Unis; le canal interocéanique; la guerre hispano-américaine. Paris, 1905.
Wilcox, Marrion. "Colombia's Last Vision of El Dorado," in *The North American Review* (New York), CLXXVII (1903), 919–933.

Williams, Mary Wilhelmina. Anglo-American Isthmian Diplomacy, 1815–1915. Washington, D. C., 1916.
—— The People and Politics of Latin America. Boston, 1930.
Winsor, Justin, ed. Narrative and Critical History of America. 8 vols. Boston, 1884–1889.

INDEX

INDEX

Abadía Méndez, Miguel, 131, 134 f.
Acapulco, Admiral Glass ordered to, 357
Accessory Transit Company, 15n
Adee, Alvey A., 117, 245, 345n
Aguadulce, Herrera's triumph at, 169, 234
Alaskan boundary dispute, 94, 96, 390
Albert, Charles S., 293
Aldrich, Nelson W., 105n
Allison, William B., 107n, 151
Amador Guerrero, Manuel, 288; offered presidency of proposed republic of Panama, 338; trip to U. S., 347; detectives hired to watch, 349; Cromwell's enthusiasm for undertaking, 349; rebuff, 350; interview with Bunau-Varilla, 356; return to Colón, 358; orders arrest of Obaldía, 363; delegate of *junta* to supervise canal negotiations with U. S., 374; in New York, 376, 377; tidings that Hay–Bunau-Varilla treaty had been signed, 378
Amaya, Ramón G., lured aboard train: placed under arrest, 362 f.; refused to accept parole, 367
American Atlantic and Pacific Ship Canal Company, 29n
Ammen, Daniel, 19n
Andreas & Company, 347, 348
Anglo-American rivalry in Central America, 67
Angulo, Fernando, reply to Caro, 304
Antioquia, population, mines, 38
April Memorandum, *see* Hay-Concha Memorandum
Arango, José Agustín, 288; conspiracy on Isthmus centered about, 337, 338, 339; leader of revolutionary party in Panama, 354, 364, 367; telegram to Hay announcing Panamanian independence, 369; plenipotentiary powers granted by, to Bunau-Varilla, 375; pledged ratification of Hay–Bunau-Varilla treaty without change, 378

Arango, Marcelino, 303; in debate on Ospina–Rodríguez-Campo project of law, 333
Arias, Pedro, 338
Arias, Ramón, 338
Arias, Ricardo, 290, 293, 338, 347, 358
Arias, Tomás, 210, 338, 374; on provisional government committee, 364, 369; signs telegram to Hay announcing independence, 369
Arosemena, Carlos Constantino, 337
Arosemena, Pablo, 210, 288, 290; Root-Arosemena and Cortés-Arosemena conventions, 391n
Arthur, Chester A., 21
Aspinwall, W. H., 14n
Astor, John Jacob, 30
Atlanta, 358
Atlas Steamship Company, 107n
Atrato River, as canal route, 34

Baker, Asher, 88
Balfour, Arthur, 99n
Bayard, Thomas F., 22
Bay Islands, 9, 10
Beaupré, Arthur M., 245, 285; quoted, 249, 250, 251, 267, 268, 282, 314; reply to State Department dispatch of April 24, 275; interview with Reyes re Hay-Herrán treaty, 299, 307, 309; asked Hay for statement of policy, 309, 310, 311; re changes in Hay-Herrán treaty, 311, 317 ff.; cable communication with U. S. delayed, 310, 317; contempt for prerogatives of Colombian congress, 320; played into Rico's hands, 322; Rico-Beaupré correspondence, 323; account of political stir in Colombia, 329; request to be kept posted as to events on Isthmus, 358; re Reyes' appeal to U. S., 371; reports lacking in penetration, 389 f.
Beers, J. R., 288; part in Panama revolution, 337, 339
Belize, 9

Biddle, Charles, 11
Bidlack, Benjamin, 12
Bigelow, John, 88
Bishop, Joseph Bucklin, 380
Black, William Murray, 339, 369
Blaine, James G., 21, 67
Bô, Marius, 118, 119, 122, 146, 213
Bogotá, 38; political scene, 40; description, 41; center of culture, 42; isolation, 43; captured by Mosquera, 47; in state of siege, 222; martial law proclaimed, 371
Bogotá, 265, 361; Panama shelled by, 364
Bolívar, Simon, 46
Boston, ordered to Acapulco, 358; ordered to Panama, 358, 362
Bowlin, U. S. minister to Colombia, 69
Boyd, Federico, 210, 338, 358, 369; on provisional government committee, 364; on executive board of Republic, 367; *junta* delegate to negotiate with U. S., 374; in New York, 376, 377; tidings that treaty had been signed, 377 f.
Brid, Demetrio H., 292, 364
Brigard, Arturo de, 109, 242
Bryan, W. J., 83, 103
Bulwer, Sir Henry, 16; *see also* Clayton-Bulwer treaty
Bunau-Varilla, Philippe, 24n, 75, 77, 79, 88n, 91, 102, 119, 122, 153n, 390; lectures, 113; propaganda a factor in success of Panama route, 148; urged ratification of Hay-Herrán treaty, 295; arrival in New York, 350; with Panama conspirators, 354 ff.; article in *Le Matin*, 355, 356; Moore's impression of, 355; asked to be entrusted with diplomatic representation of Panama in U. S., 357, 374; provided funds and program for revolution, 357; cable re arrival of United States warships, 361; appointed confidential agent of Republic at Washington, 369; *junta's* efforts to confine his duties to empty formality, 374; pressure on Arango to cable him plenipotentiary powers, 375; part in formulation of Hay–Bunau-Varilla treaty, 375; anxiety to complete negotiations before arrival of Panamanian delegation, 376, 377; *see also* Hay–Bunau-Varilla treaty
Burnside, Senator: resolution re canal, 20
Burr, William, 91, 92, 114, 149n
Burton, Allan A., 168
Burton, Theodore E., 86, 120n

Caballero, Lucas E. Nieto, *see* Nieto Caballero
Calderón, Carlos, 58n, 59, 60n
Calderón, Clímaco, 58, 59, 109n
Calderón, José Medina, 298
Calderón, Quintero, *see* Quintero Calderón, Guillermo
Calvo, J. B., 145n
Campo, Luis F., 307, 316; Ospina–Rodríguez-Campo project of law, 327, 331, 332
Canadian Pacific Railroad, 85n, 150
Canal routes, feasibility of, across Isthmus, 3 ff.; urged by Ceron, 4; problem an international one, 8, 11, 12, 17; *see also* Nicaragua route; Panama Canal
Canning, George, 9
Cannon, Joseph G., 86, 87, 88, 100n; amendment to Hepburn bill defeated, 120n
Caribbean, Britain displaced by U. S. as most active power in, 68
Caro, Miguel Antonio, 48, 52, 53, 54, 62, 224, 249, 321, 331, 372; political situation complicated by return of, 266; attack on Marroquín, 301, 304; proposed substitute for resolution of Saavedra, Arango, and Uribe B., 304; defeated, 307; denunciation of government, 324, 332
Cartagena, 289
Cartagena, 362, 365, 366
Casas, José Joaquín, 270, 271
Casey, Silas, at Panama, 171; refusal to permit shipment of munitions across Isthmus, 171, 178 f.; restrictions on use of trains removed, 172, 236; Concha angered by actions of, 176; detention of the *Bogotá*, 265
Cass, Lewis, 69, 342
Castro, Cipriano, 56; assistance to revolution, 220 ff.
Cauca, The, 38, 47, 205

INDEX   453

Cauca River, 33
Cauca Valley, 43, 71
Central America, feasibility of artificial waterway in, 3; political chaos, 8, 14; Federation, 9; interest of U. S. in politics of, 10; Anglo-American rivalry, 14, 68; Clayton-Bulwer treaty, 16, 68; de Lesseps' canal venture, 19 ff.; aggressive policy of U. S., 67; Greater Republic of Central America, 81
Central and South American Telegraph Company, 310
Ceron Saavedra, see Saavedra Ceron
Chagres River, 4, 6n, 392
Charles V, emperor, interest in Panama route, 4
Charles III, King of Spain, 7
Chatfield, Frederick, 15; Tigre Island seized by, 16
Childs, O. H., 29n
Chinácota, treaty of, 237, 246
Choate, Joseph H., 95, 96, 117
Clay, Henry, 11, 22
Clayton, John Middleton, 13n, 68
Clayton-Bulwer treaty, 67 ff., 72, 85; ratified, 16; a source of irritation to U. S., 17; Blaine's correspondence with Granville re, 21; Frelinghuysen attempts to obtain abrogation, 22; various demands for amendment or abrogation, 29; Hay opens negotiations to modify, 93; Hay's parleys with Pauncefote, 94; Hepburn attacks as obsolete, 98; and Hay-Pauncefote treaties, 105 f., 108, 117 f.
Cleveland, Grover, 22
Cobo, A. Vásquez, see Vásquez Cobo
Coghlan, Admiral, 374
Colombia, issue of sovereignty over Panama canal region, 18, 72, 132, 158, 178, 254 ff., 315; history and geographical setting, 33-74; area, 33n; population, 36; natural resources, 38; political and economic conditions, 39, 55, 201 ff., 223 ff., 247 ff., 288; waterpower, 39; isolation imposed by Cordilleras, 39; political scene in Bogotá, 40 (see also Bogotá); power in hands of aristocrats, 40; public men, 41; culture, writers, 42; systems of communication, 43, 44, 46; struggle for independence, 45; lack of experienced administrators, 45; constitutions: 1821–1901, 45 ff.; 1843, Republic of New Granada, 46; 1863, United States of Colombia, 47 ff.; 1886, Núñez constitution, 48 ff.; application of U. S. laws in canal zone contrary to, 315; political parties, 46 ff.; break-up of first republic, 46 (see also New Granada); "Regeneration," 48, 51, 52, 63; education, 50; religion, see Roman Catholic Church; financial condition, issues of paper money, 50, 55, 57, 62, 73, 204 ff., 226; neglect of foreign debt obligations, 51; Sanclemente, 52 ff., 225, 331, 332 (see also Marroquín; Reyes); revolution of 1899–1902, 56 ff., 131, 163 ff., 220 ff.; reorganization of governmental departments, 62; envoy to U. S. re Nicaragua Canal bills, 63 (see also Martínez Silva, Carlos); principal problems connected with canal from Colombian point of view, 64 ff. (see also Panama entries); protection afforded by Clayton-Bulwer treaty, 67 ff.; fear of U. S. intervention and control, 70, 229, 255, 256, 264, 320; opposition to placing U. S. in sole charge of canal work, 72; canal convention with U. S. favored, 73; fight for Panama route in Washington, 75-116 (see also under United States); attitude toward Wyse concession, 109 ff. (see also Wyse concession); failure to instruct Silva, 126 ff.; and authorization of New Company to sell to U. S., 127, 133, 146, 213, 276 ff.; apparent apathy towards canal negotiations, 130 f.; tension with Venezuela, 131, 220, 222; aim to secure canal without subordinating sovereignty, 132; noncomprehension of international situation, 134; efforts to force New Company to pay for permission to sell to U. S., 134 ff., 207 ff., 239, 263, 273, 284, 311; sacrifice of reversionary interest in railroad, 134, 135; terms proposed as bases of treaty, 138; believed its route only one possible, 145; opposition to extension of New Company concession, 149; negotiation of the Hay-Herrán treaty,

INDEX

Colombia (*Continued*)
157-99 (*see also* Hay-Herrán treaty); difficulty of communication with U. S., 162; asked intervention of U. S. on Isthmus, 163, 234 ff.; form of U. S. intervention protested, 166 ff., 175 ff.; U. S. suspected of aiding Liberals, 178; delay and indecision characteristic of diplomacy, 194, 201 ff., 232 ff.; Morgan's attacks on, 196*n*, 197; Herrán's dilemma, 200-40; ready to accept all Hay's proposals except one on compensation, 200, 203; why negotiations were not completely broken off, 204; mismanagement of dealings with canal company, 208; Cromwell's determination to avoid payment by New Company to, 211 ff., 385; danger of secession movement in Panama, 216 ff.; chiefs of revolution promise to treat with U. S., 218 f.; seeking to avoid commitment on treaty it desired, 220; reasons for failure to supervise diplomatic discussions with U. S., 222; interests at Panama suffering from war, 227; intraparty divergencies, 227; results of Fernández' methods, 228; canal diplomacy (1901-2), 229 ff.; treaties of Panama, Chinácota, and Nerlandia, 237; lost freedom to negotiate any provision except indemnity, 238; sentiment against signing treaty, 240, 248, 251 ff.; rise of protest in, 241-72; delay in calling Congress, 248, 249; basis of U. S. policy towards, 251; objections to treaty most frequently advanced, 256; discussion of constitutionality of treaty, 256, 260; disappointment caused by financial provisions, 261 ff.; political situation complicated by Caro's return to public life, 266; congress summoned, 267; cabinet crisis, 269; emission of paper money ended, 269; public order declared reëstablished, 271; pressure diplomacy, 273-97; determined not to ratify without previous arrangement with canal and railroad companies, 274, 282, 315, 317; Hay's threat to, 285, 300; congress convened, 298; senatorial debate over Marroquín's signature, 300 ff.; senate committee appointed to report on treaty, 307; scheme to liberalize financial terms of treaty, 307; government triumph in signature fight, 310; deprived of direct telegraphic communication with U. S. and Europe, 310; report of senate committee: proposed amendments to treaty, 314 ff.; plans of senate moderates disrupted by Beaupré, 320; strategy to avert political dangers of situation, 321; treaty debate (Aug. 12), 323 ff.; treaty rejected, 326; new senate committee to work out bases for new canal convention, 327; Ospina–Rodríguez-Campo project of law, 327, 331, 332; political storm, 328 ff.; denunciation of government in congress and press, 329, 330; adjournment of congress, 334; Moore memorandum on obligation to conclude canal treaty with U. S., 343 ff.; secession movement, 353 ff.; alarm as to possible action of U. S., 358; troops sent to Panama, 361; commanders placed under arrest by revolutionists, 362 f.; Panama severed political bonds with, 363; appeal to U. S.: offer to ratify canal treaty as signed, 371; determination to preserve integrity, 372; special commission created to go to Isthmus, 372; news that U. S. had entered into relations with Panama received, 373; orders issued by U. S. to prevent landing of soldiers in new republic, 374; campaign to force rejection of treaty in U. S. Senate, 378; right to make separate agreement with its concessioners challenged by U. S., 386; Roosevelt's failure to comprehend situation in, 387; recognition of Republic of Panama, 393

Colombian Memorandum, *see* Hay-Concha Memorandum

Colombian National Railway, 44

Colombiano, El, 253, 256 ff., 260, 265

Colombians, racial stocks, 36; attacked by Morgan, 197; Roosevelt's slurs on, 308, 345, 351, 352

Colón, excluded from canal zone by

INDEX

Hay-Concha convention, 141; Concha's erroneous cable re inclusion, 162; Morgan demands inclusion, 198; capture by rebels, 1901, 163; exclusion from zone insisted upon, 315; Herrán warns Bogotá on danger of losing, 349; preparations for uprising, 354; Hubbard ordered to prevent landing of Colombian troops, 362; Colombians disembark, 362; Torres threatens Americans in, 366; Hubbard lands sailors, 366; Torres leaves, 367; republic proclaimed, 369; excluded from canal zone, 377
Committee on . . . , see name, e. g., Foreign Relations, Committee on
Compagnie Nouvelle de Panama, see New Panama Canal Company
Compagnie Universelle du Canal Interocéanique, 19; controlling interest in Panama Railroad, 23; collapse, 24; achievements, 25
Compañía de Tránsito de Nicaragua, 15*n*
Concha, José Vicente, 48, 130, 249, 376; instructions issued to, 134 ff.; quoted, 139, 165, 176, 177, 183, 184, 187, 218; treaty project, 140 ff., 212 (*see also* Hay-Concha Memorandum); Hart's failure to deliver instructions to, 141 ff.; hampered by lack of authority, 162, 232; negotiations cut short, 164 ff.; orders re Hay's proposals, 164, 166, 203; attitude toward U. S. intervention in Panama, 173 ff.; resignation refused, 176, 233; interpretation of proper U. S.-Colombia relations on Isthmus, 179 ff.; distaste for continuing negotiations, 180 ff., 188*n;* position weakened by Paúl, 182, 186; audience with Hay, 182; note to Hay, 183, 186, 214; Hay's reply to, 185; decision to place Herrán in charge of legation, 185; asked credentials for Herrán, 186; commentary on Hay's note, 186; unacknowledged by Hay, 187; turned legation over to Herrán, 188; decisive steps of negotiations taken on own initiative, 203, 229; failure to secure understanding with New Company, 213

Concord, ordered to Panama, 362
Concordat of 1888, 197, 198
Cooper, Henry A., 151
Corea, Señor, 145
Correo Nacional, El, 253, 254, 255, 260-66 *passim,* 289; questionnaire, 263
Cortés, Enrique, 128, 264; Root-Cortés and Cortés-Arosemena conventions, 391*n*
Costa Rica, under British influence, 15; concession granted to Menocal for Nicaragua canal, 25; prepared to grant necessary control to U. S., 105, 189; Hay's negotiations with, 143 ff.; treaty draft submitted to Calvo, 145*n;* political advantages of dealing with, cited by Morgan, 149
Cragin, Edward F., 30; *see also* Grace-Eyre-Cragin syndicate
Cromwell, William Nelson, counsel for New Company, 32, 75 ff., 106, 109; alleged contribution to Republican campaign fund, 78, 102, 122*n;* quoted, 79, 80, 81, 99*n,* 112, 125, 274, 280; strategy, 82, 84, 273; working to block Morgan bill, 88; trips to France, 91, 353; proposal to reincorporate New Company as an American enterprise and sell control to U. S., 89, 92, 101; difficulties threatening plans, 108; dismissed, 112, 113; reinstated, 121, 123; made possible the adoption of Panama route, 122; claimed credit for Spooner amendment, 123 ff.; wish to bind Colombia by a treaty project, 133; conferences with Concha, 136; compromise scheme agreed to by Concha, 140; effort to secure consent of New Company shareholders to sale of property, 146; furnished data for Hanna speeches, 153*n;* conversations with Concha on Hay amendments, 159; efforts to defeat Morgan amendments, 198; circumvention of Marroquín's scheme, 208; determination to evade cash payment by company, 211 ff., 385; master stroke, 275 ff.; significance of success in committing U. S. government to furtherance of his aims, 283; inspired Hay's threat to Colombia, 285; contacts with of-

Cromwell, William Nelson (*Continued*) ficials of Panama Railroad Company, 287; use of contacts on Isthmus, 290; stratagem to force Colombian senate's approval of treaty, 293; artful methods used to influence Hay, 296; playing with idea of revolution in Panama, 335; support of separatist project, 339, 347, 349; Herrán's warning to, 349; fear that Colombia would cancel concessions, 350; role in fight for Canal, 385
Cuba, imposition of Platt Amendment upon, 70
Culebra, island, granted to U. S. by Bunau-Varilla treaty, 377
Culebra Cut, 31n
Cullom, Shelby, 99n, 118, 151, 154, 192, 384; quoted, 199, 340
Cundinamarca, 56
Curtis, William J., 146, 353

Danish West Indies, amount offered by U. S. for, 261; alleged German responsibility for blocking sale to U. S., 312
Darien, isthmus of: proposed canal across, 20, 29n
Davey, Robert C., 156
Davis, C. H., 29n
Davis, Cushman K., 98n, 99n
Davis Amendment, Hay-Pauncefote treaty, 105n, 106
Decker, Howell & Co., 77n
Dennett, Tyler, 281
Dickinson-Ayon treaty of 1867, 19
Disraeli, Benjamin, 18
Dixie, 358; ordered to Colón, 362; at Colón, 367, 368
Donaldson, Chester, 30n
Du Bois, ex-Minister, quoted, 41n
Duque, José Gabriel, 291, 338; offered presidency of Panama?, 347; warning to Herrán, 348; letters to Hay, 348n; Panama fire brigade, 354, 360
Durán, Facundo Mutis, *see* Mutis Durán, Facundo

Earthquakes in Central America, 147, 151
Ecuador, independent republic, 46

Ehrman, Felix, 171, 363, 365; reported creation of new Panama republic, 368, 369
Engineers, preference of American, for Nicaragua route, 29; French, 77; trend of American engineering opinion toward Panama route, 104n; *see* International Technical Commission
Ernst, Oswald, 91, 92, 115
Esguerra, Nicolás, 58, 59
Espinosa, Eduardo, 225
Espinosa B., Manuel, 338, 369
Estrella de Panamá, La, 253, 290, 291, 292
Evarts, William M., 20, 69, 70
Eyre, Edward, 30

Fairbanks, Charles W., 151
Farnham, Roger L., 293, 347
Fernández, Aristides, 61, 174, 223, 267; treatment of prisoners of war, 224; character, 226; result of methods, 228; made minister of state, 248; invited press discussion of treaty, 250, 253; ultimatum to cabinet, 270; resignation, 271
Fernández M., Julio, 255
Fillmore, Millard, 29n
Fish, Hamilton, 17; quoted, 18; attempt to revise Dickinson-Ayon treaty, 19
Flamenco, island, granted to U. S., 377
Fletcher, Loren, 156
Fonseca, Bay of, 14
Foraker, Joseph B., 105n
Foreign Relations, Committee on, 98, 99n; Hay-Herrán treaty committed to, 196
Frelinghuysen, Frederick T., 22
Frelinghuysen-Zavala treaty, 22
French, in Indies, 7; attempts to build canal, 19 (*see also* Compagnie Universelle . . . ; Lesseps; New Panama Canal Company); government disclaims intention of supporting de Lesseps, 21

Gallinger, Jacob H., 151
Garcés, Modesto, 219n
Garfield, James A., 21
Gerlein, Eduardo B., 307, 316
Germany, suspected of nurturing ex-

INDEX

pansionist schemes, 312; disclaims intention to intervene in canal question, 314
Glass, Admiral, ordered to Acapulco, 357; ordered to Panama, 362
Goethals, George W., 392 f.
Gold rush, transport routes, 14n, 15
González, Luis V., reply to Caro, 304
González Valencia, José María, 188, 316
Gorgas, William C., 392
Grace, William R., 30
Grace-Eyre-Cragin syndicate, 30, 88n, 100n
Granadan Confederation, 46
Grant, U. S., 67; "exclusive control" principle embodied in foreign policy, 17; interoceanic canal commission, 18, 29
Granville, Lord: correspondence with Blaine, 21
Great Britain, concern in Isthmus, 8; treaty with Spain, 1786, 9; efforts to secure interests in Central America, 14; alleged failure to fulfill terms of Clayton-Bulwer treaty, 22; Anglo-American rivalry in Central America, 67; displaced as most active power in Central America and the Caribbean, 68; attitude toward Clayton-Bulwer treaty, 72 (*see also* Clayton-Bulwer treaty); re her ratification of amended Hay-Pauncefote treaty, 106; rejection of Hay-Pauncefote treaty amendments, 108 (*see also* Hay-Pauncefote treaty); second Hay-Pauncefote treaty accepted, 117; willing to permit U. S. a free hand in canal, 265, 314
Greater Republic of Central America, 81; *see also* Central America
Greytown, 19; *see also* San Juan
Greytown-Brito route, 18, 29
Groot, Francisco, 206, 210, 233n, 252n; regarded treaty with U. S. as protection against European imperialism, 217
Grow, Galusha A., 89n
Grünau, Baron, 314
Guadalupe, mountain, 42
Guantanamo, 358
Guatemala, 14; under British influence, 15
Gudger, Hezekiah A., 338

Hague Tribunal, 195, 206
Hains, Peter C., 28, 91
Hall, Henry N., 76, 174, 219n, 337, 347, 357n, 359n
Hanna, Marcus A., 75, 78, 119, 133, 154, 156; championship of Panama route, 102 ff.; quoted, 104n, 114, 121, 122; carried Panama fight to Senate, 123; adoption of Panama route credited to, 151 ff.; had no part in scheme to dig canal despite Colombia, 352; death, 384
Hanna Minority Report, 146
Harding, Warren G., 393
Harris, William A., 154
Harrison, Benjamin, 26n
Hart, Charles Burdett, 131, 174, 282, 348; entrusted with Colombia's proposed treaty bases, 138, 140 ff.; failure to deliver instructions to Concha, 141 ff.; quoted, 170, 177, 182, 194, 222, 248; reply to Hay's demand for Colombian statement re canal, 238; failure to see diplomatic picture whole, 244; resignation, 245; agrees to introduce Duque to Secretary Hay, 348
Hatfield, Commander, 29n
Haupt, Lewis, 28, 86n, 90n, 91, 121n, 154
Hay, John, 93, 95, 99n, 117, 139, 145, 159, 179, 313; parleys with Pauncefote, 93 f.; hurt by press criticism, 98; protocols with ministers of Nicaragua and Costa Rica, 105; conference with Silva, 110; senatorial support on second Hay-Pauncefote treaty, 118; negotiations with Nicaragua and Costa Rica, 143; Concha-Hay negotiations, 150; task of drafting treaty, 157 (*see also* Hay-Herrán treaty); proposed amendments to April Memorandum, 160 ff.; warning to Concha, 181; dilemma re interpretation of treaty of 1846, 183; reply to Concha, 185; Concha's commentary on note, 186; failure to answer Concha, 187; cable to Hart re end of concessions to Colombia, 187; Herrán's conferences re compensation, 190; delivered ultimatum to Herrán, 195; serious distortion of fact, 202, 287; prompt statement re canal demanded, 238;

Hay, John (*Continued*)
dispatch to Beaupré one of gravest missteps of career, 275 ff.; repeated yielding to Cromwell, 281; threat to Colombia, 285, 300, 346; policy towards Colombia influenced by Cromwell, 296; on amendment to Hay-Herrán treaty, 308; asked by Beaupré for definite statement of policy, 309, 310, 311; instructions to Beaupré re amendments to treaty, 319; advising caution to Roosevelt, 340, 350; cable to Beaupré re Isthmian Canal Statute, 346; meeting with Duque, 348; to Adee re Cromwell, 352; re movement of warships towards Isthmus, 356, 357; cable to Ehrman re recognition of Republic of Panama, 370; part in formulation of Bunau-Varilla treaty, 375 (*see also* Hay–Bunau-Varilla treaty); declared treaty not advantageous to Panama, 383; allowed free hand, 386; withdrawn to advisory position, 387

Hay–Bunau-Varilla treaty, 377; negotiation of, 374 ff.; tidings of, to Boyd and Amador, 378; stormy Senate debate, 384; ratification advised, 384

Hay-Concha Memorandum, negotiation of, 139 ff.; provisions, 141 f., 158, 179 ff.; amendments proposed by Hay, 160 f.; Concha obliged to subscribe to, on own authority, 203; reception in Bogotá, 206

Hay-Herrán treaty, circumstances which shaped course of negotiations, 33; negotiation of, 157-99; sent to Foreign Relations Committee, 196; changes demanded by Morgan, 198; Herrán's dilemma, 200-240; economic benefits a factor in Colombian signature, 216; rise of protest in Colombia, 241-72; questions of sovereignty and constitutionality discussed in press, 256 ff.; objections most frequently advanced, 256, 264; U. S. shielding of New Company contributed to defeat, 283; defeat in Colombian senate, 298-334; liberalization of financial terms sought, 307; opinion that pact would be ratified with amendments, 308, 310, 311; amendments suggested, 308, 310, 311; Beaupré's opinion on modification, 311; New Company's stockholders coöperating against, 313 (*see also* New Panama Canal Company); amendments reasonable and statesmanlike, 317; Beaupré's assertion that amendments would not be considered, 318; debate of Aug. 12, 323 ff.; defeat of treaty, 326; Ospina–Rodríguez–Campo committee to work out bases for new convention, 327; project of law submitted, 327, 331, 332; Colombian senate's vote to suspend consideration of amendments, 333; defeat not a surprise to U. S. officials, 335; Colombia's obligation to continue parleys, 345; Colombian public reaction in favor of, 372; believed not legally rejected, 372; Roosevelt considers terms overgenerous, 381, 384n; Colombian disappointment at terms, 389; pressures combining to defeat, 389

Hay-Pauncefote treaty (first), 71, 96; opposition to neutrality and nonfortification provisions, 97 ff.; ratified with amendments, 105; amendments rejected by Britain, 108

Hay-Pauncefote treaty (second), negotiations, 117; ratified, 118

Hayes, Rutherford B., 20, 67, 69

Henríquez, Juan Antonio, 290, 338n

Hepburn, William P., 98, 156; Morgan-Hepburn rivalry over authorship of canal act, 86 f.

Hepburn bill, 105, 106, 118; introduced into Congress, 94; passed House, 100, 105; Senate vote delayed, 107n; adopted, 120; Spooner amendment, 123 ff., 147 (*see also* Spooner amendment); Morgan Committee's action on, 137; debate, 147; dispute referred to conference committee, 156; substitution of Hanna minority report for, 191

Herrán, Tomás, 182, 185, 193; placed in charge of canal negotiations, 188; equipment for work, 189; conferences with Hay re compensation, 190; confusion over credentials, 193n; instructed to insist upon Concha amendments, 194; kept in ignorance of new orders, 194; signed treaty, 195; ordered

INDEX

not to sign treaty, 196, 200, 239, 241, 247; Paúl's instructions to, 239; assented under pressure to meager indemnity, 284; warning against transcontinental railroads, 313; reaction to Colombian senate's recommendations, 339; cable re revolutionary movement on Isthmus, 348; events accurately predicted, 349; warning to Cromwell and New Company, 349; *see also* Hay-Herrán treaty
Herrera, Benjamín, 56, 173; insurgent army, 163, 169; signed treaty of Panama, 236 f.
Herrick, Myron, 114
Hill, David Jayne, 219n
Hill, Edward B., 146n, 242, 281, 353
Hise, Elijah, 14, 15
Hitchcock, Hiram, 30n, 89n, 100n
Hoar, George F., 154
Holguín, Carlos, 50
Honduras, looked to U. S. for aid, 14
Hornby, Admiral, 15
Hubbard, Commander, 364; order prohibiting transport of troops across Isthmus, 365 f.; landed sailors at Colón, 366; quoted, 382
Huertas, Esteban, 360, 363
Humbolt, Alexander von, 6n
Humphrey, Chauncey B., 353
Hutin, Maurice, 91, 92, 111, 115, 208; resignation, 118

Iglesias, President, 144
Indians, in Colombia, 36
Intercoastal communication, need for closer, 28
International congress to decide canal route, 19
International Technical Commission, 83, 84, 91
Interoceanic canal commission, Grant's, 18, 29
Interoceanic Canals, Committee on, 100, 103, 123, 154; action on Hepburn bill and Spooner amendment, 137
Interstate and Foreign Commerce, Committee on, 80, 86 ff.; report on Morgan bill, 87
Iriarte, Clímaco, 206, 233n, 260
Isaza, Luis M., quoted, 217
Isthmian canal, *see* Panama Canal

Isthmian Canal Commission (Walker Commission), 95, 99, 101, 105, 108, 124, 126, 153, 386; created by act of Congress, 90; membership named, 91; in Paris, 91 f.; left for Isthmus, 94n; examined by Committee on Interoceanic Canals, 100; filed preliminary report, 104; correspondence with Silva, 111 f.; failure to elicit definite figure of sale from Hutin, 115; filed final report favoring Nicaragua, 115 f.; received New Company's offer to sell, 119; convoked by Roosevelt, 120 f.; filed supplementary report favoring Panama, 121; possible share in drafting Spooner amendment, 125; questioned by Morgan's committee, 125; replies of members, cited by Hanna, 154
Isthmian Canal Statute, *see* Spooner Act

Jackson, Andrew, 11
Jesuits, expelled from Colombia, 47
Jesup, Morris K., 114n
Johnson, Emory, 91
Junta, 335, 337, 338, 358, 374, 376, 377

Kittredge, A. B., 151, 156
Knox, Philander C., 157, 197, 375

Lampré, Edouard, 119
Lansdowne, Lord, 106n, 117; rejected Hay-Pauncefote treaty amendments, 108
Latin America, British policy to prevent alliances between U. S. and, 9; trade contacts with U. S., 10; apprehension re activities of U. S., 68; effect of Spanish-American War and its aftermath, 70; Roosevelt's decisive share in isthmian coup a source of future ill will in, 380; *see also* Central America
Leo XIII, Pope, 197
Lesseps, Ferdinand de, canal venture in Central America, 19 ff.; tour of cities in U. S., 23; collapse of venture, 24
Lesseps, de, company, *see* Compagnie Universelle du Canal Interocéanique
Limón, Gulf of: canal from Bay of Panama to, estimated cost, 19

INDEX

Lindo, J. J., 376
Lodge, Henry Cabot, 70, 99n, 105n, 118, 154, 384; quoted, 106n; advised modification of Spooner Act, 351
Loomis, Francis B., 340, 363, 368; on views of Professor Moore, 341n
López, R. Valdés, see Valdés López
Ludlow, William, 28
Ludlow Commission, 28, 79
Lull, Commander, 29n

McBride, George W., 106n
McFarland, Walter, 29n
McKinley, William, 28, 81, 84, 99; supporter of Nicaragua route, 85, 88; quoted, 104n; shooting of, 115; embarrassments owing to New Company's activities, 150; uncommitted to either route, 154
McLean, Commander, marines of, accompany trains across Isthmus, 170, 175; excludes both federals and rebels from use of railroad, 170, 177; ordered to use influence to bring about peace on Isthmus, 235
MacVeagh, Wayne, 378
Magdalena River, 33, 43, 47
Mallarino, Manuel María, 12
Malmros, Consul, 363, 364, 365, 370
Mancini, Alexander, 57, 58, 59, 215, 267, 281, 331
Marblehead, ordered to Panama, 362
Maritime Canal Company of Nicaragua, 25 ff., 79, 81; American capital invested in, 29; Nicaragua losing interest in, 30; stockholders willing to sell, 85; proposal to transfer control to U. S., 87; concessions declared null and void, 88n; rights expired, 149
Marroquín, José Manuel, 53, 55, 60, 73, 74, 389; officials of his government, 41; made vice-president with executive power, 54; accession to power, 61; sends Silva to Washington, 63; quoted, 130, 218, 231, 233, 234, 236n, 246; limitations upon power, 131, 243; decision to cut short Concha negotiations, 164; cable ordering Herrán not to sign treaty, 196, 200; desire to avoid treaty conversations during civil war, 201; lacked legal authority to ratify treaty, 202; decline in popularity, 223; intraparty divergencies, 227; offer of amnesty to Liberals, 228; troubled by specter of U. S. intervention, 229; U. S. press version of position, 243; intention to place responsibility for accepting convention on legislature, 245, 247; proclaims restoration of public order, 271; address to legislature, 298; failure to place signature on Hay-Herrán treaty, 300 ff.; attacked by Caro, 301, 304; defended, 304 ff.; removal of governors, 329; manifesto, 334; resignation called for, 371; hostility to, faded, 372; Roosevelt's misunderstanding of, 387 f.
Marroquín, Lorenzo, 174, 321, 330
Martínez Silva, Carlos, 48, 60n, 62, 158, 249; mission to U. S., 63, 73, 74, 109 ff.; change in views, 112; failure to procure instructions from Colombia, 126 ff.; quoted, 126n, 127, 128, 209, 217, 221, 227; submitted treaty draft on own authority, 128, 139n, 229, 230, 232; provisions, 129; recalled, 130, 131, 230; authorized negotiations between New Company and U. S., 143; power limited to propaganda campaign, 203; analysis of canal situation, 205; desire for fixed annuity, 207; acceptance of Hutin's letter, 208; tactical blunder, 209; regarded treaty with U. S. as protection against European imperialism, 217; correspondence with Uribe Uribe, 227
Martínez Silva, Luis, 60, 225
Meléndez, Porfirio, 366, 369
Memorandum of April 18; see Hay-Concha Memorandum
Mendoza, Carlos A., 163, 293, 338n
Menocal, A. G., 19n, 25n, 29n
Merry, William L., 100n, 144, 148
Mestizos, 36
Milla, Manuel, 6n
Mitchell, John H., 153
Momotombo, Mt., 147, 148
Monroe Doctrine, 9, 20, 22
Monsalve D., F. A., 259
Moody, William Henry, 181, 357
Moore, John Bassett, 17, 98n; memoran-

dum interpreting rights of U. S. under treaty of 1846, 341 ff., 380; emphasis upon diplomatic solution of canal problem, 345, 350; impression of Bunau-Varilla, 355; assistance to Roosevelt, 380, 383n

Morales, Eusebio A., 51n, 163, 173, 338n

Morgan, John T., 26, 84, 85n, 96n, 99n, 107n, 156; passage of his 1898 canal bill by Senate, 85; Morgan-Hepburn rivalry over authorship of canal act, 86 f.; support of Hepburn bill, 100; attacks Cromwell, 100, 149 ff.; leads assault on Panama route, 147; attempt to limit period of negotiation with Colombia, 154; suggested acquisition of state of Panama, 159n; urged concluding treaties with Costa Rica and Nicaragua, 189; enthusiasm for Nicaragua route, 196, 380; attacks on Colombia, 196n, 197; assault on Hay-Herrán treaty, 197 f.; opposition to Hay–Bunau-Varilla treaty, 384

Morgan bill of 1898, adopted by Senate, 85; Hepburn committee report on, 87; attached to Rivers and Harbors bill, 89; blocked in Senate, 107

Morison, George S., 91, 92, 114

Morse, Isaac, 69

Morton, Levi P., 30

Mosquera, Tomás de, 46, 50

Mosquito Coast, 9, 10; British protectorate, 16; failure of Clayton-Bulwer treaty to force British from, 17

Murphy, Grayson M. P., report of affairs on Isthmus, 353

Mutis Durán, Facundo, 128, 130, 218n, 288

Naos, island, granted to U. S., 377

Narváez, Enrique de, 307

Nashville, instructed to maintain free transit of Isthmus, 362, 364, 365; guns trained on Colón, 366

Negroes in Colombia, 36, 37

Nel Ospina, Pedro, 231, 249, 307, 310, 316; imprisoned by Fernández, 224, 225, 307; rebuke to Arango, 307; arguments re Hay-Herrán treaty, 325; Ospina–Rodríguez-Campo project of law, 327, 331, 332; warning of new revolution, 330; a delegate to Isthmus, 372

Nerlandia, treaty of, 237

New Company, *see* New Panama Canal Company

New Granada, treaty of 1846 with U. S. (*see* Treaty of 1846–48); granted Aspinwall group concession to build railroad, 14n; part of first Republic of Colombia, 46; transformed into Granadan Confederation, 46; envoy to sound out foreign governments re canal concessions, 64; creation of autonomous zone urged upon, 69

New Panama Canal Company, 30, 72; capital, 31; Wyse concession taken over by, 57; extension of franchise, 57 ff.; requests Colombia to send diplomat to Washington, 63; lobby, 75, 287; advisory duties undertaken by Sullivan & Cromwell, 79; attempt to interest U. S. in Panama route, 82; refusal of franchise extension reported in U. S., 84; Cromwell's plan to reincorporate, 89 (*see also* Cromwell, W. N.); shareholders' refusal to transfer assets, 92; requested to submit price on property, 104; reincorporation proposed, 104n; Cromwell dismissed, 112, 113; proposal to arbitrate purchase price, 115; value of property and concessions stated, 116; predicament, 118; offer to sell, 119, 209; Cromwell reinstated as counsel, 121; U. S. authorized to purchase property of, 123 (*see also* Spooner amendment to Hepburn bill); re Colombia's consent to sell property to U. S., 127, 146, 211 ff., 276 ff., 377; Colombia forbade transfer to U. S., 133; Colombia's effort to force, to share indemnity, 134 ff., 194, 207 ff., 211, 215, 239, 273, 281; titles to property pronounced defective, 137; extension of concession opposed by Colombian Liberals, 149; Spooner Act authorizes U. S. to acquire property of, 156; legal titles endorsed by French jurists, 157; report of German offer for rights of, 194, 312; necessity of canceling contracts with Colombia, 194, 215, 273, 282, 315; extension of

New Panama Canal Company (*Cont.*) option granted U. S., 197; Colombian expectation of payment from, 207, 209 ff., 281, 283; Cromwell's determination to avoid payment by, to Colombia, 208, 211 ff., 273 ff., 385; Colombian warning to stockholders, 211; control over Panama Railroad, 213; Hay permitted confidential instructions to be inspected by, 280; approval of Cromwell's stratagem, 293; change in status of concessions viewed as violation of Spooner law, 311; Colombian conditions of transfer of concession, 328; validity of Sanclemente extension of franchise, 331, 332; implicated in isthmian secession movement, 348; confidence in Roosevelt's policy, 353; U. S. interference with agreement with Colombia, 386

Newspapers, *see* Press

Nicaragua, Republic of: ordered from mouth of San Juan, looked to U. S. for aid, 14; Hise and Squier conventions with, 15; principles of Clayton-Bulwer treaty applicable to, 17; Greytown-Brito line, 18; Dickinson-Ayon treaty with, 19; Frelinghuysen-Zavala pact, 22; American capitalists plan project through, 25; work begun, 25; part of Greater Republic of Central America, 81; cancellation of Maritime concessions, 100; Atlas Steamship Co. contract, 107*n*; Hay's negotiations with, 143 ff.; believed its route only one possible, 145; physiographical disturbances, 147, 148, 151, 152*n*; political advantages of dealing with, 149; prepared to sign U. S. terms, 189; again considered after failure of Hay-Herrán treaty, 340, 342, 345, 346, 351, 352, 386

Nicaragua, Lake, 4, 6, 147, 148, 149*n*

Nicaragua Canal Association, 25*n*

Nicaragua route, estimated cost, 12; stipulations of Clayton-Bulwer treaty re, 16, 68; internationalization policy favored by Cleveland, 22; Morgan's enthusiasm for, 26, 196, 380 (*see also* Morgan, J. T.); public sentiment in U. S. in favor of, 27, 29, 32, 75, 80, 83, 85; advantages to South, 27*n*; Walker Commission's report on, 28, 104 (*see also* Walker Commission); earliest survey, 29*n*; sponsored by Democrats, 103; Hepburn bill (*see* Hepburn bill); canal route control, 105; engineering expense, 116; scale turned by volcanoes in West Indies, 147, 152; defeat charged to Hanna, 151, 152*n*; renewed activity of supporters, 189; disparity in costs between Panama Canal and, 206

Nietro Caballero, Lucas E., 173, 223, 226, 236, 372

Noble, Alfred, 91, 114*n*

Núñez, Rafael, 47 ff., 226; new constitution, 48

Obaldía, José de, 210, 288, 300, 307, 316; at treaty debate, 326; suspected of secessionist sympathies, 329, 330; appointed governor of Panama, 329, 333; arrest, 360, 363

Obarrio, Nicanor A. de, 338

Olney, Richard, 22

Ospina, Pedro Nel, *see* Nel Ospina

Padilla, 360, 361

Palmerston, Viscount, 14, 15, 16

Panama, Bay of: canal from, to Gulf of Limón estimated cost of, 19; islands as coaling stations, 128; small islands granted to U. S., 377

Panama, Isthmus of, projects for canal across, 3-32; post road constructed, 6*n*; railroad across, 14*n*; negligence, extravagance, heroism of French, 25; events leading to separation from Colombia, 39; part of first Republic of Colombia, 46; regarded by Blaine as politically within North American sphere of influence, 67; defense, 69, 70, 161, 180 ff., 198; sea-level canal practicable only at, 78; seismic instability, 147, 148; struggle between political parties, 163 ff., 201, 202; U. S. interventions prior to 1902, 166 ff.; intervention in fall of 1902, 169 ff.; neutrality of transportation system, 169, 170; U. S. naval forces landed to guard railroad, 170, 175, 235; U. S. suspected of encouraging secession of, 178; U. S. intervention requested by

INDEX 463

Marroquín, 234 ff.; congressional elections, 288; secession threatened, 300, 329, 330; Obaldía appointed governor, 329, 333; revolution of 1903, 335-70; *junta*, 335, 337, 338; condition of country at outbreak of revolution, 336; republic under protection of U. S. advocated, 339, 347; Adee's advice to avoid precipitate action, 345; Humphrey-Murphy picture of affairs on, 353 ff.; police forces, 354, 360; secret treaty of alliance with U. S. expected, 358; revolutionary plan extended to whole of, 359; conspirators counting on aid from U. S. fleet, 359, 360; political bonds with Colombia severed, 363 f.; uprising: *de facto* government, 364; questions of Roosevelt's advance knowledge of revolution raised, 380; Roosevelt acted as his own foreign minister with regard to, 387

Panama, Republic of: established, 367; survival dependent upon recognition and protection of U. S., 367; declaration of independence read, 369; immediate consequences of creation of new republic, 371; *junta* delegation sent to U. S., 374; delegation in New York, 376, 377; Hay–Bunau-Varilla treaty, 377, 378, 384; pecuniary compensation for canal, 377

Panama, treaty of, Nov. 1902, 237, 246

Panama Canal, historical roots of story, 3 ff.; a potential source of danger to Spanish colonies, 7; neutralization of, 13, 16, 58, 65, 66, 67, 96, 106, 108, 118; applicability of Clayton-Bulwer treaty to, 17; question of international or American control, 17; sole right to construct, assigned to U. S. by treaties of 1869 and 1870, 18; Colombia's sovereignty recognized, 18; sea-level route, 19, 78, 100; French attempts to build, 19 (*see also* Compagnie Universelle . . .); excavation started, 23; system of locks substituted for sea-level plan, 24; collapse of the de Lesseps company, 24; heroism and suffering of French, 25; extension of New Company's franchise, 57 ff. (*see also* New Panama Canal Company); Colombian preference for private company, 58n; importance to Colombia, 63; principal problems from Colombian point of view, 64 ff.; defense, 65 ff.; principal leaders of campaign for, 75 ff.; not adopted solely on basis of its merits, 75; story of, replete with intrigue, 76; Cromwell and Bunau-Varilla claimed credit for adoption of route, 78; report of the International Technical Commission, 83 f.; Cromwell brings New Company campaign into open, 84 f.; creation of Isthmian Canal Commission, 86 ff.; provisions of first Hay-Pauncefote treaty, 96 f.; Walker Commission's preliminary report on, 104; growing popularity with press, 104n; Colombian attitude towards construction of, 109 ff., 132; Silva's memorandum on, 112; Bunau-Varilla's efforts to arouse interest in, 113 ff.; Walker Commission's final report, 115 f.; estimated engineering expense, 116; terms of second Hay-Pauncefote treaty, 117 ff.; triumph of route, 117-56; supplementary report of Walker Commission, 120 f.; introduction of Spooner amendment, 123 ff.; indemnity and annuity, 128, 134, 140, 190, 192n, 198, 207, 261, 284; Silva's treaty project, 128 ff.; Concha's negotiations with Hay, 139 ff.; debate on Hepburn bill, 147 ff.; minority's reasons for preferring, 152; passage of Spooner Act, 154 ff.; disparity in costs between Nicaragua Canal and, 206; right of U. S. to construct and operate, under treaty of 1846, 343, 344, 346 ff., 353; Gorgas and construction of, 392; *see also* Colombia; New Panama Canal Company; treaties under names of treaties; United States

Panama Canal zone, policing rights: sanitary regulation, 118, 128, 160, 198, 316; U. S. control of, 123, 127, 156, 158, 160, 254 ff., 284, 315 f., 377; administration of justice, 129, 141, 158, 160, 257 f., 315 f., 377; inclusion of Colón and Panama City, 162, 198; property evaluation, 261, 316; exclusion of cities demanded, 315; Hay–Bunau-Varilla treaty, 377

Panama City, excluded from canal zone, 129, 141, 315, 377; question of inclusion in zone raised, 162, 198; unsuccessful attack on, by Porras, 163; Herrera's army closes in on, 169, 234; U. S. naval vessels ordered to, 169, 356 ff.; in danger of capture by insurgents, 169, 171 f.; Perdomo permitted to send troops from Colón to, 172, 236; Herrera signs treaty of peace, 173, 237; separatist *junta,* 335, 337, 338, 358; Hay's reported interview with Duque concerning possible revolution in, 348; strategic importance to Colombia, 349; preparations for revolution in, 354; conspirators in, 358; Colombian generals lured from Colón to, 362 f.; revolution breaks out, 363 ff.; provisional government established, 364

Panama Company of America, 92

Panamanians, possibility of secession movement, 129, 139, 216 ff., 294, 336, 348 f., 353 f., 356, 359; importance of canal to, 139, 336; attitude towards civil war, 163; attacked by Morgan, 197; unanimity of support for canal, 218*n*; attitude toward Hay-Herrán treaty, 288 ff.; slight attachment for rest of Colombia, 336

Panama Railroad Company, 69, 85*n*, 150; controlling interest, 23; right to exact damages for construction of canal across Isthmus of Panama, 23, 213, 331; Cromwell counsel for, 76; price for Colombia's surrender of annuity and reversionary rights, 134 f., 190, 199, 207, 261 f., 328; granted permission to transfer concession, 141, 213, 328, 377; occupied by U. S. troops, 166 ff., 175 ff., 235 f.; Colombian insistence upon necessity of previous arrangement for transfer of concession, 187, 194, 214 ff., 273 ff., 282 f., 286, 315, 317, 328 (*see also* New Panama Canal Company); protection of by Department of State, 214 ff., 274 ff., 286; penalty for transfer of privileges to foreign government, 278; officials, 287 f.; dependence of Isthmus upon, 336; implicated in isthmian secession movement, 337, 348, 362 ff.; Cromwell wires officials on Isthmus to avoid revolutionary activities, 349; declined to transport troops, 364 f.; ordered not to transport troops, 365 f.

Pan-American Congress, Second, 113

Parra, Aquileo, 60, 61, 62

Pasco, Samuel, 91, 154

Paúl, Felipe, 131, 164, 234*n*; treaty proposals, 138; protests actions of U. S. forces on Isthmus, 177 ff.; weakens Concha's position, 182, 186; instructions to Concha, 184; failure to confide in representative, 235; instructions to Herrán, 238 f.; resignation, 247; desire to give publicity to canal question, 253

Pauncefote, Lord, 93*n*, 117; parleys with Hay, 94; *see also* Hay-Pauncefote treaty

Pavey, Frank D., 376*n*

Pedrarias, governor of Nicaragua, 4

Pelée, Mont, 147, 149*n*, 152*n*

Perdomo, Nicolás, 172, 235, 236, 271

Pérez y Soto, Juan B., 288, 289, 326, 372; objections to treaty, 316; resolution re governor of Panama, 330

Pérez y Soto committee, 307, 314 ff., 339

Perico, island, granted to U. S., 377

Perkins, George C., 153

Philip II, interest in Nicaragua route, 6; religious fear of joining oceans, 6

Philip III, interest in interoceanic canal, 6*n*

Pierce, Franklin, 69

Pinto, General, 272

Pinzón, General, 61

Piza, Nephews & Company, 376

Platt, Orville H., 114*n*, 151

Platt Amendment, 70, 312

Polk, James Knox, 66, 343; expansionist policy, 12; Central American policy, 14

Porras, Belisario, 163, 293

Potter, Commander, 169, 175

Prescott, Herbert G., 288, 339, 358, 362, 363

Press, American: attacks on first Hay-Pauncefote treaty, 97; on relative merits of sites, 120; on passage of Spooner Act by Senate, 155; comment on choice of Panama route, 241; ignorance on Colombian affairs, 243;

INDEX

rumors of Colombian opposition, 249; questions re Roosevelt's advance knowledge of Panama revolution, 380
Press, Colombian: Beaupré's reports on censorship, 250 f.; censorship lifted re canal discussions, 252 ff.; signs of bitterness increased, 254 f.; opinion expressed in, regarding canal negotiations, 256 ff.; opinion in Department of Panama, 289 ff.; pleas for submergence of feuds, 297; denunciation of government, 329; partisan attacks suspended, 372
Press, French: pro-Spanish tone, 82
Press Publishing Co., U. S. v., 359n
Prisoners of war, Fernández' treatment of, 224
Pulecio, Gerardo, 262

Quesada, Gonzalo Jiménez de, 41
Quintero Calderón, Guillermo, 310; report on Ospina–Rodríguez-Campo project of law, 331, 332

Rainey, Henry T., 76, 102, 152
Ramírez A., Samuel, 262
Reed, Thomas B., 86, 88, 90
Republican party, Cromwell's alleged contribution to campaign funds, 78, 102, 122n; change in canal plank, 101
Restrepo, Antonio José, 228
Reyes, Rafael, 58, 196n, 215, 225, 248, 308, 321, 326, 389; as presidential nominee, 52, 54, 267, 329; interviews with Beaupré, 268 f., 307, 309; amendments to Hay-Herrán treaty suggested, 307 ff.; anticipated reaction in public sentiment toward treaty, 327; appeal to U. S., 371, 372; sent as delegate to Isthmus, 372; mission to Panama futile, 374; efforts to force rejection of Hay–Bunau-Varilla treaty, 378; correspondence with Hay, 383
Rico, Luis Carlos, minister of foreign affairs, 247; re U. S. warning to Colombia, 285; counter-memorandum to American legation, 286; failure to sign Hay-Herrán treaty, 300; reply to Caro, 304; effort to draw Beaupré out, 322; Rico-Beaupré correspondence, 323; address in treaty debate, 325; denounced action of U. S., 337
Rivas Groot, José María, 307, 316
Rivers and Harbors bill of 1899, Morgan's canal bill attached to, 89
Rives, W. C., 16
Rodríguez, minister of Greater Republic of Central America, 81
Rodríguez, Celso, 219n
Rodríguez, Manuel María, 326; Ospina–Rodríguez-Campo project of law, 327 f., 331, 332
Roman Catholic Church in Colombia, 36, 42, 47; Catholicism the state religion, 49; Núñez' concordat with Vatican, 50; Morgan's attack upon influence in Colombia, 197 f.; Conservative doctrine of coöperation with, 201
Roosevelt, Franklin D., 393
Roosevelt, Theodore, 41, 70, 98, 118, 182, 283; vigorous canal policy, 115; eager to start work on Isthmus, 120, 349; in favor of Panama route, 124, 192; tactical problems raised, 124; suggested purchase of Isthmus, 160n; orders McLean to use offices for peace on Isthmus, 170; deadline for Colombia's acceptance of treaty, 191, 195; roused resentment among Colombians, 265; influenced by Cromwell, 285; interest in secession of Panama, 294, 356, 359; slurs on Colombians, 308, 345, 351, 352; interview with Cullom, 340; interpretation of treaty of 1846 influenced by Moore, 341, 350, 380; note to Hay re Moore memorandum, 345; threatening statements, 349; reply to Hay re delay in Colombia matter, 351; decision to dig canal despite Colombia, 352 f.; receives Humphrey-Murphy report on isthmian conditions, 353; talk with Bunau-Varilla, 356; aware that outbreak imminent at Panama, 359; to Bigelow re Bunau-Varilla, 359n; decision re recognition of Republic of Panama, 370; attempt to justify his course, 378 ff.; considered Hay-Herrán treaty overgenerous toward Colombia, 381, 384n; allowed Hay a relatively free hand, 386; direction of affairs shifted to, 387; inaccurate state-

Roosevelt, Theodore (*Continued*) ments in *Autobiography*, 387; never comprehended Colombian situation, 387; correctly estimated value of Panama route, 387 f.; anger and impatience, 388; interpretation of Marroquín's character, 388; isthmian affair under personal direction of, 390; would have benefited by Root's advice, 390 f.; "blackmail treaty," 393

Root, Elihu, 375, 390 ff.; regarded Germans as a predatory nation, 312; task of restoring Latin-American confidence in the U. S., 391 f.; Root-Cortés and Root-Arosemena conventions, 391n

Saavedra, Indalecio, 303, 307
Saavedra-Arango-Uribe B. resolution, 303, 307; Caro's substitute, 304, 307
Saavedra Ceron, Alvaro de, 4
Salazar, Governor, 171 ff., 176, 178; asked to prevent intervention by U. S., 175
Salgar-Wyse concession, *see* Wyse concession
Salisbury, Lord, 99n, 108; favored negotiations re Clayton-Bulwer treaty, 93
Salvador, looked to U. S. for aid, 14
Samper, Miguel, 52
Samper, Rudolfo, 207
Sanchez, Nicaraguan foreign secretary, quoted, 163n
Sanclemente, Manuel Antonio, 52 ff., 225, 331, 332
San Juan River, British in temporary possession of mouth of, 10; British order Nicaragua to withdraw from mouth of, 14; Palmerston's motive in seizing, 16; steam navigation rights, 107
Santander, Francisco de Paula, 46
Seitz, Don C., 102, 359n
Seward, William H., 17n, 168, 343
Shaler, J. R., 288, 350; prevents transportation of Colombian troops to Panama City, 362, 364; ordered by Hubbard not to permit troops to use the line, 365 f.
Shaw, Albert, 375, 380
Sherman, John, 89n

Silva, Carlos Martínez, *see* Martínez Silva
Simmons, Edward, 122
Soto, Foción, 56, 60, 219
Soufrière, La, 147, 152n
Spain, attitude toward canal project, 3 ff.; grip on New World relaxed, 7; treaty with Great Britain, 1786, 9
Spanish-American War, 28, 31, 70; emphasized strategic advantages of isthmian canal, 82
Spooner, John Coit, 107, 146n, 151, 154, 158, 159, 190, 198, 274, 340, 383; introduced amendment to Hepburn bill, 123 f.; authorship of amendment, 125, 149 f.; in debate on Hay–Bunau-Varilla treaty, 384
Spooner Act, 75, 157, 191, 195, 198, 229, 233, 254, 285, 286, 345, 385; passage, 155 f.; terms, 156; terms compared with those of April Memorandum, 158 f.; terms not known in Bogotá until August, 162; Hay's contention that assessment of New Company would be a violation of, 275 ff.; Beaupré's opinion that provisions of, were complied with when Hay-Herrán treaty was signed, 311; references to, inappropriate in pact between sovereign nations, 315; modification suggested by Hay, 341; president's obligations under terms of, 346 f.; modification advised by Lodge, 351; Roosevelt's view of spirit of, 352; Roosevelt complied with, 381 f.
Spooner amendment to Hepburn bill, 123 ff., 147, 386; Cromwell claimed authorship of, 123; instigated by Roosevelt, 124; Morgan Committee's action on, 137; Morgan's suspicions as to origin, 149; Senate vote on, 154
Squier, E. G., transit treaty with Nicaragua, 15, 16; treaty re Tigre Island, 15
Stephens, John L., 12
Stimson, Henry L., 393
Suez Act, 99n
Suez Canal, 18, 96
Sullivan & Cromwell, 77n, 79, 80, 109, 121, 147, 349

Tascon, Captain, 360
Taylor, Zachary, 13n, 15, 16

INDEX 467

Tehuantepec, principles of Clayton-Bulwer treaty applicable to, 17
Teller, Henry M., 151
Terán, Oscar, 210
Thompson-Urrutia pact, 393
Tigre Island, England's desire to possess, 14; ceded temporarily to U. S., 15
Tiradores Battalion, 362, 364, 367
Tobar, Juan B., 361; Tiradores Battalion at Colón, 362, 364, 367; lured aboard train: placed under arrest, 362 f.; refused to accept parole, 367, 369; lost opportunity, 368
Torres, Eliseo, efforts to transport his men, 364, 366; threat to burn Colón and kill Americans, 366; accepted bribe and withdrew, 367, 369
Tower, Charlemagne, 312
Treaty of 1846–48, U. S. with New Granada, 12, 18, 46, 66, 340; ratified, 14; Colombian uneasiness concerning, 67 f., 70; Abadía Méndez proposes international guaranty of neutrality of Panama as substitute for, 134; basis of employment of U. S. naval forces on Isthmus, 166, 235; Article XXXV re free transit across Isthmus, 168, 182, 185; precedents of enforcement violated by U. S., 173*n*; guaranties of Colombian sovereignty, 179; fear that U. S. might abrogate, 218; abrogation by U. S. reported under consideration, 294; Moore's interpretation, 341 ff., 350; Roosevelt's interpretation influenced by Moore, 341, 380; Roosevelt's application of Article XXXV during Panama uprising, 360; action of U. S. denounced as violation of, 373
Tribunals, establishment of, by U. S., 158, 160, 315; to decide differences of treaty interpretation, 316
Tribunals, joint: Silva proposes, 129; Hay amendment to April Memorandum provides for, 161; Morgan asks abolition of, 198; Colombian protest against, 257 f.; opposed in Colombian congress, 315 ff.; Beaupré warns against amendment suppressing, 318; Ospina–Rodríguez–Campo committee endorses principle of, 328; no provision for, in Hay–Bunau-Varilla treaty, 377

United States, interest in Central American politics, 10; trade contacts with Latin America, 10; interest in construction of an isthmian canal, 11 (*see also* Nicaragua and Panama entries); negotiations with other nations re canal favored, 11; expansionist policy of Polk, 12; Central American countries look to for aid, 14; right of transit across Nicaragua acquired, 15, 19; Clayton-Bulwer treaty (*see* Clayton-Bulwer treaty); attitude toward all canal projects in Central America, 20; Frelinghuysen-Zavala treaty, 22; work on Nicaragua Canal begun, 25 (*see also* Maritime Canal Company); partiality for Nicaragua route, 27, 29, 32, 75, 80, 83, 85 (*see also* Morgan, J. T.; Nicaragua entries); need for closer intercoastal communication, 28; public demands action, 29; Zelaya influenced by State Department, 30*n;* treaty with New Granada, *see* Treaty of 1846–48; treaties of 1869 and 1870 with Colombia re canal, 65, 66 (*see also under* names of treaties); possessive attitude toward Isthmus, 66, 68, 69; Clayton-Bulwer treaty a check upon, 67 ff.; most active power in Central America and the Caribbean, 68; protocol signed with Colombia re defense of Isthmus, 69 f.; growing taste for imperialistic expansion, 70; Colombians oppose control of work by, 72; battle of the routes, 75-116 (*see also* Bunau-Varilla; Cromwell; Hanna; Hay; Hepburn; New Panama Canal Company; Spooner; Walker Commission); Panama lobby, 75, 150; maintenance of Colombia's sovereignty over Isthmus, 113, 315; passage of the Spooner Act, 117-56; Hepburn bill, 118 ff.; Spooner amendment, 123 ff.; New Company authorized to sell to, 127, 146, 211 ff., 276 ff., 377; Tenure on Isthmus, 128, 135, 140, 158, 160, 183; sailors and marines in Colombia and on Isthmus, 132, 170, 175, 235, 254, 382; reaction to Colombian terms, 139; negotiations with Nicaragua and Costa Rica, 143; negotiation of the Hay-Herrán treaty,

United States (*Continued*)
157-99 (*see also* Hay-Herrán treaty); issue between control by, and Colombian sovereignty, 158; intervention on the Isthmus, 163, 166 ff., 175 ff., 234; guaranteed right of transit across Isthmus, 170; restrictions upon transportation of Colombian troops, 170, 177, 180; suspected of encouraging secession of Panama, 178; sovereignty over canal demanded, 199; right to acquire rights of New Company, 213, 276 ff.; ignorance of Department of State on Colombian affairs, 244; facts upon which policy towards Colombia was based, 251; pressure diplomacy, 273-97; committed to support of New Company's financial interests, 275, 283, 386; confidential instructions communicated to New Company, 280; warning to Colombia, 285; defeat of treaty, 298-334; would not consider any modifications of Hay-Herrán treaty, 311; rights of tenancy in canal zone, *see* Panama Canal zone; minister outmaneuvered by Rico, 323; policy during revolution in Panama, 335-70; rights under treaty of 1846, 341 ff., 346 ff., 353, 380; three choices facing administration, 346; support of revolution, 356 ff., 361 ff., 368 ff.; ships ordered to Panama, 356, 357, 358, 362; purchased generals from Colombian army expect support of, 360; recognition of *de facto* government of Panama, 370, 371; legation at Bogotá guarded, 371; action denounced: threat of war, 373; orders issued to prevent landing of Colombian soldiers in new republic, 374; intensity of effort which characterized signing of treaty with Panama, 375; plan to divide indemnity between Panama and Colombia advocated, 376; guarantees independence of new republic, 377; rights granted by Hay–Bunau-Varilla treaty, 377; criticism of administration's decisive share in isthmian coup, 380; Reyes' accusations against, 383; permitted agent of private company to jeopardize momentous diplomatic arrangement, 386; might have obtained Panama route without revolution, 388 f.; grants indemnity and privileges in use of canal, 393

United States of Colombia, 47; *see also* Colombia

United States *v.* the Press Publishing Company, 174n, 359n

Universal Panama Canal Company, 277

Uribe, Antonio José, 51, 113; quoted, 61n, 70n, 205; resignation, 126, 131, 224, 230, 231; opinion on pecuniary importance of canal to Colombia, 205; reaction to indemnity clause of Hay-Concha memorandum, 206; opinion on transfer of New Company's concession, 210; speech, July 10, 305 f.

Uribe Uribe, Rafael, 56, 74, 233n; surrender of army, 172; visit to Castro, 221, 224; correspondence with Martínez Silva, 227 f.

Uribe B., Joaquín M., 303, 307, 316

Uricoechea, José María, 288, 307, 316; call upon Grünau, 314

Valdés López, Ramón, 338n
Vallarino, Carlos, 259
Van Buren, Martin, 12
Vargas Santos, Gabriel, 56, 60, 219, 228
Varón, Ruben, 339, 360
Vásquez Cobo, Alfredo, 173, 270, 361
Vélez, Joaquín F., 298, 307, 326, 330n
Vélez, Marceliano, 51
Venezuela, set up as independent republic, 46; tension with Colombia, 131, 220, 222
Vergara y Velasco, Francisco J., 263

Waldeck-Rousseau, P. M. R., 157
Walker, John G., 28, 91, 112, 113, 115, 119, 158, 208 f., 274
Walker Commission, 94, 101, 105, 115, 117, 125, 126, 128, 153, 154, 207n, 209, 222, 339, 385, 386; constituted, 90 f.; visit to Europe, 91 f.; examined by Morgan Committee, 100, 103; preliminary report, 104, 108; correspondence with Silva, 111 f.; final report, 115; New Company cables offer to sell, 119 f.; supplementary report in favor of Panama, 120 f.

Walker-Hains-Haupt Nicaragua Canal Commission, 28, 29n, 81n
White, Henry, 93, 99n, 117, 120n, 312
Williams, John L., 27n
Wilson, Woodrow, attempt to adjust Colombia's grievances, 393
Wisconsin, 169, 171, 173; treaty of Panama signed on board, 237
Woolsey, Theodore D., 99n
World, New York, 97, 104n, 174n, 249, 271n, 293, 313, 380; prediction of revolution on Isthmus, 293 ff.; source material on U. S. *v.* The Press Publishing Co., 359n
Wyse, Lucien Napoleon Bonaparte, 20
Wyse concession, 63, 64, 109, 388; extensions secured from Colombia, 30; forbade transfer to foreign government without consent of Colombia, 31, 82, 276, 279; stipulation for opening canal, 57; taken over by New Company, 57; Colombia's attitude toward transfer of concession, 109 ff.; sale of, in return for stock of Panama Railroad, 210

Young, Lieutenant-General, summary of Humphrey-Murphy observations, 353 f.

Zelaya, José Santos, 100n; promise of contract with Eyre and Cragin, 30; suggested indemnity, 144